THE KID STAYS IN THE PICTURE

THE KID STAYS

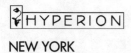 HYPERION

NEW YORK

ROBERT EVANS

IN THE PICTURE

MARINKA PESCHMANN,
PROJECT EDITOR

LIBRARY OF CONGRESS CATALOGING-IN-PUBLICATION DATA

EVANS, ROBERT
THE KID STAYS IN THE PICTURE / ROBERT EVANS.—1ST ED.
P.   CM.
ISBN 0-7868-6059-6
1. EVANS, ROBERT.   2. MOTION PICTURE PRODUCERS AND
DIRECTORS—UNITED STATES—BIOGRAPHY.   3. MOTION PICTURE ACTORS AND
ACTRESSES—UNITED STATES—BIOGRAPHY.   I. TITLE.
PN1998.3.E98A3   1994
791.43'0232'092—DC20
[B]   94-7782
CIP

Designed by Kathy Kikkert

FIRST EDITION

10 9 8 7 6 5 4 3 2 1

To Joshua.

By far the greatest production of my life.

Craig Nelson,

I thank you. You were far more than my editor, rather the captain of my ship. Your combative passion for excellence streamlined my thousand-page manuscript into, hopefully, a page-turner.

ACKNOWLEDGMENTS

Charles Michener, whose editorial expertise afforded me a crash course in autobiographical structure. Never once was he judgmental of my idiosyncratic behavior. His encouragement inspired me to tell it all. Without him *The Kid* would still be in my head.

Ed Victor, my literary agent, psychiatrist, and friend. Each time the pain of putting life to paper became excruciating, he "Billy Grahamed" me. "It's therapeutic, Bob. Get it out of your system." Ed, you're one hell of an agent, but Billy Graham you're not. It's still hurting!

Jeff Berg, an extraordinary man who personifies everything an agent is *not* supposed to be. Through *thin* and *thin,* he's always been there, never once asking for anything in return. Including commission! That's friendship with a capital *"F."*

Robert Goldberg. Forget he's my business manager, accountant, and friend. Let's talk "hat trick" inventive. How else could he have pulled me through a cash drought that made the Sahara Desert look like Niagara Falls. It was close, but he did it. Buying me the time I needed to write, rewrite, and rewrite my bumpy road of life. Now that's talent!

Steve Frankfurt. For a quarter of a century, his magic eye has never failed to come up with the extraordinary. You did it again, Steve, helping me get *The Kid* dressed for the party.

Arnold Newalu. With no gainful purpose, the purity of his objective overview brought with it confrontation, making the painful pages of rewriting *The Kid* even more painful. But he was right. That's all that counts.

Michael Binns, my top executive lady. For over a year, seven days and nights a week, she forced me to get *The Kid* off the ground. By far, it was the most exhausting endeavor of her life. Finally she had it, needed time away. She sure in hell deserved it.

The next victim, *Linda Davis,* was excited to take on the challenge. Together we scratched out a thousand-page first draft. Did it take its toll on Linda? Let's just say she left town with no forwarding.

Without my consent, before me stood a "hired gun." Me the bounty, she the hunter. "Write or die" was her daily dictate. What could I do? I wrote. Write her name down, one day she may cross your path. Quote me if you want, she's lethal, *lethal good!* Her name? *Marinka Peschmann.*

To Charles. Though diametric our beliefs on many a subject, you stand alone as the major influence in my life's destiny. Knowing *The Kid* was no "musical," never once did you press for the kindness of a read. That's style! That's you. That's one telling the other not to compromise. Stick to the integrity of his thoughts.

Know, dear brother, that second act trauma makes for third act magic. That's theater. That's life. That's us.

FOREWORD

My fifth-grade teacher used to admonish his students that by the time we all reached adulthood we would have forfeited three fourths of ourselves in order "to be like other people."

From the moment I met Robert Evans, I realized that he was one person who hadn't played the forfeiture game. He played by his own rules and lived according to his own scenarios. His unwillingness to bend or forfeit a piece of himself cost him dearly at various times in his life, but it also lent him uniqueness.

For better or worse, Evans was and still is an original. It made him famous, it made him infamous. Many say they know him, few do. I am one of them.

Robert Evans's appointment as production chief of Paramount Pictures in 1967 was regarded by most of Hollywood's power players as utterly hallucinatory. Here was an actor who had never produced a picture, much less run a studio, being awarded sweeping responsibility over one of Hollywood's most fabled movie factories. It was bizarre!

But it was also fascinating. These were the 1960s, remember, and hallucinations were in vogue. The studio Evans was taking over was hardly a studio, rather a sleeping giant. One that had been in Hollywood's cellar for a decade. His appointment was accompanied by the promise that Gulf + Western, which had recently acquired Paramount, would pump hundreds of millions of dollars into an expanded production program. This meant jobs for actors, writers, and technicians—good news for Hollywood, even if it was Bob Evans doing the hiring.

When Evans brought me in as his right-hand man, the prognosis only worsened. How could a writer for *The New York Times* possibly help this wannabe Thalberg thread his way through the minefields of Hollywood? No sooner had Evans and I moved into our offices than items started appearing in the trade papers and gossip columns predicting our imminent demise. The silver-haired studio apparatchik who was in charge of office furniture declined to refurbish mine or Evans's. "You won't be here long enough to bother," he said reassuringly.

The fact that eight years later, he was long gone, and Evans and I were still ensconced at Paramount, had as much to do with the times, perhaps, as with the talents and tenacity of the principals.

If our "act" seemed unlikely, it nonetheless reenergized a fading studio with a new voice. Bob and I were strangers to the Hollywood establishment, but there were many others as well, brilliant ones, demanding to be heard. And heard they were. Soon a new spirit of filmmaking emanated through the once decrepit Windsor gates of Paramount. *The Odd Couple, Rosemary's Baby, Harold and Maude, Goodbye, Columbus, Paper Moon, True Grit, Love Story, The Godfather, Chinatown,* were but a few.

Paramount had come back from the dead and Evans had been

transmogrified from goat to folk hero. For that brief moment in time, it was wondrous to behold.

Soon the ridicule that had greeted Bob Evans halted. I recall watching him arrive at the Bistro, the top place for power lunches at that time, a couple of days after *Love Story* had opened to record numbers. Upon recognizing him, the diners broke into applause. Evans looked behind him to see if some superstar had shown up, then realized with astonishment that the applause was for him!

For nearly ten years we were to work side by side, driving to and from the studio in one car—mine. He couldn't drive, or wouldn't. We were, indeed, a study in contrasts. I plowed through scripts and deal memos, trying to figure out how things got done. Evans really didn't care. He was a true maverick who was driven to take the big risks, to do things his way.

The road was by no means easy. Evans was constantly being second-guessed by the domineering Charles Bluhdorn, the Austrian-born financier who owned Paramount and an instant expert on everything, from what stars should be paid to what films should cost. There was another instant expert in the wings as well. Martin Davis had been a press agent at Paramount when he came up with the idea of luring Bluhdorn into buying the studio. Taut and conspiratorial by nature, Davis had become an important force in the company but by the late 1960s was using his power to try to sell the back lot and move the studio operation to New York, where it would function under his direct control. Bluhdorn wanted to use the studio as part of a massive real estate deal involving a shady cluster of Italians—a key figure was the infamous Michele Sindona, who ultimately was to die in jail. Bob Evans was the only person at the studio who fought Martin Davis to keep the studio open. Threats and insults bothered Evans little.

I vividly recall the day Evans asked me to try to persuade Mike Nichols to do a special directing gig for us. His assignment: to direct Evans in preparing his filmed presentation to the board of directors. "What's the purpose?" Nichols demanded. "To save the studio from becoming a cemetery." It was vintage Evans—the unexpected—and it worked.

From that moment, the New York hierarchy left the making of films to their creators. Evans himself began to change. He became fascinated with the minutiae of post-production—the editing, the mix of music and effects, etc. *The Godfather* was a seminal experience in that Evans was dissatisfied with Francis Ford Coppola's cut and spent months working round the clock with him on the film, even postponing its release date. Now the gossip in town was that Evans was intruding on the prerogatives of young filmmakers. The reality was quite the opposite: I watched as a superbly shot but ineptly put together film was transformed into a masterpiece.

After *Godfather,* Bob Evans became increasingly obsessed with his work. His Gatsby-like image began to fade. In the office all day, in the cutting room all night, he became somber and reclusive, increasingly dependent on painkillers for an acute back condition and on so-called vitamin shots dispensed by a friendly studio physician. By the mid-seventies, the dream had begun to fall apart.

Needless to say, I found all this saddening. Working with Evans had been a roller-coaster ride. He was a man devoid of pettiness; he could never criticize a colleague's mistakes, however grotesque. He was willing to take artistic risks, however outrageous. But now, with his marriage to Ali MacGraw shattered and his substance-abuse problem worsening, I decided to move on to another job in the industry. Evans ultimately surrendered his power position at the studio and turned to producing and then, as this book chronicles, fell upon difficult times.

Memories of the good years at Paramount under Evans soon became frayed. The town forgot that through the Evans years a studio was reborn, extraordinary talents were nurtured, superb films were created. The American film emerged as number one in every country in the world. Suddenly the financial barons paid attention, legitimatizing a new industry for Wall Street to embrace. When I started with Bob in 1967, Paramount accounted for less than 5 percent of Gulf + Western's revenue. In less than a decade, it was closing in on 50 percent. Five years ago, Gulf + Western changed its name to Paramount Communications.

His autobiography recounts his bizarre life in often embarrassing detail.

The biography's voice is very much that of Evans—robust, audacious, original, though sometimes he minimizes his own hard work and achievements. Perhaps he never truly understood how much he gave of himself or comprehended the positive influence he had on others. The book relates many conflicts and clashes; it leaves out the countless kindnesses he dispensed.

But perhaps this was to be expected, I never felt Bob really understood his own innate ability. There were times, many times, when he was his own worst enemy. Given his propensity for doing good, it was amazing how much evil he allowed to penetrate his life.

Looking back, I too sometimes wonder if it all really happened. But happen it did. The films are there to prove it. Miraculously, so is Bob Evans.

—Peter Bart
Editor-in-chief, *Variety Magazine*

PREFACE

There are three sides to every story: yours . . . mine . . . and the truth. No one is lying. Memories shared serve each differently. Be it day or decade, recall still remains the one ace I've been dealt from life's deck.

In the spirit that the least spared in these pages be myself, I make no apology to those chronicled. At least you've been remembered—made a dent in another's bumpy road.

THE KID STAYS IN THE PICTURE

1

March 14, 1972.

"Sidney, guess who's coming to dinner."

"Yeah?"

"Henry."

"Kissinger?"

"Yeah!"

"You sure it's right?"

"It's *great!* Why?"

"It ain't no ordinary film. That's why. It's about the boys—the organization. It's a hot ticket."

Was I hearing right? These words were coming from Sidney Korshak. The man whom *The New York Times* called one of the five most powerful people in the United States. For close to twenty years Sidney was not only my *consigliere,* but my godfather and closest friend.

In the past year alone, two phone calls of his saved my ass. Literally. The first, to stop the heavy muscle from threatening not only my life, but my newborn kid's as well.

"Get the fuck outta our town, will ya? We don't want nothin' to happen to you or your kid. Go to Kansas City or St. Louis if ya wanna, but New York ain't opening up for ya," was the threat from New York's families five.

One call from Korshak, suddenly, threats turned to smiles and doors, once closed, opened with an embrace.

Al Pacino had signed for another picture, *The Gang That Couldn't Shoot Straight,* and was contractually unavailable. A second call from Korshak—Pacino became available. Why was he now giving me heat?

"C'mon, Sidney. It's a fuckin' movie. It'll be a bash—the biggest opening of the decade!"

"Yeah, and he'll make it bigger."

"So what. It's my coming out party. He wants to be there. What's wrong with that?"

"Nothing and everything." Silence. "How's Ali?"

"Fine."

"Is that all you can tell me?"

"Yeah. Why?"

"Just asking. Did you fuck her yet?"

"No . . ."

He hung up.

I looked in the bedroom. Ali was still asleep. Or at least pretending to be.

The night before, she had flown in from El Paso on the Gulf + Western private jet without a moment's rest—starting with a six A.M. wake-up call on Sam Peckinpah's *The Getaway.* It was after one in the morning when she finally landed at Teterboro Airport in New Jersey, during the worst March snowstorm in New York's memory.

For the past hour I'd been on the phone to Marlon Brando's agent, Marlon Brando's lawyer, Marlon Brando's manager, trying to persuade Marlon to fly from L.A. to New York for the world premiere of *The Godfather.*

Brando had never gone to a premiere in his life. But months before, he'd agreed to godfather the premiere of *The Godfather.* It would be his "fuck you" to the world—his comeback in spades.

What a coup! It didn't last long. Anna Kashfi—Marlon's crazed ex-wife—kidnapped their son, Christian. Marlon canceled out. Two days before the premiere, Christian was found. I tasted the drama. It had to work.

Only one person could persuade Brando to make the opening—Christian's psychiatrist. I was waiting for her return call when the loudspeaker announced the arrival of Ali's plane. I rushed to the gate to greet my lady who but two months earlier, against her strong wishes, I'd packed off to Texas to star with Steve McQueen in *The Getaway.*

Two months had passed, and I hadn't once bothered to visit her on location. The very lady who but hours before we married had whispered, "I love you, Evans. I love you . . ."—then, curling up beside me—"forever."

"Forever," I whispered back.

"Never leave me. Promise?"

"Promise."

"Not even for two weeks."

"Not for one."

"I'm a hot lady, Evans."

"Never change."

"Then never let anything get between us, promise?"

"Promise."

Pale and windblown, she entered the terminal. Quickly, we embraced. Instead of kissing her, I whispered, "Wait here. I'm expecting a call."

"I'm exhausted, Evans. Can't you call from the hotel?"

When I told her I couldn't chance missing it, because it was a call from Brando's kid's psychiatrist, she looked at me as if I were the one who needed a shrink.

She was asleep before she hit the bench. Ali MacGraw, the biggest female movie star in the world, curled up in the waiting room of a freezing, two-bit airport, while her husband waited for the fuckin' phone to ring.

It rang! For the next hour Ali could have been back in El Paso as I went back and forth with Christian's psychiatrist, trying to make her an offer that even Marlon couldn't refuse—a private jet for him and Christian. Father and son sharing the accolades together. What better reunion? The doctor wavered.

"I'll call you back."

"I've got him. I've got him," I said to myself, pacing back and forth, waiting for the phone to ring. It did. Anxiously, I grabbed the receiver. Brando? He passed!

By now, it was almost three A.M. I hustled Ali through the falling snow, into the waiting limo. Before the door closed, she was asleep again—this time on my shoulder. I was glad as my thoughts had little to do with her—only, "How do I better Brando?" Would you say I was sick?

The next morning, the alarm blasted at 9:30. Instead of turning over to make love, I rushed to the phone in the living room. Weeks ago I had invited Henry Kissinger to the premiere. My timing couldn't have been worse. The North Vietnamese offensive had just begun. Naturally, he begged off.

"Hello, this is Robert Evans. May I please speak to Dr. Kissinger?"

"Dr. Kissinger is with the President, Mr. Evans. He'll have to call you back."

"Have him call me as soon as possible, please. It's urgent."

Quicker than a junior agent at the William Morris agency, within ten minutes, Kissinger was on the phone.

"Bob, what's the urgency?"

"I need you in New York."

He laughed, "When?"

"Tonight."

"The Paris peace talks—they've just blown apart."

"I know—it's on every channel. But I need you with me tonight, Henry—real bad."

"Why?"

"*The Godfather.*"

"What?"

I couldn't tell him I was calling because Brando flaked out.

"Tonight *it's* for me, Henry. It's the premiere. Win or lose, it would be worth it if I could walk in with you."

"We're in the middle of a blizzard. . . ." He paused. "I'm in with the President all day." Again, he paused. "I have a seven-thirty breakfast that I can't get out of." A cough. "I'm leaving the country tomorrow."

"Henry, I need you tonight."

Only later did I learn that his "leaving the country" was in actuality a secret mission to Moscow; that his 7:30 breakfast was with Joint Chiefs of Staff to resolve the mining of Haiphong harbor.

A long pause. "I'll get back to you."

The phone rang. It was my boss, Charlie Bluhdorn, chairman of Gulf + Western, the conglomerate that owned Paramount Pictures. As usual, Charlie wanted to take my head off for something I had no control over. *Life* and *Newsweek* were on the stands with cover stories about *The Godfather*. Where was *Time*?

"We need a triple blitz, Evans. A triple blitz. You can do it. I know you can."

"I'm trying, Charlie."

"Try harder. For me, Evans, for me."

The Carlyle operator interrupted, "Mr. Evans, the White House on the line."

"The White House? What White House?" Bluhdorn screeched.

"Call you back, Charlie."

It was one of Kissinger's assistants. Blizzard and all, the Doctor was flying in to be with me.

"What time?" she asked.

Protecting myself, "Six-thirty," I said.

"Would you mind if the doctor changes at your hotel?"

Quickly, I dialed Bluhdorn back.

"Charlie, Kissinger's coming!"

"Kissinger? Kissinger? Evans, I love you! I love you!"

The management of the St. Regis Hotel rued the day they accepted to take on the opening night party. Celebrated, highly profiled? Yes. But nothing was worth the grief of having to deal with the likes of me!

With less than twenty-four hours till post time, I called for a full dress rehearsal. On inspection, I made them change the napkins, silverware, candles and—oh yes—the food.

After tasting it, I shook my head, "No, it's too bland. Get me a new chef. A Sicilian." Then I took on the orchestra leader. "Play *The Godfather* theme over and over until everyone is seated."

"But Mr. Evans—"

"Don't argue!"

He didn't. He knew I'd fire him.

Finally, I gathered together the eighteen security guards I'd hired to protect the party from crashers. In keeping with the spirit of the night, all were dressed in double-breasted, striped gangsters' suits and large-brimmed hats, rented from Strock Theatrical Costumes.

The fire ordinance of the St. Regis ballroom would not permit more than 470 people at the post-premiere bash. When more than 2,000 people are invited to the premiere, "the Crash Factor" becomes the paramount factor in protecting the bash from a potential disaster.

Protection being only as good as its weakest link, one by one, I placed each striped suit at his immovable stations—starting with the outside revolving doors, then to the lobby itself, to every elevator, back and front, every staircase, back and front, to every lavatory and terrace. Did I plug every hole? I'd know in twenty-four hours.

I shook Ali awake. "Better get some breakfast, baby. There's a car waiting. You've got to make it to Halston and back by four. Gotta go. Love ya." She crawled back under the covers.

There was a rap on the door. It was Mary Cronin, a reporter from *Time.* She was there to see Al Pacino. Since Pacino lived in a cellar— no joke, a cellar—I'd arranged for them to meet in my suite for the interview.

Al showed up a few minutes later, unshaven, wearing a Navy pea coat and a knit hat pulled down over his ears. A second-story man? Possibly. But not the subject of a *Time* cover.

Quickly, he pulled me aside. "Can you loan me a fiver? I need it for the cab tonight."

I slipped him two crisp C notes, which he pocketed without blinking. With that, I left, scratching my head. This kid's the star of *The Godfather?*

Was my ass on the line! It was me who fought the entire Paramount organization to cancel the Christmas opening, give us time, get it right, touch a bit of magic. Not unlike a parachute jumper, a picture gets one shot—if it doesn't open, it's dead.

"Come on, fellas, back me!" No one did except Bluhdorn. Even my so-called loyal cabinet begged me not to press my luck. "Fuck luck, fellas, it's instinct. If I can't press it, I should fold." Luck fucked me—a blizzard in the middle of March.

Outside, the storm was getting worse. I trudged to Meledandri, my tailor, for the final fitting of my new dinner suit—black velvet jacket and gray flannels. Then to the St. Regis, where I completed the seating plan as well as tasted the new chef's rigatoni. Then by foot all the way across town to Loew's State, where I was greeted by Al Lo Presti—Paramount's ace acoustic guru.

"Is that you, Evans? You look like a fuckin' snowball."

"Fuck you too. Let's get the sound right, okay?"

"Don't worry, no one's gonna show anyway. There ain't no way to get here."

Both of us burst out laughing. How could this be happening to us?

Not trusting anybody but ourselves, we planned our strategy to ensure that the sound levels would be correct for our now questionable night of triumph. (During the premiere, Al would bicycle between the two projection booths, listening to my instructions from the walkie-talkie neatly tucked in the inside breast pocket of my velvet dinner jacket.)

Back at the hotel, Ali came in from Halston's. Being tired did not stop her from being accommodating, as she tried on various outfits for my appraising eye to pick. After settling on black feathers over a simple black sheath, we added a tight-fitting black "ostrich" hat, since she didn't have time to get her hair done.

The Bluhdorns, my brother, Charlie, and his date, and a few others were invited over at 6:30 for a taste of caviar and champagne. My first guest arrived early—Henry Kissinger.

At 7:45 Ali and I joined Henry in the backseat of the limo. Pulling up to the theater, Henry leaned over. "Bobby, will there be a lot of press?"

"A *lot*." Somberly, shaking his head.

"The President's going to love this."

The doors opened. Enough flashbulbs went off to light up New Jersey. On one arm—Ali MacGraw—the ravishing Mrs. Evans; on the other, the most charismatic statesman in the world. Was this really happening to me?

The paparazzi became so unruly that extra police were called in to physically push them back.

"Dr. Kissinger, why are you here tonight?" one of them yelled.

"I was forced," he smiled.

"By who?"

Looking at me, "By Bobby."

"Did he make you an offer you couldn't refuse?"

"Yes."

When the lights went down and Nino Rota's music swelled, my whole life seemed to pass before me. Here, sitting between Henry and Ali, watching this epic unfold, I felt that everything my life was about had led up to this moment.

Two hours and fifty-six minutes later Diane Keaton asked Pacino if he was responsible for all the killings.

"No," he lied, then walked into the family library, leaving her behind to watch two of his hit men, Richard Castellano and Richard Bright, come in to kiss their new godfather's ring. The doors slowly closed on Keaton's face—the screen went to black—the credits started to roll. No applause—not a sound—just silence. Scary? No, eerie.

"It's a bomb," I said to myself. I looked at Ali, then Henry. Their faces too were solemn. "Let's get out of here."

In the backseat of the limo, Henry shrugged. "Reminds me of Washington; just different names, different faces."

No compliment. He must have hated it.

Squeezing my hand, Ali whispered, "Evans, I'm so proud of you. It's brilliant." What else could she say, she was my wife.

Am I an idiot giving a party? It's a mob picture, not a musical.

Wrong again. It was a blast! I played master of ceremonies, introducing anyone and everyone. From Mario Puzo to Francis Coppola, they all made it to the stage.

The screaming, the fights, the threats that never let up since day one of filming, were worth it. Even Francis Coppola, the director whom I'd hired over Paramount's objections and then personally fired four different times during the post-production editing, came over to hug me, closing the book on two years of terrible battles— from casting to music and the final edit.

Two jarring moments put a slight dent in the evening. Spotting Sidney and Bernice Korshak at a table across the floor, I rushed over and kissed Bernice.

"Without the big man, none of this could have happened. Join our table, will you?"

Not cracking a smile, he shook his head. "No."

"Why?"

"And give the fuckin' press a field day?"

"Come on, Sidney, it's your night too."

Like a vise, he grabbed my arm. "Don't ever bring me and Kissinger together in public. Ever! Now go back to your table, spend some time with your wife, schmuck."

I hadn't been back at my table for more than five minutes when Jimmy Caan, who exploded into stardom that night, rushed over. An embrace? No! He grabbed my other arm. "You cut my whole fuckin' part out." Did I hear right?

Sure. An actor is an actor is an actor is an actor.

Ali never looked more radiant. For the rest of the night we danced as one. Holding her tightly in my arms, I felt I was the luckiest man in the world. It was the highest moment of my life.

Was I dreaming it? I was. It was all a façade. The beginning of the end.

2

"Hey, pretty boy!"

Six staccato punches—that's all it took for Jimmy Cagney to finish off Humphrey Bogart and his two henchmen. Then he straightened his tie, flashed his cocky grin, and walked out as if he'd just left church. . . .

I had Cagney's strut down perfect as I came out of *Angels with Dirty Faces* at the Regency, sauntered up Broadway, then turned into my block on West Eighty-third Street.

"Your wallet, pretty boy!"

He must have been a half foot taller and eighty pounds heavier, but, thinking I was Cagney, I punched him in the gut before he had a chance to grab my lapels. From behind, the other guy grabbed my hair. I let out a scream that could have been heard in Yonkers. Flash! A blade slashed down my left cheek. They took off like lightning.

I ran down Eighty-third Street, past Mike the doorman, into an empty elevator. The door closed. Before my eyes in the mirror, blood gushed like a fire hydrant down my face.

My mother took one look at me and screamed, "Archie! Hurry!" She burst into tears. "Bobby, Bobby, my poor baby!"

Pop ran out in his undershirt and shorts.

"What happened?" His face ashen. "Who did it? Who did it?"

Cagney would have stayed mum. So did I.

"Florence, get Dr. Anderson!"

He pulled me into the bathroom, pressing the wound with a towel to make the bleeding stop.

"Florence," he called out, "don't get Anderson. He'll want to put stitches in. Bobby doesn't need them. Bring me some ice."

Pop was right. The bleeding stopped. Thanks to Jimmy Cagney, the thugs didn't get the seventy-five cents in my pocket. Thanks to Jimmy Cagney, I still have that scar running down my left cheek. As for Dr. Anderson's stitches—I think I needed them in my head!

I was born in New York City on June 29, 1930, in Women's Hospital just as the Depression was sinking in. My name was Robert J. Shapera, the *J* sounding good but standing for nothing I know of. After a few days I was brought home to live at 825 West End Avenue with my parents and my brother, Charles, who was four years older.

I don't remember much about the Depression except that my pop had to work seven days a week at his dental clinic in Harlem to keep us housed, fed, and clothed. He was always the provider—not only for us, but for his mother and three sisters as well. Both my parents were second-generation Jews. That was all they had in common.

Pop grew up with a father he never saw and a mother and three sisters needing him to bring home the bacon. He was a brilliant pianist, talented enough to play duets with Rachmaninoff. But he never gave himself the chance to become the next Rachmaninoff. Instead he paid his way through Columbia University's dental school giving piano lessons. Rather than using the brilliance of his fingers to fill concert halls, he used them to fill cavities. Because his father had been an indigent, a nonprovider, his family always came before his dreams. Responsibility, rather than fantasies fulfilled, became his life. Poor Pop, he was dealt a hand he couldn't win.

Conversely, my mother's family rolled in green, but was empty on education. One of nine children (five boys and four girls), she was the beauty of the Krasnes. While others went without food during the Great Depression, her brothers were driven around in chauffeured limousines.

Abe, the eldest and richest, owned Krasdale Foods. He must have been one popular guy sitting in the backseat of his custom-built six-teen-cylinder, open-chauffeured Cadillac limousine, passing hundreds of people on most every corner waiting in breadlines.

His younger brothers, Izzy, Julius, Ben, and Sam, were in business together—competitors of Abe, owning Bernice Foods. All of them together weren't as wealthy as Abe. They only had Packard limousines. Only two of the five could write anything but their name on a check.

The five brothers shared one thought: their beautiful sister, Florence, had married beneath her. How could she compromise, marrying a dentist—in Harlem, no less? One day, when I was fourteen, I found out.

Whenever my parents left town, I would sneak girls into the apartment. My parents were vacationing in Boca Raton, Florida. One night, after spending hours with a girl in my bedroom, she asked if she could borrow a comb, brush, and lipstick. She didn't want to look like a tramp, which she was, walking past the doorman.

Quietly, I slipped past the maid's room into my parents' bedroom, opening my mother's vanity. Gathering together a comb, brush, and lipstick, I spotted a hatbox I'd never noticed before. Curiously, I untied the ribbon and opened it. Inside were letters, all in my father's handwriting.

The first thing next morning, I snuck back into the bedroom. The hatbox was filled with love letters, more than a hundred of them from Archie to Florence, starting after their first date. No wonder she'd fallen in love with him! My father was more than a dentist—he was a romantic. A poet. How could she not be swept off her feet?

My parents were the classic marriage of opposites. Mom was the personality of the two—quick to laugh, expressive with her feelings, friendly with strangers. When she was home, the phone never stopped ringing. When she took a weekend off with the girls, it never rang at all. Certainly not for Archie. Pop's entire life was us—his wife and children. (Later, when I was twelve, another child was born, my baby sister, Alice.)

Pop lived a double life. To his social contemporaries, a nameless dentist. But once north of 110th Street, Pop was a king. Almost everyone knew of his full-floor dental clinic on the corner of 133rd Street and Lenox Avenue. Just below was the hottest club in Harlem, owned by Madam Queen of the numbers racket royalty.

Pop had the first fully integrated dental clinic in America. He had six dental rooms, staffed by four dentists and four nurses, split evenly between black and white. Not bad for the thirties, huh?

It was two bucks an extraction. Every patient was black, except for Charles and me. My mother's family insisted she go to their dentist on Central Park West.

Ernest, the black superintendent of the building, was my father's best pal. During the winter he made sure the clinic was fully heated. During the summer he kept an air-cooling system filled with blocks of ice. My father had the only air-conditioned offices in Harlem and his business thrived because of it. Ah, but Ernest sported the pearliest whites in Harlem—gratis from Archie. When he died, Pop paid for his best friend's funeral.

At least one Sunday a month, I took the subway up to 135th Street and Seventh Avenue and walked the three blocks to his office. Sunday was usually a half day, but Pop and his staff stayed as long as it took to see every patient.

Locking up, he then opened the safe in the X-ray lab and took out the week's earnings. There was nothing but cash—mostly two-dollar bills, some ones, a rare fiver. I helped him separate the bills into nine stacks and watched as he personally paid each nurse and dentist. Once I saw one of the nurses—she was a beauty, a black beauty— squeeze his hand and whisper something in his ear. His face beamed. It was my only glimpse into what could have been a secret life. The ninth stack of bills he put into his own pocket, which bulged like a softball—and off we were.

Lenox Avenue was his. Everyone knew him, from the cop on horseback to the vagrant on the stoop. "Hiya, Doc, how's it goin'?" Or

"Sorry I'm late, Doc, I'll bring the two bucks in on Monday!"

We walked from Harlem to Riverside Drive. To this day, I treasure that time alone with him. How different the city was then! Here we were, a man and boy, white, walking through the Depression days of black Harlem, and never for a second did we feel threatened.

My imitations of Cagney, Bogart, Cooper, Gable, and Stewart made him laugh. Putting his forefinger down under my chin, he tilted my head up. Our eyes met.

"You're some character, kid!" Through the eyes of a nine year old looking up, even though he was only five foot eight or nine, he looked like a giant. He was.

Putting hand in pocket, he pulled out a crisp two-dollar bill. Dropping it into the hat of a young soldier with no legs wheeling himself down Lenox Avenue. The soldier smiled up.

"Doc, without you I couldn't smile." Then taking out his upper and lower dentures, he started to laugh. "Couldn't eat either."

Then with the zest of a relay sprinter he went into high gear down Lenox Avenue, laughing like he hadn't a worry in the world.

Many Sundays later, taking a walk down Lenox Avenue, I told Pop of my dream.

"What do you think about me becoming an actor?"

He laughed. "Sure, sure." But he didn't say no.

Back home, he'd take out his wad of cash.

"Bobby, break it down, count it, give me the total." It felt better than stealing home plate. For a flash, I was a pit boss in a gambling casino, giving him the final total while he sat eating his canned salmon and saltines at the kitchen table.

One Sunday in December 1941, my brother and I picked Pop up in Harlem, splurged on a cab, and headed to the Polo Grounds. The Giants were playing the Dodgers. In those days, the Dodgers were not only a baseball team, but a football team as well. The stadium was packed. The favored Giants were upset by a score of 37–17. But the guys in uniform were not there to see the end.

In the cab home, we heard why: the Japanese had bombed Pearl Harbor. Imagine, they never even announced it during the game.

That night a family meeting was called at my Uncle Abe's. I was always uncomfortable visiting my rich uncles, especially Abe. They were perfectly nice to us, but it is no high being looked down upon as a poor relative—which we were. The only one more uncomfortable than me was Pop. As soon as he entered the wood-paneled elevator to ascend to Abe's eighteen-room penthouse overlooking Central Park, he began to shrink. He knew no one there was interested in hearing about the gold tooth he'd put in the mouth of some *shvartzer* that day, or about Rachmaninoff's new prelude or one of his historical theories on the subject of religious genocide.

That night, all they were interested in was, first, how to keep their kids from going to war; second, how to expand their wealth; and third, how to protect it.

We were the first to leave. As we were going down in the elevator, I remember, Pop said in a voice barely above a whisper, "The wealthy will get wealthier and the young will die."

Just as my father wanted to be everything his father was not, I wanted to be everything my father was not. My dreams would become realities no matter what.

Radio in those days was king. No matter how poor you were, everyone in America had a church-shaped Philco or Edison in their living room—it was the family hearth. Starting at nine in the morning, fifteen-minute soap operas filled the air with the latest installment of "Young Widder Brown," "The Right to Happiness," and so on. In the evening, the shows ran longer, from thirty-minute soaps like "Henry Aldrich" and "Gangbusters" to hour-long dramas like "Lux Radio Theatre." Radio employed more actors than theater and films combined.

My only friend at Joan of Arc Junior High was Larry Frisch, another loner who wanted to be an actor. Larry's dad was a radio executive, and from him we learned how to get our foot in the door.

"Make up a résumé," he said, "a pack of lies—credits that can't be checked."

In the summer of 1942, my family rented a house on the ocean in Long Beach, Long Island. Instead of hanging around the beach clubs, I became a commuter with my copy of "Radio Registry," which listed the week's available parts, tucked under my arm.

From nine to five, June to September, I hit every audition room in New York, making up one story after another about my brilliant career to date. I got my foot in the door, but that was as far as it got.

Rejection breeds obsession. How could I break in? I had one talent, an ear for accents. I couldn't speak German, French, Italian, or

Spanish, but there was no one better at faking it than me.

When school started up, I went right on filling out audition blanks. Finally I got a part—a Nazi colonel in a concentration camp for "Radio Mystery Theater."

Here I was, a twelve-year-old Jewish kid, within six months labeled the top Nazi in town—in radio that is. The trouble was I couldn't stop playing it in life. From the age of twelve, until the day Pop died, I always called him the Führer. Whenever Pop came through the front door I'd click my heels, *"Sieg heil mein Führer."*

Call a spade a spade, but I was the only one south of 110th Street who looked up to him.

Being hailed as the Führer didn't rest well with family or friends—all of whom, naturally, were Jewish.

"Archie, your kid. Is he a little off?"

"Let's Pretend" was the show to be on; it was every radio actor's goal. On Saturday mornings from eleven to twelve, every kid in America was glued to these adventure stories—a new, original fantasy every week. By the time I was fourteen I was a regular. Playing everything from a German baron to a Spanish buccaneer and a stuttering Italian waiter, I was the accent kid.

My father always resented not being called by his proper surname, "Shapera" rather than "Shapiro." His sensitivity concerning a pronunciation mistake so slight seemed totally foreign to his persona. In fact, it had nothing to do with pronunciation. *It was far more complicated.* Call it thwarted revenge, harbored resentment toward a father who would go out to buy a newspaper and return home three weeks later—broke. A degenerate gambler who was always away, leaving his family on empty.

Late one evening, Pop walked into our bedroom, his face pained. "Boys, I need a favor. It's about my mother. She's got six months left, maybe a year. Her whole life's been one big sacrifice. Never a luxury, a good year, a good month. All that mattered to her was her Archie. I suppose I filled the gap for a husband she never had." What was he getting at?

"Her maiden name was Evan. That should be your calling card. Why carry his moniker? He was never there. I wanted to do it myself, but I couldn't. I was afraid he'd hurt her. For me, it's too late. But for you, life's just starting. For Grandma, for me, let her know her Archie loves her"—his voice cracked—"before she passes on."

Our name now started with an *E*. We kept the *S*, however. It became the last letter of our new moniker. Without it, again our last name could have been mispronounced as "even" and the one thing we didn't want was to go through life with our surname mistaken for an adjective or adverb.

Here we were, a family divided, everyone with a different name. Divided in name only, though. If anything, it brought us closer. And me, I was now Robert Evans—"Nazi actor" for hire.

After junior high I wanted to go to Professional Children's School. At PCS, classes ended at noon, which gave you the afternoon off to get on with your career. My mother wouldn't hear of it. Her elder son, the conformist, had gone to Horace Mann, a college-prep school. Her younger son, though a bit peculiar, should at least get what's considered a "normal" education.

My father's attitude was a bit different. Outwardly, he didn't approve of my acting ambitions, but at least I had a goal. And in some ways, inwardly, I think it was a new beginning for him, living out his thwarted dreams through his little Bobby's adventures.

One night I joined him in the kitchen, where he was hunched over his usual salmon and Saltines.

"I know why you waited up to talk to me," he said. "It's about school, isn't it?"

"Yes."

"If you want to go to PCS, you're going to have to earn it."

"Sure, that's okay. How?"

He thought for a minute while he finished off the last of the salmon. "I want you to take an admissions test for Bronx High School of Science."

"C'mon, Pop! It's in the Bronx, and I'm not looking to be a scientist."

"Hear me out, Bobby. First you have to get in. Only five percent make it. If you do, and get an *A* in every subject for one year, you can go pick any school you want."

"What if I don't get in?"

"If you don't, you can't get *A*'s."

"Pop, that's not fair . . . !"

"You're right. If life were fair, I'd be playing Chopin at Carnegie Hall."

I took the test. I got in. I hated it more than I thought. Not only did

I have to travel an hour each day to the Bronx, not only was it academically the toughest school in the city, not only did I have nothing in common with one kid in the entire school, but I had zero interest in every course. Yet, to get the hell out, I had only one goal— The big *A* across the board.

Before the ink dried, my final report card was before my father's eyes—The only letter on it was the big *A*. Though two had minuses next to them, he couldn't deny there was no other letter on the card.

Did I resent it? Sure. Was Pop right? Sure! If I could get through that, nothing could stop me now.

Charles and I were walking down Broadway. Suddenly he pointed to a girl. "What a beauty."

"Do you want her? She's yours."

Charlie looked at me, his kid brother, as if I were crazy. "Sure," he'd laugh.

Maybe it was his laugh that gave me the adrenaline to go up to the girl, sheepishly saying, "Someone dared me to try to meet you."

Was I from another planet? She'd walk a little faster. I'd keep up with her—a step, a block, two blocks, whatever it took. If nothing else worked, I'd go into one of my imitations—Cagney, Gable, Grant, Cooper. When I got a smile out of her I'd say, "I do this for a living. Ever hear of 'Let's Pretend'?"

If she said, "Sure," or anything sounding like it, she was a goner.

"I'm on it every Saturday. I'm a radio actor. How'd you like to watch the next show? Bring a couple of friends." If she opened her mouth yes, like a fish, she was hooked. "I'll send you the tickets. Come backstage if you'd like. Where can I call you?"

Once I got her number, I said a quick good-bye. Though I was only fourteen, my batting average was better than Ted Williams's.

Instinct cannot be taught, bought, or acquired. Either you have it or you don't; it does not come with age. Till this day, I can't switch from TV to cable. Yet before I could shave, I was as instinctive to a woman's thoughts as I am today.

Danger was my turn-on. The thrill of sneaking a girl into my parents' apartment was greater than getting her into bed. That ended at one o'clock in the morning on New Year's Eve of 1944. My parents were away for the weekend, Charles was in the army, and the girl next to me in bed was Patty Wheeler, daughter of Bert Wheeler, the great comedian. Only eighteen but already the toast of Broadway, she thought I was seventeen.

Suddenly, a knock on the door. It was Daisy Diggs, our nosy housekeeper. "You in there with some tramp, Bobby?" Quickly, I put my hand over Patty's mouth. "Shhh."

"You hear me? You get outta there with that white trash. Your daddy's gonna give you some whippin' in the mornin'."

Patty gave me a double take. "How old are you?"

I cringed. "Fourteen."

At noon on New Year's Day, I was greeted with a smack across the face by Pop, the only time he ever hit me.

"Don't ever be disrespectful in our home again, ever!"

I wasn't. I found a more dangerous turf—the banquet room on the top floor of the St. Moritz Hotel. It was my cousin's wedding. Others were congratulating the bride and groom. I was checking out my new digs.

Not bad. Great view, terrace, lounges, privacy, no upkeep. When we left, I checked the elevators, staircases, entrances, and exits. "Can't beat the price," danger told me.

Like a second-story man, the next afternoon, and for a week to come, I checked the place out, doing a dry run from the hotel entrance to the thirty-first floor, passing the doorman, to the elevator, getting off two floors from the top, a quick left to the back staircase and up two flights by foot, find the one keyless door, which I did, and there it was—my home away from home.

Dangerous? Sure. That was the turn-on.

"Go up the elevator to the twenty-ninth floor, turn left and open the back stairwell," I'd whisper to my love of the night.

"It shouldn't take longer than seven minutes. Wait, count to a hundred. I'll be there. Got it?"

Did she get it!

Whether it be a debutante or a showgirl, my M.O. was the same. I used the place so often I could have done it blindfolded. Ah, but whoever the lady of the night might be, she thought we were sharing something together for the very first time.

During the week, I'd zero in on showgirls, and for good reason— they only had two hours off. It's what's called "between shows." To me a triple blitz. Danger, dropping my pants, and home in time to finish my homework. My sumptuous terrace suite at the St. Moritz remained my private paradise for almost two years.

One night in the middle of a rather intimate embrace, four hands grabbed me from the back. It was the manager with two guards behind him. Embarrassing? The girl I was with just happened to be on the cover of *Life* that week: THE DEBUTANTE OF THE YEAR.

My new best pal, Dickie Van Patten, was the top juvenile actor in town. At eighteen, he had appeared in more than twenty Broadway plays, and had six or seven running parts on radio soaps. We made a great team: me, dark-haired and swarthy; Dickie, blond and fairskinned. We were the same size and constantly exchanged each other's clothes to make people think we had twice the wardrobe we really had. Dickie was almost two years older than me, but we shared the same addictions: gambling, girls, and danger.

At the time, Dickie had the juvenile lead on Broadway in Terence Rattigan's *O Mistress Mine*, starring Alfred Lunt and Lynn Fontanne. On Saturday night, I'd meet him after the show backstage at the Empire Theater. With Jeremiah, Alfred Lunt's black valet, we'd hop a cab to Harlem.

The Red Rooster was a gambling parlor and whorehouse. Dickie and I were the only white faces in the joint. The poker tables were downstairs, the bedrooms upstairs. We never ventured upstairs, but we didn't have to. All the waitresses could do it: you'd hold out a dollar bill, and in one movement, they'd lift their skirts, squat, and pick up your tip with their pussies. Through the eyes of a fifteen-year-old, it was tantamount to discovering an eighth continent.

For years, Dickie had the juvenile lead on "Young Widder Brown"—radio's top soap. Through him, I got a running part on the show as his best friend. During rehearsal breaks, we'd hang out with all the other soap actors around the third-floor stairwell of NBC.

Dickie knew that the one thing I couldn't say no to was a dare. One day, he pointed to the railing over the stairwell. "A buck says you can't hang by your fingers for five minutes."

It was thirty feet down, enough to kill me.

"You're on."

Everyone gathered around. And there I hung, and hung, and hung.

While Dickie counted off the minutes, I shut my eyes and counted off the seconds, trying to block out the pain. Finally, four hands pulled me up. There was no applause, but it sure filled up my little black book with more numbers than I had pages for. Only the day before, no one even knew my name.

Haaren High, located on Eleventh Avenue and Fifty-ninth Street, smack in the middle of Hell's Kitchen—was the roughest school in Manhattan. An all-boys prep school for jail. After my year at Bronx Science, I thought I'd won the right to go to Professional Children's School. My father said okay, but my mother still insisted on a "normal" school.

Nobody in his right mind would ever choose Haaren—that is, if he wanted to come out alive. I did. It was the one place I could matriculate and be out by 11:40 in the morning.

The only thing I learned there was survival. It didn't take long to figure out my only shot to make it out alive was not to show fear, and not to let on I was an actor. Luckily, the toughest kids in the school were the dumbest. That was my ace. Suddenly, their homework was done, and cheating became an art. For this, I ascended to a king without a throne. Without it, my next address could have easily been the morgue next door.

Haaren High was an embarrassment, especially for my folks. But by bus, it was ten minutes to Rockefeller Center. Once the bell rang, I was out the door and off like a sprinter to the bright lights of big Broadway.

The gusher decade of the eighties was a fizzle compared to the postwar forties. Watch out 1945, here I come. Close to ninety shows a year hit the Broadway boards. The eight major film studios each turned out between fifty to sixty flicks a year. (Today, the eight combined don't turn out that many.) Each studio had between forty to seventy actors under contract. Broadway was the mecca—Hollywood the next stop. There were more agents in New York than police and more actors than cockroaches.

Now fifteen, attending Haaren finishing school, scratching out a buck or two on radio, I copped a big one—the co-lead on "Henry Aldrich," the most popular half-hour family comedy on radio, with a paycheck of $175 a week to boot.

Next, the lead in the stage production of Booth Tarkington's *Seventeen* at the Equity Library Theater, New York's most prestigious showcase for actors. The pay was zip. The exposure, unbuyable.

My parents attended opening night. Just two weeks later, they were sitting across a large, oval oak desk from Charles Abrahamson, New York's most prestigious film agent, head of Famous Artists.

"Your son's got a presence. That's the key in film. More than talent; more than looks. With your permission, I'd like to put him under personal contract, get him on the boards, do a play or two, test the waters, sign him with Warners, Twentieth, or Metro—whoever shows the most interest."

Mom and Pop were in shock. Me! I was now a Famous Artist.

Chamberlain Brown was the oldest, most revered, and by far the most snobbish purveyor of talent in the theatrical world. Whether it be W. C. Fields, Clark Gable, or Douglas Fairbanks, every actor on his way to them Pearly Gates of Hollywood passed through his doors. He must have been in his seventies when I met him. A foppish man on a couch, he didn't smile but pointed to a bookcase.

"Walk over there, pick out a book, and bring it to me." I obeyed. "You move well. Sit down." I sat. "What have you done?"

"Mostly radio." I reeled off my credits.

Looking me over. "How old are you?"

"Fifteen."

"Huh. Abrahamson was right. Your voice—who trained you?"

"Nobody."

"Well, we'll find out just how good you are. We'll fit you in at our New Amsterdam Theatre showcase. Find a scene—ten or fifteen minutes max."

With a sarcastic laugh, "Let's see how that untrained voice of yours responds to pressure." Walking out, his high-pitched voice squeaked. "You're sure your voice is not trained?"

"Wish it were," I smiled.

On Tuesday afternoons, the New Amsterdam Theatre, seating more than eight hundred people, was the hottest ticket in town. Credentials, not money, allowed one entrance.

Chamberlain Brown, the guru of tomorrow's stars, presented his showcase—twelve to sixteen actors, all with ticker tape credentials, presenting their wares before an array of directors, producers, writers, talent scouts, and every top Hollywood mogul in town. Each seat was filled with a "somebody," seeking to discover the next Humphrey Bogart, Lana Turner, or Cary Grant.

There I stood backstage—my big break. Hollywood, here I come! Only a month before, Chamberlain Brown gave me the big news of my big break, that I was gonna be front and center at his New Amsterdam Theatre showcase. Excitedly, I called Abrahamson, my mentor. "Don't stretch," he advised.

I looked through play after play, realizing the one way to be underwhelming was to give a road show performance of a remembered performance. Why not write an original?

My brother, Charles, had just gotten out of the army and was unemployed. Why not do a scene between brothers—one confronting the other? The elder comes back from the army, finds out his kid brother's been playing around with his "lady" while he was landing at Normandy.

Didn't Abrahamson say "Don't stretch?" Well, I wasn't.

Charlie had never worked professionally, but so what—he had only four words to say: "Why'd you do it?"

Then for nine pages, I copped to the truth about his so-called lady. Furious, he pulls a gun out and blows me away.

Each day, for the next month, we rehearsed, rehearsed, and rehearsed; by now, my nine pages of dialogue down that pat, I could have done them backward.

From behind the curtain I look out. There's Charles Abrahamson in the third row, next to him, Jack L. Warner, "Mr. Big" of Warners. Watch out Hollywood—here I come. Half a dozen actors already had done their gig. From center stage, Chamberlain Brown's high-pitched voice echoes through the theater. "May I now introduce Robert Evans."

I jab Charlie with a left, "Okay, let's give it to 'em."

The curtain parts. From stage left Charlie walks to center. From stage right, I do the same. I'm standing there. He's standing there. His lips part—nothin' comes out.

The fucker's frozen.

I shake him, whispering.

"Give me the fuckin' line, will ya." He's a glacier.

I grab both his arms:

"Tell me I'm no good, tell me I'm a piece of shit, tell me anything." Nothing.

"Kill me if you wanna!"

He takes his gun out *and shoots me.* Is he fuckin' nuts? What about my nine pages of dialogue? Now, I've gotta drop to the floor dead. I did.

Suddenly Charlie's defrosted, but it was too late. I was dead, so was my career. He looks down at me. I look up at him. I wanna kill him, instead both of us burst out laughing.

There we are, center stage, two hyenas in hysterics. The audience loved it—a new comedy find—the next Abbott and Costello. They're laughing too. Yeah, but we couldn't stop.

Wham! The curtain closes.

It's Chamberlain Brown, he's screaming.

"Throw 'em out! Throw 'em out!" His temple vein was about to burst. "Lunatics! Lunatics! You're never work on Broadway as long as Chamberlain Brown's alive."

That did it. Laughter turned to convulsions.

"Garbage, garbage!" as blood began pouring from his nostrils. "Throw 'em out! Out! Out!"

Like garbage, four stagehands grab us and throw us out into the back alley. Was it worth it? Yeah, it was the longest laugh of our lives.

Did Chamberlain Brown keep his word? Forget Broadway. I couldn't get an audition for summer stock. Was I angry with Charlie? That's what you call love.

"If your feet are as fast as your hands, you could be one hell of a scrapper—maybe make the pros. There ain't many white kids around. Maybe I'll even manage you, call you Pretty Boy Floyd."

"Thanks, but no thanks. I'm an actor, not a fighter."

"Good for you, kid. Your hands, usin' 'em right, is as important in acting as it is in fighting—that's if you wanna make the pros. So keep 'em up."

The words were coming from Mike Todd, who was getting a kick out of watching me punch the bag at the Gotham Health Club. Me, I enjoyed nothing more than showing off in front of him, for in total awe was I of this adventurer, gambler, entrepreneur, showman, and, oh yes, cocksman to boot. And there he was watching me.

Many a day, we would leave the Gotham Health Club, walk up Sixth Avenue to Central Park South, and grab a quick sandwich at Rumpelmayer's; never sitting at a table, but at the counter—it was faster. He always ordered the same thing: a chicken salad sandwich on rye toast and a strawberry soda. Naturally, I ordered the same, not caring, just wondering why he wanted to break bread with me—a sixteen-year-old kid.

As years passed, his myth only grew, marrying some funny-looking dame, Elizabeth Taylor, at the height of her career, and accomplishing the near impossible, raising his own financing and independently producing *Around the World in Eighty Days*, which won the Academy Award for best film of the year.

At the pinnacle of his success, he was killed in a plane crash over Palm Springs. He died the way he lived—dangerously.

One Saturday afternoon, we left the club and walked to our usual sandwich hangout. Ordering the usual as well, Mike took out a big cigar, then lit it with a wooden match.

"You've got too much moxie, kid, to be an actor. It's okay for a dame, but not for a guy. Unless you make it big, real big, it's a lousy life. After a while you start losin' your *cojones*. There's nothin' more boring than hangin' with some half-assed actor, talkin' about himself." Finishing his sandwich, he quickly got up. "Gotta go. I'm late for a gin game."

"Could I play?"

He burst out laughing. "You? Play in this game? Are you nuts? These guys will take your pants off and not even blink. What will you pay 'em with? Your dick? Come up and watch if you wanna. Just don't be a wise ass."

The game was next door at 40 Central Park South. Mike was late. Five guys were waiting. It was a six-handed game. The group played once a week. No one wanted to be paid by check, only by cash. At the start of every session, the prior week's tally would be settled—in cash, of course.

There was a problem, a first. The guy responsible for keeping the tally sheet lost it. All six agreed that there were two winners and four losers, but no one agreed as to how much each one owed to whom. They were all friends. No one was looking for an edge. Rather, everyone's recollection was different.

Mike, one of the four losers broke in. "Fuck this, fellas. I've only got four hours and I came to play gin. You say I owe $2,100, right, Nick?"

"Yeah," Nick nodded.

"Well, I brought $1,400 in cash. That's what I remember losin'.

There's a $700 dollar spread. What the fuck, let's split it."

Taking a check from his pants pocket, he filled it in for $350. "Don't cash it, will ya? I'll bring you the cash next week." Then turning to the others, "Will you guys do the same so we can start the fuckin' game?"

Reluctantly, they all agreed. The game started. The stakes were set at a dollar a point. One could easily lose ten or fifteen thousand in an afternoon, which, by today's standards, would be like losing a quarter of a million. As much in awe as I was in watching, I was equally eager to be part of the action. But this was a game for the pros. And me, I hadn't even started to shave.

The four hours were up; no one wanted to quit. Bending over, Mike whispered to me, "Go into the other room. Call David Niven at the Pierre. Tell him I'm in an important meeting. Ask him to pick up Susan Hayward. She's at the St. Regis. I'll meet them both at Le Pavillon at nine o'clock."

Nine o'clock rolled around. Nick Conte, the guy Mike gave his check to at the beginning of the session, who at the time was a big Hollywood movie star, better known as Richard Conte, suggested one last set.

Without any thought that people were waiting for him, Mike said, "Start dealing." In the next hour, Mike hit it big. A triple blitz. From being a small loser, he was now a big winner.

It was way past ten by now. Again, it turned out there were four losers and two winners. This time though, Conte and Todd were the big winners. Mike won about $4,700, and Nick, well over $7,000.

Tallying up the wins and losses, Mike looked at the scorekeeper. "Take $350 off of mine and put it in Nick's column. Now tear up my fuckin' check, pretty boy."

Conte laughed. "You're more than an hour late. The broad's gonna' be pissed."

"So what! I won, didn't I? I'll keep the tally sheet this time, fellas. See you next Saturday. Same time, same station. Let's go kid, we're late."

Going down in the elevator, Mike lit his cigar again. "That cocksucker Conte's a fuckin' pro. He never loses. If he acted half as well as he played, he'd have copped two Oscars by now. Walk me to the restaurant, kid. It's only three blocks away." Strutting down Central Park South together, Mike began laughing, "It's a good thing I didn't lose; the check I gave Conte would have bounced."

Did I hear right? His $350 check would have bounced and he's playing for a buck a point?

Before I had a chance to ask, he laughed, "That's what gamblin's all about, kid. It ain't no fun unless you play for more than you can afford to lose."

Approaching the restaurant now. "Being a good player ain't enough. For a buck you can buy 'em by the dozen. It's all handicappin'. Gotta know who you're playing with. Good players come and go. Good handicappers seem to always pick up aces." Under the restaurant canopy, he put his arm around me. "Don't forget, if it ain't written down, it ain't collectible; everyone remembers things different." He feigned a left. My hands went up to block it. "That's it, kid," he laughed. "Keep them dukes up; it's cold out there. Got it?"

Got it I did. He hurried into the restaurant more than an hour late. Ah, but far more important, *a winner.*

A few months later Dickie Van Patten and I were sparring on the beach when a little fat guy with a cigar walked over.

"Either of you fighters?"

"No," we laughed, "we're actors."

A beady-eyed look, "You're good, kid. Fast. How'd you like to fill in as a sub novas in Forest Hills on Tuesday? With your speed you could make the Golden Gloves."

"Thanks, but no thanks."

"Ten bucks says you're scared," jabbed Dickie.

"Where do I show?"

Once again, Dickie and I were the only white faces in the joint. They put me into black satin trunks and told me I was fifteenth on the card. For the next two hours, I sweat it out watching one loser after another come back into the locker room with his teeth knocked out, his nose broken, his eyes slashed.

What the fuck am I doing here? I'm an actor.

I got the nod.

I'm next. This is nuts. This ain't no theater. It's a fuckin' hole in the wall in black Cambodia.

Entering the ring with Dickie behind me, I saw for the first time the guy I was to fight. This animal with no teeth wasn't looking to get into flicks. Except for his white trunks, he was as black as I was white and he tasted this honky fruit across the ring.

This ain't fair.

Gong! Three rounds—two minutes each. Six minutes to stay alive. Throwing everything he could, he came at me like a wild man. Mike Todd's words "Keep them dukes up" came in handy. By the end of round one, the only thing that got hurt were my arms. They were ready to fall off.

Gong! Round two. The animal came out charging again. A roundhouse left, it hit the air. I got off my first punch—a right to the ribs. A second—a left I never knew I had to the jaw. His legs wobbled. He was ready to go. His arms were down. There were still thirty seconds left. There was one problem—I couldn't lift my arms, I couldn't catch my breath, I couldn't even sit down when the round was over. If I did, I'd never get up. Gong! Round three. Again he came at me. A roundhouse punch—wild. I saw my opening—threw a right.

Twenty minutes later I opened my eyes. All I could see was white. Was I in heaven? A tenner dropped on my stomach.

"Thank God," said Dickie. "I thought you were dead."

A few years passed. It was now Dickie's turn to be on the other end of a knockout punch.

On my third callback for a juicy role in *Fourteen Hours,* a flick Twentieth Century–Fox was shooting in New York, I met a real looker. She, too, was on her third callback. She got the part (her first), I didn't. But I got her, at least in the figurative sense.

Persistence, and being a good dancer, got me several dates. Being older and much sought after, she had little interest in an aging teenager. Though she did enjoy sharing a few hours with me every so often, dancing up a Latin storm at the Plaza Hotel's Rendezvous Room.

What the looker didn't know was that she had a hundred-dollar bounty on her head. Months before, Dickie and I did everything imaginable to meet her, stalking the Barbizon Hotel for Women trying to bribe the doorman, Oscar. No luck, no chance meeting, zero on all counts. "A hundred dollars to the one who has her on their arm first," blurted a frustrated Dickie. Now, here she was dancing in my arms to the beat of the samba.

Dick, at the time, was costarring in Broadway's new smash hit, *Mr. Roberts*. One Friday night I caught the show with Miss Hundred-Dollar Bounty. Later we paid my pal Dick a visit backstage.

Makeup and all, his face paled seeing Miss Hundred-Dollar Bounty on my arm. The three of us left backstage together. Congratulating him on his performance, the Bounty and I climbed into a horse and buggy and trotted down West Forty-fifth Street, leaving Dickie behind, knocked on his ass, way past the count of ten. The Bounty? Oh, some wannabe actress . . . Grace Kelly.

From the mid-1940s, television was the new medium. "The ticket to fame," echoed an enthusiastic Abrahamson, who still believed in me. I was front and center for every audition.

I couldn't wait to finish school. That summer I took extra courses so I could graduate six months early. By December 1947 I was free—skipping graduation, never saying good-bye, for there was no one to say good-bye to.

No star yet, but my credits, both on TV and radio, made me a legitimate contender. Except for Broadway, which was off-limits as long as Chamberlain Brown was breathing.

The jackpot! I got my first part in a movie, a gang flick at Universal. Hollywood, here I come. Come April 1, I was to report to wardrobe. Between acting, actresses, models, showgirls, poker, and the racetrack, I wasted little time on sleep.

"Bobby," my mother hastened, "I'm not letting you go out to California until you get a good rest. You're coming to Florida with your father and me. Get some sun, put on some weight. Look like a movie star."

A week later, we broke in my pop's new Pontiac and headed for Palm Beach. In Wilmington, North Carolina, stopping for gas, I hopped out for a Coke. My left side went numb. A local doctor examined me, diagnosed indigestion, and gave me an enema. The farther south we traveled, the more the pain. Pulling up to the hotel in Palm Beach, I could hardly get out of the car and was rushed to a hospital, where X rays showed that my left lung had collapsed. The doctors were surprised I was still alive. Suddenly, Hollywood was very far away.

There was one cure—*rest*. My parents rented a house on an isolated island off Palm Beach. There, for the next six weeks, I did nothing but lie in bed and feel sorry for myself. Now it was God talking to me, not Mike Todd. What he was saying was "Slow down, or you'll be dead."

For the first time in my life I was a watcher, not a doer. It felt good.

After six weeks, my lung was again healthy. The doctor strongly suggested caution. Also for the first time, I liked the word. When my parents left for home, I told them I'd like to try something new: be a beach bum for a while. Not that I'd found God, but at least I'd heard him. They thought it was a terrific idea.

It took but two weeks, and I was on local radio doing news, sports, and weather. You can't get into any trouble doing that! Really?

A guy from Miami showed up one day. He'd heard my voice and liked it. Doubling my salary, a week later I was in Miami Beach, the youngest disc jockey in America. "The Robert Evans Show," brought to you from the glamorous lounge of the Caribbean Hotel. Everyone was on, from Rosemary Clooney, Tony Martin, Frankie Laine, Phil Silvers, Dick Shawn, to the local big spenders.

"Put the Diamond Jims on the air," my boss prodded. "Make 'em feel like celebrities."

I wasn't yet eighteen, but I thought I knew it all. I didn't. Miami Beach was a town where there was nothing to do but play, play, play. It was crawling with women looking for trouble. And me—I couldn't stay out of it. Being the beach's new celebrity, I never said no more times, yet never had so much action.

I'd been at the Caribbean six weeks when Havana called. One of the owners of the Copacabana Club had caught my act at the Caribbean. Again, an offer doubling my salary, but that wasn't the attraction. Havana was the gambling capital of the world. Need I say more?

In Havana, women faded into the background. I only had eyes for guys, the guys who ran the action, that is—the mob. Meyer Lansky, Frank Costello, you name the nose, he was there.

My gig was celebrated but very short. Accidentally one night I witnessed something I shouldn't have. A guy you don't say no to grabbed and blindfolded me, then took me for a ride. Taken out of the car, a pack of green was handed me.

"Forget you were ever here." I did.

Suddenly, I'm in another seat. It was to either oblivion or a small plane. Luckily, they must have liked my smile—like luggage, I was dropped off by seaplane on a beach north of Key West. My head still bleeding, but with five thousand of good-bye green in my pocket. It was time to go home.

Absence does not make the heart grow fonder. Gone less than a year, I was no longer a juvenile, yet too young for romantic leads, and suddenly tough to cast. But it mattered little since, for the first time, I fell in love. Her name: Elaine Stewart. Beautiful in looks, heart, and giving, her face graced every fashion magazine imaginable. Get this—a virgin to boot. Me, I wanted her to stay one. For morality? Uh-uh. For immorality. That way I could still play and not feel guilty cheating.

Elaine's career soon overshadowed mine. One night, we joined Benny Medford, a top Hollywood agent, at Danny's Hideaway. Elaine's golden future in films was all he could talk about. She held my hand tight, knowing how much I wished it were me he was talking about. Benny had spotted Elaine on a magazine cover and showed her picture to producer Hal Wallis, who offered to fly her west for a screen test. Within a week, she was signed to a seven-year contract. When she called to say she'd be coming back east to get her things before taking off to La-la Land, the good news I was eagerly waiting to tell her suddenly shrunk into the background. I had just gotten the plum role of my career, playing young Lord Essex in NBC's live TV special *Elizabeth and Essex.*

She spent her last night in New York backstage, watching my performance as the romantic young Lord Essex, a dashing young nobleman on stage, while in life I was a wannabe left behind by my own virgin princess.

For months, I courted her long distance. By now Elaine had become filmland's female find of the year, making the cover of *Life.* I couldn't get her out of my head. Buying a three-carat diamond ring, I flew west to surprise her. From the airport, I went straight to her address, rushing up the steps and ringing her bell. The door opened. It *was not* Elaine, but one handsome motherfucker. An actor named Scott Brady, who at the time was the screen's hot new tough guy.

Up an octave. "Is Elaine here?"

Coming to the door in a bathrobe, with her hair dripping wet, was my virgin princess, giving me a look as if I were an Auschwitz refugee.

"Bob, what are you doing here?"

"I thought I'd surprise you. . . ."

"Never pull a surprise on a lady," she smiled. *"Ever!"*

My college education.

3

"Change into the three-piece single-breasted pinstripe."

Off came the Harris tweed jacket, the cavalry twill trousers, and into the pinstripe, rushing back into the showroom, where the buyer and merchandise manager from Saks were sitting. I unbuttoned the jacket to show the vest, turned slowly around, putting my hands in the pockets.

"Great look," said the buyer from Saks. "We'll take it in brown, navy, and gray from 38 to 46. Double up on the 40s and 42s. Let's look at the sport coats."

I was now a model for L. Greif, one of the more prestigious men's clothiers in America, earning sixty-five bucks a week. My acting career had come to a standstill, leaving L. Greif's showroom my only stage. In three months, not only did my salary triple, but I was made a house salesman with a dozen small accounts of my own. Still it was less than half the green I had been making just two years earlier as an actor. It was a new beginning, yet being an actor still haunted my every thought. How could I be over the hill at nineteen?

One morning in the elevator, a man tapped me on the shoulder. "Nat Moskow—Cardinal Clothes. Hear you're one helluva salesman." Before I got a word out, he blabbered, "How'd you like to rep my line on the West Coast?"

Opening up California for a clothing company was not the route to stardom I had dreamed about, but it was a route. Arriving in Tinseltown, the first person I called was not the buyer at Bullock's, but Benny Medford.

"Have I got a shot?"

"No. With broads you can always make a deal. With guys it's different. You've gotta have talent. But I'll try."

Hollywood was another planet. Everything looked different, smelled different, tasted different. Movies were booming—television trying to catch up. Benny and I became good pals. Out of friendship, he busted his ass trying to get me in front of the camera. I was interviewed, auditioned, and screen-tested for everything from hoods to cripples. It always came down to me and another guy. The other guy always got the part.

Meanwhile I was busting my ass for Moskow trying to get Cardinal Clothes in any store I could. Every other week, Willy Loman would get into his secondhand Buick and hit the road. I was getting orders, but my commissions barely kept my Buick in gas.

William Michaeljohn was the head honcho of talent at Paramount, the man responsible for building the studio's stable of stars. His eye for a new face was reputedly the sharpest in the business. A nod from him could get you into "the fishbowl," the circular arena at Paramount where all screen tests and auditions were held. This room was lined with two-way mirrors behind which sat the studio chief, the producers, the directors, the writers.

Getting Michaeljohn's nod could take years. Getting in to see him could take months. Benny somehow arranged an audience with "his holiness" in a matter of weeks.

Michaeljohn had the looks and manner of a British banker as he cryptically eyed me while I filled him in on my New York experience.

"Benny, I'll send the script of *This Gun for Hire* over to your office this afternoon. Scenes 86 and 128." Looking at his calendar, "Susan Morrow will test with him. Wednesday, a week, ten A.M."

What a break, what a trap. How could I possibly look good in a role that made Alan Ladd an overnight star?

"Get out of my life, and stay out!" smacking Susan Morrow across the face.

"Cut," the director blurted.

"Terrific, kid," Benny interjected.

This time he was right. By afternoon's end, I was the newest member of Paramount's "golden circle."

For the next months, I went to college, "Paramount style," studying everything from fencing to riding bareback. There were twenty other male actors under contract, each of whom had bluer eyes, whiter teeth, and a better physique. None of whom, however, had to play Willy Loman on the side, schleping his new spring line from San Diego to Sacramento. Six months later, instead of graduating, I was left back.

Benny gave me the bad news over lunch at the Brown Derby. "They dropped your option, kid. Michaeljohn's still hot on you, but there's some new dame running the show. You ain't her type. Henry Willson's guys are—the Troys, the Rocks, the Tabs." Shaking his head, "You know the type."

"That's it then?"

"At Paramount, yeah. But fuck it, we've got some great test footage on you. In a month, we'll be in action."

The test was seen at every projection room in town. The only interest came from Eagle-Lion, where a B film was big budget. A long way from the majors, but better than being on the road selling Moskow's new fall line.

I was about to sign with them to do a gangster film when my parents arrived on the scene. Mom and Pop treated me to my first dinner at Chasen's. It wasn't me they wanted to talk about, it was my brother. Two years earlier Charles and a tailor named Joseph Picone had started Evan-Picone. With very little capital, they began manufacturing women's skirts. Now they were selling to the best stores in the country and their sales were touching the million mark. Charles wanted to expand into something new. Both Mom and Pop thought it was a great opportunity.

"Who could launch it better than you?"

"But I'm an actor, I'm only twenty. I'm not washed up yet."

I was in my sixties, wearing a rumpled suit, frayed shirt, shoes five years too old, hungry for work, hungry for food, desperately needing a gig. I waited, waited, waited to read for a two-scene part in a minor movie. I didn't get it. Jumping up in a cold sweat from the recurring nightmare that I had witnessed time and time again through the eyes of a teenaged wannabe actor. It never ceased to haunt me. I vowed to myself then, I would never let it happen to me.

New York here I come.

4

"Charlie, we've made it! We're on Fifth Avenue!"

What a high. Frances Loeb, the buyer at Lord and Taylor (now Frances Lear, who later became the editor of *Lear's* magazine), was putting our slacks in the window.

"How'd you do it?" Charlie laughed.

"I made her try them on herself. She looked great."

It was the end of a year's journey of preaching the gospel: "Women in Pants."

It was easy to do—I believed it. I never pretended macho. A ladies' man, not a man's man, was my future to be.

Insightful always to a "void" most women share, that of a male embracer—not sex, affirmation. Being a positive influence to their needs, their goals.

Conversely, in the crunch, women have always been there for me. Men? Sometimes.

What better proof? Women were responsible for making me a millionaire before my mid-twenties. From east to west, from department to specialty store, 60 percent of the buyers in our showroom were women. However, 90 percent of our volume came from them. That says it all.

From Filene's in Boston to Rich's in Atlanta, Halle Brothers in Cleveland, J. L. Hudson in Detroit, Marshall Field in Chicago, Neiman-Marcus in Dallas, Frederick and Nelson in Seattle, I. Magnin in San Francisco, Bullock's and Robinson's in L.A., it was "Women in Pants." Really? Without exception, it was taboo with a capital *T*. Selling bibles to the Hell's Angels would have been an easier sell.

Needing a hook, I came up with the unexpected. Every major city in the country had at least one or two local breakfast shows on TV. Each desperately needed to fill time without spending money. That's it! Fuck it! I'm an actor—use it.

Systematically, I contacted the person at the top TV station in every major city who did local morning programming. Without exception, each had a breakfast show. Acting as my own manager, using a different name, I offered the station the opportunity of having Bob Evans, a radio and television personality, present a breakfast fashion show to the women of their city, free of any production cost.

"Mr. Evans would use hometown models, supply the music, and emcee the fashion show himself." Saving the last for best, "It's not a fashion show you'll be offering your audiences, it's a fashion explosion, news—'Why shouldn't women be wearing the pants in the family?' "

Did it work? Within two months I was a fashion celebrity. I would arrive in Cleveland, Detroit, St. Louis, you name it, a day ahead to interview local models. Height and long legs were a necessity. A flat chest was okay; a flat ass wasn't.

I rehearsed the girls for two hours before the show, which was usually nine in the morning. From toreador pants to gray flannels to silk lounging trousers, the models moved to the music. My commentary followed their every turn, ending with "If Dietrich and Hepburn can look glamorous in pants, why not you? Don't let men be the only ones wearing the pants in the family."

Did it work? Gusher time. Suddenly every top store wanted me to put my fashion segment on their prime TV breakfast show. As my act got better, my orders got bigger. Within a year, pants became a fashion contender. What was once taboo now was in. Today, Evan-Picone is among the most important signatures in the fashion world—its imprint certainly outlasting the movies I've produced.

For the first time, heavy green began making a heavy dent in my bank account. Charles and I were inseparable. We laughed together, cried together, gambled together. I would have stopped a bullet for him, and he for me. When a mutual friend stole his girl, I not only vowed never to speak to the prick again, but made sure he lost the girl, and any other girl he made a play for. Call it brother's revenge.

Double-dating was a catastrophe. Charles and I were so turned on by each other's company that our dates felt like ornaments. One night, some smart-assed broad slammed the door in my face. "Why don't ya just go home and fuck your brother?"

Evan-Picone was a trendsetter. *Harper's Bazaar, Vogue, Mademoiselle, Glamour,* all agreed. Before long we had expanded to a plant specially built for us in North Bergen, New Jersey. Employing more than four hundred Sicilians, it was Joe Picone's kingdom.

Joe was more than my brother's equal partner in the overall company. He was the maestro. (My partnership and equity was limited to the pants division.) No work was contracted out. Everything that bore Evan-Picone's label was made under Joe's demanding eye. He ruled with an iron hand, but such was the loyalty he commanded that our factory remained the only one in New Jersey the unions couldn't organize. Of course, it helped that no one spoke English, only Sicilian.

Harlem never recovered from the war. The old had become older, the dirty dirtier. By the early fifties, Lenox Avenue was a war zone. Depressed by the neighborhood's decline, Pop closed shop, never to practice dentistry again.

Meanwhile my mother had found a new life. Every morning she came to work at Evan-Picone, calling herself "Mrs. Stone," leaving her identity as our mother behind. With her warmth, energy, and astute eye, she was more than just the star of the showroom, she was a voice to be reckoned with, her opinions sought by buyers and fashion writers across the country. She traveled with Charles from Hong Kong to Milan, looking to break barriers in fashion and fabric. Yet my father had no place to hang his hat. Though he had introduced Charles to Joe Picone and given them seed money to start the business, he was now the only one in the family who didn't enjoy a part of its success. His dentistry behind him, he was now the one left out in the cold.

His self-esteem shrank; his rage grew. Family dinners now joyless, tension was all that prevailed. There wasn't a day Charles and I didn't talk about how to make Pop feel part of our success. We gave him various responsibilities, knowing they were only Band-Aids. He knew it, too. Charles would sadly shake his head, "Poor Pop, from the Führer to Archibald to Archie to 'A.'" For the rest of his life, we referred to Pop as "A"—a secret sadness Charlie and I shared for the muted dreams of a man we loved.

Pop was never short on vision, only on luck.

"Charles. Bobby. There's more money to be made on the west coast of Florida than anywhere else in the country. Miles and miles of undiscovered beachfront with nothing on it, not even electricity. The sand is like silk. It's only a dot on the map now, but in a decade it will make Palm Beach look like Coney Island. Boys, if you want to hit the jackpot, this is it—let's lock it up."

In the spring of 1953, Charlie and I agreed to make the trek. On reflection, we were only patronizing him. If I hadn't been very close, in the biblical sense, with the top showgirl at the Latin Quarter in Miami, I doubt that we would have gone at all. I told her Charlie and I would be there for the weekend and to fix my brother up with the greatest pair of legs in the line and "Look out; we're not coming there for a tan."

With a great weekend to look forward to, we went off in search of Pop's mountain of wealth. Pop was right. Stretching before us were miles and miles of white sand, blue water, and palm trees. Nothing else was there except a trailer. Out of it stepped a man with a shark's smile and a neck as red as the Russian flag.

"Riley the land agent."

Pop stuck out his hand. "Evans from New York."

"Nice seein' ya, Doc," Riley answered. His eyes lit up as though Pop were Diamond Jim himself.

Hours of negotiations later, papers were drawn. We were to become the land barons of more than a mile of empty Florida beach front for $318,000.

"We'll close tomorrow?" sharked Riley.

I sneaked into the trailer to call my squeeze at the Latin Quarter in Miami, whispering that I couldn't get there until the next day. She didn't take it kindly.

"You fucker, I took the weekend off. I fixed your brother up with the best legs in town, Chicky Jones. Now you tell me you're a no-show? If you're not here tonight, forget it!" Bang.

Whispering the update to my brother, he looked at his watch. "The last plane's at six-thirty. We can still make it."

"But, Pop told Riley we'd close tomorrow."

"Okay, big shot, you decide."

Coming up with a brilliant idea, I whispered back, "With property, we're buyers; with pussy, we're sellers. Let's make the plane!"

"How about putting the closing off until Monday?" Charles suggested to Pop. "Just to be sure everything checks out."

Riley's neck got redder. He wasn't happy. "There's a time to close and a time to close." He glared back.

"It's too late for us to check with our bank, Mr. Riley," my brother interrupted. "We want to be sure everything's in proper order for the check transferral. Is Monday all right?"

"Have to be in Tampa on Monday," Riley icily blurted out. "It'll have to wait till Tuesday."

Great, I thought to myself, gives us an extra day to play.

Well, Pop did his homework, checking out every possible negative. There weren't any. Charlie and I did our homework as well. For the next three days in Miami, we never saw the sun.

On Tuesday morning, promptly at 11:00, with check in hand, Pop, Charlie, and I were back on the empty Naples beach in Riley's trailer.

"Sorry, fellas. No deal." Riley had done his homework too. "Remember what I said, Dr. Shapiro, or is it Shapera?" snickered red-neck Riley. " 'There's a time to close and a time to close.' Well, ya missed the train. Just as well. Your kind don't belong on this side of Florida anyway." As he closed the door in our faces.

Today, that mile-plus of Naples beachfront, known as "the gold coast of the Gulf," is worth not millions, but billions.

Poor Pop, another extraordinary vision, another unrequited dream.

5

Putting pussy before property changed the course of my fortunes. Putting pussy before patriotism changed the course of my life.

November 5, 1956. I was in Beverly Hills setting up Evan-Picone boutiques at Bullock's. Staying at the Beverly Hills Hotel, I had graduated to a suite and cabana by the pool. Theona Bryant, an actress under contract to MGM, was helping me pack. The next day was the Eisenhower/Stevenson runoff for president and I wanted to get back to New York to vote.

"Bob, I need quiet time alone with you more than Ike needs your vote," purred Theona. "You've been married to the phone since you've been here. Stay please," taking two of my fingers in her mouth. "It'll be better than voting any day. Promise."

It's a good thing I wasn't born a girl, I'd have been the town pushover. Naturally I stayed, lying by the pool on election day, sucking up the sun. Theona by my side.

"Excuse me, young man, my name is Martin Arrogue," a voice interrupted. "Are you an actor?"

Squinting through the sunlight, I half laughed. "A long time ago."

"It couldn't have been that long," he laughed. "My wife and I have been watching you by the pool these past few days. Her name is Norma Shearer. She'd like to meet you."

"Why?"

"Let her tell you."

Norma Shearer, one of the few remaining icons of Hollywood's legendary aristocracy, was a petite blonde in a striped short robe. Raising herself on her chaise, she repeated her husband's question.

"Are you an actor?" I gave her the same answer. "Pardon me for being curious, but why are you always on the phone?"

"I have to pay my bills."

"You're not a bookmaker?"

"No, I'm in ladies pants."

She laughed. "I was right, Marty. Young actors don't have his presence, authority. He's perfect. He's Irving." Then looking to me. "Would you like to play my husband?" I quickly looked at her husband. "No, not Marty," Norma giggled. "My *deceased* husband, Irving Thalberg."

Flashing through my mind, That guy was the boy genius of Hollywood.

"They're making a film at Universal called *Man of a Thousand Faces*. My friend Jimmy Cagney is playing the title role of Lon Chaney. It was Irving who discovered him and made him the biggest star in silent film. He was only twenty at the time, too young to sign the checks, but not too young to run a studio. Would you consider playing Irving, Mr. Evans."

This had to be a gag.

"Thanks, but no thanks. I'm already a day late. I have to leave for New York this evening."

"Then it's not too late. Aren't we lucky, Marty? We still have this afternoon to set a meeting up with Jimmy and the producer, Robert Arthur."

"Why me?"

"I have the approval of who plays Irving, Mr. Evans, and every actor the studio's brought over for me to meet looks like a young actor. Watching you on the phone, I said to Martin, 'Now that's Irving.' Would you consider playing him?"

Thinking to myself, Cagney owes me one—the scar down my face is still there. "Sure, why not? Cagney's the one guy I've wanted to meet."

Robert Arthur's office was a bungalow next to Cary Grant's at Universal. Waiting for him in the anteroom, Marty whispered, "Norma's been impossible. She's turned all of their choices down, so don't expect a hero's welcome."

Wearing a three-piece Harris tweed suit and thick horn-rimmed glasses and smoking a pipe, the distinguished producer Robert Arthur tolerated my presence for as long as he thought was professionally polite to satisfy Miss Shearer's desire.

Picking up the phone, he dialed. "Jimmy, Norma's found a young man that she thinks is perfect to play Irving. We'd like to put the two of you on film together. Would you mind?"

All the years I had been trying to get in the door, something like this had never happened. Within minutes, I was on the set with the director of the film, Joe Pevney. Then, appearing beside me was the man responsible for the knife slash that scarred my left cheek close to twenty years before.

"Jimmy Cagney," he said, offering his hand. "Nice to meet you, kid."

"I've told Mr. Evans what the scene's about," said Pevney. "Let's improvise. Get the two of you together and see how you look."

I knew they were going through the act just to patronize Norma. What the hell. At least I'd have in my scrapbook being on film with Cagney.

The set was a replica of Thalberg's office when he was the "boy wonder" boss at Universal. Cagney assumed the nervous air of an actor meeting the head of the studio for the first time. Me? I don't remember what I did.

When it was over, Cagney gave me a quick look.

"You did good, kid." Then, with equal quickness, he disappeared.

Theona was right: a landslide victory, Ike didn't need my vote. Twenty-four hours later, I was packed and ready to fly via the 11:00 TWA sleeper to New York when the phone rang. It was Robert Arthur.

"Congratulations. I've just called Norma and thanked her. We need you in wardrobe tomorrow."

"What?"

Martin and Norma were permanent residents of the hotel, their suite but ten doors away from mine. Before calling my family with the news, I called Norma. Triumphantly, she said, "Join us for dinner."

BIG SPLASH:
N.Y. BUSINESSMAN DIVES IN POOL
AND COMES OUT MOVIE STAR!

Variations of this headline appeared on entertainment pages around the world from Louella Parsons's column to *The New York Times*. The *Times* story began, "The real and reel worlds of Hollywood were merged unexpectedly when . . ."

Norma personally worked out my contract. At her insistence, Universal was not allowed options on me. Ten thousand dollars for four weeks of shooting. A favor.

"Please come out two weeks before principal photography starts. I want to help you prepare for the part."

In the twenties and thirties Norma Shearer had been the queen of Metro-Goldwyn-Mayer, the studio Irving Thalberg had helped make the most prestigious in the world. She had appeared in more than fifty films, including *The Barretts of Wimpole Street, Romeo and Juliet,* and *The Women.* Nominated for five Academy Awards, she won her Best Actress Oscar for *The Divorcee* in 1930. She was royalty. Hollywood royalty.

Back in New York, every big honcho from Saks Fifth Avenue to Neiman-Marcus and Marshall Field was cramming the showroom, interested not in my new spring line, but in my new role in life.

Arriving back at the Beverly Hills Hotel early, as promised, I started working with Norma, learning everything about Irving from the day he was born in 1899 till the day he died in 1936 at the early age of thirty-seven. Though 98 percent of what she told me about the love of her life would never show up on the screen, at the very least I'd know the man I was playing. Her letters were not merely a biography of Hollywood's boy wonder, but rather a crash course of what constitutes a filmmaker's brilliance. Thalberg had an obsession for excellence and endless patience with talent. He fought continually with Louis B. Mayer over not rushing a film into the theaters—"an artist needs time to complete his canvas." His heart was that of an artist, his mind was that of a mogul.

The script called for *Man of a Thousand Faces* to open with Lon Chaney's untimely death in 1930 and Thalberg's eulogy to the great actor. Norma had agreed to write the eulogy as she remembered it. For days we worked on the speech, Norma coaching me so I would sound and look as much like Irving as possible. She was obsessive about every detail, every inflection of his voice, every pause, every movement of his head and hands. It wasn't a performance she was after, it was a resurrection.

One thing was crucial. "You must not allow them to put makeup on you, Bob," she said. "I don't want you looking like another pretty-boy actor."

After one of our sessions she told me she was negotiating to buy the film rights to F. Scott Fitzgerald's *The Last Tycoon*, his unfinished novel about the Thalberg-like Monroe Stahr. She hoped to produce it herself for MGM. "I've always thought," she said, "that Tyrone Power would be perfect for Monroe Stahr. But Ty's too old." She smiled. "Now, Robert, you understand why I've been spending so much time with you."

Was I lucky? Sure. But luck doesn't happen by mistake. If I hadn't had the experience of working with the pros as a pro in radio, television, and theater, I never could have gone eye to eye with Cagney. Conversely, if I had stayed an actor, Norma never would have given me a second look. What caught her eye was a young go-getter, sure about himself, persuasive, a subliminal reminder of the man who was once her mentor and her husband.

What a turn-on to have Pop fly out to L.A. to share my dream.

The night he arrived, we dined with Norma and Martin at Chasen's. Norma turned on the star power. How fortunate I was, she said, to have a father who had encouraged his son to strive for goals! For hours they spoke. Her poetic admiration toward Pop made the night among the most memorable in his life.

The next morning at six, Pop and I arrived at Universal.

"Okay, Mr. Evans, into makeup," said the assistant director.

"I'm sorry, Miss Shearer instructed me not to wear makeup."

"I'm sorry too, but Miss Shearer is not directing this picture. Into makeup."

Here I am at a standstill before I even start.

Joe Pevney, the director, quickly entered the scene.

"Maybe Norma's right, Bob, but the scene is just between Cagney and you and he's in heavy makeup. Without you in makeup we won't be able to light it—make the by-play match." Into makeup I went.

For some ungodly reason, they pick the longest and toughest scene in the film to do first. Five pages of dialogue between Cagney and me. Not only was it my first shot on the big screen. But to make it worse, the crux of the scene was me teaching Jimmy Cagney how to act!

The scene begins with the arrival of Lon Chaney in Thalberg's reception area. He has been summoned by the studio boss, whom he has never met, to discuss his portrayal of Quasimodo, the lead character in *The Hunchback of Notre Dame*. Nervously, he announces himself to the receptionist. Next to her stands a young man in shirtsleeves who ushers Chaney into his luxurious office and then walks behind the desk. Chaney's jaw drops. "Is this kid the head of the studio?"

The publicity being derived from Norma Shearer allowing Thalberg to be portrayed for the first time—by an unknown, no less—had made news throughout the entertainment world. My luck, the fuckin' press of the world plus the entire brass of Universal was on Stage 15 to see Thalberg re-created.

"Rolling, quiet please, *bells.*" Suddenly one could hear a pin drop.

A guy comes out in front of my face with a clapboard.

Slate slams.

"Scene 140, Apple, take one."

Through his bullhorn, director Pevney, who's perched on top of a ladder, bellows *"action!"*

I usher Cagney into my office. Timidly he glances around. I cross around to my desk, button my vest, slip on my jacket. Take my chair.

"Please sit down, Mr. Chaney."

Incredulously, Cagney looks around the office, then at me.

"Mr. Thalberg?"

I look at Cagney. Not unlike my brother at my near fatal audition for Chamberlain Brown, nothing comes out. Camera continues to roll.

Cagney gives me a quizzical smile. Nothing.

"Okay, let's do it again!" Pevney says through the bullhorn. Cagney walks back to his marker. I stay frozen in the chair—Thalberg's chair. Pevney walks over to me. "Don't wait so long to react, Bob. Pick up the action." Again, through the bullhorn, "Okay. Take two. Action!"

Cagney and I walk into my office together, I go around to my desk, I button my vest, Cagney does the same incredulous look around the office, then at me, Mr. Thalberg.

Looking at Cagney, I open my mouth. Again, there's one problem, nothing comes out.

From the bullhorn, "Cut. Okay let's try it again."

Cagney throws me an encouraging wink. We try it again. Then again. Then again. Then again. The result is the same. Every time Cagney says *"Mr. Thalberg?"* I freeze.

The stage is a buzz. Pevney, Cagney, and Robert Arthur huddle. Me, I'm standing behind the desk. I've waited fifteen years for this shot—now I can't even open my mouth. They'll have me on the noon plane to New York. I look over at my pop, his head down, another dream vanished.

Cagney walks over, does a quick "Yankee Doodle Dandy" dance step.

"Let's take a walk."

Now, outside in the blinding light, the Yankee Doodle himself puts his arm around my shoulder. "Let me tell you somethin', kid. I'm only five foot five. When I came to Hollywood my first scene was with a guy six foot four; when the scene was over, I was six four, he was five five. Now don't be scared of me. Let's go back in . . . get it on."

Cagney knew the feeling of looking up to somebody, knew the feeling of being scared. That's a *real* tough guy.

"Stop the film, please! Stop it right now!"

Norma Shearer jumped to her feet, livid. It was the first day of dailies, and everyone was there to view my screen debut.

This was a Norma I'd never seen. "How dare you wear makeup, Robert! I specifically gave you orders not to. You look like a *girl* up there, not the head of a studio!" She stormed out.

Feeling like Benedict Arnold, I downed six mai tais at the Luau, then back to the Beverly Hills Hotel. Awaiting me at the reception desk was an envelope. Inside was Norma's letter of apology. Joe Pevney took the heat, explaining to her he would not have shot the scene unless I followed his orders to wear makeup because of matching problems with Jimmy Cagney. The real blast, though, was how she started her letter: "Dear Irving. . . ."

Pop went home feeling great about his Bobby, but more important, about himself. Me, I became great pals with Cagney and remained so until he died.

"Everyone", said Norma, "will be at Romanoff's New Year's Eve party—Clark Gable, Gary Cooper, Jimmy Stewart, Fred Astaire, Van Heflin, Bogart and Bacall, Mike Todd and Elizabeth Taylor and especially David Selznick. I want him to meet you. I told him that you're going to play Monroe Stahr in *The Last Tycoon* and that more than anything I would like him to produce it with me. Merle Oberon is joining us too. Would you mind escorting her?"

I was passing through the lobby of the Beverly Hills Hotel with my rented white tie and tails when my old pal, Benny Medford, grabbed me.

"I've got a New Year's present for you, Bob. She's in the Polo Lounge."

There sat a combination of Sophia Loren and Brigitte Bardot. An Italian beauty on her first trip to Hollywood to star opposite Mario Lanza. Her name—Marisa.

After finishing a bottle of Dom Perignon, Benny vanished. Was I drunk, maybe, but I sure in hell was in love. Finishing off the second bottle, Marisa purred in my ear.

"Let's bring in the New Year making love."

Not drunk enough to forget my command performance of the evening, I whispered, "We'll meet at one."

"No, no. We must bring in the New Year making love."

"Turn your clock back an hour"—kissing her on the ear—"we'll make believe it's midnight."

"*Amore,* change your plans. My family will not understand me leaving home that late." As her hand went slowly up my thigh. "Roberto for Marisa."

The closer her hand, the quicker my decision.

"Where are you staying?"

"At the Chateau."

"Do you drive?"

"No."

"Meet me at the hotel at eleven-thirty. Take a cab."

"*Amore,* I am not American. I feel, *come se dice,* uncomfortable, walking into the hotel alone."

Totally disregarding my black-tie plans for the night, "Meet me at eleven, corner of Fairfax and Sunset, Thrifty Drugstore. Take a cab. I'll be parked in a white Corvette."

"Norma," I lied, "I have terrible stomach cramps."

At 11:00 on the dot, there I was in my white Corvette, both motors running, parked smack in front of Thrifty's on Sunset. Coincidentally, it was not only the last, but by far the coldest night of the year.

At 11:25, there I was pacing, looking at every passing cab. "Damn it, why didn't I pick a simpler place?"

Now five minutes to midnight, a cab pulled up on the other side of the street. At last! Almost getting run over, I ran as fast as I could, took a tenner out of my pocket for the driver, and anxiously opened the back door. Marisa? No. Two black hookers.

"Wanna party, honky?"

Stood up? No. Frozen up, making it back to my hotel and under the covers alone. Romantic, huh. My first New Year's eve in Hollywood as a movie star. Marisa? I never saw or heard from her again— but I did get pneumonia.

6

Even though the beginning of spring was but three weeks away, subzero weather still plagued New York. Arriving at my new apartment at 2 Sutton Place South after a fourteen-hour day at the office, I looked forward to only one thing—a *hot bath*. Lying on my bed, I must have fallen asleep, clothes and all. Two hours later, the ring of the phone awakened me.

"Bob, where the hell are you! It's after midnight."

"I'm a basket case, Charlie. Get me out of it, will ya?"

"I can't, the broad's a countess. It's below zero. She came out specially to meet you. I'll look like an idiot."

Twenty minutes later, unbathed, wrinkled suit and all, I made my entrance into El Morocco, New York's plushest supper club. Charlie Kahn, the guy who was on the other end of the phone, ran over.

"She's royally pissed, Bob."

"Fuck her. Where are we sitting?"

At the table sat Countess Christina Palozzi, whose *Harper's Bazaar* cover, and the multipage, bare-ass layout inside, had made her the talk of the country. She could have been a nun for all I cared. I wanted to be back in bed, under my covers, taking a long Z. Downing two martinis, in the hope that it would be a shot of adrenaline, didn't work.

To say she was less than thrilled with my company would be self-serving. "It's only another fifteen minutes," I said to myself, "talk or dance." Conversation wasn't coming easy, so: "Let's dance."

Impress her I didn't. We sat down. I was about to say *au revoir*, when Charlie quipped, "The guy in the corner with the big cigar—he's been staring at you all night. Do you know who he is?"

I looked around. "No."

"It's Zanuck, Darryl Zanuck. He's only the top producer in Hollywood."

"So what!"

"He hasn't taken his eyes off you."

"Cut it, Charlie, will ya? He ain't no fruit. If he's been looking at anybody, it's her" (referring to my turned-off countess).

And with that, it was *adios*.

Sixteen hours later, my secretary interrupted me with a note: "Call Joe Pincus. Urgent."

"Joe Pincus?"

"He says he's with Twentieth Century–Fox."

"I'll call him later."

I didn't. But two hours later he called me.

"Mr. Evans, we don't know each other but it's imperative that we meet tonight. I'll wait as late as you wish, but it must be tonight."

An hour later, I was sitting across the desk from Joe Pincus, who was Twentieth Century–Fox's top honcho of talent. His reputation was notorious—that of an iceberg.

Strange, I thought, Cary Grant couldn't be more charming.

Graciously smiling, he got up from his desk. "Have you ever acted?"

"Just finished a picture opposite Jimmy Cagney."

"D. Z.—he's amazing, what an eye. Well, young man, now how would you like to play opposite Ava Gardner?"

Is this fucker nuts?

"You were in El Morocco last night, right?"

"Right."

"At noon D. Z. called me to his office—'I saw a kid on the dance floor last night doing a tango. He's perfect for the part of Pedro Romero. The captain gave me his name. Find him. Today!' " Excitedly, Pincus picked up the phone and dialed Zanuck. "I found him, D. Z. You're right. He's perfect. He's a pro too; just finished a picture opposite Jimmy Cagney. What an eye, D. Z., what an eye. Leave it to me, D. Z., I'll work everything out." Hanging up the phone, "Who's your agent, kid?"

I eyed him. "Don't have one. What's going on, mister?"

"What's going on? I'll tell you what's going on. You've just been set as Ava Gardner's Latin lover in the biggest picture we're making this year, *The Sun Also Rises*. D. Z. himself is producing it."

"I never read it."

"It's only the best part in the picture. You steal Ava away from Tyrone Power, Errol Flynn, and Mel Ferrer. Not bad, huh? Ever see a bullfight?"

"No."

"You're playing a bullfighter."

"Me? A bullfighter? Why don't you use a real one?"

"They don't look real. We've been testing for a year. The ones who looked like bullfighters can't speak English and the ones who speak English don't look like bullfighters. You're it."

"I've never seen a bull in my life."

"Don't worry, we'll teach you."

"Sure!"

By Friday, I was back in California in makeup at Twentieth, testing for the part of Hemingway's Latin lover, bullfighter Pedro Romero.

Because it was a star-making part, the studio insisted I sign a "test option" agreement, giving Zanuck the option to use me for two pictures a year over five years. Knowing Norma's feelings about options, I called her.

"As long as the contract is nonexclusive, I'll approve it," Norma said. "Bob, let's not forget *The Last Tycoon*. Lew Wasserman is a close friend. As a favor I'll ask him to personally handle your contract to make sure it's nonexclusive."

Within two days, more paperwork was shuffled on an option contract than on the Versailles Treaty. Nonexclusive contracts for young actors were unheard-of. Once the studio invested in you, they owned you lock, stock, and barrel. Because of Norma and agent Lew Wasserman's muscle, I was the exception. I was to be paid $25,000 for *The Sun Also Rises*. My subsequent commitments, if used, would escalate north to $150,000 a flick.

There was a problem. A big one. First I had to get the part. When I heard John Gavin was also being tested, I felt my chances were slim to none. At the time he was very hot, very handsome; he was also half Spanish and spoke the language fluently. Also testing was a well-known Spanish movie star, plus a new entry—*the real thing:* a matador who looked like one, and spoke English as well.

When I met Henry King, Twentieth Century–Fox's top epic director *(The Song of Bernadette, The Gunfighter,* and *The Snows of Kilimanjaro),* he was professionally cordial but far from impressed. Of the four potential Pedros, in his mind I had to be fourth.

It's a long story, so I'll cut to the chase. I got the part. Why? I found out later: after Zanuck looked at my test, he never bothered to look at the others.

"The kid's perfect. Sign him."

It's what's known as "sense of discovery." An emotion so important, yet so unheralded. As beauty is in the eye of the beholder, discovery is in the eye of the brain. It has little to do with you, the object, but has all to do with the ego of its discoverer.

After a 5½-hour drive from the Mexico City airport, I arrived in a town known as Morelia, which more aptly should have been called "Nowhere." Though it was only March, the temperature soared past 100 degrees every day in the shade.

Rising out of a shantytown, the hacienda-style hotel at the top of a scrubby hill looked like Xanadu. Zanuck had taken over the entire facility for his all-star cast.

Ushered to my hacienda on the grounds, I met Bill Gallagher, who was my bunkmate and Tyrone Power's longtime personal assistant. Awaiting me was a message from Peter Viertel, the ultrachic screenwriter of *Sun,* asking me to drop by for a visit. He was looking forward to meeting me, and me him. After all, this guy's words were going to make me a star.

Our meeting didn't quite turn out the way I had hoped. He opened the door, looked at me, didn't invite me in, just looked, not even hello. Till this day, he is the only person I have ever met who cut me down from near six feet to three feet without even saying a word.

With a shit-faced grin, he started laughing. "You play Pedro Romero? Uh-uh, not in my film." With that, he slammed the door in my face.

"Dinner's at nine. Fuck Viertel. He's a snob. You'll meet the whole cast tonight, they're a hell of a group. You'll enjoy it. Promise," said well-meaning Gallagher.

Everyone was there—Ava, Tyrone, Mel Ferrer with spouse Audrey Hepburn, Errol Flynn, Eddie Albert, Henry King, the director, and my new good friend, Peter Viertel.

Was I embraced? I might as well have been invisible.

"Where's Zanuck?" I nudged Gallagher.

"Oh, he's in London making another film."

"Great, just great."

"Sit down, old boy. Have a drink!"

It was Errol Flynn. He was tanked, but so what, it was still an embrace.

"Fuck 'em," he said, "they're all jealous. Tyrone, Mel, both of them played bullfighters."

Then, loudly, "Now, they're just too fuckin' old."

Then he burst out laughing. But no one looked up. No one wanted to talk to Errol because by two in the afternoon, every afternoon, he was drunk. Certainly, no one wanted to talk to me. Together we made a great combo.

"Boring here, isn't it? Show you a bit of the local color."

As we got up to leave, in a voice loud enough so everyone could hear, "As long as you're here, ole chap, don't forget—don't touch the food, the water, or the ladies. They'll all give you dysentery."

Roaring with laughter, he led me out to his car and driver. Down the hill we went directly into the red-light district. Ordering the driver to stop in front of a hole-in-the-wall club, he told him to jump out and take care of business. Then he pulled out what looked like a bottle of gin, taking a long swig of it.

Handing it to me, "Go on, go on, it's the only way to stay alive down here."

Why not? I took a good-sized swig myself. A bomb went off inside me. This ain't gin; it's mustard gas.

Slapping my back, Flynn couldn't stop laughing. "The fun's just starting."

"I think I'll pack it in."

"No way, ole boy."

Twenty minutes later we were back at his bungalow. His driver must have closed the deal. Three girls were waiting for us.

"Undress, undress," he laughed.

Sweeping everything off the table, he switched on a phonograph. Hot Latin music blasted out.

"Now, on the table my little sweet *muchachas*"—he continued to laugh—"on the table, on the table, that's it, dance, dance!"

Settling back into a chair, hysterically laughing, he turned on a tape recorder and began speaking into the microphone.

"I'm doing my autobiography, ole boy."

The wilder the music, the wilder the dancing, the wilder Flynn's memories became—none of them printable. But it was the beginning of a beautiful friendship.

Alfredo Leal was among Mexico's best-known bullfighters. He never smiled, nor did I blame him. He was very handsome, a top matador who was commissioned to make me look like him. What I didn't realize is that he was tested three times for the part, but no cigar. Desperate to suck up as much knowledge as I could, I stuck to him like a cheap glove, but with one eye always checking my back. I knew everyone wanted me off the film. And who could take me out better than Alfredo?

Between the 100-plus temperature and the rubber girdle around my midsection, I dropped close to twenty pounds. Next to Alfredo, I was still a plump-in-the-middle Jew boy. It hardly mattered; even the director didn't bother to come and see if I was making progress.

A Neanderthal would know something was brewing. Ten days before I was to start shooting, a cable was sent to Zanuck in London. The gist of it could not have been more clear: "With Robert Evans playing Pedro Romero, *The Sun Also Rises* will be a disaster," signed Henry King, Ava Gardner, Tyrone Power, Mel Ferrer, Eddie Albert, and lastly, my good friend Peter Viertel. Errol Flynn refused to sign it. Word came back that Zanuck would be arriving in Morelia in five days and I was to report to the bullring in my suit of lights, so that my mentor could view his new discovery in full regalia.

Knowing about the cable worked the wrong way—not for me, for them! By the time Zanuck got to Morelia, Zanuck's folly was ready to take them on.

"Action," yelled Henry King through the bullhorn.

Stride by stride, with a real matador on either side, I crossed the ring, finally stopping at the *barrera* in front of me. Was that D. Z.? I couldn't tell. The cigar in his mouth was half the size of his body. On one side were Ava Gardner and Tyrone Power, on the other Henry King, Mel Ferrer, Eddie Albert, and Errol Flynn.

Doffing my hat, I looked up. "For you," in my most baritone voice. Quickly turning my back, I threw the hat over my shoulder into his hands. Then into action I went. Doing my various *quites* and *veronicas,* swirling my *muleta,* all of course to a fake bull. Then bowing to him again, I took my *muleta* and turned to face death in the afternoon, but I was stopped. Zanuck, all five foot three of him, stood—bullhorn in hand.

"The kid stays in the picture. And anybody who doesn't like it can quit!" With that he turned, walked up the steps, and left.

It was then I learned what a producer was—a Boss. It was then I learned I wanted to be D. Z., not some half-assed actor shitting in his pants, desperate for a nod of approval.

That night a fiesta was given honoring D. Z.'s arrival. I walked in late, alone. Errol immediately came over, putting his arm around me. "I told you, sport, once D. Z. gets here you'd be in like Flynn. Come, say hello to your mentor."

"I've never even met the guy."

"You will now," laughed Flynn. "Remember, don't say yes until he finishes talking."

There sat Zanuck, cigar and all. Ava, who in two months hadn't said two words to me, was by his side. She wanted to enchant Zanuck into replacing me with Walter Chiari, her boyfriend, an Italian movie star. I use the word "enchant" since Ava never stopped talking about Zanuck's pride and joy.

"The only thing bigger than his cigar is his cock," she always laughed, "which he's not shy to show or put into use."

My hello to Zanuck was indeed brief. I wanted it that way.

The music started. The mariachis did their turn. Now the music really heated up. I made my move. I walked to Zanuck's table and, without asking, took Ava by the hand and onto the floor. The Barefoot Contessa was somewhat shocked, but not for long. For the next forty minutes we danced as one. In a total sweat, without a single word between us, we made it back to Zanuck's table. The silence was eerie; so were the stares. She sat. *I left.* From that moment, it wasn't only Zanuck who thought I was Pedro Romero.

Suddenly it was tennis with Tyrone Power, driving for antiques with Mel and Audrey, playing the guitar with Eddie Albert; but best of all were the nights with Errol. If I were to be reborn, however, I'd like to come back as Tyrone Power. Not for his extraordinary black Irish looks, but for his complete lack of narcissism. Tyrone was a man's man, a ladies' man, an adventurer, artist, athlete, compulsive reader; competitive, but never boastful; genuinely, not theatrically, concerned; never afraid to admit his fright. Over dinner one night he told me how scared he was when he appeared on Broadway in *John Brown's Body.*

"A movie star on Broadway is suicide."

"Then why did you do it?"

"Because, damn it, I'm selfish. I wanted to beat the odds."

Without knowing it or acting like one, Tyrone Power was a true aristocrat. Conversely, Ava, the world's most beautiful woman, was a haunted soul—haunted by her poor childhood, stormy romances, fading beauty. She, unlike Tyrone, never inhabited her beauty, always feeling nondeserving of it.

There were two weeks when my ego thought we were in love. In reality, Ava, the professional, was just trying to make our onscreen chemistry more convincing. Not that she lorded it over me. Ava was wide open about Ava, blaming herself for her failed love affairs, telling me the most bizarre stories about how she'd screwed up her marriage to Frank Sinatra. I think she was still madly in love with him. Was I nuts about her? Who wouldn't be?

Ava had a thing for matadors. They weren't movie stars, they were gods who played with death. She'd recently ended a torrid romance with one of the supreme bullfighters, Luis Dominguin. We shot our interior scenes together in Mexico City. Afterward we'd go to the bullfighters' hangouts. When Ava walked in, she got a matador's cheers.

A great Spanish bullfighter was there one night. Ava recognized him, leapt to her feet, clicked her heels, and with her scarf executed several perfect *veronicas*. The matador got down, his knees nearly touching the floor, and charged her like a bull. Snorting, laughing, sweating, they did the first two acts of the *corrida*—everything but the kill. Finally he stood up, faking a terrible pain in his back, and she finished him off with a laugh and a kiss. It was by far the most exciting bullfight I've ever seen.

Tossing back her triple vodka, straight, Ava wiped her brow. "Pedro?" she said. "You know who sent the first blast about you to Zanuck? Me. You looked like a fool." She leaned close, playing with me. "Hate me?" she whispered.

Six months later we celebrated her thirty-sixth birthday at the Harwyn Club in New York. It was sure in hell different from the smelly, steamy matador hangouts. And it sure in hell was a different Ava.

"It's over, Pedro."

"It was never really anything to begin with. You were just using me."

"Don't flatter yourself, I wasn't even thinking of you."

I raised my glass. "Happy thirty-six, Lady Brett."

She closed her eyes. "Happy! I'm over the hill—I know it, you know it, the industry knows it."

She was right! In 1958, it was over for a leading lady touching her mid-thirties.

Wild! Women have grown into their own in the last thirty years more than they have in the last three hundred. In the mid-sixties I met Faye Dunaway in Miami. She was starring in her first flick *The Happening*. No high school cheerleader she, rather a femme fatale. Now thirty years later, still a femme fatale. A working one too. Things do change—today most every top leading lady on the big screen is north of thirty five.

Put that in your pipe and smoke it!

"How can I meet Lana Turner?" I pressed Joe Hyams. Both of us were at Universal Studios. Me to do an afternoon of post-production looping with Jimmy Cagney and he to interview the glamour queen herself, who was starring in a flick called *The Lady Takes a Flyer* with Jeff Chandler.

"After you finish looping with Cagney, come by Stage 7. I'll be there all afternoon catching her between takes," said ace Hollywood reporter Hyams.

Three hours later, there I stood beside him watching fake clouds blow into a fake cockpit hooked twenty feet in the air. In it was my fantasy lady since I was a teenager—*the* Lana Turner. The take now completed, the cameras and clouds stopped rolling. Being helped down the ladder from the cockpit and walking toward us was my fantasy come true. Not to see me, but to pick up with Joe on his interview.

"My name is Lana Turner," greeting me with her hand.

My legs shook. My voice hardly audible, "Robert Evans."

"I know." A seductive smile. "How is Ava?"

Wow, if ever there were cat claws, that was it. But who cared? Certainly not me. She cared as much about me as Ava did—nothing. But she didn't know how Ava really felt toward me and I sure as hell wasn't going to tell her. It was a unique key to a very short-lived romance. Before my first flick's release, my name was all over the tabloids dating two of Hollywood's most glamorous legends. Both considerably older. Both considerably infamous. Did it help catapult my newfound career? You bet your ass *it didn't*. A gigolo possibly. A playboy for sure. An actor? No way!

7

It was a long hot summer. Flashbulbs were popping wherever I went. *Man of a Thousand Faces* and *The Sun Also Rises* were opening within three weeks of each other. I couldn't leave my apartment without a camera going off in my face. My presence in the Evan-Picone showroom was a negative. All they wanted to talk about was Ava Gardner or Errol Flynn, not the new fall line.

Man of a Thousand Faces was Universal's choice to commemorate their fifty years in the film business. How proud I was that night walking into the Palace Theatre with my entire family to its world premiere. On full blast, the klieg lights filled the sky. Cops were brought in to hold back the eager fans from breaking through the ropes. Radio and television were there en masse—from Barry Gray to Jack Eigen; from CBS to WPIX—all to cover Universal's Golden Jubilee. Best of all, walking in beside me, was Yankee Doodle Dandy himself, Jimmy Cagney.

The lights went down, the screen lit up, and I was Irving Thalberg, driving through the Universal gates on his way to eulogizing the late, great Lon Chaney. For the next two hours, it could have been Groucho Marx or Laurence Olivier up there, I wouldn't have known the difference.

By far, that night was the highlight of my life. A payback to Mom and Pop, who took so much heat from both family and friends about their offbeat kid.

Why is it that affirmation from your family always remains the one approval you never stop seeking? A mother and father who embraced my idiosyncratic behavior, a brother who was my closest friend, and a sister who looked up to me as if I were the Almighty.

That balmy summer evening of August 6, 1957, was as high a high as one could ever hope for.

From the premiere, off to El Morocco we went, all of us, from the top honchos of Universal to Yankee Doodle Cagney, making one of his rare public appearances. Forget *my* high! The honchos of Universal were really flying. The picture, both artistically and commercially, was a surefire hit. And did they need it. Universal in the fifties was low man of the majors. Finally, an oasis. Even Cagney seemed to be having a great time.

Being a nervous Jew, I couldn't sit back and wallow in the night's joy. The reviews must be on the stands by now. Using the excuse of going to the john, I slipped out the front door and around the corner to a newsstand. All the morning papers had just been delivered. The *News,* the *Mirror,* the *Herald-Tribune.* All of them raves. I was batting three for three, getting very special notice no less.

Picking up *The New York Times,* I quickly turned to Bosley Crowther, the dean film reviewer in the country. Wow, my picture, not Cagney's, attached to the review. It must be the best of all.

Robert Evans as Irving Thalberg, the famous producer, is unspeakably poor. It is, indeed, a shame that one of the most professional per-

sons ever to work in Hollywood should be played so amateurishly as Thalberg is by this monotonous actor.

It can't be. It must be a mistake. It wasn't. Did it bother me? I wanted to kill myself! Instead, I slid back into El Morocco thinking, Schmuck, you couldn't wait until tomorrow, could you?

For the rest of the evening, I gave by far the best performance of my life. That is, until I got home. As soon as the door closed behind me . . . I started to cry. Curling up under the covers, I shut the phone off and stayed in a fetal position for seventy-two hours.

A telegram arrived: "Trying to reach you. No reply. Please call. Alan Hall. *Time* magazine."

I tore it up. They're after me—all of them.

The next day, another cable: "You were hung by Crowther. Want to clear the record. Please call."

Two days later we met for lunch. Alan Hall was *Time*'s movie reviewer.

"Why did Crowther do it?"

He laughed. "He just finished writing *The Lion's Share*. It's about Thalberg and Louis B. Mayer. He probably thinks only Orson Welles could play him."

"*The Sun Also Rises* opens in three weeks. He'll kill me again."

"He'll probably make it up to you."

"Sure."

Close to three weeks later, the *Sun* premiered at the Roxy. Hall was right. Romero, wrote Crowther, is "perfectly personified by Robert J. Evans."

The reviews in the *News, Mirror,* and *Trib* were mixed to good. Toward me, however, all were an actor's dream; I was described as everything from "electrifying" to "mesmerizing."

The following Monday, *Time*'s review hit the stands. To begin with, the picture accompanying the review was a large picture of Ava Gardner and me in an embrace. The review went on to say,

The difficult role of Brett's ultimate conquest, young bullfighter Pedro Romero, is played with fierce intensity by handsome newcomer Robert Evans. In the movie's arena sequence, actor Evans conveys Hemingway's paradoxical feeling of affection for what he kills ("The bulls are my best friend"), just as Brett always momentarily loves the men she ruins.

Following the review was a two-column feature devoted solely to the bullfighter.

Evans is the most exciting young man since Valentino,

Zanuck was quoted as saying.

But Valentino died at thirty-one!

8

It was Easter Sunday. The temperature, 103 in the shade. I was one of many watching a mixed doubles tennis match at the Racquet Club in Palm Springs, California. Being a guest at the Racquet Club was tantamount to being in *Who's Who in Hollywood*. Founded by Charlie Farrell and Ralph Bellamy in the thirties, it attracted the *crème de la crème* of what was then glamorous Hollywood.

Playing were Pancho Segura and Lew Hoad, two great pros, each partnered with a blonde. The occasion: a celebrity/pro mixed doubles tournament. One lady I knew. Her face was on television every week—Dinah Shore. I had never seen the other lady, but she was a real looker!

Was I having sunstroke? Looking up, I saw a ruggedly handsome man, at least six foot three, walking past me, not in tennis shorts, but wearing a black silk shantung suit, with a starched white shirt and tie. Wiping my eyes, I took a second look as he took a seat nearby. He wasn't even perspiring. Who was this guy? In all the years I'd gone to Palm Springs, never had I seen anybody dressed this way.

The set now over, the heat so intense, all four players decided to continue the match once the sun went down. It was eerie—all four walked over to the big man as if they were looking for approval. He barely smiled. Then all five walked into the air-conditioned clubhouse. Me, I walked to the reception desk.

"Who's the big guy, the one in the black suit who just walked in?" I asked the desk clerk.

He stuttered, "S-S-S-S . . . Sidney K-K-K-K . . . Korshak."

"Who is he? What does he do?"

He turned and rushed into the back room. Obviously, it wasn't any of my business. Obviously, I wanted to find out. It didn't take long.

He was known as the Myth, from the Racquet Club to the "21" Club in New York. Many said they knew him; few actually did. One thing was for sure, he was one powerful motherfucker.

Incident brought the Myth and me together; from the moment we met in the early fifties until 1980 we were as close as two friends could be. What did he do? He was a lawyer living in California, without an office. Who were his clients? Well, let's just say a nod from Korshak, and the Teamsters change management. A nod from Korshak, and Santa Anita closes. A nod from Korshak, and Madison Square Garden stays open. A nod from Korshak, and Vegas shuts down. A nod from Korshak, and the Dodgers suddenly can play night baseball. Am I exaggerating? Quite the contrary. In the spirit of confidentiality, it's an underplay.

Born in Chicago, Korshak, by the age of twenty-one, was one of Al Capone's top *consiglieres*. By the early fifties, he represented more than twenty companies on the New York Stock Exchange. Was he a mobster? No, he was a lawyer. Was he crooked? Not only was he not, I doubt whether he has ever been charged with a misdemeanor. Was he a myth? Yes, with a capital *M*.

In his midthirties, Sidney married a beautiful blonde from the Ice Capades named Bernice. Arriving back from their honeymoon, many a message was awaiting the big man. His new bride began reading them off.

"George Washington called, everything is status quo. Thomas Jefferson called, urgent, please call ASAP. Abraham Lincoln, must speak with you, important. Theodore Roosevelt called three times, must connect with you before Monday."

She began laughing. "Your friends sure have a strange sense of humor. Who are they?"

"Exactly who they said they were. Any other questions?"

Fifty years later, Bernice has never asked another question. Nor, for that matter, has she ever asked him where he's been—even when he goes out for a shave and comes back three weeks later.

Being one of the fortunate ones invited to celebrate their fiftieth anniversary together, I suggested Bernice should bottle her secret potion. After all, how many couples have been married for fifty years and look forward to their fifty-first?

Till 1980, when a specific incident cooled our relationship, not a day passed without Sidney and I spending at least an hour alone together. When separated by geography, our time alone was spent by phone. His affection unconditional. His legal wisdom and time unbilled. Was there reciprocity? Yes, but the scale tipped way to his side. What memories we shared.

For openers, it was 1958. *The Sun Also Rises* had opened and me, I was the next Valentino. Sidney invited me to join he and Bernice for dinner at Le Pavillon in New York, which at the time was the finest and most elite French restaurant in the city. (The restaurant's proprietor, Henry Soulé, had barred Jackie Kennedy from entering for lunch. Why? She was wearing pants.) Naturally, I accepted.

Korshak was a different story. Soulé was like a buck private standing before his drill sergeant. Quickly I was ushered to his table. Sitting beside Sidney and Bernice was a couple I had never met. The guy made John Gotti look like a fruit. The girl was a different story. A knockout. Blond hair, blue eyes, great smile, and fetching with a capital *F*. I'm seated between Miss Fetching and the big man. During the first course and into the second, Miss Fetching couldn't take her eyes off me—giggling, questioning me about *The Sun Also Rises*, being a bullfighter, a Latin lover.

Suddenly, a shot to the shins almost took my leg off.

"Bobby, you're late." Looking at his watch, Sidney said, "The script—you were supposed to pick it up twenty minutes ago."

"What script?"

With that, my other leg gets it—a kick that made the first feel like a kiss. If I wanted to get up, I couldn't. Then I got the look, the Korshak look. Did I leave? Hardly able to walk, Houdini couldn't have disappeared quicker. The morning after, the big man called.

"Schmuck, if you'd stayed one more minute, you'd have gotten it to the stomach. Not a punch—lead."

"Who's the guy?"

"It's none of your fuckin' business. His broad's got one tough road ahead. Been married a week and the doorman don't even say hello to her—that's how tough the guy is. And you, schmuck, you're coming on to her. Tony was gettin' hot—I could see it. You're lucky your eyes are open."

Was Korshak right? Ms. Fetching and Mr. Nice stayed married for a few years. He divorced her, married someone else, had two children. She continued to live in her hometown, Chicago. There was one problem. Not even a vagrant would take her out. Frustrating? It's just the beginning. Being colder than the weather, she decided Chicago was not for her. She moved to Los Angeles. Strange, but not one guy in L.A. would take her out either. Mind you, this is a great-looking chick. Hawaii. Ah, that's the place to live. It's a different world, different people. Who would know her there? Nobody! Till this day, Miss Fetching is still dateless.

But me, I was coming on to her when she was still on her honeymoon.

9

I never had a press agent, but I was always in the press. Contrary to the popular belief that being publicized is an asset, in reality it is a handicap, both personally and professionally. Professionally you are plummeted into being a celebrity before you've made your bones as an artist. Personally undressing your life for the world to see is the quickest way to mayhem, unhappiness, and ending up an 8-×-10 glossy. Conversely, it is mystery that sustains your career and affords you some peace of mind. Unfortunately, both my career and life fell into the former not the latter. Except for Elvis Presley, I was getting more fan mail than anyone at Twentieth Century–Fox. Troy Donahue was getting more fan mail at Warners than Paul Newman. Today, it's Troy who? Heralded as the next Tyrone Power, the next Valentino, I was in reality becoming the next Troy Donahue.

I was set to star in the remake of *Blood and Sand*—first made with Valentino and then Tyrone Power. My co-star was Sophia Loren. It was a natural, so the fan magazines said. It didn't matter. They canceled it.

Across the headlines of almost every newspaper's entertainment page: "EVANS STARRING IN ZANUCK'S NEW PRODUCTION, 'COMPULSION.' " A hit Broadway play about the murder case of Leopold and Loeb, the thrill-killers whose trial shook the country in the twenties, I was to play the Nathan Leopold character. A Zanuck production, yes, but it was the wrong Zanuck. Not Darryl, but his son, Richard, freshly discharged from the army. Darryl, my mentor, was now living in Paris, leaving his son to protect his interest at the studio. As much as Zanuck Senior wanted to see me become the next Valentino, Zanuck Junior wanted to see me back at Evan-Picone.

I first met Dickie in the luxurious bungalow Zanuck Productions occupied on the Fox lot. He was the spitting image of his old man, but thirty-two years younger and no cigar.

"I'm not sure you're right for it," said young Zanuck.

(Is the kid head-fucking me?) "I'm already announced for it. I'm under personal contract to you."

"I know, but something bothers me." Then he looked at me, smiled; a sick sense of enjoyment came across his face. "Don't know what it is."

"Don't worry," George Chasen, my agent, said later. "It's yours."

A week later, Brad Dillman was announced for the part. It was the beginning of young Mr. Z getting his nuts off on young Mr. E.

Back in New York, an excited George Chasen had me on the phone.

"Bob, it's been worth the wait. Fox is remaking *Kiss of Death* into a western. We've got you up for the Widmark part—it made him an overnight star. The crazo, ex-con who pushes the old lady in a wheel-chair down a flight of stairs."

"It ain't no romantic lead, George."

"You're damn right it ain't. Let me give it to you straight, Bob. We need legitimacy."

His words were a tough reminder, but the truth. I was an overpublicized, overglamorized pretty boy, a fashion tycoon turned actor. Outside of my family, no one took me seriously, not even at Evan-Picone, where everyone thought my head was in Hollywood. In Hollywood, everyone thought my talent was on Seventh Avenue. What others envied as having the best of both worlds, was in reality my downfall. To paraphrase the great philosopher Rodney Dangerfield, "I didn't get no respect."

At the screen test the director, Gordon Douglas suspiciously looked me over. "It's a helluva stretch—you playing Tommy Udo in spurs."

Again, I didn't know I was only one of five being tested, along with Tony Perkins, Eli Wallach, Sal Mineo, and my pal Ray Danton. The part was originally intended as a star vehicle for Elvis Presley, then Steve McQueen; both of them jumped at it at first, but then turned it down upon reflection, not wanting to be compared to Widmark. They were right. You're never compared favorably, even if you're better, when you fuck around with a classic.

"I don't want you to even *look* at the script," said Douglas. "First let's see what I can get from you—inside you." Little by little, he got inside me, to talk with my eyes. "That's it! Don't lose it. *Now* look at the script."

Again, cutting to the chase, I got the part.

Without realizing it, I soon became the biggest fraud in town. Starring in: *The Hell-Bent Kid, Rope Law, Enough Rope, Quick Draw,* its sequel, *Quick Draw at Red Rock,* and *The Hell-Bent Kid II.* There was one problem, they were all one flick. The studio kept changing its title every other week, but no one in town knew it.

"Is this guy Evans hot." Wherever I'd go, every actor asked me who was my agent.

Instead of pushing the old lady down the stairs, I put an arrow through her heart.

Gordy Douglas told me to live the part and I did. I was the guy. Away from the cameras I still couldn't stop my lisp. At the time, I was going with Kathryn Grayson, the MGM musical star, who, as the weeks went by, began having second thoughts about our relationship because I was becoming as peculiar in life as I was in film.

Edward R. Murrow, the dean of television journalism, saw the final cut with his staff and pressed Twentieth Century–Fox to have me, of all people, as an interview subject for "Person to Person." This program was not only the first network interview show, but number one in ratings as well. Rarely did his prestigious format embrace the world of entertainment; when it did, it was on the level of Elizabeth Taylor, Audrey Hepburn, Elvis Presley, or Frank Sinatra, not someone as low down the totem pole as me. When the chain-smoking Murrow predicted on network television in his famous voice of doom that *The Hell-Bent Kid* would make Robert Evans the next major star in Hollywood, all hell broke loose.

The film was to open in two months. The morning after "Person to Person" aired, next to Paul Newman, more scripts were sent to me than any actor in town.

George Chasen called. "Bob, Lew and I are working out a production company for you. The next picture you make will be under your own banner."

Barrington Productions was formed. Three weeks before the picture was to open, the film's producer, Herbert Bayard Swope, called me with the news.

"I don't know how to tell you this, Bob. It's hard for me to get it out of my mouth, but they've changed the title again. You're not *The Hell-Bent Kid* anymore. You're *The Fiend Who Walked the West*."

Charlie Einfeld, the Neanderthal marketing and distribution genius at Fox, brilliantly concluded that with westerns and horror flicks both being hot at the box office, why not change the title again to fit the mood of the movie-going public? It was not by mistake he was the second highest paid executive at Twentieth Century–Fox. Who else but a genius could come up with *The Fiend Who Walked the West*?

"You can't do this, Mr. Einfeld. I'd rather sell ladies' underwear than go out as *The Fiend Who Walked the West*."

"Hold it, kid, you act in 'em. I sell 'em. The title, it's brilliant. We'll get both audiences—the rednecks who go for oaters and the horror freaks."

"Yeah, and I'll become Fatty Arbuckle."

He didn't even hear me.

"Tomorrow I want you in wardrobe and makeup. We're gonna shoot a new trailer."

Excitedly he held up the new ad campaign. It was a huge picture of me looking like Freddy from *A Nightmare on Elm Street*. The letters hit me boldly in the eye: "Don't turn your back on the kooky killer with the baby face—**The Fiend Who Walked the West**."

"We're gonna shoot a new trailer with you like this, as the Fiend. It's gonna scare the shit out of everyone."

Knowing my career was as good as over now, I lashed back. "You know where your brains are, fuckface? In your ass! Go sit on 'em!"

Walking out, I slammed the door in his crimson face.

Two days later, the new title was officially announced to industry and press. The scripts stopped coming. Barrington Productions was now a name without a company. Changing the title changed my life, even though my reviews were an actor's dream. *Time* predicted that my "exceptional performance will be long remembered." It wasn't. *The Fiend* died a fast death. Charlie Einfeld got promoted to an even higher echelon—that of executive vice president. And me? Well, I suppose it was meant to be. The role that made Richard Widmark a star overnight made me all but an unknown.

"Forget it, Rona, he's a homosexual. It'll show up on the screen."

Listening in on the extension, I wanted to crack up. Jean Negulesco, the director, was talking about me. Rona Jaffe was the author of the year's hottest novel, *The Best of Everything*. A few hours earlier over lunch at the Harwyn, the hottest new face in literature had told me that one of the novel's main characters, Dexter Key, was fashioned after me. Had I read it? No. But every chick in town I knew had.

"Thanks for the compliment, Miss Jaffe, but I don't understand it, you've never even met me."

"But I've done my homework," she blushed. "I know more about you than you'd like me to."

No compliment. Dexter Key was every girl's nightmare, a playboy bastard. I had a good reputation, huh?

Still on the phone with Negulesco, Rona was pitching me for the part.

"He's a homosexual, Rona," laughed Negulesco. "Everyone knows it. They'll never believe him as a cocksman."

Her hand over the mouthpiece, she looked at me, surprised. "Is it true?"

Deadpan, I nodded yes.

"Jean, I have to call you back." Now in total shock.

"You're a homosexual?"

I couldn't hold it back. I broke out laughing.

"Is Joe DiMaggio? If you're not everything to everybody, you're nobody in Hollywood. Monty Clift stole me away from Rock Hudson and that's from top sources, Rona. But I'm also being kept by Ginger Rogers. There's one problem—I never met any of 'em."

"Then why did you nod yes?"

"It was too good. I had to. I wish I had a picture of your reaction."

"Evans, you *are* Dexter Key; you're a real bastard."

After days of prodding from Rona, Negulesco was willing to reconsider my sexuality, but again I'd have to test for the part. Again, paraphrasing philosopher Dangerfield, I was still getting no respect.

I read the novel. *This part I wanted!* Unlike *The Fiend, The Best of Everything* was an A-picture all the way. Not only was it the top-selling novel of the year, but it was being produced by Twentieth's best, Jerry Wald, with an all-star cast from Joan Crawford to Stephen Boyd, to Suzy Parker to Louis Jourdan to, hopefully, Robert Evans.

It wasn't that I was hungry for a gig. Just three weeks earlier, I turned down the title part in *The George Raft Story.* A month before, I turned down the title part in *Legs Diamond.*

Not that I was in demand, but I didn't like the road I was on. It's called "goin' south." When you start out in the majors, it ain't a fun ride ending up in the minors. My instinct must have been right. My pal Ray Danton took both parts. Poor Ray, he never became Redford.

Wicked was my smile after reading Rona's book. "This dame's got me down pat." A matador I ain't; Dexter Key I am. This part I could call in, but I sure in hell don't want to lose it. It meant getting back into the big leagues again. Protecting myself, I called Stella Adler, a great pal, and a greater teacher. She agreed to coach me for the test. Since I had to leave for the coast in three days, time was of the essence.

"Come to our apartment." She was married at the time to Harold Clurman, the great Broadway producer. "We'll work from there tonight—eight P.M. sharp."

In the living room of their luxurious Fifth Avenue apartment, we rehearsed my test scene. It was one where I walked into the apartment only to be shocked.

"Do it again; do it again. It's not coming from inside you. It's not real."

For the eleventh time I opened her living room door. Instead of walking in, I all but jumped out of my skin. Humongous breasts and all, there was Stella, nude from the waist up.

"That's it—*that's* what I want—shock—real shock!"

It's the best hook I'd ever gotten on how to play a scene. And, with it, I got the part.

From the moment we met, Jerry Wald and I became fast friends. Jerry was by far the most entrepreneurial producer in Hollywood. No one had a greater flair with both industry and press. Best of all, he even respected me as an actor and he wasn't shy in telling anyone. From the *Saturday Evening Post* to *Photoplay,* to television, radio, and print, the industry was well aware that I was Jerry Wald's pick as "the romantic rage" of the sixties.

It didn't happen. As a bullfighter, the head of a studio, or a crazy killer, at the very least, I was believable. Playing myself, I was a dud. Why? I was a better imitator than actor.

Jerry Wald felt different. Maybe because he had already gone out on a limb announcing me for the second male lead in *The Billionaire,* opposite Marilyn Monroe and Yves Montand. Who was I to argue?

The title is not the only thing that got changed. Now called *Let's Make Love,* principal photography kept getting pushed back and back. Monroe was being her usual indecisive self. Meanwhile, Jerry Wald offered me a co-starring part in *Return to Peyton Place.* What's worse than being in a sequel to a piece of shit? Playing the same part I had just finished, that's what. Only this time it was "Dexter Key Goes to New England."

"No thanks," I said.

"Fine," said Lou Schreiber, who ran business affairs at Twentieth. "You're on suspension."

"Dumb move, Evans. You're only an actor. Being on suspension, Twentieth cast someone else in the Monroe film."

Not wanting to play the third lead in a B gangster movie, I turned down *Murder, Inc.,* even though May Britt, my lady at the time, had the female lead. Again, I was put on suspension. May Britt dumped me, and the guy who replaced me in the film, Peter Falk, was nominated for the Academy Award. Good judgment, huh?

In the months that followed, I was set and unset in more films than I have fingers and toes. But none of it mattered. Finally, I got the break I needed—one of the lead parts opposite Audrey Hepburn in John Huston's *The Unforgiven*. There was one problem. Two years earlier, in the lobby of the Beverly Hills Hotel, I had met a statuesque, five foot eleven Japanese beauty, Eiko Ando. She must have been extraordinary. After all, she was John Huston's discovery to play opposite John Wayne in *The Barbarian and the Geisha*. What started out in the lobby didn't end up there. What to me was a passing fancy was to John Huston one of the loves of his life. Naturally, I didn't know. I was in wardrobe, ready to leave for location, when I got the call from my agent.

"It's over."

"What's over?"

"Huston's found out about Eiko—*you're Unforgiven!*"

"Call Sam, will ya, Kurt? I'm perfect casting."

"He's in London."

"I know. They're starting the picture soon. They've gotta cast the part."

Kurt Frings, my new agent, got Spiegel on the phone. Though I wasn't on the extension, I could tell Spiegel was less than excited. He told Frings he was going to Paris to speak to Alain Delon. If it didn't work out, he'd think about it. I followed up on it like a private eye. Ten days passed, and through my network, I was tipped that Delon wasn't available. Again, I prodded Frings to call Spiegel. He did and Spiegel suggested I go into makeup and wardrobe at Twentieth and have a photo shoot, in costume, as an Arab warrior.

Excitedly, I went over to see my old pal, Dickie Zanuck. After all, I was still under personal contract to his old man.

"I've got a shot for the second lead as the Arab warrior in *Lawrence of Arabia*. Spiegel just wants to see pictures of me in costume to show them to David Lean."

With all earnestness, Dickie got on the case, setting up the makeup, costume, and photo shoot at Twentieth. Together, we picked out the shots to send to London.

A week later, I received a call from Owen MacLaine, Twentieth's head of talent. "Bob, I've just received a cable from Sam Spiegel. I don't quite know how to handle it; let me read it to you: 'Please have Evans fly to London immediately. With him on scene, I am sure I can secure the role for him. Will work out details of contract with D. Z. personally. On no condition involve Kurt Frings. He will only complicate transaction. Sam Spiegel.' What should I do?" asked MacLaine.

"I've got to tell Kurt. He's my agent."

I did and he blew.

"That no-good Spiegel. I told you I didn't trust him. He wants options on you—for nothing. Fuck 'em. We're flying over together!"

We did, taking the newly inaugurated polar flight directly to London.

First, I called my mother, father, sister, and brother, telling them it looks like I've got the lead in *Lawrence of Arabia*. They were as excited for me as I was for myself.

Upon arrival, reservations were awaiting me at the Grosvenor House, where Sam resided. I had missed him by just a few hours—he had left for the weekend. Kurt flew off to Paris to visit his client Elizabeth Taylor, while I paced for two days and nights awaiting Spiegel. By Monday, I needed a nail implant on eight of my ten fingers.

I telephoned Spiegel's suite. "Sam, I'm here."

Frings pushed a note written in capital letters in front of me: "DON'T TELL HIM I'M HERE."

"Good, Bob, good. Let's play some gin? Nat Cohen's free, so is Frankovich, we'll get a foursome."

"Fine, Sam, can I come up to see you now?"

"Of course, come on up."

I looked at Kurt. "He didn't bring anything up about *Lawrence.*"

"That's why Frings is here. He wants options. He wants to steal you for nothing. He's a *gonif!* Go up. See him. I'll be by the phone."

Walking me to the elevator, Frings grabbed my arm.

"Don't let him bluff you. Play him like you play gin. Got it?" The elevator door opened. "Got it."

Into Spiegel's apartment I went.

Sam greeted me with his usual graciousness. Hot tea and heated scones were waiting (a very English practice).

"What brings you to rainy town? No one's here this time of year unless they have to be."

"You."

Sipping his tea, "Me?"

"*Lawrence.*"

Enjoying the taste of the scones, "Like a feather . . . only in Londontown." Swallowing the feathery scone, "Lawrence who?"

"*Lawrence of Arabia.*"

"What about it?"

"Sam, the cable . . . David Lean . . . you want me to meet with him."

"What cable? I never sent you a cable. I got pictures from you, yes. You're totally wrong. I've just signed Omar Sharif; he's an Egyptian actor. Ever hear of him?"

"Can I use the john in the bedroom?"

"Sure."

Slamming the door behind me, I didn't know whether to throw up or call Kurt. I did both.

Kurt barked, "I told you he'd do this! I'm coming right up!"

Kurt arrived.

Opening the door, Sam greeted Kurt. "Why didn't you tell me you were coming, Kurt? What are you doing here?"

"What am I doing here? I'm here with Bob! That's what I'm doing here."

Sam was not smiling.

"I have no idea what either of you are talking about."

"You can bluff the kid, but you can't bluff Frings," as he angrily shook the cable in Spiegel's face.

"I did not send any cable!" Spiegel barked back.

"You didn't? Then read this," screamed Frings.

Quickly Sam read it, then turned it over. Purposefully angering Frings, he asked, "How many years have you been an agent?"

Frings chuckled. "Longer than you've been a producer."

"Look at the back—it's a fake."

For the first time, both of us looked at it, then at each other. Spiegel was right. The message was authentically stripped Western Union style, with a minor difference: it was the instruction form for sending a cable, not the cable itself.

To make it worse, Sam began laughing. "A moron could see it's a fake."

Kurt angrily interrupted, "No one knew about it."

"Dickie did," I whispered.

I looked at Kurt, and he at me.

In duet, "That little cocksucker."

To this day, Dickie has never dared to admit he sent the cable.

I spent the summer in New York. Rather than go out to the Hamptons, I spent weekends playing gin with the Wagners—R. J. and Natalie. Natalie Wood was having a difficult time helping a young actor play his first big screen role—Warren Beatty—in *Splendor in the Grass,* a picture being shot in Connecticut in which she was starring.

One Sunday, dressed ready to join R. J. and Nat to celebrate her getting the lead in *West Side Story,* I was surprised by my doorbell. No one at my new digs at 36 Sutton Place South ever rang it without first being announced by the doorman.

Looking through the peephole, "Who's there?"

"Robert Gordon."

"I don't know who you are. Please leave."

I put my ear to the door and heard the sound of strange scraping footsteps. Robert Gordon . . . the name came back to me. Could that be the kid who'd lived next door to us on Riverside Drive, who'd gone to camp one summer and returned crippled with polio?

I called the doorman, "Is the guy who's just leaving crippled?"

"Yes."

"Please have him come back up right away."

The Robert Gordon I let into my apartment was a young man in his twenties with heavy braces on both legs. Both his parents had died, he said, and he didn't know where to turn.

With an ingenuous laugh, he said, "All my friends think I know you well. But I didn't come here to get an autograph. I need your help."

"How'd you find me?"

"When you have to, you find a way."

I was impressed. Here was a studious, serious guy with a terrible handicap, humble, obviously bright, looking at a guy who on the surface had everything.

"How can I help?"

A quick cut to a very long chase. For more than three years I paid for Robert Gordon's tuition through law school, during which time he got married and had a baby—all on Godfather Bob, averaging $600 a week. But I did get letters upon letters of gratitude, snapshots of my new godson, who was named after me. Though a hundred Gs in, I rationalized that it was well worth it. Graduating with honors, it was celebration time. I invited the Gordons to New York. Robert showed up alone.

"My namesake . . . I was looking forward to meeting him. Where's Katy and Bobby?"

"I have to talk to you alone, Bob. Katy and I decided I should take up accounting law. It's one more year of school. I'd like you to take care of us for another year."

Didn't sit well.

"It's been over three years now, Bob. Don't you think it's time to go out and test the turf? Go to school at night?"

His face changed completely. Staring at me was a monster. "It's easy for you to say—you've got everything!" He began to tremble. "I hate you," he screamed. "I've always hated you!" Reaching into his pocket, he pulled out several snapshots of his kid and flung them at me. "Look at them. Look at them! He wasn't named after you! He was named after *me!*"

I never heard from Robert Gordon again. I never learned from the mistake.

"You've always wanted to be a producer, right?"

"That's right."

"Well, this is your chance to start at the top."

Over dinner with Kurt Frings, at Trader Vic's, he told me his wife, Ketti, who had recently won the Pulitzer Prize for her dramatization of *Look Homeward, Angel,* had just finished writing her new play, *The Umbrella.* It had three acts and only three parts. Each part was already cast with a major star—Geraldine Page, the biggest star in the theater; Franchot Tone, among the biggest male stars in the theater; and Tony Franciosa, a theater and Hollywood heartthrob at the time. Also attached was the top Broadway director Gene Frankel. Kurt and I toasted to *The Umbrella.* How could it miss?

That night, I read *The Umbrella* straight through. Maybe I had had one too many mai tais, but I didn't understand it. I read it again. On the second time around, I was even more confused. Better get some shut eye.

I woke up in the morning, my brain clear, as I turned page after page of *The Umbrella,* I still didn't know what I was reading. (What the hell do I know to argue with Ketti Frings, Geraldine Page, Franchot Tone, and Tony Franciosa.)

"It's brilliant," I told the investors.

Within a month I raised the money, including some from my brother and some of my own. But, so what, here I was Robert Evans, Broadway bound.

We tried out the play in Philadelphia. The opening was the biggest thing to hit Philly since Ben Franklin. The scalpers were having a heyday. You couldn't hear a pin drop when the curtain parted. By the close of the third act, you couldn't hear a pin drop either. There was no one in the theater. No one else understood it either. *The Umbrella* closed after one performance in Philadelphia.

No longer was I Robert Evans, Broadway bound.

10

"I now pronounce you man and wife. . . ."

Our chapel was an ancient oak tree on the grounds of a romantic carriage house on La Colina in Beverly Hills. All my family were there, along with a host of friends—Cary Grant, Elizabeth Taylor and Eddie Fisher, Natalie and R. J., Felicia and Jack Lemmon, Anne and Kirk Douglas, and more—gathered to witness the breaking of my marital virginity.

None of them, I doubt, had ever seen a bride more beautiful than

Sharon. I remember Rossano Brazzi telling Douglas Fairbanks, Jr., in his most charming Italian manner, that my raven-haired bride was the brush of Michelangelo.

I had met Sharon Hugueny on a dare. At the time she was Warner Brothers' entry as the next Elizabeth Taylor playing a starring role in *Parrish*. It was her first picture and for some strange reason she was being protected as if she were the Hope diamond. No one could get near her. No one knew why.

One day, Ray Danton, while shooting a film at Warners, dared, "Even you, Evans, won't be able to get to her."

That's all I needed. The next afternoon, she was shooting a scene with, that's right, Troy Donahue. After each take, she would disappear into her trailer, surrounded by a phalanx of bodyguards. I couldn't get within twenty feet of her.

The following day I came back with Ray. "What are the odds?" I asked.

Ray said, "Name it."

While the hairdresser was putting her hair in a bun, I went up and introduced myself.

"This is my second day on the set," I said, "I just wanted to watch you."

She smiled sweetly. "You're the bullfighter, aren't you? Are you really a bullfighter?"

"No, just a lousy actor."

She laughed.

"When do you finish shooting?"

"I have one more shot. Then I'm off for the day."

"Let's take a drive to the sea."

"Really?"

We eluded the bodyguards and spent the afternoon on the beach, just talking. For me, Sharon was from a different planet. She had been raised by loving, affluent parents in the San Fernando Valley, educated by private tutors, never allowed to touch money. (Her allowance was twenty-five cents a week.) She was so pure I felt guilty kissing her.

Sharon fell madly in love with me, yes, but it could have been anyone who was the first to touch her. That's how protected she had been every day of her life until that moment.

Nine months earlier my own family had been hit with the horrible news—our mother had cancer. It was lodged in her jawbone. So devastating was its tentacles that it traumatized our family's every waking moment.

No one deserves the indignities my poor mother had to suffer. Being among the first to serve as a guinea pig to chemotherapy, (better described as mustard gas), she was the victim of excruciating pain, losing her hair, her beauty, but not her dignity. It angers me that more than thirty years have passed, yet we haven't found anything resembling a cure for the most dreaded disease of all. It's still death the hard way.

Was I in love with Sharon? I didn't know. What I did know was my mother's one desperate wish. To have her overly adventurous son, me, settle down to a life of normalcy. Just as my father before me gave his mother something prior to her passing, so did I want to give something to my mother. What better gift could there be than mother of the groom.

Literally, I swept Sharon off her feet, proposing to her and setting a date. Her parents were vehemently against it—and rightfully so—but I wasn't thinking of their daughter. I was thinking of my mother. My mother, who barely had the strength at the time to make the trip, traveled west for her shining moment.

The night before the I dos, my mother wanted to meet her new daughter-in-law, and meet her alone. After she saw Sharon, my mother asked to see me alone too.

In a voice hardly above a whisper, she said, "You can't marry her, Bob. She's a baby; she's untouched. It's unfair to her."

I lay down beside my mom and cradled her. "I love her, Mom. I'm a changed man. It's going to be wonderful. A year from now you'll see a little Bobby running around."

We both knew that would never be. What she didn't know—and what I couldn't tell her—was that I was only marrying Sharon for her.

From Walter Winchell and Louella Parsons to *Photoplay,* Sharon and I were the couple of the moment. Together, we were a fan magazine's dream. Being with me was far more important to Sharon than being in front of the cameras. This beautiful, genteel innocent not only was a virgin when I married her, but had never been on a date. Her family's strict rules were not without reason.

Still under contract to Darryl Zanuck, who had now become more active and was showing renewed interest in my career, I was signed to two of his most ambitious projects: *The Longest Day* and *The Chapman Report*.

At the same time, I was feeling guilty living in Los Angeles while my mother withered away back east. Then came the ultimatum. Evan-Picone, unlike my career, was making huge strides. Though I owned a decent chunk, my brother, Charles, and Joe Picone were the major partners. Justifiably, they both confronted me. "Either come back or sell out."

Looking at yourself in the mirror, calling a spade a spade ain't easy—Evans, you're not good enough to make it all the way. The parts you're offered you don't want, and the parts you want you're not offered. Paul Newman? No shot. Tab Hunter? More like it. Not for me. I wanted to be the next Darryl Zanuck, and I paid the price, making the most difficult decision of my life. I gave up the glamour of Hollywood, two firm pictures with Zanuck, a storybook existence, and returned to New York City with my child bride, back to Evan-Picone's showroom on Broadway.

New York was a disaster. Every morning I would get out of the cab at 1407 Broadway, wishing I were going through the gate at Twentieth Century–Fox. Every evening, sitting in a restaurant entertaining an executive from Saks, Bloomingdale's or Bullock's, I was thinking how much I missed my actor, director, and writer pals. I hated the Hamptons. I loved Malibu.

For my child bride, it was worse. One afternoon, my secretary buzzed me. Sharon was on the line, urgent.

"Darling, what's the problem?" All I could hear was weeping. "What is it, baby, what is it?"

Childlike, "I don't know where I am."

"Where are you calling from?"

"I don't know. I'm so scared!"

"Sharon, darling, are you in a phone booth?"

"Yes . . ."

"Inside or outside?"

"Inside . . ."

"What street are you on?"

"I don't know. . . ."

"Listen carefully, darling. Open the door and look at the street sign."

"I can't. I'm too scared!"

My heart dropped. What had I been thinking, bringing this child to New York? It was like setting a Persian cat loose in the Amazon.

"Please, darling. Just read the street sign. Tell me what it says and I'll be there in five minutes."

"Don't hang up! Don't hang up!"

I heard her open the phone booth door and say to a passerby, "Please, mister, where am I?" Apparently he thought she was crazy and kept walking.

"Ask a lady."

I heard a woman answer, "You're on Fifty-fourth and Lexington, dearie."

"You're only four blocks from home, darling. Walk down to First Avenue, turn left, go one block, and you're there."

"I can't! I can't! I'm too scared!"

"Stay where you are—I'll be there in ten."

My mother was right. How could I have been so insensitive to think this fragile flower could survive, no less me, but New York as well? I told Sharon I couldn't stand by and watch her be hurt anymore. It was unfair to her. Listening like a child, she understood.

Together we went to Mexico for a quickie divorce. Almost six months to the day of our wedding, we kissed good-bye. It was like the first day we met.

11

"Fuck goin' public! We're goin' private, fill our pockets with green, not stock!"

If ever my brother was right, it was then. For months, Eastman-Dillon, Lehman Brothers, and Loeb, Rhoades—three of the biggest firms on Wall Street—had all been competing to bring Evan-Picone public.

"Let me follow through with Charlie Revson," said my brother. "If he wants us, it's payout time. No papier-mâché shit."

Charlie Revson, founder and owner of Revlon, wanted to buy us out. None of us knew why, but who the fuck cared. My brother was the seducer and quite a lover was he. Akin to a sex-starved Victorian groom, the more time the two Charlies spent together, the more Revson wanted to get in Evan-Picone's pants. The negotiations lasted over six months.

Each Charlie thinking he was playing the other like a fiddle. Ahhh—but baby brother came up with the cat. Her name, Sheika Mosher—better known as Yellowbird, the only stripper on the Vegas strip to get equal billing with Milton Berle. We had known each other for a month and had fallen deeply in lust. For her, leaving Vegas for New York was a step in the wrong direction, but she wanted to change her style of life. I was there to accommodate that wish—from $2,500 a week at El Rancho Vegas to $140 a week at Evan-Picone as a showroom model, where she was more seductive putting her clothes on than she was in Vegas taking them off.

One day Charlie Revson came in to look at our new fall line. It was the first time I'd ever seen him smile. And it wasn't our clothes he was smiling at. Revson had never liked me and let everyone know it.

My brother snuck into my office. He whispered, "Bob, do you mind if Revson takes Sheika to dinner?"

A smile crossed my face. "Charlie, the price of poker's just gone up for Evan-Picone."

Revson's life was his work. Dining out each night with six to eight of his top lieutenants, strategizing their next move to gobble up Evan-Picone, he never realized that Mata Hari was smack in the middle of his high command. My little Sheika became Revson's constant girl Friday, each night listening, listening, listening.

In June 1962, the deal was closed. Our sale price on signing was $12 million in cash. The only hitch was that Charles, Joe Picone, and I had to sign five-year employment contracts. Some hitch. By today's standards, those numbers would equate to several hundred million.

Sheika was right. Her talents lay in New York. Where else could she strip several million out of one pocket into another? Thank you, dear Sheika, thank you again. Proving the prophecy true that it's a woman's world! While men think it's theirs.

What should have been a triumphant time was not. My mother died, mercifully. In the last year of her life we had tried every known cure, experimental or illegal, including pure enzyme shots administered by the infamous Dr. Max Jacobsen, who had administered addictive amphetamine mixes to John F. Kennedy, Eddie Fisher, Alan Jay Lerner, and scores of others on his cure-all, which was nothing more than a highly addictive form of speed.

It's strange, but women are so much stronger. Had my father died first, I'm sure my mother would have recovered in time and gone on with her life, possibly a better one. But Pop, who had stayed by his Florence's bedside throughout her illness, never recovered. He retreated further and further into his shell. The tentacles of Alzheimer's had struck. Within a few years he couldn't walk, talk, or express pain.

Charles and I refused to put him in a home. For the last ten years of his life he had round-the-clock nursing at 737 Park Avenue. In 1982 he finally passed away. Pop was dealt a bum deck. He never once picked up aces. Yet the indelible memory of both my mother and father's moral standards remain deeply imbedded in Alice, Charles, and me. Rarely does a day pass without a loving thought toward Mom and Pop. We were lucky kids.

Thanks to the combination of Hollywood notoriety and newfound green, New York became far more friendly. When my mother passed away, I moved into a town house on East Sixty-seventh off Fifth Avenue, complete with elevator, two terraces, and three skylights. It was there I discovered a new passion—interior design—and learned that background makes foreground. If I was paid too many compliments on the tie I was wearing, it would immediately go into a shredder. The tie is there for me to look better, not for me to make the tie look better. If my drawing room's eighteenth-century armoire was given too much attention, off to Sotheby's it went. Again, the armoire is there to enhance the drawing room, not the reverse. That's what background makes foreground is all about.

My new pad was akin to a corner of Paris in New York. Maybe it was because, for the first time, I had "fuck you" money in my pocket, but I began feeling better about myself. Living on the East Coast, even being a so-called movie star puts you on the A list. Combine that with being a fashion tycoon and you end up on the A+ list. I never made that. A Jew never does. The A+ list is boring anyway. The A list is good enough for me. Certainly, it dealt more of an action hand.

I became great pals with Porfirio Rubirosa. I met him with Darryl

Zanuck a year earlier. This legendary cocksman and sportsman, ex-husband of three of the richest women in the world (from whom he asked nothing after divorcing them), was the best company in the world: wonderfully self-deprecating, intensely focused on whomever he was with. A man's man, that's for sure. A woman's man? There was never anyone like him.

In the winter of 1962 we went together to the International Red Cross Ball in Palm Beach. There were movie stars galore there—from Cary Grant to Yul Brynner. When Ruby walked in, the word "background" is what fit their presence. Ruby was the star. Excitedly, every woman's eyes turned to him, then to his crotch. That was his legend. In the forties and fifties, the popular quote was "in like Flynn," referring to Errol. In the fifties and sixties it was "How's your Rubirosa?" referring to my pal. Strange I should know both guys!

A few months later, Ruby was in New York. Would I dine with him and his wife? By the way, he added, an extraordinary-looking girl from Brazil would be joining us. A half hour later, the four of us were at Côte Basque, a great French restaurant. The girl didn't speak a word of English and my Portuguese was even less. But her beauty and charm made up for it.

Naturally, my ego told me, She really digs me. Ah, possibly the next Mrs. Evans.

Better we don't speak, it'll last longer, I thought to myself.

Gianni Agnelli, the Italian industrialist, joined us for dessert with the actress Julie Newmar on his arm. After the soufflés, Gianni suggested we try out a new private disco called Le Club. Though the weather was bitter cold as we took off on foot, I felt the warmth of heaven.

"Florinda Evans," I kept repeating to myself, "sounds good, sounds good," as we entered the newest hot spot in New York.

Florinda and I danced till we were drenched in sweat. Once we sat, Odille, Ruby's wife, leaned forward across her husband, the century's greatest lover, put her hand on top of mine and shocked me like I had never been before, which ain't easy.

"Forget her, Bob. She's *mine.*"

Months later, Alan Jay Lerner invited me to a small after theater party for his old roommate, Jack Kennedy, and his wife, Jackie. My date that evening was one of Eileen Ford's top models, Renata Boeck, whom I'd been seeing for several months. Renata and I were just about the only people there who'd never met the Camelot couple. I would have liked to believe that the President really knew as much about me as he pretended, but he'd undoubtedly had somebody do his homework. We shook hands and he recited my screen credits and asked me about the stars I'd worked with—especially Ava Gardner. Wow, I thought. What a terrific guy!

Renata and I were sound asleep when the phone rang at three in the morning. I picked up the receiver.

"This is Jack Kennedy calling. Can I please speak with Renata?"

"The President?"

Without a slight raise of voice, "That's right."

I woke up Renata.

"It's the President on the phone. . . ."

I handed her the phone—what else could I do? They chatted a few minutes and no chat was more charming than Renata's purr. After hanging up, Renata nestled close to me and fell back to sleep. As tempting as it was, I never asked her what they talked about. Nor later did I ask her if she ever saw him. She wouldn't have told me the truth anyway.

From the moment Revlon took over Evan-Picone, its business went south. It was run by a committee that knew everything about fragrances but nothing about fashion. Soon our bottom line was lipstick red. In November 1963 a sit-down was called in my brother's office. Revson and his honchos were there, along with Charles, Joe Picone, and me.

Outside the temperature was chilly. Inside it was freezing. Adolf Revson was terrorizing the group when my brother's secretary ran into the office.

"The President's been shot!"

All of us jumped up and rushed to the television. Not Uncle Charlie.

"Sit down," he demanded. "This is not a social call. I don't like looking at red numbers. Let's get down to business."

I pulled my brother aside. "I hate the motherfucker and he doesn't like me either. Help me get out of my contract, will ya?"

It was easy. Revson was glad to get rid of me.

As brothers, Charles and I were so alike yet so different. Charles ultraconservative, me a gambler. Today, Charles is a millionaire a hundred times over. Me, I'm still in hock.

Our first investment, after selling Evan-Picone, was in a speculative mutual fund. Charles, the far richer, put in $25,000; me, a quarter of a million. Two months later, the fund went bust, I mean bust—zero back on the dollar. How depressing it would have been to know then that it was a portent of our financial futures. Even in the gold-rush eighties, I came up a loser.

12

In the late fifties, Warren Beatty was playing second fiddle to Dwayne Hickman in the TV series "Dobie Gillis." Me, I was playing opposite Ava Gardner in Cinemascope. Five years passed. He's was now a top movie star and I was back selling ladies pants. Even then we were competitive as to whose pants we were in the night before.

Warren kept a pad in New York, which he shared with Charlie Feldman, his mentor and friend.

Over lunch at P. J. Clarke's, Warren, Charlie, and I were discuss-

ing Charlie's new flick, which Warren was to star in, written by a
rising comic named Woody Allen—*What's New Pussycat?* The title
was taken from real life—Warren's life, that is; it was his opening
line to whichever new girl was on the other end of the phone. Charlie
was telling Warren and me how brilliant this new kid, Woody Allen,
was.

"The kid's a genius. We went to Danny's Hideaway for a steak last
night. I laughed so hard, I couldn't eat."

"Yeah," said Warren, "and I had the most boring night of my life
with the new Miss Iceberg."

When he told me how he'd batted out with Eileen Ford's latest
Scandinavian discovery, I knew this was a girl I had to meet.

Her name was Camilla Sparv. The moment she arrived in New
York, she was a star model. A tall, leggy blonde, she had a natural
patrician quality money can't buy. After many calls to the Ford
agency, the best I could land was a Friday breakfast. I had a forty-
minute shot at her. Like a fool I broke my old rule against talking
about myself.

We met in the coffee shop around the corner from her hotel—she
in curlers, me in a three-piece suit with my hair slicked back. I never
saw anyone so skinny eat so much. I babbled. She ate. Finishing off
the last of her eggs, pancakes, and bacon, she gave me a quick good-
bye.

Not liking her attitude, "Suppose the more you eat, the taller you
get."

"That's right," laughing in my face. "Too tall for you, Mr. Smooth-
ie."

Royally opening her cab door, I half-whispered, "Really."

Within twenty-four hours we were together and stayed that way
until the day we divorced.

Within a year we were married. I knew then it was time to get
serious or get in trouble. It was safer to get serious. I had everything
going for me. A sensational new wife, my pockets bulging with green,
and for the first time in my life I was unemployed, with no less than
a rainbow of options to pick from.

Big screen parts were still being offered me. Opposite Mamie Van
Doren not Elizabeth Taylor. Going for broke rather than going back-
ward had always been my style. I wanted to be the next Zanuck.
From my town house in New York, I set up a nonexistent Robert

Evans Production Company. Through a friend, I met a reviewer at *Publishers Weekly* named George Wieser who had access to every new book before it went anywhere. Though his position was influential, his salary wasn't. For $175 a week, he agreed to moonlight as my literary scout.

Before his second check, he gave me a sneak look on the manuscript of a new novel, *Valley of the Dolls,* written by a then unknown author, Jacqueline Susann.

"It's hot pulp, Bob," he said. "Make a quick deal on it. Lock her up on her next three books."

Five years earlier I became friends with a producer at Fox, David Brown. Under contract to the studio at the time, he wanted me to be one point of the triangle in an erotic screenplay, *The Chinese Room.* Monty Clift and Brigitte Bardot were set as the other two points. Announced to be made, it was pulled at the last minute. Distribution thought it was too hot to handle. Now David was based in New York and married to the brilliant new editor of *Cosmopolitan* magazine, Helen Gurley Brown. I had always thought of David as a fan. Naïvely, I went to see him.

Laying the galleys of Jackie Susann's novel on his desk, I said, "David, I think I have Fox's next big picture. I can get a lock on the author too."

David glanced at the title page. "Thanks, Bob. I'll get back to you in a week."

A week later, Fox bought the film rights to *Valley of the Dolls,* but they didn't buy Bob Evans to go with it. Instead they assigned one of their staff producers, David Weisbart, to produce it. Money talks and bullshit walks. For five Gs, I could have had an option on the film rights to what was to become not only a best-selling novel, but a smash film to boot. Once a mistake—twice a failure. It never happened again.

If ever a guy was worth his $175 a week, it was George Wieser. Less than a month later, he brought me another first novel, this one written by an ex-cop, Roderick Thorp.

Holding up the manuscript, he said, "It's gonna be big, Bob, I can smell it. The guy knows what he's talking about. It's called *The Detective.*"

For five Gs, I was the proud owner of an option of a new manuscript written by a totally unknown author. But for some reason, knowing that possession is 99 percent of ownership, I had the balls of Goliath when I went back to see David Brown.

"I didn't do too badly with *Valley of the Dolls,* did I, David?" I dropped *The Detective* on his desk. "Insiders say this is the sleeper of the year."

Again, David glanced at the title page. "Hmmm, I'll get back to you in a week."

"Thanks, David. Oh, by the way, I own this one."

Within a week I was offered a cockamamie deal where I'd get billed as the associate producer. It was understandable. I'd never produced a movie before. But fuck 'em, I owned it; they didn't. I turned their offer down flatter than any performance I had ever given. California, here I come. Keeping my town house intact, with bride in hand, I rented a romantic hideaway in the hills of Bel Air.

George Wieser kept sending me book after book. For another five Gs, I bought another option. This time, F. Lee Bailey's account of his successful defense in the sensational Dr. Sam Sheppard case (after serving nine years for the murder of his pregnant wife, the Ohio osteopath was retried by order of the United States Supreme Court). Was it dumb luck, or was Wieser this bright? First *Valley of the Dolls,* then *The Detective,* now the Sam Sheppard murder case. *The Detective* had already worked its way up to the top of the best-seller list. Who says the writer ain't the biggest star? Suddenly, every leading actor, director, and writer in town wanted to be part of bringing *The Detective* to the screen. For the first time, the guy holding the aces was me.

"David Brown's on the phone," said my part-time secretary.

His charm more lethal than ever, "Twentieth's been your home, Bob. Let's keep it that way."

Negotiations had started. As a favor to Korshak, Greg Bautzer, Hollywood's most highly profiled attorney, represented me. What Bautzer thought was an afternoon's work took close to three months. Fox offered half a mil, but that was to buy me out. I wanted my foot in the door. I told Greg that to get *The Detective* Fox would have to give me a three-picture development deal, a suite of offices with secretaries located in the select administration building, and two back-page ads in the trade papers with a picture of me signing my deal with the new head of the studio, Dickie Zanuck.

Ego? You bet! Revenge? Even more so.

"Is he crazy, this half-assed actor?" screamed Lou Schreiber, Fox's top business honcho. "He's lucky to get in the gate! I have to tell Mr. Zanuck he has to pose for an ad in the trades with him? Nothing's worth that. Forget it!"

The news was a turndown, but Greg's flamboyant account of his meeting with Schreiber made us laugh so hard that everyone in the Polo Lounge looked around to see what the joke was. It was no joke. I had no deal.

One of the scripts collecting dust on my desk was *Chevalier,* an original screenplay about the life of the French entertainer Maurice Chevalier, centering around his love affair with the legendary cabaret singer Mistinguett. I didn't think much of it as a script, but for a thousand bucks I'd taken a thirty-day option on it because the writer, Maurice Richlin, had won an Academy Award. From Alain Delon, an old pal, I heard that Chevalier himself was in town for a couple of weeks. When your back's against the wall, the impossible becomes possible.

Alain was preparing an American picture, hoping to become the next Charles Boyer. A reclusive loner, he was one of the most unapproachable people in the world. Yet we seemed to share a common bond as brothers.

He, at the time, was among the world's biggest film stars. I was a producer who had never produced and was without an office, but it didn't matter. When I asked him to arrange an introduction with Chevalier, he said of course. Better yet, he said he'd like to play Chevalier himself.

We went to the great man's hotel. Only the French could turn on the charm like Alain. He told Chevalier he'd always had a "fascination" with playing him on the screen. Hearing this, Chevalier dropped thirty years. For the first time, he noticed the kid with the script.

I was rolling sevens. "Mr. Chevalier, do you have any pictures of yourself with Mistinguett? Something startling that would jump off the page?"

Chevalier looked at me strangely.

"*Chevalier* is not going to be just another picture, we're going to make it an *event*. Alain, I want to give a press conference—the Bistro would be the perfect backdrop. Mr. Chevalier—and Alain, if you wouldn't mind—I'd like you both to be there."

As showmen, they agreed.

Two days later at eleven A.M. I walked into the Bistro with the script of *Chevalier* under my arm. "Hey," I whispered to Alain, "what if I announce Bardot as Mistinguett?"

"Why not?"

All the movie press was there, foreign as well. Not to see me, but Alain Delon and Maurice Chevalier.

I had hardly got a word out when Walter Winchell's stringer got up. Grinning sarcastically, he said, "I don't understand, Mr. Evans. Are you talking as a *producer?* To the best of my memory, you're an *actor,* aren't you? And also in the *dress business?*"

Everyone laughed.

"Mr. Seidman, I sold my dress business for several million dollars—cash. I gave up acting when I turned down parts in *The Chapman Report* and *The Longest Day.* Presently I'm in negotiations with a major studio for a multipicture deal. The first picture is *The Detective,* based on the novel by Roderick Thorp." I stopped them cold. Call it the unexpected: no one knew I owned the best-selling novel. Then I held up an old picture of Chevalier and Mistinguett, which I'd had blown up and glazed with an antique veneer. "My second project is *Chevalier,* starring Alain Delon as the great entertainer and Brigitte Bardot as the love of his life, the legendary singer Mistinguett. Unfortunately, Miss Bardot could not be with us because she is filming outside Paris. But Mr. Chevalier and Mr. Delon are here to answer your questions."

The response was so explosive, I never announced my third project. Lucky—I didn't have one.

The next day, "BARDOT, DELON IN 'CHEVALIER'" was in headlines across the country. Way down in the text were the words "to be produced by Robert Evans."

Over at Fox, Lou Schreiber was on the phone to Bautzer. Greg got me everything: three-picture deal, great office, and my picture on the back pages of both trade papers—with my good friend Dickie Zanuck, no less.

Camilla had been one of the most in-demand models in the business, a favorite of Scavullo and the other top fashion photographers. Now she was only "Mrs. Robert Evans," but she loved it. My skinny Swede was the perfect wife; wonderful around the house, wonderful as a hostess, wonderful as a companion—with a great flair for a raunchy story.

Everyone saw Camilla as "the next Audrey Hepburn." She had the same ingenuous smile and coltish grace, the same champagne effervescence, the same innate projection of style.

"How about doing some acting, baby?"

She laughed. "Of course, there's a very big demand for a tall, skinny Swede with no tits."

"Let me make some calls."

She shrugged.

Me, Camilla's Svengali? Not at all. I didn't care about her becoming a movie star any more than she did. I just wanted her to get some work so she'd be out of the house and I could get my freedom back. Good husband material!

I invited Billy Gordon, head of talent at Columbia, and his wife over for dinner. To say they were enchanted with Camilla is an understatement. The next day Billy asked if he could test Camilla, using a scene from *Sabrina*. Camilla would be in the Audrey Hepburn role; Cliff Robertson in the Bogart part. Richard Brooks would direct.

Camilla's reaction was "Bob, I'd rather not." As a lark, she agreed to it. Driving to the Columbia lot, she said, "If you laugh at me I'll hit you right in your *cojones.*"

Maybe it was the fact that she just didn't give a damn that made her so alive. When Columbia's hierarchy saw the test, they immediately wanted her for a long-term contract. With luck, I thought, she would get a good long-location picture. And I would get my freedom back.

Camilla would rather play gin than read scripts. Alain Delon had stayed on to make *Texas Across the River* with Dean Martin, and almost every night he and his wife, Natalie, would come over with their infant son, Tony, for the high-stakes action. Camilla and I weren't necessarily better players, but we had an edge because we were playing by home rules. No ace around the corner. After a month, we were up $26,000 in green.

One night Kurt Frings arrived with Eddie Fisher. Alain and Natalie knew Kurt well and had met Eddie once before. All six of us were there to play gin. The game began. Three against three, Eddie and Kurt switching sides after each set. I bent down to pick up a card that I dropped and thought I was seeing double. Natalie's hand was on Eddie's crotch. This dame, married to Europe's most attractive male star, was making a play for this over-the-hill singer, with more ridges on his face than the Grand Canyon.

Was I hallucinating, or was it a setup? If it was, it worked. It was the first time Camilla and I had lost—and lost big—about $11,000. But it wasn't a setup. The next morning a very distressed Alain called. Would I quickly come over to his house? Once there, I listened to one of the most unbelievable stories of my life. Natalie, kid and all, had just taken off for Miami Beach, not to get the sun, but to be with Eddie Fisher, who was appearing at the Hotel Fontainebleau.

"Let's get on the next plane to Miami," Alain urged.

"You're on."

Off we went—Camilla, Alain, and myself—to bring Natalie back to her senses. We arrived at five in the afternoon. By eight, we were sitting front and center at the Fontainebleau, waiting for Eddie Fisher to come out and perform. He did, spending the entire hour on the stage, crooning to his new lady love, Alain's wife, Natalie.

When it's over, it's over. Poor Alain. All he kept saying in his broken English on the flight back was "Eddie Fisher, Eddie Fisher, Eddie Fisher."

My brother Charles and his wife, Frances, had taken a house in Miami Beach for the winter. I had to be back in L.A. for some meetings. Alain had to return to get on with his flick. I suggested Camilla stay on for a week—spend a bit of time with her new in-laws. She bought it!

Good, dutiful husband that I was, I promised to call Camilla every night. It's one of the few promises I kept. I had been home about a week, and I dialed Camilla in Miami. My brother answered.

"Is Camilla there?"

"I'm not sure."

"Where will you be tomorrow about noon?"

"At the Palm Bay Club."

"I'll call you there. Boy, have I got some wild stories for you."

When it came to kiss-and-tell, Charlie was my only confidant. On the phone the next day, I rattled off, one by one, the graphic details of my week's escapades.

"A cashmere sweater if you can persuade Camilla to stay another week."

Laughing, Charlie hung up the phone. So did Camilla, who wasn't laughing, and certainly wasn't supposed to be listening. Call it woman's intuition, but the night before, she had picked up the phone early and heard me tell my brother about the wild stories I had for him. It motivated her to pay a hundred bucks to the hotel operator to be hooked up to our clandestine noon call. What a difference a call makes.

The skinny Swede was so cool about it. As angry as she was, she kept her secret to herself for nearly a month.

I'd been invited to play in the amateur/pro tennis tournament at the Palm Springs Racquet Club and I asked Camilla to join me.

"No," she said, "I'll just be a distraction. Be a winner."

Wow! A weekend off.

Disqualified in the first round, I could have gone home that day. But not me. The town was packed. Without a racquet, I was ready for everything.

When I got back to our love nest late Sunday, the cool Swede was cold.

I tried for a smile. "Just because I lost, you don't love me anymore?"

"Like a drink?" She brought me a mug of ice-cold beer. Then she took my hand. "Let's sit down and talk."

Maybe she wanted a bigger house. . . .

"How could you do it, Bob?"

"Lose? Easy, I'm a lousy player."

"You're a loser."

What?

"A loser? That's one thing you know I ain't, baby."

She looked straight at me. "I should hate you, but I don't. I *pity* you."

"What are you talking about?"

One by one, she named the friends of hers I'd fucked on the sly.

"Are you crazy? What are you talking about?"

"How do you think it makes me feel, walking into a room, knowing everyone's laughing at me because I'm married to the town whore?"

Early in life, I learned never to cop to a woman, even if she catches you in the act.

"Are you crazy?" I repeated.

"I know all about it, Bob. I heard you on the phone with Charles."

I could jump out the window and roll down the hill. Or I could be a coward and get to the nearest phone. I was a coward. I made it to the phone booth at the east gate of Bel Air in a minute and a half.

Charles wasn't home in New York. His butler said he was dining at The Little Club. Warren Beatty couldn't have dialed The Little Club's number any faster.

"Charles, it's a bad dream. Remember that phone call to the Palm Bay Club about a month ago?"

"Yeah. So what?"

"Camilla just read me the riot act. She heard the whole thing."

"She couldn't have . . ."

"If she had three private eyes on my tail, she couldn't have been as accurate. What the hell's going on, Charles?"

"I don't know."

"Well, you better know! Ask Frances."

"Settle down, will you, Bob!"

"Thanks for the advice. What do I do now?"

"Deny everything."

I couldn't. Instead, I copped to everything. What the hell. I'd already told her I wasn't marriage material. But in truth, I couldn't look myself in the mirror without total disdain.

Camilla was the ultimate Swede—a pragmatist. "Bob, I want you to see a psychiatrist. I want this marriage to work."

"Psychiatrist? Come on! I've never been to one in my life and I'm not going to start now."

"You're sick. You need help!"

She was right. I was sick, but it wasn't help I was looking for.

After three visits to Dr. Hacker, the psychiatrist of Camilla's choice, he called her.

"Forget it, Mrs. Evans. It's a waste of time. He'll never change. My advice to you is go out and have an affair yourself. You deserve it."

Our breakup caused a far deeper depression than I ever imagined. Los Angeles suddenly lost its glamour. Naturally, I blamed the town, not the person, as the culprit.

13

You live by the press, you die by the press. Who would have thought a journalist would change the entire course of my life and career? On reflection, I don't know whether I should love him or hate him.

I met Peter Bart, the West Coast correspondent for *The New York Times,* through Abby Mann, whom I'd hired to write the screenplay of *The Detective.* Peter and I hit it off as opposites. I was fascinated by this intellectual straight arrow, who was writing stories about hippies and antiwar demonstrations in California—"Indian country" to the people back east—and getting them printed in the ultrasquare *Times*. Peter must have been fascinated by a type of guy he'd never met before. We were both new boys in town.

I couldn't believe it when Peter said he wanted to write a feature about me for the Arts & Leisure section in the Sunday *Times*. I had yet to produce my first picture.

"Is this a joke, Peter?"

"No, Bob. You're the first person I've met out here who makes things happen."

"Okay. If you say so."

One night Peter Bart took off his horn-rims after a day of interviews and said, "I started this story about your energy. I'm thinking of changing it."

"To what?"

"The Outsider—you, Bob Evans, the ultimate one. The ex-actor, laughed at, ridiculed by the so-called power players, but as they laughed, you figured out a way to beat them at their own game. You know you have, Evans."

"If you're right, pal, I'm on my way."

"You're the only one I've spent time with since I've been in Tinseltown that isn't tinsel. You know who the real star is—the material. What's interesting about you, Evans, and why you're worth writing about, is that you're beating the so-called big guys at their own game." Bart laughed. "You could become the guy you played."

If I was smart, I would have retired after Peter's article in *The New York Times,* calling me the next Thalberg.

Instead, Greg Bautzer said, "Pack your bags, Bob. We're going to New York."

"I got plans, Greg."

"Break 'em. Charlie Bluhdorn, who just bought Paramount, wants to meet you. He read that article about you in Sunday's *New York Times.*"

"What does he want to meet me for?"

"He's as tough and bright a guy as I've ever known, Bob. He's a doer, not a talker. He wouldn't ask me to waste my time if he didn't have something specific in mind. Now get packed."

Within five minutes of meeting Charlie Bluhdorn, I knew this was no kibitzer. Before I finished trying to answer one question, he was asking me another. Strangely, I didn't have to answer any of them.

Before I could open my mouth, he answered the questions himself.

With him was Martin Davis, his top *capo,* who was the one responsible for the go-go conglomerate, Gulf + Western, buying the aging "mountain" (Paramount). During the hour's barrage, Davis never once turned his deadly Doberman eyes away from me. Forget Bobby Evans; the two of them together could have intimidated Bobby Kennedy. After an hour of being a Ping-Pong ball I looked at Greg.

"Between the two of them, they'll eat me for breakfast and still be hungry."

Was I perceptive? Never more. Except that they also ate me for lunch and dinner.

There were eight major studios at the time, and Paramount was ninth. Though Bluhdorn had bought it at bargain-basement prices, everybody thought he was nuts to get involved in a business he knew nothing about, much less a business as crazy as show business.

Secrecy being the M.O., I began to feel like a CIA agent, flying back and forth from New York to Los Angeles for more than a month. Summoned to New York on a Sunday, I was greeted by Marty Davis.

Without cracking a smile, Marty gave me my marching orders. "We're making you head of European production. You're going to be based in London. That's where the action is. Writers, directors, actors. It's fresh, not stale like Hollywood."

Bluhdorn burst in. "I want twenty pictures a year from you. The Paramount *caca* in charge there now is ninety years old. He saw *Alfie* and couldn't even hear it."

"Gentlemen, I've got a deal at Twentieth and—"

"Get out of it." Marty said. "You'll be running Paramount in three months. Is that right, Charlie?"

"That's right, Marty."

"My Fox contract, it may not be that easy."

Marty gave me a look.

"If you're gonna run Paramount, you better be tougher than you are now."

I got the message. Two hours later I was walking on Sutton Place with David Brown. When I told him what had happened his eyebrows arched.

"You haven't even made your first picture yet. Do you have any idea what you're getting yourself into?"

"Truthfully, David, I don't and I don't give a shit. I've been on a real low since busting up with Camilla. Just living in another city could be exciting. Most of all London."

His tone changed, from family to steel. "Is this a negotiation?"

"No . . . no, David."

"Have Bautzer call me tomorrow."

"David, you gave me my chance. You can keep *The Detective.* You can keep everything. I don't want a dime for my projects."

By eleven the next morning, David had sent over the papers. The terms were simple: walk away, give up all financial participation in my projects at Fox. Only an Okie would have signed—I did. The next day I called David to say good-bye.

"I just hung up from Dick Zanuck," he said. "When I told him the news he couldn't believe it."

"I'll bet he couldn't."

"He couldn't stop laughing. 'David,' he said, 'let me understand you correctly. Did you say Robert Evans will be based in London as head of European production for Paramount Pictures?' I said, 'That's right. And the odd thing is I don't think he's ever even *been* there!' Then Dick said the strangest thing: 'Yes, he has . . . *once!*' "

There I was in England. Is this a dream? It was a nightmare. I spent about five months in London and never even saw Big Ben. I was an inpatient at the Connaught Hotel, just like a hooker, always on call.

It wasn't only the time difference between London, New York, and L.A.; I was in the middle of a revolution. Charlie Bluhdorn and Marty Davis were restructuring the whole Paramount mountain. Between the politics, the managerial upheaval, the confusion over what films to make, and the fact that I had two tigers by the tail, I had one life—the phone. It didn't matter whether it was three P.M. or three A.M., I had to be there, waiting for the ring.

Paramount's executives in London were overage, overpaid, and over-British. To my face they bowed, to my back they laughed. Within a month, I fired half of them. The others knew their days were numbered. I was too new at the game to be sure of what I wanted. But I knew what I didn't want—which was everything my Dark Age compatriots were excited to see get to the screen.

To protect my back was one thing, but how do I protect my front? Six thousand miles away, Peter Bart, an avid reader, became my unpaid right-hand man. Peter could read more over a weekend than I could in a week. I burned up the transatlantic wires. Every night I called him for his report. Peter had no idea how good he made me look before the aging Paramount House of Lords. The audacity putting this philistine, an American, not even with the credentials of a master's degree, an uneducated indigent actor no less, to preside over us! They were right. But, thanks to Peter, they never knew how right they were.

One of the old guard's pet projects was *Half a Sixpence,* adapted from the hit musical, starring Tommy Steele. I had liked it onstage. But a movie? Who would see it in Kansas City? I was not shy in voicing my opinion.

If I was to lose that battle, I wouldn't go down easily. One night I was on long distance with Charlie and Marty, taking one last shot at killing *Half a Sixpence.*

"I'm going on record, Charlie. This picture's going to be a disaster."

"*Told* you, Marty," Charlie said. "The kid's got *balls.*"

I got a weekend leave. The studio's most expensive picture in years, *Is Paris Burning?,* was opening in Paris. Every top executive, from production to distribution, advertising, and publicity, had been summoned to Paramount's night of glory.

Two days before the premiere, there were round-the-clock meetings. The buzz was that Bluhdorn was going to close down the studio and sell off its assets. Being the new kid on the block, I knew enough to keep my mouth shut. It wasn't easy when I heard all the posturing. Everyone was there to protect their jobs, it was all that mattered.

Another thing was clear—the people to please were not Charlie

Bluhdorn or Marty Davis, but the heads of international distribution. They'd been there forever and they shared one philosophy. A calendar had to be filled. They didn't care how as long as it had stars, stars, stars. The phone book would be green-lighted; that is, if it starred John Wayne, Paul Newman, or Elizabeth Taylor.

Somehow nobody brought up the fact that last year's *In Harm's Way*, with John Wayne, Kirk Douglas, Henry Fonda, etc. had been a colossal dud. After all, Paramount had three "blockbusters" on the way: *Assault on a Queen*, with Frank Sinatra; *Promise Her Anything*, with Warren Beatty and Leslie Caron; and, the biggest one of all, *Is Paris Burning?*, featuring a who's who from Orson Welles, Kirk Douglas, and Charles Boyer to Alain Delon, Simone Signoret, and Yves Montand. How could we miss?

I'd seen them all. *Assault on a Queen* was a B-picture inflated to A status only because it had Sinatra. *Promise Her Anything* promised onscreen chemistry between the year's hottest offscreen couple, but since it had no story, it had no oxygen. *Is Paris Burning?* was a historical fashion show.

Yet only a few months earlier, Paramount had released, almost by mistake, a beautifully written "little" picture called *Alfie*, starring an unknown Cockney actor named Michael Caine. So what if *Alfie* cost less than John Wayne's asking price and captured the imagination of the world? To the prima donnas in distribution, it was no more than a fluke. Their dictate remained intransigent—"stars, stars, stars."

The morning of the premiere, I requested a breakfast meeting with Charlie and Marty.

"You know this business better than me, Marty," I began, "but from all the bullshit I've been hearing it seems that distribution is running the business, not production. We're going the wrong way, fellas. If the product stinks, you can't sell it. Certainly not these dinosaurs."

"You're right," Marty growled. "I'd like to fire the whole bunch of 'em, close the studio."

This was the real Marty Davis talking. I knew one thing. As long as I was at Paramount, I wanted to be on *his* side.

"Maybe we will, Marty," said Bluhdorn, "maybe we will. Is Evans right about distribution?"

"He's right about distribution, but production stinks, too. Would you excuse us, Bob? I want to speak to Charlie alone."

He didn't seem to care that my bacon and eggs had just been served.

It was a big night for Charlie Bluhdorn: his first world premiere as a film mogul. His wife, Yvette, was not only French, she was Parisian. Opening this film about the liberation of her city from the Nazis—and at the opera house!—was an incredible high. A year ago, Charlie would have been lucky to get a reservation at Maxim's. If he had, they'd have seated him near the kitchen. Now the entire restaurant was his for the asking—bows and all.

Our night of glory was nearly a washout. Paris wasn't burning, it was flooding. The rain all day was torrential. Traffic was at a standstill. Would anybody be able to get to the premiere? Well they did, from every half-titled Charlie in Europe to all the famous faces in the film, including Leslie Caron, who was on the arm of little mogul Evans.

My night with Leslie was about as romantic as the picture. For a girl who said she didn't care, she couldn't stop talking about her baby boy ex-lover, my old pal Warren Beatty.

It was a setup. How could the picture *not* play well in Paris? When the lights went up, Charlie Bluhdorn was like a kid in a candy store.

The next morning all the candy was gone. He was in his suite with Marty, pacing the floor. "Marty, how much did last night cost us?" When Marty told him the number (with the coldness of an IRS investigator), he took off his thick-rimmed glasses. "Marty, you're right. Let's close the whole place down."

Sitting between these two guys I couldn't help thinking, Why didn't I listen to David Brown?

Charlie Revson, the baron of Revlon, was tough, but at least you could read him. He liked you or he didn't. These guys were in a different league. These guys made Revson look like Santa Claus. They're major-league motherfuckers—and I'm on their roller coaster with no way off.

They didn't close Paramount. Worse. They launched a third world war. Heads rolled faster than marbles. Paranoia became the name of the game. Politics first, films last.

Awakening me at three in the morning from the first good dream I had in months was Marty Davis barking my marching orders. "Be in New York Monday morning, ten A.M."

"Marty, if I left right now I wouldn't get there in time."

He didn't answer me; he hung the phone up.

Monday morning at ten there I was sitting across from him at his desk. Without looking up to smile, he said, "You're leaving tomorrow to run the studio."

"Run the studio? I've got all my clothes, my stuff in London."

"They'll be sent."

"What about Howard—"

Bluhdorn burst in the room, cutting me off. "Did you tell him, Marty? Did you tell him?" Taking his glasses off, he squinted in my eyes. "Well, what do you think?"

"Do I have a choice?"

"No," Davis answered.

I looked at the two of them. "It's suicide, fellas. There isn't anyone in Hollywood who's better liked than Howard Koch. It's not fair! It's not fair to him; it's not fair to me. You haven't even given him—"

Davis cut me off. "It's not fair, huh? Would it be fair if there's no studio next week? Don't worry about him. Worry about yourself. Koch will have it better than he's ever had it. We're setting up a tandem operation. You take care of the picture end. Bernie Donnenfeld will take care of the business end."

In machine-gun style, Bluhdorn overlapped: "Go by the seat of your pants, Evans. Make pictures people want to see, not fancyschmancy stuff people don't understand. I want to see tears, laughs, beautiful girls—pictures people in Kansas City want to see."

"But I—"

"That's all, Evans. Marty, what else do we have to go over?"

David Brown, where are you? What the hell did I get myself into? Fifteen years earlier, I had gone through the Windsor Avenue gates at Paramount as a would-be contract actor. A long shot then, but a shoo-in compared to now.

For everyone from the guards at the gate, to the actors, directors, writers, and producers, there was no one as popular as Howard Koch. Schmuck. No wonder I got the nod. Who else would take the job?

At first Howard was devastated, not only that he was being replaced, but the indignity of turning his reins over to some half-assed actor turned producer. To this day, we both laugh about its being the luckiest day of his life. It didn't take long before Howard was one of

I didn't know it then, but Korshak was right. Craps was a safer bet than flicks. Not wanting just to survive, but to win, I handicapped my chances. One thing was for sure, I wasn't gonna grab the brass ring in Vegas.

That was close to thirty years ago. Only once have I picked up the dice in Vegas since. I rolled for a million dollars and won.

Hal Wallis, the producer of *Casablanca, Yankee Doodle Dandy, The Maltese Falcon,* and *Gunfight at the O.K. Corral,* was now having to report to me? If this was a joke, it wasn't taken as such. Only ten years earlier, Norma Shearer brought me to his office to discuss my playing Monroe Stahr in *The Last Tycoon.* He was underwhelmed then.

I heard him tell his right-hand flunky, Paul: "Who is this little shit calling me down to his office?"

To add insult to injury, I canceled the western he was going to make at the studio. He slammed the door behind him with such anger that the hinges gave in. Pleasantries now antiquated, hostile exits flourished.

Being served a shrimp rémoulade at Chasen's one night, George Hamilton laughed. "Bluhdorn offered me the part first, you know. But I was too busy testing for an important film, *Gidget Goes to Hawaii,* but he saw you play Thalberg and thought you knew the role well."

Was I taken as a joke? Worse—a Polish joke. But fuck 'em, fuck 'em all. The more they laughed, the tougher my resolve.

Who could I count on? Who is brighter, better read, no, *much* better read? Even more important, where could I find loyalty in an industry where loyalty is not even in Webster's? Peter Bart stood alone on all counts. Even more important, it was his article in *The New York Times* that got me into this fuckin' mess.

There was one problem. Everyone at Gulf + Western and Paramount thought bringing Peter Bart in as my right-hand man was unconscionable. A nosy, smart-ass journalist in a conglomerate?

"No way" said everyone.

"Why?" said Bluhdorn.

"He's not tarnished, that's why. He's not Hollywood. He doesn't read synopses—he reads the entire text. Where he can read six books over a weekend, I am pressed to finish one in six days. It's my ass on the line, Charlie. If you're giving me the store, let me run it."

Thriving on conflict, Bluhdorn agreed. "Marty, I told you the kid's got balls." He laughed.

They all laughed. From the press to the industry and Wall Street. An actor and a journalist running "the mountain"—it had to crumble. Well, fuck you too.

The first to feel my lethal charm was distribution.

"It's a new ball game, fellas. Let's cut to the chase. I don't care how good you are as salesmen. For better or worse, you're only as good as your product."

With chalk in hand, standing with a blackboard behind me, I stood before all the distribution managers who represented Paramount across the country. I had one point—and one point only—to instill.

"There's no worse sound than chalk on a blackboard, fellas. So don't make me have to do it again."

Then turning my back, facing the blackboard, I made a line straight down the middle. On one side I wrote in large letters, "DON'T TELL ME WHAT TO MAKE." On the other side: ". . . AND I WON'T TELL YOU HOW TO SELL." Then, turning back to them, "Are there any questions?" There weren't any, nor was there any love, but I wasn't looking to get married.

Peter and I caucused in Palm Springs for a full week trying to strategize how an actor and a journalist could turn a white elephant into a contender.

Patience was a quality neither Bluhdorn nor Davis claimed to have and the clock was already ticking.

"Let's go back to basics, Peter. If you build a house, no matter how well you paint it or furnish it, if the structure's not there, it doesn't hold up. It's no different in film. You can have stars up the ass, but if it's not on the page, it's not on the screen. Enough fuckin' around making half-assed announcements just to be fashionable. It's no mistake Paramount's been in ninth place for five years. It's time to pick up new dice."

With the little experience we had, we knew one thing—the property's the star. How the hell else would I have had a suite of offices at Twentieth as a producer if I hadn't owned *The Detective?*

"We can't get lower than ninth, so what's the worse that could happen? They'll fire us!"

Peter laughed. To his credit, it was far easier for me to be cavalier than him. What did I have to lose? I had no wife. I had no kids. I had plenty of green and was holding the dice as well. For me, the worse thing that could happen is that I'd crap out. Luckily for me, Peter had no idea the gambler his partner-in-crime was. Nor, for that matter, did anyone else at Paramount.

From the day I arrived, the rumor mill had me packing my bags. *Time* ran a story saying my firing was imminent. Friends, columnists, agents, lawyers, all let me know that they were sure I wouldn't make Christmas. When *Variety* printed a front-page headline confirming the reports that my tenure would be over by the end of the month, I called Charlie Bluhdorn. He was in Spain.

"Charlie, I hate to bother you like this, but on the front page of *Variety* it says I'm being fired by the end of the month."

"That's why you pulled me out of the meeting?"

"It's that or not sleep, Charlie."

He didn't laugh. "Get this straight, Evans, and I'm only telling it to you once—as long as I own Paramount, you're head of the studio . . . unless you call me like this again!"

Down went the phone, my eardrum a bit battered.

Ten days later Bluhdorn was in Los Angeles. I picked him up at the Beverly Hills Hotel and drove him to the studio for a meeting with Clint Eastwood. Clint was known in Europe for spaghetti westerns, but he had not yet become a giant on the American screen. Convinced he had the makings of a big international star, I wanted Bluhdorn to meet him and persuade him to make his home at Paramount. On the way to the studio, Bluhdorn talked nonstop.

"I'm going to be spending more time out here. I just closed a deal to take over a California oil and gas company. Evans, I'm losing a fortune at Paramount. Get yourself a house where I can have meetings. I need privacy. Build a theater in it. I want to look at everything we're making without anyone asking me for a job."

Heading toward my office now to meet Eastwood, Bluhdorn turned the wrong way.

"Charlie, my office is this way."

"Don't think I don't know it, Evans, but if I don't take care of what I have to do, you won't be in an office."

I followed him down the corridor to the office of Bernie Donnenfeld, head of business affairs. Quickly, his feet were off the desk. Just as quickly, he hung up the phone. Even quicker, he stood at attention.

"Yes, Mr. Bluhdorn."

"Get the Evans contract out now."

"Yes, Mr. Bluhdorn."

Am I getting fired? He just told me to get a house.

Bluhdorn grabbed my contract from Donnenfeld's hand. "From this moment on, I want his contract to stipulate that for every day that he's in Paramount's employ, he has a chauffeur on call twenty-four hours a day. I'm not gonna let this kid spend hundreds of millions of dollars of Gulf + Western's money to have him killed in a year. He's a menace. It was less dangerous getting out of Germany before the war than making it to Paramount this morning. Take his license now and put it in the vault. A chauffeur, twenty-four hours a day. Is that clear?"

For eighteen years, twenty-four hours a day, I had a private chauffeur gratis from Paramount. It was by far the most generous gesture—and for the wrong reasons—the hierarchy of Paramount ever extended to me during my tenure. Though he was on the ledger as chauffeur, this arrangement gave me the opportunity to hire a top major domo to run my home, David Gilruth. That hour drive to and from the studio was the most constructive hour of each day. In that era before car phones, Peter and I could discuss the thumbs-up or thumbs-down of the day without interruption. The silence of the car gave us the luxury to do everything—from cogitate to altercate. Without Peter's figurative chauffeur's cap, *The Sterile Cuckoo, True Grit,* and *Harold and Maude* might possibly have never made it to the screen.

A decade before, Norma Shearer took me for a short walk. Within ten minutes of the Beverly Hills Hotel we entered a hidden oasis, protected by hundred-foot-tall eucalyptus trees. It was Greta Garbo's hideaway whenever she snuck into town. The French regency home was owned by James Pendleton, considered one of the finest interior designers in the country. His wife was heir to the Paragon oil fortune.

Designed in 1940 by John Woolf, the "court architect of Beverly Hills," the miniature palace combined French classicism with California casualness. The house, a formal pavilion with a mansard roof, was beautifully proportioned. But what really got me were the grounds—nearly two acres of towering eucalyptus, sycamores, and cypresses, thousands of roses, and all behind walls.

If Bluhdorn wanted privacy, this was it. Was it for sale? No. But in L.A., there's nothing that's not.

The real estate agent called Mr. Pendleton, who was now a widower, living there alone. "A young man he had met with Norma . . . could he come by?" Mr. Pendleton was gracious.

Since his wife's death, the house had deteriorated, but it still had great style. More important, the setting was as I'd remembered it—a world away from Beverly Hills. When Mr. Pendleton told me how lonely he was, I didn't waste words.

"Would you like to sell it?"

"Why not?"

For $290,000 the place of my dreams was mine.

Paramount took over. Under Bluhdorn's orders, an army of studio engineers, carpenters, painters, electricians, and plumbers expanded the pool house into a luxurious screening room with state-of-the-art projection facilities, including the largest seamless screen ever made—sixteen feet wide. A new, winding driveway was installed off Woodland Drive to create a second, more private entrance. A greenhouse was constructed. A north-south, day-and-night tennis court was designed by Gene Mako, the premier designer of hard surface courts.

Nature couldn't be improved on when it came to the garden's prize. Standing among over two thousand rosebushes was an enormous spreading sycamore, several centuries old, with branches covering half an acre. Anything that's been breathing that long needs lots of help. It's been operated on more times than the Pope. For the circumference of the half acre, every three feet the roots are intravenously fed. Many a time I've given it an anxious look: "You're one hell of an expensive lady." But it's more than a tree—it's a piece of art. I'd take a night job to keep its leaves aglow. Twenty-one weddings have been blessed under its far-reaching branches. I'm sure its batting average is higher than any altar in the world. Nineteen for twenty-one. Not bad, huh? Only two have failed—*mine.*

I couldn't afford the upkeep of being bicoastal. With a bit of sadness I rid myself of my little corner-of-Paris town house in New York, selling it to Alan Jay Lerner and shipping a truckload of French antiques westward. Paramount offered me the key to their Gold Room—a huge sound stage filled with a fabulous assortment of signed antique pieces acquired over forty years. It wasn't me they were doing it for, it was by order of the Führer, Herr Bluhdorn. What I didn't realize was that it wasn't for me to enjoy either. It was background for clandestine meetings for historic deals—both legal and illegal.

Everyone has a dream; mine was to be the proud possessor of great art. While in New York closing up my town house, I ventured over to the Wildenstein Gallery, the most prestigious in New York, seeking to find the love of my life—a canvas that I could spend nights alone looking at. Paul Mano, one of the gallery's honchos and a personal friend for years, opened room after room, each one filled with canvases of celebrated artists.

After Mano unlocked another door, before me hung my new bride—a six-by-twelve-foot canvas of water lilies.

"This is what is known as an original," Mano chimed in. "In art, there's no price on an original. It's Monet at his best."

Was I in love? Very. Was it an expensive love? It was tagged at $580,000. Having learned something from Bluhdorn, I was not timid to negotiate. After two hours of cat and mouse, Paul called his boss, Mr. Wildenstein. Even Mr. Wildenstein was not shocked by the word "negotiate." From $580,000 we settled at $436,000. I was now the proud owner of Monet at his best.

Abruptly, my stay in New York was cut short. By order of the Führer, I was ordered back to Los Angeles to host a very important lunch under the sycamore. Though the setting was very French, the cuisine was not. German wieners, with sauerkraut and mustard, served on heated onion rolls, with cold tap beer was the menu of the day.

The cast, well, that's a different story. The table under the tree was set for eight. Each of its guests had flown in to L.A. in his own private jet. Each at a different time. Each minutes apart. Each a bit concerned as to the privacy of his surroundings. I was the host, yet I was not introduced to the other seven men, nor was I invited for lunch, I wasn't even allowed near the table. Every time I got close, Bluhdorn quickly ushered me away.

With lunch now over, the men began leaving one by one. Each shaking my hand at the door thanking me for my hospitality, though not one gave me his name. The last to leave put his arm around me. "You're a charming young man. Sorry you couldn't join us." Then he whispered, putting his finger to his lips, "Don't tell Charlie. I'll fill you in. Put some bacon and eggs on for breakfast. I'll be here Monday at eight."

At breakfast Monday, Santa Claus told me the purpose of the lunch. The eight men were part of new corporate America—the go-go conglomerate giants of the sixties. The purpose of the lunch? To architect the gobbling up of United States industry. Each one assured the others he would not infringe on their meals.

Gobbling up the last of his breakfast instead of America, my entrepreneurial friend whispered, "Got any cash?"

"Some. Why?"

"It's private!"

"Yes, sir."

"Promise?"

"Promise."

He leaned forward, "I'm General Host; name's Kliener. Listen carefully. Our stock opened this morning at forty-three and an eighth. Next week I'm buying Kennicot Copper, then Pittsburgh Iron and Steel. In a month I've got clear sailing to pick up, dirt cheap, Pan Am Airlines. Even taking over something in your business, kid. This Canadian, Tommolison, doesn't know his ass from his elbow, owns MGM. Has no idea what it's worth, but it's up for grabs. As of Saturday, it's in Kliener's pocket. Six months from now," he laughed, "my stock will still be selling at forty-three and an eighth, only it will have been split, four for one. Shhh . . . don't say a word to Bluhdorn. Thanks for the breakfast, kid."

Well, it didn't take long for the idiot, me, to cancel the Monet. Within twenty-four hours I was the proud owner of 11,500 shares of General Host.

Three years later, General Host was taken off the board of the New York Stock Exchange and Kliener, well, he moved to India to become a guru. The General Host certificates? Oh, they're in a Kleenex box in the attic. The Monet—forget the fact that for a quarter of a century my eyes would have feasted on the lilies of my life. The canvas, considered one of Monet's greats, has been resold twice. Its last bidder paid a mere 36 mil for the lilies' fragrance.

Quoting the great Rodgers and Hammerstein's lyrics from *South Pacific:* "This nearly was mine."

15

It had to happen. I was ready now for Hitler himself—Otto Preminger—a man whose dictatorial skills far overshadowed his directing abilities. He was about to start shooting a zany comedy called *Skidoo!* Not only wasn't it zany, but it was a zero on every level. Preminger doing a comedy was akin to George Foreman dancing *The Nutcracker.*

In my most persuasive manner, "Otto, we need bigger canvas films from you. Distribution is desperate for a Preminger Christmas film."

Hollywood's top producers. It didn't take long for me to be the biggest joke in town.

I was called "Bluhdorn's Folly" by *The New York Times* and "Bluhdorn's Blow Job" by *Hollywood Close-Up,* a local scandal sheet read by all.

Army Archerd, the encyclopedia of the industry, was once asked: "In forty years of writing for *Daily Variety,* which of your columns caused the most outrage?"

Without a moment's hesitation, he answered, "The day I printed Bob Evans would become head of production at Paramount! This actor from Twentieth Century–Fox! With no experience!"

I watched the dice roll from my hand. "Eight the hard way!" I barked.

"Seven," the croupier icily responded, quickly clearing the chips off every number on the green felt.

A hard tap on the shoulder. "The plane's waitin'. We're leavin', Vinnie. How much did the schmuck lose?"

Counting the markers, "Forty-three thousand, Mr. K."

Suddenly, a blank check was put before me. "Sign it. I could take the markers and use 'em as toilet paper, but you're payin' every fuckin' cent." It was the voice of Sidney Korshak, the silent owner of the Riviera Hotel in Vegas. "Before you shaved, you shot crap better than you do today. No one stands at the table all night and ends up winning."

"Cut it, Sidney, will ya?"

"Listen, schmuck, if I didn't brass knuckle ya' now, within a year you'd not only be out of a job, you'd be on the lam from the collectors. Flicks is a tougher gamble than craps. Instead of doing your homework, you're standin' here like a pigeon."

Just fourteen hours earlier, Sidney had invited Mike Frankovich and myself down on a private jet to be at Ann-Margret's opening at the Riviera in Las Vegas. It was command performance time for me; Ann-Margret was an important star at Paramount.

But, as they say, "a funny thing happened on the way to the forum." A quick $200 on the line. Win. Doubled it. Won again. Doubled it. Won again. Twelve hours later, not having seen either of the two shows, I was still standing at the table having blown half my yearly salary.

His bald pate turned scarlet. "Who do you think you're talking to!" He stormed out.

"Marty, the kid's crazy . . . taking on Preminger," Bluhdorn chuckled.

"Better him than me, Charlie. I'll pick up the pieces tomorrow."

"I'm not going down because of Preminger, Marty. The guy's cost us a fuckin' fortune. His new entry belongs in the sewer, not on the screen. He's such a prick; he gets his nuts off seeing us sink. I don't mind him calling your money vulgar, Charlie, but then he shouldn't take it."

Silence, then an almost inhuman growl. I knew Charlie was about to explode.

"Hey, I'm just a kid, maybe I'm wrong about the script. Read it yourself—I'll get it off to you tonight."

Bluhdorn slept only two hours a night. He had time to read everything. Preminger's script hit the bull's-eye.

Apoplectic? "I want to vomit," he screamed. "I won't put Gulf + Western's name on it."

"Not so easy, Charlie. I've checked it with legal. It's too late. We can't stop it."

Now close to cardiac arrest, "Marty was right. We should have closed the studio down."

With little regard for my eardrum, he hung up.

I made sure the word "vomit" got back to Otto. It was a big mistake. He retaliated by accelerating the starting date of *Skidoo!*

Peter and I couldn't help laughing. The third world war was now in full gear. This time it was kraut versus kraut.

Looking at the rushes of *Skidoo!,* I was the one who almost had cardiac arrest.

"Go back," I told the projectionist, "I want to see it again."

There in a prison scene was a face I'd never seen on screen before. But I knew to whom it belonged: Jaik Rosenstein, publisher, editor, and writer of *Hollywood Close-Up.* The guy who'd coined the phrase "Bluhdorn's Blow Job" was getting a weekly paycheck from Bluhdorn. It was so sick, I had to laugh. I couldn't tell Bluhdorn. If I did, he would close Paramount down before I could zip up my fly.

We had come to a standstill in a do-or-die negotiation for a major project at the studio. Only his nod, which he refused to give, could make it work. I knew that the only way I could get him to California was to finally tell him of Preminger's play. When I did, all I could hear was heavy breathing. It didn't sound human. An hour later I got word he was flying out from New York with Marty Davis. Neither knew I had other plans for them.

I'd like to say it was me, but it was Howard Koch who acquired an option on all the plays written by the most prolific playwright of our time, Neil Simon. *Barefoot in the Park* was the first of Simon's plays that Paramount had the rights to. A big success on Broadway, and a respectable film. Simon's next at-bat was an out of the park home run, *The Odd Couple*.

Bluhdorn had seen the play a dozen times. Such was his pride of ownership that he laughed harder every time. For the film version, Charlie wanted to use the Broadway stars. Howard and I wanted to use movie stars. We'd come up with the perfect odd couple: Jack Lemmon and Walter Matthau. And the perfect director, Billy Wilder.

As every good gambler knows, the only way to be a winner is to press your winnings. *The Odd Couple* was the studio's one asset—it had to be pressed. It became my first major stand at Paramount. If I couldn't get Matthau, Lemmon, and Wilder, I would quit. Never make a deal unless you're prepared to blow it, and I was prepared.

Charlie and Marty thought they were coming out to throw Preminger off the lot. First, I wanted them to resolve *The Odd Couple*. For Bluhdorn, it was a brand-new battlefield against a new enemy—agents.

He arrived on a Friday afternoon. To read the one-page deal memo, he took off his glasses, as he always did to read anything. The more he read, the whiter he got. Finally, he put on his glasses. "Three million dollars and fifty percent of the profits? Evans, I'll go back to coffee futures before I accept this blackmail!"

Bluhdorn was like a bronco. To stay on, you had to know how to ride him. This was a tone of voice you didn't argue with. Instead, you massaged it. Then challenged it.

"Charlie," I said, "you've negotiated the most complex deals in America. Are you telling me you can't sit down with a bunch of agents and make a deal for two actors and a director? Do it for me, Charlie, for Christmas. Please."

Then he growled, "You really want it, huh?"

"Badly, Charlie, badly. Make it happen. I know you can." He too was a kid and I knew the buttons to push.

The seventy-two-hour war started. The battleground was Charlie's suite at the Beverly Hills Hotel. The chambermaids must have thought the suite had turned into a miniature brothel as one male agent after another came in and out morning, noon, and night. Bluhdorn was unrelenting. The more he negotiated, the more turned on he became.

"I want everybody to get rich, but don't rape me."

After the first day, everybody was exhausted except Charlie. The real love of his life wasn't family, sex, or even business. It was *negotiating*. Charlie would negotiate for anything from an airline to a potato. His edge was his energy. The one thing he never accepted was "no."

After the first all-nighter, he said with disgust, "Hollywood—I thought it was glamorous. Everyone I meet is under five feet tall!"

He'd met the "minutemen" of the William Morris Agency. Abe Lastfogel, who headed William Morris for half a century, was barely over five feet and he didn't want anyone to look down on him. Only one agent was over five feet two, six-foot Lennie Hirshan. Lennie, who was Jack Lemmon's agent, stood out like Mt. Everest.

"I'm doing this for you, Evans, you know that don't you? You sure you want it?"

"I can taste it, Charlie . . . please."

He really wasn't doing it for me. He was enjoying every minute of negotiating on a new turf.

Pacing the floor, his eyes suddenly lit up, "There's one weak link: Billy Wilder!"

"They won't make it without Wilder."

He walked over to me. His nose touched mine. He took his glasses off. So close now our eyelashes almost touched.

"Greed, Evans . . . *greed.*"

Bluhdorn was right.

Lemmon got his deal. A million against 10 percent of the gross. Matthau, who at the time was a far lesser star, got a paltry $300,000 and no percentage. And poor Billy Wilder? He had to buy a ticket to see it. Gene Saks was brought in to direct for a mere salary.

I got my way. Bluhdorn got his way. *The Odd Couple* became the studio's biggest hit since *The Ten Commandments.*

Charlie still had Preminger on his agenda. Silently, he paced back and forth in my office. He then took his glasses off, squinting, and standing less than an inch away from me, said in a whisper more intimidating than any scream, "As long as I own Paramount, Preminger will never make another picture here."

Half enjoying it, half scared, I told him the truth.

"Easier said than done, Charlie. Otto's got three more years on his contract."

Putting his glasses back on, he looked at me as he were if an actor playing Iago.

"I want you to give Mr. Preminger a very slow death, very slow, understand? If you don't, you're going to have a very quick one."

If ever orders were followed to perfection, Preminger's demise was. It took three years. His arrogance finally broken, Preminger exited the Paramount gates for good, one shattered kraut.

James Coburn was a perfect leading man for the late sixties—rugged but irreverent. I thought it was a great coup getting him for an anti-establishment black comedy, *The President's Analyst,* in which he would play a White House shrink so besieged to reveal state secrets that he ends up escaping to a hippie commune for privacy. For the next quarter century, *The President's Analyst* would cost me *my* privacy.

The real heavies of the script were the telephone company and the FBI. One day my secretary buzzed me with the message that two gentlemen were waiting to see me—from the Hoover Agency.

"It must be a mistake, I'm not looking for a butler." I buzzed back.

"No, Mr. Evans, not the Hoover Agency. It's Mr. Hoover's agency, the FBI."

Was it something I'd done in Havana?

Starched collars and all, they entered my office. No smiles, just gorilla handshakes and proper identification.

"I think you've got the wrong Bob Evans, gentlemen."

"You're making a picture called *The President's Analyst.* Correct?"

"Correct."

"We don't like the story."

"Then don't see the picture."

"Then don't make it."

"Then get me a Paul Newman picture to take its place."

"Mr. Hoover doesn't appreciate having the FBI being made fun of."

"Well, that's show business, fellas."

"Mr. Evans, I don't think you understand."

"No! I don't think *you* understand. The picture goes as is. Got it?"

Within twenty-four hours, a half-crazed Marty Davis was on the phone screaming.

"Are you crazy? You don't play games with Hoover. You don't play games with the FBI."

"Fuck 'em. It's a free country, isn't it?"

"No, it's not."

The order was to change it. I did: to the **FBE.** I refused to compromise further, but I made sure anyone who read a paper knew the story behind the story.

Smart? Dumb, with a capital *D.*

It's been over a quarter of a century now. Still my thirty-two phones at home and office share one thing—a silver anniversary of bugging. I hope what they've heard has made their faces as red as their necks.

Irving "Swifty" Lazar, in a moment of weakness, promised me a first look at the next important literary property he controlled. I had been in the hot seat less than three months when Little Caesar was on the hot line.

In a whispered voice, as if I were a retard, "Vladimir Nabokov just completed the first draft of his new manuscript."

He didn't know that Nabokov was possibly my favorite author. Forget *Lolita,* which was great, but *Laughter in the Dark* was one of my five favorite books.

"You'll have to move quick, kid. The Nabokovs live in Montreux, Switzerland. Hop a plane, get there quick as you can, read it. You're getting a look even before me. Did I come through for you?"

Flying from L.A. to Montreux, Switzerland, wasn't nearly as romantic as it sounded. Twenty-four hours and many planes later, I arrived at the Palace Hotel in Montreux. It was off-season. I think the Nabokovs were the hotel's only residents.

Not having a moment's sleep in almost two days, I tried to pull myself together. Certainly in awe was I as I walked through the virtually empty two-hundred-foot-long dining room, where sat Vladimir Nabokov, the maestro himself, with his wife. Introducing myself, I joined them for morning coffee.

Quizzically looking at me, "You're the Mr. Evans from Paramount?" Mrs. Nabokov asked.

"Yes." I smiled.

"You're sure?" the maestro asked.

"Honestly, I am."

"You're a child." He smiled.

"You can't be more than twenty," interjected Madame Nabokov.
"You're really head of Paramount?"

"Here's my passport. See?"

Both of them looked at it, still not believing me. When you're that
high up the ladder in age, one loses perspective looking at someone
half a century younger. Compared to them, I was still an embryo.
However, I was certainly not old enough, nor presumptuous enough,
to call him Vladimir. To me he was always Mr. Nabokov. To him, I
was a boy, not a young man. But so what, I was still getting the first
crack.

After an hour at breakfast, both of them still felt somewhat skepti-
cal handing me the maestro's new manuscript, as well they should
have. Not many people would have the strength to pick it up. It
weighed more than my luggage.

I went to my hotel room, not to sleep, but to read, and read, and
read, and read, and read. There was one problem, I didn't know what
I was reading. Maybe it's jet lag? I took a Dexamil, at that time a
popular amphetamine. It didn't help; I still didn't know what I was
reading. I was too excited to fall asleep, yet too numb to know what
was on the page. From throwing cold water on my face, to a gallon of
black coffee, I did everything to keep my cerebellum on alert. At ten
that evening I finally finished it. I took a cold shower, then looked at
myself in the mirror and screamed. "God damn it, Evans, you finally
got a shot at a big one and you don't know what you're reading."

Now going into my seventy-second hour of being awake, I read the
900-odd pages yet again. It was torture. I became so angry at my
inability to understand it, I got up from my bed and began knocking
my head against the door.

"God damn it, Evans, it's Nabokov. Are you this dumb?"

Then back to reading. I might as well have stayed in L.A. After
twenty-four hours with manuscript in hand, I didn't understand or
remember a fuckin' thing I'd read. It was now 11:00 A.M. Time to
meet the Nabokovs for breakfast. What the hell am I going to tell

them? I told them the truth. In my own way, that is.

"It's fascinating, extraordinary. I've never read anything like it." It's true. I never had.

Fool me once shame on you—fool me twice shame on me. Only seven years before I was the victim of snob appeal. Trying to produce *The Umbrella,* I read and reread the play, not understanding a word of what it was about. But what the fuck did I know? It was an expensive lesson finding out no one else understood it either. It was then I decided, no matter whose pen it was, if I read something once and then read it again and still couldn't understand it, it ain't for me. Let someone else enjoy its success.

I flew directly to New York from Switzerland where Charlie and Marty were anxiously awaiting the result of my Nabokov coup—possibly the most prestigious piece of material Paramount had been offered in years. What an announcement! I prefaced my critique telling them in detail of *The Umbrella* experience. Then, taking a deep breath, I told them that I read the book, not once, but twice and didn't understand one fuckin' chapter in the entire story. The manuscript to me was one big Rorschach test.

Both Marty and Charlie gave me a look I didn't like. I knew my credibility was on the line.

"Fellas, every success I have had has been for a different reason and every failure for the same—I said yes when I meant no. At the cost of losing my job, I won't say yes when I feel no."

Silence ensued.

Finally, "The kid's got balls, Marty."

Marty looked at me. "You may have balls, Evans, but if someone else buys it, I'll have your ass."

Two weeks later, Columbia bought Nabokov's new masterpiece for the unheard-of price of one million dollars. Me . . . I was a hair away from being sent back to makeup.

A quarter of a century later, Nabokov's novel not only *did not* make it to the screen, but was never adapted into a screenplay. Not one screenwriter could understand it. Neither did the most avid Nabokov diehards. Certainly no one at Columbia understood it. They bought it for all the wrong reasons—they wanted an announcement. It's called star-fucking at its most expensive.

The name of the novel—*Ada.* And Allah must have been looking over me.

Charlie Feldman was more than a close personal friend. In many ways he looked upon me as the son he never had. He was not a bad guy to call your friend. Not only was he a big shot in the industry, but he represented all that was glamorous in the world of film. He was handsome, dashing, self-deprecating. As an independent agent, he had by far the top client list in town and was a successful producer as well. He also had one of the town's most prestigious art collections.

I doubt whether there was a handful of people in the entire industry who genuinely wanted me to prove everyone wrong. Luckily for me, he was one of them.

Behind the desk only four months, I felt like it was four years. But there I was still on top of the mountain.

"Eat *those* bananas, motherfuckers."

I was awakened on a Sunday morning. It was Charlie Feldman. "Something's come up. It's gonna put you over the top, kid. Get your ass over here quick."

Mario Andretti couldn't have made it to his home faster.

"Meet Ray Stark," Charlie said to me.

We shook hands. We had met once before, in France at the world premiere of *Is Paris Burning?* To say Ray's relationship with Paramount and Bluhdorn was strained was an understatement. Bluhdorn and Stark shared something—mutual animosity toward each other.

Is Paris Burning?, which was Ray's film, broke Bluhdorn's virginity into the film business. It almost broke Bluhdorn as well. Ray was by far the most entrepreneurial producer in Hollywood. Columbia Pictures was now his playground. Paramount was certainly the last place Ray wanted to be partnered with in the making of his Hope diamond, *Funny Girl.*

As producer of the Broadway musical, Ray had discovered the then unknown Barbra Streisand. Whatever Bluhdorn's feelings were toward Stark, it didn't stop him from seeing the show more than half a dozen times. How vividly I remember him telling me that *Funny Girl* was the best entertainment he'd ever been afforded since landing in America as an Austrian refugee.

Feldman started in. "Bob, *Funny Girl* just fell out at Columbia. Serge Seminenko is having a tough time with the Banque de Paris. They're not giving him enough financial leeway to cover the production budget and marketing costs for Ray's film. Seminenko's asked Ray for another week to secure the funds. Ray's not concerned with them coming up with the production money . . . they will. His worry, and he's right, is that they won't have enough in the till to promote it the way Ray wants it marketed. He's got a forty-eight-hour out in his contract. There's a bank holiday tomorrow. You've got forty-eight hours to make it a Paramount film."

Stark interrupted. "The kid must mean a lot to you, Charlie. The last place I want to bring it to is Paramount."

"It's for me," said Charlie.

"There isn't a major in town who wouldn't kiss my ass for it. What's the kid got on you?"

"He introduced me to Clotilde. Without him I would never have met her." Clotilde was the love of Charlie's life, whom he later married.

Stark immediately understood that a Feldman chit was as valuable as it was rare.

"Okay, it's yours. Don't trip."

Off-limits, taboo, call it what you want, but there were only two hours during the entire week that those words were operative in the life of Chairman Bluhdorn. On Sunday afternoons between two and four, Bluhdorn was incommunicado to the world. Everyone knew it; everyone abided by it. Those hours were reserved for a lengthy hot bath and an hour of uninterrupted discussion with his two kids and Yvette, his wife. At 2:40 Sunday afternoon, the phone rang at the Bluhdorn residence. It was me—an intrusion that could have cost me a quick exit. Since she didn't believe in servants, Yvette herself picked up the phone.

"Bob, hang up quickly," she whispered. "I don't want him to know it's you." Click went her phone.

Maybe I should wait? No, I can't. I dialed again. Again Yvette picked up the phone. "Bob," she whispered. "You're crazy. You know the rules."

"It's life or death," I answered back. "Not for me, but for the company."

As she gently put the receiver down, I heard yelling in the back. Nervously, I waited for over five minutes. Getting Charlie out of the bathtub on a Sunday afternoon was akin to persuading Ted Kennedy to become a Republican.

Suddenly, an almost inhuman snarl, "Evans, this better be important!"

"Funny Girl."

"What about it?"

"It's ours."

He hung up. Immediately, I called back. Knowing his M.O., I knew he was getting off on my anxiety. This time it was he who picked the phone up.

"You're crazy, Evans. Columbia owns it and it's the only ticket they have to put them back in the black. You're crazy, Evans. Ray Stark—he hates me." Then a long silence. "Do you really have it?"

"Would 'Bluhdorn's Blow Job' bullshit you, Charlie?"

"I could kiss you, Evans. I could kiss you! Was it blackmail?"

"No, loyalty, Charlie. Every so often it comes back to embrace you. It has nothing to do with Ray; it's Charlie Feldman. To make your bath even hotter, Charlie, Barbra Streisand's going to star in it too. It all happened this morning. I'll fill you in later. We've got forty-eight hours to say yes, that's it. I'd like to call 'em back in forty-eight minutes and give 'em a yes. The budget's not even that high, Charlie. It's between six and seven."

"Stay by the phone, Evans." He hung up in my ear.

An hour, then two, then three, then four, no call. What the fuck's going on. I called him back.

He picked up.

"Charlie . . ."

"Did I say stick by the phone?" Before I could get a word out, he hung up.

It wasn't until 11:00 that night, 2:00 A.M. New York time, that he called back. His voice was more subdued than I'd ever heard it, and not because of the lateness of the hour. "We can't go forward with it."

"Did I hear right? Charlie, don't tease me; it ain't funny."

"I'm not."

"If we don't make *Funny Girl*, Charlie, we shouldn't be in the business. It's our ticket out of the basement."

"Listen carefully, Evans, what do you think I've been doing these last twelve hours? From London to Johannesburg to Hong Kong to Rio I've been on the phone with all the heads of distribution. They know their territory, Evans, better than we do. Not one of them want the picture. With Shirley MacLaine, maybe. But with Barbra Streisand, there wasn't one thumb-up. I even called Charlie Boasberg," Bluhdorn said, referring to the head of U.S. distribution for Paramount. "He said the same. Outside of New York no one's gonna want to look at that yenta. Try to sell her in Kansas City. Forget it! That's

Boasberg's feeling and he's our top guy in sales. What can I do?"

"Fuck 'em, that's what! Charlie, you know it and I know it—they're wrong. Christ, it's your favorite and mine too. These are the same guys who put the company in last place. What the hell do they know?"

A long silence. "Evans, I have no choice. I've taken enough heat over you already. If you'd been there four years, not four months, I could make a case. But I can't go against the entire organization. It's too big an investment."

"Go by your instincts, Charlie. That's what this business is all about. Take the gamble, back me, please."

He didn't. He never forgave himself. Until that moment, at best, I was always suspect of letting the honchos of distribution have a say in what we were going to make. From that moment on, however, and until this day, suspect turned to disdain concerning distribution's approval of a creator's dreams. The distribution mavens not only cost Paramount *Funny Girl,* but their mistake compounded itself tenfold and all but caused the gates at Paramount to close forever.

Calling Charlie Feldman back, telling him I didn't get the go, was as difficult a professional call as I've ever had to make. Ray Stark was thrilled. Within a matter of days he got the funds, plus, from Columbia to go forward with *Funny Girl* full blast. Its international success made it the savior of Columbia Pictures.

Conversely, with *Funny Girl* not being ours, Bluhdorn had a competitive yearning to make up for what he knew was a mistake. Everyone was on alert. Paramount had to make the musical of musicals. At that moment in time, only one musical female star had the magic to capture the attention of the entire world. With *Mary Poppins, The Sound of Music,* and *Thoroughly Modern Millie* behind her, Julie Andrews was it. It could have been the phone book—Bluhdorn had to have her.

We got her all right. Her new husband, Blake Edwards, had written a thinly disguised romantic comedy that took place during World War I. It was titled *Darling Lili.* No darling was she. I had already turned the project down when Bluhdorn called me in a huff.

"As a comedy, Evans, you're right. But, add twelve songs to it, then put Julie Andrews into the mix to sing them, and we've got ourselves a musical. I mean a *musical!* Barbra Streisand—who knows? Julie Andrews—the world knows!"

"I still don't like the story, Charlie."

It didn't matter. For all anyone cared, I could have been on top of Mt. Everest. No one wanted to hear me.

Darling Lili was Blake Edwards's wedding gift to his lady love and Paramount paid the bill. The film's losses were so exorbitant that, were it not for Charlie's brilliant manipulation of the numbers, Paramount Pictures would have been changed to Paramount Cemetery. The film business was going through tough times, as was the country. Ah, but the cemetery business was booming . . . never having a losing year.

16

"Bob," said Robert Redford, "there's only one girl I want to use in *Downhill Racer*." His big blues were looking right at me.

I thought he was about to say Elizabeth Taylor, whose asking price then was a mere million.

"Camilla Sparv." Redford smiled.

I said to myself, "If this is another Zanuck sicko trick, I ain't fallin' for it."

It wasn't. For some reason, still unknown to me to this day,

Camilla was Redford's only choice for the part.

Giving me his whites, Redford smiled. "You don't mind, do you, Bob?"

"Mind? From one Bob to another, it's great casting, Mr. Redford. It's about time someone gets to bat, be inventive, use creative casting."

I had to get Redford out of my office. I didn't want him to run into my next appointment—Roman Polanski.

William Castle, a veteran director and producer of low-budget horror movies, had optioned the film rights to *Rosemary's Baby*, Ira Levin's new novel—a surefire best-seller. Castle insisted on directing it!

"Sorry, Bill. Produce it, yes; direct it, no."

"Sorry, Bob," Bill snapped back. "I own the property personally and I'm gonna direct it."

Knowing the novel had a real shot at becoming a big film, I played hardball.

"Sure, that's fine with me, Bill, but we've got an exclusive three-year deal with you. If you want to hold it until your contract's over, then you can set it up someplace else. Or you can start tomorrow as the producer and I'll double your deal."

Suddenly Castle only wanted to produce it.

The director I had in mind was the Polish creator of *Knife in the Water, Repulsion,* and *Cul de Sac,* three *really* offbeat thrillers. Roman Polanski, a top director in Europe, had just made his first Hollywood film, *The Fearless Vampire Killers,* for producer Marty Ransohoff. No disrespect, but whatever Ransohoff liked, I hated, and vice versa. When I heard Marty ranting all over town about what a no-talent Polanski was, I knew Roman was the man for me. But how to get him?

Hearing he was an avid skier, I'd lured him to my office with Redford's *Downhill Racer,* even though I already had a director for that one, Michael Ritchie.

Redford had been gone a couple of minutes when Roman walked in. Right away, I knew this was some character. He picked up the ashtray and turned it over. He looked at the titles of the books on my shelves. Within five minutes he was acting out crazy stories—somewhere between Shakespeare and theater of the absurd. We clicked immediately because we both came from the same school of drama, the drama of life. Almost three decades later, our friendship is still electric. Roman stands in my book of life as being one of the most extraordinary people I've ever had the good fortune to meet, know, befriend, and love.

I didn't want to bullshit him. *"Downhill Racer* was just a pretext to get you here. Would you read this?"

I shoved the galleys of *Rosemary's Baby* across the desk.

"This isn't about skiing."

"Read it. If you don't like it, you're next ski trip is on me."

Roman loved it. Then the fights began. Fighting is healthy. If everyone has too much reverence for each other, or for the material, results are invariably underwhelming. It's irreverence that makes things sizzle. It's irreverence that gives you that shot at touching magic.

Casting, by far, is the most subjective aspect of filmmaking. When two people agree that there's only one person to play the part, with rare exception, both are wrong. For the title role of Rosemary, Roman wanted Tuesday Weld. I wanted Mia Farrow. Tuesday was more experienced in film and technically the finer actress. She would deliver just what the part seemed to demand—all-American healthiness. Mia was more complex. On the surface she was the quintessential flower child, the ingenue on TV's "Peyton Place" who had just married Frank Sinatra.

Roman was worried that Mia's ethereal quality might evaporate on film. I argued that this was exactly what would give the picture something unexpected—real magic. Roman gave in. For the part of Mia's husband, Roman wanted Redford. But Redford was feuding with Paramount's legal department over *Blue,* a western he'd walked out on, anticipating, rightly, disaster. Anyway, Bob's real passion was *Downhill Racer.* When Warren Beatty heard about Redford, he asked why he hadn't been offered the part first. I knew he only wanted to be asked so he could say he'd turned it down. He's still that way. "It's yours, Warren," I said. "But you're not right for *Rosemary* unless you play it in drag."

We ended up with John Cassavetes, a terrific, intense actor but hardly ideal casting for the all-American husband.

By the end of the first week's shooting in New York, Roman was a week behind schedule. His dailies were brilliant, but everyone from Bluhdorn to Bill Castle wanted me to throw him off the picture because he was such a perfectionist. Bluhdorn had his nose in everything. When he learned that Roman had rejected a red cab for the cemetery scene and ordered props to produce a yellow cab, he went nuts.

"This crazy Polack doesn't like the color of the cab" became Charlie's favorite line whenever Roman's name came up. Roman wasn't crazy. He was right in insisting on an authentic yellow banner.

Roman's dailies touched an ominous sense of fright—one I'd never seen on film before. At the same time, Bill Castle was pressing the right buttons getting the New York brass unnerved over my Polish discovery.

"Fire the Polack" was the word from New York.

I flew to New York and confronted the accusers. "If he goes, I go." And I would have. You can't make a deal unless you're prepared to blow it. For a moment, I thought I'd have to pay my own plane fare back. Not with a smile, they acquiesced.

That night I grabbed Roman aside. "Pick up the pace, will ya, or we'll both end up in Warsaw."

Bluhdorn and company weren't the only ones screaming about Roman. Another power entered the scene. Marty and I were in a meeting with Bluhdorn when a secretary interrupted with an urgent message for me. Frank Sinatra was on the horn. "Must speak with you," was the message. Ole Blue Eyes was married to Mia at the time. Me . . . I'd known Peck's Bad Boy for years, I put him on the speaker phone. He wasn't crooning.

"I'm pullin' Mia off the fuckin' film, Evans, if it ain't finished by November 14. She's starting my picture on the seventeenth."

His picture was *The Detective*, the project that had launched my producing career. Now it was about to sink it. Sinatra wanted to start shooting by Thanksgiving.

"Sorry, Frank. She won't be finished with *Rosemary's Baby* until mid-January."

"Then she's quittin'."

Frank didn't bark; he bit. He let Mia know in no uncertain terms that if she didn't walk off *Rosemary's Baby,* he would divorce her. Hysterically, she came into my office, telling me of her dilemma.

"I love him, Bob. I love him. I'm going to have to quit."

"Mia," I said, "if you walk off in the middle of my film, you'll never work again."

Now crying hysterically, "I don't care. I don't care. I just love Frank."

"Screen Actors Guild will enjoin you from doing his picture too, Mia."

"I don't care. I don't care. I just want to be with Frank."

Years of knowing what makes the head of an actress tick finally found its purpose.

"Mia, come with me."

Into the executive screening room we went. I showed her an hour of *Rosemary's Baby* cut together. We watched it in silence. The lights came up.

"I never thought you had it in you. It's as good, no, even better than Audrey Hepburn's performance in *Wait Until Dark*. You're a shoo-in for an Academy Award."

Her tears gone, her face lit up.

"Do you really think so?"

"The one thing I'm *not* is prone to exaggerate. You're a shoo-in, Mia, a shoo-in."

Suddenly, a smile. Suddenly, she didn't take a hike. Just as suddenly, Frank served her with divorce papers, right on the set, delivered by Mickey Rudin, his attorney.

It's strange how quickly women recover. It took her a full week. Suddenly, her only interest was to see *Rosemary's Baby* outgross *The Detective*.

What irony. To Mia's satisfaction, *Rosemary's Baby* and *The Detective* opened on the same day. While *The Detective* opened to good box office, *Rosemary's Baby* was *the* smash hit of the summer. Overnight, Mia was a full-fledged star. I couldn't fill her one request— taking a double-page ad in both *Variety* and *The Hollywood Reporter*. On one side she wanted in bold numbers the theater gross of *Rosemary's Baby;* on the other, the theater gross of *The Detective.*

"Bob," said Sharon Tate, "the baby's kicking!"

"How does it feel?"

"It's the best feeling in the world."

"I'll tell Roman."

"While you're at it, tell him he'd better be home for his birthday. Remember, it's the eighteenth."

"He'll be here, baby."

Just about the only really happily married couple I knew in Hollywood were Roman Polanski and Sharon Tate. Coming from a child-hood of horror in Nazi-occupied Poland, Roman couldn't believe he was the husband of this milk-fed American beauty. Sharon's movie career was just beginning to heat up after *Valley of the Dolls*. In Roman's eyes, she was already the brightest star in the world. Around his gentle, sun-kissed bride he was like a child who's just seen his first Christmas tree light up.

In the spring of 1969, Roman had asked me if Paramount would put some money into a low-budget film he'd written called *A Day at the Beach*, which a friend of his, Simon Hessera, was directing in London. When he got Peter Sellers for a small part, I persuaded Bluhdorn to cough up $600,000. I flew over to London in July to look at the rough cut. It was unreleasable, but Roman wanted to stay on and reedit it. We spent a wonderful week together shopping for a vintage Rolls Silver Dawn, a surprise present to Sharon for their first baby.

Before I took off for L.A., Roman said, "Look after Sharon for me, will you, Bob? Tell her I love her. I'll be home in a few days."

Now Sharon was on the phone from the house they were renting on Cielo Drive, up in Benedict Canyon. She loved feeling the baby kick, but she felt cooped up. How about joining her and a few friends on Friday night? It would just be her house guests, Gibby Folger, of the San Francisco coffee family, and Gibby's boyfriend, Wojiciech "Voytek" Frykowski, a Polish rogue and great friend of Roman's. Dinner at a nothing place like El Coyote on Beverly.

"Sounds great, baby. I'm working in the editing room. I might be a little late."

At nine o'clock on Friday, August 8, 1969, I was still in the editing room. I called Sharon.

"I'm stuck, baby. Count me out. Sorry."

"Don't be silly, Bob. I can always get Jay." Jay was the star hair-dresser Jay Sebring, an ex-boyfriend who was still devoted to her.

"Sweet dreams."

"You too."

The success of *Rosemary's Baby* hadn't been enough to turn Para-mount around. Charlie Bluhdorn was flying out that night for week-end meetings. This time the threats sounded real: the studio would have to be closed down. At ten on Saturday morning I picked him up at the Beverly Hills Hotel. When we returned to Woodland, David, my major domo, was standing at the door. Joyce Haber, the *L. A. Times* columnist, was on the phone. Bluhdorn frowned.

"I thought I said no calls this morning, David."

"She said it's urgent, Mr. Evans. She sounds terrible."

I took the call in my bedroom.

When she heard my voice, Joyce started wailing. "You aren't dead! You aren't dead!"

"Joyce, what are you talking about? Of course I'm not dead!"

"You didn't hear?"

"Hear what?"

"It's on the radio. Last night at Sharon and Roman's house on Cielo. They're all dead. . . ."

"What are you talking about?"

"They're all dead."

"Joyce, what is this?"

"Sharon, Jay Sebring, Gibby Folger, that Polish Voytek what's-his-name . . ."

"I know. I was supposed to be there."

"They've all been killed!"

My body went numb. "A landslide?"

"No, they were murdered—some kind of massacre."

"Joyce, are you making this up?" From the sound of her voice, I knew she wasn't. "What about the baby?"

She couldn't go on.

Charlie had been pacing my living room impatiently. "Come on, Evans," he said when I walked in. "Let's go outside and get started."

"I can't, I can't, Charlie."

I started to cry.

He came over and put his arm around me. "What is it, Bob? What happened?"

I told him what happened and we went out to sit under the tree.

When Roman arrived from London, I knew he mustn't go home. I arranged for him to be driven to Paramount and installed in the suite that had recently been Julie Andrews's dressing room for *Darling Lili*. There he hibernated for a few days, heavily sedated by a Paramount doctor.

Not wanting to leave him alone at Paramount, Roman moved into my guest house. Sounds simple; it wasn't. Every crackpot in the state wanted to get a jab in. It necessitated having around-the-clock guards for the duration of his stay. The LAPD put their own tap on my phone, which became an integral instrument in their investigation. How I remember cradling Roman as if he were a child. I loved him. I felt his pain. Even though criticized, I went the extra nine yards, doing whatever I could, *whatever* to ease his suffering. Though I could do little, at least I was there.

The horrific murders of Sharon and her friends by the insane followers of Charles Manson sent a shock wave through Hollywood that is still felt today. What made them even uglier was the media orgy of lies, all of which came down to one outrageous innuendo: because of their "decadence," the victims had somehow brought it on themselves. Typical was a *Newsweek* story calling the massacre not a tragedy but a "fascinating whodunit" and reporting, among other ridiculous speculations, that the murders might have ". . . resulted from a ritual mock execution that got out of hand in the glare of hallucinogens."

The press even implicated Roman. It didn't matter that he was six thousand miles away when the tragedy occurred. Somehow the "master of the macabre" had to have been involved.

Roman's good friends—Warren Beatty, Richard Sylbert, I, and a few others—took turns keeping him company. Roman threw himself into helping the police investigation and with his incredible strength he got through it. Many of the biggest names in Hollywood turned out for Sharon's funeral. Later, Roman wrote that "it was like some ghastly movie premiere."

Leaving Holy Cross Cemetery, he said something that would come back to haunt me: "The only one of Sharon's good friends who didn't come, Bob, is Steve McQueen. Sharon loved that cold son of a bitch."

Starting my bumpy road with a smile.

Pop worked seven days— and nights—a week to keep his family winter- warm. With my brother, Charles, and our mother during the Depression days of the thirties.

Mom and Pop circled the world when the world was tough to circle. Together in Havana circa thirties.

Sweet sixteen. Me, not the girls. Both were Copacabana showpieces and my "between show" regulars for midweek rendezvous at my St. Moritz clandestine pleasure pad.

Celebrating Mom and Pop's new Park Avenue digs with brother, Charles, and sister, Alice.

Charles, the professor. Me, the student. The course? Fashion. The campus? Evan-Picone.

Zorita: No queen of the high-school prom—rather crowned queen of the strippers. One hell of a date to share my eighteenth birthday with.

A BACHELOR IS A BACHELOR IS A BACHELOR IS A BACHELOR.

Strike I—Sharon Hugueny

Strike II—Camilla Sparv

Strike III—Ali MacGraw

Strike IV—Phyllis George

AND OUT FOR GOOD!

My mentor, Hollywood royalty Norma Shearer. Knighting me to portray the legendary boy wonder Irving Thalberg, her deceased husband, on the big screen in A Man of a Thousand Faces.

My first scene in flicks. Going eye to eye with my idol, Jimmy Cagney. Me telling him how to act. Now that's comedy, colored black.

The Sun Also Rises.
To all I told: "I was lucky to come out alive."
Shhh…it was bullshit, I only fought the camera.

Ava Gardner giving an Academy Award performance during intimate off-screen moments with me. For two weeks I thought it was love with a capital L. Was I wrong!

Seductress Gardner during intimate on-screen moments for The Sun Also Rises *with ME— her young prey, Matador Pedro Romero.*

Journal

NEW YORK

American

L · AN AMERICAN PAPER FOR · THE AMERICAN PEOPLE · R

No. 25,296—DAILY   WEDNESDAY, JULY 10, 1957   10 Cents

THE VOICE OF BROADWAY:

Bob Says Yes to Lana

By DOROTHY KILGALLEN

LANA TURNER
Auditioning Bob Evans

AVA GARDNER
with her new heartthrob Bob Evans

*Not a bad parlay for a guy who
had just started to shave.*

FASHION TYCOON / MOVIE STAR   ROBERT EVANS

*Sounds
good, huh?
It worked
against me.*

HANDSOME HOLLYWOOD ACTOR Robert Evans, who is also vice
president of the Evan-Picone women's sportswear firm, shows Maggi McNellis
where to look when she poses. She wears a tiger Nehru coat by Ben Kahn
and a brown suede Emme hat.

Together with Dolores Hart in 1958, both of us winning the Outstanding New Personalities of the Year award presented on CBS television. Dear Dolores, it was her last public performance. She became a nun.

Together with dear Joan Collins that same year. She didn't become a nun!

IT AIN'T EASY STAYIN' IN THE PICTURE!...EVEN IN FLICKS!

Hugh O'Brian saying good-bye in The Fiend Who Walked the West.

Hope Lange saying good-bye in The Best of Everything.

Mel Ferrer saying good-bye in The Sun Also Rises.

IF WE START NOW PROMOTING THIS SENSATIONAL OFF-BEAT OUTDOOR SCREENPLAY IT CAN BECOME ONE OF THIS YEAR'S LEADING GROSSERS

HE LEARNED THERE IS NO SHORT-CUT TO SECURITY

FOR HIM KILLING WAS A JOY IN A LIFE OF HATE

LOOK FOR A NEW TOP STAR IN OCTOBER

THAT IS INDICATED BY ROBERT EVANS' PERFORMANCE IN "THE HELL BENT KID"

Told ya! If only I had hit the theaters as the "Hell Bent Kid," not "The Fiend," **"I could have been a contender."**

But never Brando! Onwards and upwards.

Career change: Starting my climb up a mighty treacherous mountain: Back page announcement in both Variety *and* The Hollywood Reporter:

"Hollywood, Calif.... Richard D. Zanuck, 20th Century–Fox vice president in charge of production, signs Oscar-winning screenwriter, Abby Mann, to script the celebrated best-selling novel The Detective. *Robert Evans (left) will produce and famed director Mark Robson will helm the production for 20th Century–Fox release."*

AGAIN...THE **BIG NEWS** COMES FROM 20th CENTURY-FOX!

Hollywood, Calif. ... Richard D. Zanuck, 20th Century-Fox vice president in charge of production, signs Oscar-winning screen writer, Abby Mann, to script the celebrated best selling novel "THE DETECTIVE." Robert Evans (left) will produce and famed director Mark Robson will helm the production for 20th Century-Fox release.

The prize-package of the year!

The **Detective** A NOVEL BY Roderick Thorp

A MARK ROBSON-ROBERT EVANS PRODUCTION

FOR 20th CENTURY-FOX RELEASE

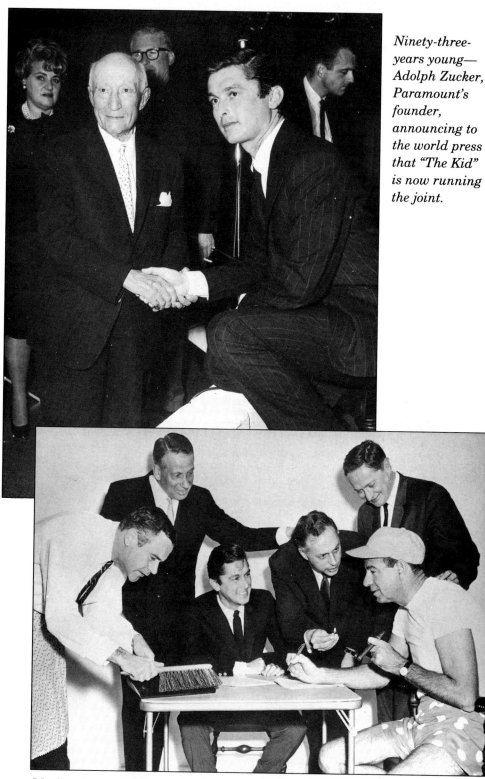

Ninety-three-years young—Adolph Zucker, Paramount's founder, announcing to the world press that "The Kid" is now running the joint.

My first big coup at Paramount, The Odd Couple. *From left to right: Jack Lemmon, producer Howard Koch, myself, director Gene Saks, head of business affairs Bernard Donnenfeld, and Walter Matthau.*

Sandwiched between mentor Charlie Bluhdorn and Martin Davis the day of the world premiere of Is Paris Burning?

How young we looked, circa 1967. Peter Bart and I preparing to announce our film slate to the press.

How young we looked, circa 1968. Stanley Jaffe and myself at the post-premiere party of Franco Zeffirelli's Romeo and Juliet.

How young we looked, circa 1967. Clint Eastwood and I at Super Bowl Number One at the LA Coliseum.

How young we looked, circa 1968. Warren Beatty and I at the Directors Guild screening of The Odd Couple.

Getting camera-dodger Sidney Korshak to pose for a picture was no easy feat. Left to right: Sidney Korshak, his wife, Bernice, Annabel Garth, and me.

The stars *are back at Paramount! Front (left to right): Lee Marvin, myself, Barbra Streisand, Bernard Donnenfeld, Clint Eastwood. Rear (left to right): Rock Hudson, John Wayne, Yves Montand.*

Looking in on maestro Roman Polanski directing Mia Farrow pregnant with Rosemary's Baby.

Joining Sharon Tate and Roman Polanski at the first screening of **Rosemary's Baby.** *(Courtesy Peter C. Bosari)*

October 24, 1969. Moments after getting hitched to Ali MacGraw in Palm Springs, with high hopes of hitting a grand slammer not a third strike. Sharing our joy were Tollie Mae Wilson and David Gilruth, our housekeeper and butler.

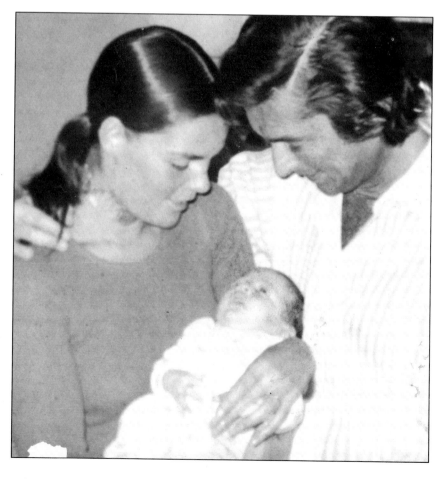

Sharing the most magical moment of our lives— Joshua!

Celebrating, Boston style, at Sumner Redstone's theater. All toasting the success of the Harvard-Wellesley charity premiere of Love Story. *Left to right: Sumner Redstone, Frank Yablans, Howard Minsky, Arthur Hiller, Mrs. Redstone, and me. Today Sumner not only owns the theater but owns Paramount as well.*

From the palace they came! MacGraw and Evans being formally introduced to the Queen Mum at Love Story's *royal premiere in London.*

17

Midafternoon, July 3, 1968—the studio, already half empty, most everyone was off and running to a festive July 4. After the last of my secretaries had given me her good-bye, she rushed back into my office, her face a-blush, her voice a-stutter.

"Mr. Evans. I've just gotten off the phone with Mr. Cary Grant."

Her stutter so pronounced now, I couldn't make out what she said.

"What?"

"Mr. Grant would like to see you."

"Why didn't you put him through?"

"He . . . he told me not to. He wanted to know what your weekend plans were. I, I hope I wasn't out of place. I, I told him you didn't have any. Mr. Grant . . . he laughed. Could you spare a moment for him later this afternoon?"

"Call him. Tell him I don't have one plan, zero, till July fifth. Whatever time he wants to come is fine with me."

A moment later, she returned, stuttering, "He, he's coming here Mr. Evans—at six. Can I stay?" Her face now a Delicious apple. "Please?"

"I thought you were off to Catalina."

"Catalina can wait. Cary Grant!" Her eyes said it all.

"Sure, stick around."

A few hours later, Cary and I were sitting at opposite ends of my coffee table being served tea by the trembling hands of my now flustered secretary.

She whispered in my ear, "Could I . . . could I ask Mr. Grant for his autograph?"

There was only one Cary Grant!

"My secretary's blown her weekend to check out your smile. Write down the old CG for her, will ya?"

Before he could take a pen out from his inside pocket, a still photo was placed before him by my secretary—an 8-×-10 glossy from *Indiscreet,* a film made a decade before opposite Ingrid Bergman.

"Dear, dear. Where *did* you find this one?"

"From the film library—it's my favorite film."

Looking closely at the picture, he flashed it to me, "How young I looked. No wine has ever aged as well. It was such fun with Ingrid. Own the negative, you know."

With pen in hand, Cary looked up, flashing his cleft-chin smile again.

"My dear, what is your name?"

"J-J-Jennifer."

He stood up, "It can't be!"

She stuttered back, "D-D-Did I say anything wrong?"

"My favorite name. It's my daughter's name. Jennifer, Jennifer. Isn't that something!"

He wrote across the 8-×-10 glossy, "Jennifer, my favorite name of all . . . Cary."

No fireworks could have matched the glow of Jennifer's face. Fireworks? Forget it. The most colorful firecracker of her life had just splashed across her world.

Was Cary here to tell me that he wanted to work again, come out of retirement, do his first gig at Paramount? Would *that* be a coup!

"Isn't it marvelous? One of us running a studio," referring back to a decade before when we met as fellow actors at Universal. He, the most glamorous star in the world. Me, a contract player at $175 a week. Most every day we'd pass each other on the lot. Though at the time we had never met, I couldn't help myself, staring at him in awe.

What was the connective tissue that caused the most glamorous star in the world to become friends with a fledgling young actor?

A Yugoslavian basketball player. A guy? Uh-uh, a girl. Luba Otashavich by name, later changed to Luba Bodine. Cary met her while making *The Pride and the Passion* in Spain with Sophia Loren and Frank Sinatra. Cary fell madly in love with Sophia. Sophia, who was married to Carlo Ponti, broke off the relationship. Her marriage came first.

Sophia's stand-in and double was Luba. Not quite a carbon copy, but who could be? Yet she was a lovely remembrance who could match Sophia's spark, energy, and charisma better than anyone. She was put under contract to Cary's company at Universal. At first, I had no idea of her relationship with Cary. In my eyes Luba was a young Sophia Loren—a knockout. To Cary, Luba was but a shadow, a remembrance of a lost love. To me, she was what love could be all about. Because Cary was her mentor, it was important to her that he approve of me. Our kinship started almost the moment we met. For more than a year, several nights a week, the three of us would go out together. A drive-in movie, with sandwiches to go from Nate 'n Al's, a night ball game, an industry function, there we were—Luba, Cary, and myself.

For two or three years Luba played a very important part of my life. Her relationship with Cary stayed the same—*not platonic*. All three knew what the action was. All three wanted one thing—to make one another's lives a bit more fun, with no questions asked.

Now, a decade later, Luba's married to one of the world's wealthiest men. Cary's married to dynamic Dyan Cannon. I'm between gigs, a momentary bachelor. Cary and I were more than friends, we were close friends. Sipping our tea, I couldn't help but think how exciting it would be to get Cary out of retirement and back on to the Paramount lot. When you're an original, you owe it to the world—you can't retire simply because you can't be duplicated. Everything about Cary was stamped "original."

How many times had Cary chuckled "As an actor, I don't know how good I am. I just play myself to perfection."

Katharine Hepburn jokingly said, "Cary? He's just Cary. He's a personality functioning."

Fashion is temporary. Style lasts forever. Till this day, Cary's the only man I've ever met who could walk into a room backward with more grace than anyone walking forward.

Suddenly, dead serious, he said, "Need some advice, dear Robert."

Great! He's going to ask me what picture he should do.

"Why doesn't Dyan love me?"

He's asking me? I don't even know her. Being overly aggressive, "Would making a picture together help?"

"I'd be on my knees in broken glass if I thought it would help." Sadly, he shook his head.

My first and only look-see at a crack in Mr. Grant's sterling armor.

"Does she like you, Cary? Do you like her? Are you pals? Don't answer me, please. Think about it. Answer it, but only to yourself. That's what it's all about."

With full aplomb, changing the subject beautifully, Grant cleft-smiled me, "Dinner tonight?"

"Sure. Why not?"

"Chasen's—nine P.M.?"

"Woodland—got a great duck in the oven, give you a sneak peek of *Rosemary's Baby*. It's the final print."

"Is it as good as they say?"

"We'll find out tonight."

"Can I bring Dougie? He's in town."

That night of July 3, 1968, Douglas Fairbanks, Jr., Cary Grant, and I finished off two ducks, wild rice with plum sauce, followed by a lemon soufflé. *Rosemary's Baby?* We never saw it. We talked, laughed, talked, laughed, about every imaginable subject regarding relationships between men and women, except—a *big* except—the one Cary and I had discussed earlier at our clandestine meeting at Paramount.

The afternoon of July 4, an envelope marked "Personal and Confidential" was delivered to the front door by special messenger. Inside was a three-page handwritten poem, not from Cary, but from Dougie, about the magic of Grant, Evans, and Fairbanks bringing in the July 4 fireworks together.

What I had tried to get across to Cary that afternoon about like, about friendship, conditional and unconditional, was answered not by his words, but rather by Dyan's action. A few months later, poor Cary was sued for divorce, Dyan claiming he used to beat her—in front of the servants, no less. Me, like a schmuck, was asking the same guy "Do you like your wife?" Apparently, her like for him was minimal at best. A bitter child-custody fight ensued. The most valuable jewel of Cary's life—his daughter, Jennifer—was now his only to visit, not to have.

When I was first put into the catbird seat to run Paramount, the one thing I knew for sure was that every eye in the joint was on alert to see how "the womanizer" operated.

Knowing that, my deportment was conservative. With purpose, at my daily lunches at the studio commissary my chair, without fail, always faced the wall. I knew full well that if I sat facing out into the room and gave a smile here or a hello there, the gossip windmill would start turning a smile into a romantic interlude.

Hollywood is a town where most people are looking for work, rather than working. It propels gossip into a major industry. By the way, gossip is never good. Why should it be, who would listen? By the time an eighth of a truth gets back to you, it is so exaggerated it is laughable or even harmful.

I don't know why but before my first shave, I already landed right smack in the center of gossip. After a while it doesn't matter. It's been said that when people stop talking about you, that's the time to worry. I wouldn't know—it's never happened.

For three years, from 1966 to 1969, I had a lover, a mistress. I was obsessed with her: the Paramount mountain. It was a seven-day-a-week, eighteen-hour-a-day affair. It got worse. From obsessed, I became possessed. I doubt whether there was one night a week for three years that I left the studio before midnight. I couldn't help it. I didn't want to fail.

Every so often, between the time the sun went down and the time I left the studio, a director, actor, writer, or producer pal would drop by the office, many a time with a beautiful girl by his side. Whether it be for twenty minutes or an hour, they'd have a drink, talk, and a laugh. During those three years, almost every woman who dropped by with a pal shared a connective tissue. All of them came from different parts of the country, all dreamed of becoming actresses, all were studying. All had legitimate jobs—salesgirl, waitress, or dental hygienist—all shared the same dilemma: *no wheels.*

Without exception, all of them were given an ultimatum by their parents: "Stay at home—anything you want that we can afford, you can have. But if you leave and go out to Hollywood, you're going to have to make it on your own. We will not support you."

How dumb and shortsighted parental decisions can be. A son is one thing, a daughter another. If it meant taking a night job, I'd make certain my daughter was covered no matter where she wandered. When things get tough, rent not paid, electricity turned off, little or no food to eat, and too scared to ask her judgmental parents for help, sadly, no matter how decent a girl is, she ends up spreading her legs in the world's oldest profession.

Not having a car in Los Angeles is tantamount to not having shoes in New York. One has to drive, not walk their way up the ladder to success.

From time to time, even if it was a casual hello, I'd pick up a magnetic quality of a car-less wannabe actress. With no strings attached, I'd rent her a Mustang convertible. Cost—$148 bucks a month from my pal, David Shane, who owned Hollywood-U-Drive-It. Was I looking for reciprocity? No, I didn't have the time. Was I propositioned? By some, because they thought it was necessary. Did I have liaisons with any? A few. Was my gesture altruistic? No, selfish. What greater turn-on is there than knowing that at a moment in time in another's life your presence made the difference between growth or compromise?

Ali MacGraw and I were getting married in October 1969. How could I tell her that I was renting cars for fourteen girls? Try to explain it! I couldn't. Instead I called David Shane.

"Get the cars back—I'm getting married."

"You can't," David shrieked. "You're my biggest customer."

"I may be eccentric, David, but I ain't crazy. I'm marrying Ali, and I don't need no front-page tabloid shit."

Why do I tell the story? Today, of the fourteen girls, six have become internationally famous stars, none earn less than a million bucks a year. Four married men whose wealth is such that their state tax is more than I make a year. The others I've lost track of. Yet back then, a $148-a-month car made the difference in the paths their lives took.

18

"Sign her. Make a multiple picture deal," I told Andrea Eastman, my head of casting and talent.

Andrea agreed, "She has a shot at being the next Julie Andrews."

I had just seen a new Disney picture, *The Happiest Millionaire*. Lesley Ann Warren was the first girl I had put under contract. My nose told me she could go all the way. She sang, she danced, she was beautiful and had a flair for comedy that was very difficult to find. Immediately I thought of a piece of material sent to me by a young producer, Stanley Jaffe—a terrific screenplay by Arnold Schulman, adapted from a Philip Roth novel, *Goodbye, Columbus*. We closed the deal with Stanley in a matter of days and Stanley then attached a brilliant young director, Larry Peerce, to helm it. In less than a week, the package was put together, with Lesley Ann set to star.

Two months before filming, Lesley visited me at the studio. It was good news for her, bad news for me. She was four months pregnant. My first discovery, a mother-to-be.

Next!

Wisely, Stanley began looking for unknowns. Me, I went the Hollywood route. The script was submitted to every star and half-assed star in the business. All of them turned it down. Maybe they didn't want to play Brenda Patimkin, a Jewish American Princess. Or maybe because it was just good. No one seems to know the difference out here. The best proof being that every actress who turned it down went on to make a picture that turned out to be a disaster or near disaster.

Still, it was getting close to post time and we hadn't found our star.

Jaffe and Larry Peerce called me from New York, and they were excited. They had found their Brenda.

Was it Susan Strasberg? I thought to myself.

No, they said it was Ali MacGraw.

I couldn't believe what I'd just heard.

"Stanley, are you nuts? Ali MacGraw, an eighteen-year-old, spoiled Jewish American Princess? She's a twenty-eight-year-old over-the-hill shiksa."

"We've read her, Bob. We think she's dead on."

"Dead on wrong, unless we're thinking of two different pictures. Nat Goldstone brought in some sexy Jew broad who's on 'Peyton Place,' Michelle something, I forgot her name, but she read really good. That's someone we should test."

"Why don't you test her out there," Stanley said, "and we'll test MacGraw here?"

"Okay, Stanley, but you're wasting your time."

I remembered this MacGraw broad—vividly. Ten years earlier I'd spotted her while she was being photographed for an ad. It was on a terrace, directly across from my terrace at 36 Sutton Place South. Though it was in the middle of August and 95 degrees in the shade, she was modeling a white mink coat. Great-looking chick; I gave my elevator man ten bucks to go over and get her name.

Eileen Ford, her agent, was a good friend of mine, so she arranged a luncheon date for us at the Harwyn Club. Ali was a coed from Wellesley, the *Mademoiselle* girl of the year, and a star snot-nose. All she could talk about was how vulgar the Harwyn was. I remembered her saying "Look at all those fat asses lined up at the bar." Not wanting to get into a fight with her, I had a phone brought over to the table and started making calls. Her look said it all: Talk about vulgar!

She dropped me off in a cab. Before I slammed the door, I said, "You sure have big feet." I was sure she'd never speak to me again.

Ali MacGraw as Brenda? Are they nuts? First, we looked at the test of the girl from "Peyton Place" whom I thought was right. Then we looked at MacGraw.

Before her test was even over, Peter Bart stood up. "Thank God, we found a real nineteen-year-old for the part."

"No wonder Paramount's in last place," I said to myself.

But there I was, standing alone. From the secretaries to the top brass, everyone agreed. Ali *was* Brenda.

Never wanting to be in a position to be prey to the scavengers, those agents and managers who are constantly at your door exaggerating their client's talent, I knew I had to take a crash course in knowing the turf, and not in synopsis style. There's only one way to do it. It's called "doing your homework." It became a ritual. Every night after an early dinner, I would go out to my projection room, watch dailies of the pictures we were shooting, then watch two films currently playing the circuit. No phones, no interruptions, but concentration with a capital *C*. After studying the work of everyone— from the cinematographer to the costume and set designers, to certainly the director and the actors, from bit character players to above-the-line stars—I felt sure that no carpetbagger would pull the rug from under me.

Watching the dailies of *Goodbye, Columbus,* sitting beside me most every night was my *consigliere,* the man himself, Sidney Korshak. He was getting a kick out of his Bobby running a studio. He was also getting a kick watching take after take of Ali disrobing on the lawn outside a country club, running across the lawn, bare-ass naked, to jump into a pool and swim across it. Whatever dailies I had to watch, or films set up to run later, each night we'd run those takes of Ali in the buff. There we sat like two horny kids—the Myth and me.

After about the tenth night of watching the same takes, Sidney grabbed my arm.

"You're gonna end up marrying the broad, Bobby."

"She's a hippie; lives in New York with some male model. Forget it, Sidney."

His grip was now all but breaking the veins in my arm. "She's the first broad I've seen you turned on to since I've known you. You'll see—you'll end up with her."

Charlie Bluhdorn couldn't get enough of *Goodbye, Columbus,* which was the first picture Paramount shot in New York since he bought it. He was always on the set. Afterward he'd call me in L.A.

"I was on the set today. I watched some kind of Jewish dance. I got so excited, I wanted to join in myself."

This was coming from a man who never once in all the years I knew him admitted to anyone that he was Jewish. Whether he was or not, I never found out. Whatever meeting Charlie was in, Marty was by his side. When Charlie got up to take a leak, Marty would guard the door, and for good reason. Everyone wanted a peek to see if the chairman was circumcised!

Both in New York and at the studio, there wasn't anyone who didn't flip over *Goodbye, Columbus,* yet nobody knew how to sell it. This was 1969. It was protest time against the war, against the establishment, against parents. How could we interest anyone to pay two bucks to watch a contemporary story of family set in the world of nouveau riche Jews?

For months now, we had tried and failed to come up with a hook to sell the picture, to interest an audience to watch two unknown actors play a Yiddish *Romeo and Juliet.*

With hardly any money left in our advertising budget to hire an outside agency, Stanley Jaffe and I paid a visit to Steve Frankfurt, the youngest and most brilliant hotshot on Madison Avenue. At thirty, he was the president of Young and Rubicam, the largest advertising agency in the country. We told Frankfurt we had no budget to fail again.

"Fine," Frankfurt said. "I'll do it for nothing. It's my gamble. If you want to use it, though, it's a hundred Gs."

Stanley's face turned beet red.

"A hundred Gs. Are you nuts? That's more than five percent of the film budget!"

"I'm taking the gamble, Stanley," said Steve. "I get zip if it's not used. What's the percentage—one in a hundred?"

Nudging Stanley, I whispered to him, "What the fuck do we have to lose!"

Plenty!

Frankfurt's campaign was right on—a saintlike profile of Ali, holding a single rose. Calligraphed across the page, the caption read, "Every father's daughter is a virgin." In 1969, every father thought his daughter was a virgin.

"Are you crazy, Evans?" Bluhdorn screamed. "A hundred Gs for one line. I won't pay it. That's it. I won't even look at it."

He looked at it; he paid the two bucks (a hundred thousand). Frankfurt's extraordinary one line hit a nerve of moviegoing America. Extraordinary too were the reviews and the business. Suddenly, Ali MacGraw, whom I had astutely pegged an "over-the-hill shiksa," became the "new fashionable girl" on the silver screen.

19

The Alfred Eisenstaedt photograph ran across two pages in the March 3, 1969, issue of *Life*. It showed me in bed, surrounded by film scripts and breakfast on a tray, doing business on the phone. Over it was the headline:

WHY SHOULD HE HAVE IT
Robert Evans is an outrage. He has no more right to be where he is than a burglar. He has no credentials, none of the requirements for

membership. Robert Evans has never even produced a film, doesn't know that about movies, and so why should he be a boss of Paramount, with control over 25 pictures a year, costing $100 million, influencing the cultural intake of millions of Americans? He is entirely too good looking, too rich, too young, lucky and too damned charming. The playboy peacock of Paramount. Who the hell does he think he is? If there's anything Hollywood wants out of Robert Evans, it's to see him fail.

It went on and on—five thousand words, eleven pages illustrated with Eisenstaedt's pictures of my princely lifestyle. If I had been the new chief justice of the United States, they wouldn't have given me one tenth the space.

I had cleared the article in advance with Charlie and Marty, but I should have known I couldn't control Jim Mills. Notoriety in the fashion business sells clothes. In show business, it sells tickets. For an executive in a conglomerate like Gulf + Western, it's suicide. I called Bluhdorn to see if I still had my job.

"Evans, from now on stay home. Keep your name out of the papers. I can't take it any longer."

"Charlie, that's all I do is stay home."

"Evans, why is it that since I've met you, I have no life anymore? Half my day is spent defending you—the other half is praising you. Why did I ever meet you?"

"If I'm too hot to handle, Charlie, you've got no problem. I'll make an exit. I'll even—"

"Did I say anything about you leaving?" Bluhdorn screamed. "You leave, I close down the studio. Is that clear, Evans?" Again, slamming down the phone in my ear.

I've never been an office person. Call it habit. Call it picking up traits from your mentor, mine being Darryl Zanuck. He always did business from wherever he was living. Ah, but Zanuck was the employer, the largest stockholder of Fox, a real boss. Me? Though my title was prestigious, I was still an employee. My idiosyncratic behavioral patterns—working from my home, working from my hotel suite, starting late, working very late—have always been looked upon as suspect. One is never independent in this business unless it's one's own money at stake. When you're overpaid, as I've always been, not unlike everyone else in the business, you're up for grabs when it comes to criticism.

I've lived on Woodland Drive now for quarter of a century. More deals have been conceived and consummated in my projection room than in all of Paramount; not in numbers possibly but certainly in importance.

Three years ago, the six leather chairs I had in my projection room for more than twenty years were worn through. Even though I had turned the seats over two years before, cotton was coming out from the arms and the seats as well.

"I can't keep them any longer," I said to my secretary. "Business ain't good, but this ain't the Salvation Army."

I didn't want to replace them with merely ordinary chairs. Naturally, that would be the right thing to do. Me . . . I had to design my chair of delight—six of them to be exact. Five months and many arguments later, they were finally delivered.

There is no chair on any airline in the world, or any private aircraft for that matter, that is half as comfortable or as beautiful as the ones I designed—all in black Italian leather; tufted on the back, the seats, and the sides; with a side button that makes the chair turn into all but a bed. The only negative about them, if you could call it one, is that they offer such comfort that if the film ain't good, your eyes close quickly.

A few days after my six prizes arrived, Nicholson came over to see *Silence of the Lambs.*

"Them blackies, whaddya do with 'em?"

"Tryin' to give 'em away as a tax deduction. The Motion Picture Relief Home won't even take 'em. Try this chair, Irish, it's pure heaven."

When the flick was over and the lights came up, the Irishman gave me a wink, not about the flick.

"Can I have 'em?"

"Sure, if you pick 'em up."

By 9:00 A.M. the next morning, a truck was there to pick up the blackies.

Three nights later, when the lights came up after watching Kevin Costner's new epic, *Dances With Wolves,* the Irishman gives me a wink—not about the flick.

"Them blackies, Keed. The greatest gift I've ever palmed. More people have called me begging for one than have ever called for seats for the Laker playoffs."

A raucous laugh. "Don't get it, do ya? Them blackies, Keed, made history, changed all our lives." Shaking his head on full smile. "Ain't it the truth, though?"

20

On a Clear Day You Can See Forever came as part of Bluhdorn's acquisition of Paramount. An Alan Jay Lerner and Burton Lane Broadway musical with one great song in it—its title number.

As we fervently searched for a brass-ring musical, it was brought out of the cobwebs when Barbra Streisand agreed to play the lead. The very girl, mind you, whom the Paramount distribution frauds from around the world called "suicide" only two years earlier was now the hottest ticket in town.

Turning down *Funny Girl* haunted Charlie until the day he died. In Charlie's mind now, Streisand could do the Yellow Pages and he'd make the deal.

Did I like *On a Clear Day*? As close as Alan Lerner was to me, I couldn't help but tell him that I hated it. My feelings were equally blunt about not making it into a film. It didn't matter. Charlie was haunted by Streisand. Not only did I have little to say, I had nothing to say about bringing it to the big screen. Charlie was so excited to have Streisand on the Paramount lot that he himself flew out to L.A. to deliver 2,600 shares of Gulf + Western stock to her; this was a sentimental birthday gift from the chairman of the board to the star, 100 shares for every year of her life. With Paramount selling at $34 a share, it was nearly a $90,000 hello. In those days a big number.

On a Clear Day, the plush musical extravaganza, turned out to be everything I thought it would: Streisand's first flop—a total disaster.

But it was all worth it. When it came to casting, there was never anyone more impossible than me. Possibly it was my background as an actor. No part, no matter what size, could be cast in any Paramount picture without my approval. Was it autocratic? Yes. I wasn't running a democracy. Among half a dozen pictures that were in preproduction casting, I couldn't help but turn down everybody I had seen film on who was a contender for the part of Tad, Barbra Streisand's stepbrother in the flick. Producer Howard Koch, director Vincente Minnelli and my head of talent, Andrea Eastman, all of them thought I was impossible. It ain't their money, but it was my ass.

"Next!"

"Hold it!" I stood up. "That's the guy."

"I think he's terrific too," said Eastman. "Could be the next Jimmy Dean."

"No, not him. The other guy. The one who didn't talk. The smile."

"I never saw him before."

Before she had a chance to go on, I shouted "Find him!"

At 9:00 the next morning, Andrea Eastman was in my office.

"His name's Nicholson, forget him, he's some nut who works for Roger Corman, writes, directs, acts, cleans toilets . . ."

Cutting her off quick. "I didn't ask for his credits. Find him!"

"Okay, okay."

Two hours later, Eastman's back in my office.

"Sorry to be the bearer of bad news, but your future star is out of the country." She began to laugh. "Tryin' to sell two of his cockama-mie films at the Cannes film festival. Together, they both cost under ten Gs. Do you still want to meet him?"

"Did you hear me say different?"

"Okay, okay. Well, if he doesn't cut it in acting, put him in sales, we could sure use him there."

"Good-bye, Andrea, find him."

A week passed. After looking at more than fifty other possible con-tenders, I sounded like a parrot: "Not right, not right, not right."

Suddenly I was called to New York for an emergency meeting. Was it an emergency? I'd say so. They just wanted to close the studio down again, that's all.

The phone rang in my suite at the Sherry-Netherland Hotel.

"Hi, Bob. It's Bernie Sohn."

"Nice to hear from you, Bernie." I hadn't seen or heard from him in fifteen years.

"I'm with the Morris office," he said with as much pride as if he were the U.S. secretary of state.

"Good, Bernie, good for you."

"Jack Nicholson just came back from the Cannes Film Festival. He's in town for the day."

"Jack who?"

"The guy you saw film on for the part of Tad. I heard you wanted to meet him."

"Oh, the guy with the smile?"

"Yeah, that's him."

I looked at my watch. It was 10:15. In two hours I had to be at the Gulf + Western Building for an S.O.S. meeting with the board of directors to stave off closing the studio gates.

"Can you make it over here in the next hour?"

"Are you kidding?"

At 11:00 on the dot, in walked Bernie Sohn. Wow, had he gained weight in fifteen years. Next to him was the Smile.

"Thanks for getting here so quick, fellas. Come on in."

In typical agent form, Bernie had diarrhea of the mouth, telling me how brilliant his client was. Nicholson had already lost his smile, he was so uncomfortable.

"Hold it, Bernie," I said, putting up my hand. "What's the last picture you made, kid?" Imagine me calling someone else kid.

"I've just finished a flick that could be a real winner."

"Really. Tell me about it." I wanted to hear him talk.

"Been in the can for just a month. Somethin' about it's real interestin'."

"Who's in it with you?"

Back came the smile, "Hoppy; the Pete."

"Hoppy? Hoppy who?"

Then a wink. "Dennis the Menace."

"Oh! I see."

Blasting off with a laugh, "It'll turn ya upside down."

I didn't understand a fuckin' word the guy was saying, but it didn't matter, the guy was an original. He must have been. It sure in hell was a first for me, mesmerized by another guy's smile. I didn't even know if the kid could act. Imagine, signing a guy to a leading role opposite Streisand on a smile.

"Listen, kid, put the motorcycle pictures behind you, will you? How would you like to co-star with Barbra Streisand—play her stepbrother."

"Don't know. Haven't read it yet."

Bernie Sohn was ready to explode. "He'd love to play it. Are you making us an offer?"

The Irishman just looked at Bernie, shaking his head, smile and all.

"Yup," I said, "ten thousand buckaroos for six weeks, plus two free."

The most the Irishman had ever been paid for a flick was $600. Suddenly I was "Mr. Evans" to agent Sohn.

"Thank you, Mr. Evans, thank you."

The Smile interjected, "Bernie, I'd like to speak to Mr. Evans alone."

Angrily, Bernie looked at him. "Jack, stop it!" Then, turning to me, fake smile and all, Bernie said, "Thank you, Mr. Evans. It's confirmed?" I nodded my head yes. "I'll wire the Coast immediately."

"Hold it, Bernie, hold it," I said. "If your client wants to speak to me, let him speak to me." Anxiety crossed his face, thinking, I'm sure, he's gonna blow it, he's gonna blow it.

Together, the Irishman and I walked to the window. My suite had a panoramic view of Central Park. It *was* a clear Day.

"Pal, you don't know me, but I sure know who you are. Could you do me a big favor?"

"Shoot."

"Ya see, I just got a divorce. I gotta kid, gotta pay alimony, gotta pay child support and I'm on empty. Could you make it fifteen?"

"How about twelve-five?"

His billion-dollar smile lit up. "Thank ya, pal, I'll never forget it."

The beginning of a remarkable friendship.

21

To anyone who didn't know me (which was everyone), Evans had it all. The only bachelor in Hollywood running a studio. Power, glamour, money. In reality I was in the hot seat seven days a week eighteen hours a day working my ass off not to get the boot. A week never passed without a knock from the press that the axe was about to fall on Evans's neck.

My social and sex life were next to nil. To protect my reputation as a stud rather than a spud, even midnight rendezvous were put on hold. News travels fast when you fall asleep before dropping your pants.

On a Saturday night in the middle of November 1968, the gates were closed and the phones shut off. It was script-reading time. I was in the middle of reading a real winner by James Poe, a top Hollywood writer, when I noticed the red button on my phone blinking. Fuck it. English accent and all, "The Evans residence."

"Good thing you gave up acting," said the voice on the other end. It was Lee Anderson, Hollywood's top socialite, inviting me to a last-minute get-together.

"Thanks, but I'm in bed for the night with a script."

"Sure," she laughed. "Too bad. It's for Princess Soroya. She's here for one night. A stopover from Hawaii to Paris."

Why did I pick up the phone? She must have known this was the one broad I'd crawl over broken glass to meet. Divorced from the Shah of Iran, she was the most sought after woman in the world. Her wealth enormous, her beauty more. Why waste my time? Why not?

"When and where?"

"It's already started."

"Thanks for the notice."

"You never show anyway."

"Okay, Okay. Where?"

"Two hundred yards from your house . . . you can walk it." She laughed, giving an address on Alpine, the next street over.

"Pajamas okay?"

"Sure, if you want to be left out in the cold."

"Black tie?"

"Black socks."

Eighteen minutes later I rang the doorbell. More than a hundred people were already there. Yet there wasn't a face in the room I knew. A first; still is. Old money filled the room, rather than Hollywood glitz. Making a U-turn out, I caught a royal glimpse. A quick 180 in search of Miss Society Anderson. Found her, kissed her cheek.

"No pajamas," I said, lifting my left pant, "black socks too—dressed to meet the princess."

Shaking her head, she took my hand, guiding me to meet the lady of my life.

"Soroya, dear. This is Robert Evans," then in half a whisper, "boy genius of Hollywood."

Interrupting her quickly, "I'm no boy and I'm no genius."

A royal smile.

What the princess didn't know was that I, and I alone, held the secret key to her royal highness's weak link.

"Ah, but what I *am* is a wand, a magic one, who grabs a shooting star and makes it light up the screen. . . ." She looked at me as though I was crazy. "I saw your film in Rome."

Suddenly, there was no one else in the room.

"You couldn't have. The film's never been released. I wouldn't let it be. No one has seen it."

I interrupted, "But me. Dino de Laurentiis asked me to, told me of your demand, asked my opinion—I gave it to him. You were right; the picture's unreleasable"—a purposeful pause—"but you were unforgettable."

A forty-carat emerald couldn't have made her face more aglow. Then I completed my one-two punch, throwing a white lie. "Dino sent me the only print he had; I asked him to. I still have it, show it to all my execs at Paramount, tell them this is what a movie star is all about. Now go out and find me someone like her. And here you are."

Jim Poe's script? Never finished it. Paris? Soroya didn't quite make it. Woodland became her home away from home. From tennis bum to movie star, all my guests were treated royally. After a month, it was time for her to go. She, the world to travel. Me, a ladder to climb. We toasted to St. Moritz at Christmas time, but both of us knew it was a fucking lie, rather our last good-bye.

22

The big honchos, Harry Cohn, Louis B. Mayer, Jack Warner, were all gone now. They had been owners, not employees. Now the new game to play in Hollywood was musical chairs. No longer moguls for decades, rather kings for a day. Power was not ours to dictate, but rather be dictated to us. Film was no longer an art to be nurtured, but a commodity to be sold. The Zanucks were gone—the boards of directors were in. Making announcements to save jobs came before the passion to create.

I was a throwback, but, unfortunately, not an owner. Lew Wasserman said it all on the phone one evening.

"Where are you, Bob? You're late."

"*Godfather*'s in deep shit, Lew. I'm in the editing room."

"You're head of a company, not an editor. Get your priorities straight!"

Was Wasserman right? Today he's a millionaire 500 times over, while I'm breaking my ass finishing the book to pay back taxes.

From 1967 to 1970, my instinct said no but my survival said yes. I star-fucked with the best. At one time, I had seven of the top ten box-office stars making pictures at Paramount. I batted one for seven—Duke Wayne came through with *True Grit*. Even with a grand slammer, one for seven ain't a good average.

How could we miss with Alan Jay Lerner and Fritz Loewe? With *Gigi, My Fair Lady,* and *Camelot* (all for other studios), they'd batted a thousand on the big screen. We got Lerner and Loewe's *Paint Your Wagon,* which cost megabucks, and struck out—*Paint Your Wagon* painted Paramount's wagon bright red. After its disastrous premiere, the clouds never opened for *On a Clear Day*. And neither did they for *Darling Lili, The Adventurers,* or *Catch-22.*

In film as in life, I've always believed that, when forced into a crisis, do the unexpected. I went back to basics. Instinct, stories— where the written word was the star, such as Shakespeare's *Romeo and Juliet*. "Strictly for television," they said. Thirty years earlier my mentor, Norma Shearer, starred as Juliet opposite Leslie Howard. Both were more than twice the age of the characters they played. But their unrequited love brought unrequited lines to the theater. As a kid, I had seen various versions on the stage of *Romeo*. Never once, though, were the actors the actual age of the characters they played.

How brilliant director Franco Zeffirelli was, finally a *Romeo and Juliet,* played by actual teenagers. Olivia Hussey and Leonard Whiting, who were sixteen and seventeen, respectively, during filming, were certainly not stars, but they were perfect for the roles. The picture went through the roof.

From British to Yiddish with *Goodbye, Columbus* was next. This time Juliet was a Jewish American Princess and Romeo, her librarian love; both critically and commercially, it was a four-star hit for Paramount. *Downhill Racer* was Redford's labor of love. No studio wanted a ski picture. But Redford did. For $1.4 million, my money was on him. To this day Redford considers it one of his best, which it is.

A real cuckoo was *The Sterile Cuckoo*. Alan J. Pakula, a fine producer, now wanted to direct. There was one problem—no one wanted to take a chance with him. Especially when he insisted Liza Minnelli play the misfit college girl. If ever there was a case of two negatives making a positive, it was *Cuckoo*, which launched Alan as a major maestro and Liza as a major movie star.

And me, I was still a minor nut. Especially when I announced a film written by a pool attendant and directed by an editor whose first picture had yet to be released. That was bad enough. But try to tell your distribution honchos that you're making a love story where an eighteen-year-old boy falls for an eighty-year-old woman! When Bart first brought me the script, written by the pool boy of producer Eddie Lewis, a kid named Colin Higgins, I began having second thoughts about Bart.

"Peter, I ain't readin' it. Don't tell me how brilliant it is. I don't want to hear. If it was dug out of Shakespeare's vault and no one had seen it yet, I still wouldn't read it."

"Bob, you're wrong."

"Pull the car over, will you, Peter. I want to walk to the studio. An eighteen-year-old kid making love to an eighty-year-old woman? I can just see me telling Bluhdorn the story. He'll take his glasses off, squint, and state eloquently: 'I want to vomit!' "

"Take an hour—read it. Please."

"Fuck you. I'm not!"

"Stanley Jaffe's brother, Howard, gave it to me."

"You sure know how to push my buttons, you prick."

Two hours later, I walked into his office. "It's gonna get me fired, you know—an unknown director, a pool boy writer, two impossible-to-cast parts. It's gonna give Marty Davis the shot he's been waiting for—straightjacket time."

Bart laughed. "If it doesn't work, we'll blame it on Ashby, say he went crazy."

I looked at Bart. "Is Ashby crazy? He must be, wanting to take this on. Peter, I gotta ask you something. How come a conservative guy like you has more weird ideas than Timothy Leary?"

He thought for a moment, took off his glasses, eyed me. "Good cover, huh?"

Harold and Maude was the pool boy's script. Hal Ashby was a then untested director. Bud Cort was a teenager, and hardly a recognized actor. To play the eighty-year-old eccentric, who better than Ruth Gordon, who had just won the brass ring, the Academy Award, for *Rosemary's Baby*. The connective tissue was Cat Stevens's extraordinary music from *Tea for the Tillerman*.

It was an impossible dream. The dream became the longest-playing cult picture in cinema history. It opened at Christmas time more than twenty-three years ago. Today, in cities all over the world from Minneapolis to Paris, the picture has never been off the screen.

Two pictures I insisted on making almost got me barred for life from the Gulf + Western building. One was *Medium Cool,* directed by cinematographer Haskell Wexler, using actual footage of the riots during the 1968 Democratic Convention in Chicago. Controversial? The Republicans thought it was democratic demagoguery. The Democrats thought it was radically Republican. Gulf + Western thought it should never have been made. It had a wide release . . . one theater.

Walking the edge is one thing, but jumping rope on the edge is another. Henry Miller was a personal friend of mine. Someone with whom I'd played Ping-Pong most every weekend. He was in his eighties. Not even twenty years before, his books weren't allowed in stores because of their lustful subject matter. I would beat him at Ping-Pong nine out of ten games. He was setting me up. One Saturday afternoon, after losing 21–10, 21–12, he threw me a dare.

"You say you're a gambler, huh?"

"No, I'm a handicapper."

"Handicap this one, kid. I beat you the next two games and you don't reach ten either game."

"That's not handicapping, Henry, that's stealing. Come on."

"Bet?"

"What?"

"I win—you get *Tropic of Cancer* onto the screen."

"I can't make the fuckin' film and you know it, you prick."

"I can't beat you 20 to 9 either, and you're a prick too."

"When I win, what do I get, writer?"

"Twelve handwritten raunchy letters to twelve pussies, or twelve raunchy letters to one pussy—your choice. Each *pussero* who gets a letter will yearn for your balls. If a dozen letters go to one, she'll walk the streets to please you."

"You're a hustler, Henry, but you're old. You don't stand a shot. You're on."

He beat me 21–6, 21–7. The old motherfucker should have spent his years in Vegas, not in Paris. He would have come out a helluva lot richer.

"Okay, junior, start thinking how to get it on the screen. No weather reports, nitty-gritty, hand-picked crabs, right from the lady's crotch. That's the book, that better be the film, junior."

"Henry, you're one sick fuck."

"Uh-uh, kid, just a fuck."

Tropic of Cancer got to the screen. Joe Strick directed and produced it—brilliantly. Raunchy? Ellen Burstyn, who later won an Academy Award, lay in a Paris bed, bare-ass naked, her legs spread, pulling crabs from her crotch. The scene went over very big in the Gulf + Western boardroom.

"Fire him," they said. "Burn the negative."

They didn't burn the negative. It played in one theater and disappeared for good. Because of Henry Miller, I traveled a back elevator for the next two months. Henry, you got the last laugh, wherever you are, and I'm sure it ain't heaven.

An executive I was not. That's why Bluhdorn hired me. But now that "the mountain" was beginning to see light, it needed a chief executive in New York, Gulf + Western's main office. It sure as hell wasn't me, nor did it bother me that the corporate title of the person Charlie and I chose be over mine.

"Who better to fill it," I said, "than Stanley Jaffe?"

"He's hardly old enough to shave." Bluhdorn started to laugh.

"That's the reason."

That evening Charlie and I met to discuss it further at Frankie and Johnny's Steak House. By cheesecake time, Jaffe was the guy. By the end of the week Stanley was Paramount's president—the youngest president in the oldest place, New York; for a moment, the New Hollywood.

If ever one plus one equaled eleven, it was with Stanley and myself. We were opposites on every level, except for handshake honor and loyalty to each other—an emotion we share to this day. He wasn't looking to be me, nor was I looking to be him. Whatever capabilities I lacked in being corporate, Jaffe had in youthful spades.

He was pragmatic—tough and straight—while I was romantic, a pushover, and not so straight. Our bond in film was instinctively

sharing a priority to the power of the written word—though unheralded to most, to us it was sacred.

Stanley, Peter Bart, and I spent time together strategizing the
future of Paramount.

"Every half-assed guy in the business is making films about where
it's at," said Stanley. "Let's take a different road, Bob . . . give the
audiences something they haven't had for a while—stories about
how it feels."

Paramount's strategy of telling stories about how it feels was the
secret flag we were going to carry in the years to come.

Peter was still the devil's advocate.

"I'm not disagreeing with your philosophy, Stanley. Let's get down
to facts—like agents, managers, lawyers, money. Writing about
where it's at is easy pocket money; about how it feels, that's different.
Not only does it take talent, which most of these penholders don't
have, but writing about feelings takes a helluva lot more time. Stanley, you know it better than me—we're in the business of deals, not
excellence. The ten percenters know their clients can write three
concept scripts a year. To write texture takes time; time is money
and money is what pays their light bills."

"You're right, Peter. That's why we're all overpaid. If we can't accomplish what we think is right, let someone else be overpaid. We
don't deserve it."

"What the hell's wrong with this dame, Larry? Is she jerking me off?
Does she ever want to work again? I give her the biggest break a
dame can get, a lead in her first flick. Don't I deserve a break? I've got
a five-picture deal with her and it's worth shit. She turns down everything."

Larry Peerce lit up his pipe. "That's her," he grinned. "Want it
straight?"

"You're damn right, got a big investment in this broad. I offer her
the lead in *The Adventurers,* tells me she doesn't like the script. It's
only the biggest picture we're making this year."

Peerce couldn't hold back his laughter.

"Hate to tell you. You've got one bad investment. She hates Hollywood and couldn't care less if she ever works again."

"That's bullshit!"

"That's true," Peerce said. "She's the real thing, a total *meshug-*

geneh. She was working for one hundred and twenty-five bucks a week as a stylist when she could have been making thousands as a model. Told you she's a *meshuggeneh.* I think she enjoys being poor. You wanna her for a picture? You got her." Larry smiled.

"Damn right I do. Bluhdorn enjoys givin' me heat. 'What kind of business is this? You invest and own something cheap, but you can't use it. We own her for twenty thou a film. She's already turned down three.' "

"I got a script she'll pay to do." Larry laughed.

"Is it in Hebrew?"

"Might as well be."

"That bad?"

"Worse."

"She likes it, huh?"

"Doesn't *like* it—thinks it's great!"

"Can I read it?"

"You'll hate it."

It was a rainy Saturday afternoon. Larry Peerce and I were having lunch at my home. Both of us were looking for a project for him to helm. After *Goodbye, Columbus,* Larry was one of the new hot kids in town, with at best a half-assed allegiance to me since I broke his big screen directorial virginity with *Goodbye, Columbus.* Walking back into my sitting room with a rumpled script, the top page half torn off, he handed it to me, laughing.

"When you call her, don't be too tough on her—she's a good kid. Now can we get down to business. *The Sporting Club:* let me get my teeth into it, will ya, Bob?"

"Let me give it to you straight, Larry. I read *The Sporting Club* and I didn't understand it. Because it came from you, I read it again and I still didn't understand it. I'm not Mr. Intellectual, but when I read something twice and still don't understand it, let someone else make it a hit."

"It's brilliantly written."

"That's why I don't understand it."

Less than forty-eight hours later, Larry Peerce was on the horn.

"You weren't too tough with her, were you, Evans?"

Silence.

I finally said, "I want to make it."

"You want to ruin her career. That's it, huh?"

"You got it. And I want to ruin yours too. I want you to direct it."

"I'm losin' my fuckin' mind with you, Evans. You won't make *Sporting Club*, but you'll make this piece of dreck."

"I read *The Sporting Club* again. Still didn't understand a fuckin' word. This piece of dreck made me laugh. Get this, Larry—it made me cry too. Not a bad parley, huh, Mr. Director?"

"Don't do it to me, Evans, please. I direct this and I'm back on the tube again."

"Who owns it?"

"An agent from William Morris. His name is Minsky. He's schlepped it all over town. I don't think it's gotten past one reader."

"How come Paramount didn't get a crack at it?"

"They did. It was turned down. No one had the guts to give it to you."

It was the easiest deal I'd ever made. Howard Minsky believed in this supposed piece of dreck with such conviction that he resigned his position at the Morris office to go for it and get *Love Story* onto the screen.

Poor guy. By the time it got to me, he was a beaten man. I think, in all of filmland, mine were the last eyes to see it. His dance card still totally on empty, Minsky was quick to his knees to close the deal. I give the guy great credit, giving up a cushy job to wildcat. Howard did and hit a gusher. A gusher so big that he never had to work again for the rest of his life.

The starlet-turned-star, whose undying belief in the potential of this one-on-one story of two young kids falling in love, was Ali Mac-Graw. Erich Segal, the author, was at that time a Harvard professor. His pulpy, somewhat autobiographical, love story was already packed in his summer luggage. No one wanted it. The heroine of the piece was a J.A.P., as she had been in his life. While Ali, the quintessential WASP, had gotten away with playing a J.A.P. in *Goodbye, Columbus,* I didn't want to press my luck. Our heroine's moniker suddenly changed from Cohen to Cavileri—this time an Italian American princess. Did it bother Erich Segal? She could have been an Arab princess. From the trash can, it now had a chance to end up in a film can.

Larry Peerce, having a tough time putting *Sporting Club* together, desperately needed a gig. Between alimony and child support, he was running on empty. Closing his eyes, he reluctantly agreed to helm this "piece of shit." After a month of collaborating, there he was across my desk, shaking his head.

"I can't be a hooker, Evans. I wake up in the morning, look at myself in the mirror, and *I don't like what I see.* No matter how you put it in the mixer it comes out shit. I'm passing. I'd rather do daytime soaps; at least no one will know I'm doing it." Hunching over the desk, his face almost touching mine, he said, "You wanna fuck her, right? That's why you're makin' it."

"It never entered my mind, but maybe he's right," I said to myself.

That night I sent the script to Jaffe, Davis, and Bluhdorn, telling them that Larry Peerce just quit. Davis had little interest in reading it. Jaffe had a big interest. After all, he was mentor to both Larry and Ali.

Within forty-eight hours, Charlie and Stanley reluctantly admitted that it not only got to them, but got a tear from them as well—not an easy feat.

Separately, I said to each of them, "If I can get a tear from you, that's the picture I want to see on the screen."

Enter Tony Harvey. The previous year he'd won everything for *The Lion in Winter,* from the New York Film Critics Circle Award to the Directors' Guild Award; at the time he was the only director in the history of the Academy who didn't cop the Oscar after winning the nod from the Directors Guild. Hooked by MacGraw, *Love Story* was his to helm. After weeks of collaboration with Erich Segal revising the screenplay, he too walked off. Suddenly *Love Story* was no love story at Paramount.

The dictate from the forty-third floor in New York was simple and direct: "Go forward" with a big asterisk. If you go over the budget even with one telephone call over $2 million, no love.

Though he was not yet thirty, Jaffe's eye was as keyed to the top sheet of a budget as a Vegas pit boss's was to a blackjack table.

"Over $2 million, Evans—it's from your pocket."

Damn it, I should have taken him up on it. For a $2 million dollar put, I could have cornered at least 10 points on the back end of the picture. The picture came in 1 percent under budget and the 10 points would have given me "fuck you" money for the rest of my life.

In the spring of 1969, holding *Love Story* sure as hell wasn't holding aces. I went to New York to find Mr. Right to helm my flawed jewel. I batted a thousand—turned down by all.

I set up a lunch date with *Love Story*'s mentor and star, MacGraw, at La Grenouille. By the time dessert was served, I would have made the phone book with her. Would you say she got to me? I sure in hell knew I didn't get to her. With all my props, my position, my "boy wonder" rep, she was as turned off to me as I was turned on to her. My competition was a model/actor she had been living with for three years, sharing the bills in a 3½-room apartment on West Eighty-seventh Street. Almost purposefully, she kept on interjecting how in love she was. Leaving the restaurant, I hailed a cab. As it pulled up she gave me her last zinger.

"Hope we shoot in the summer. Robin and I are getting married in the fall. We plan to spend October in Venice. Ever been there?"

"Nope."

"Then wait. Only go there when you're madly in love."

That's it. I grabbed her arm, whispering, "Never plan kid. Planning's for the poor."

She tried to snap back. "No way—"

"Let me finish, Miss Charm. An hour ago, *Love Story* was even money to end up in the shredder. You win, I lose. Got it? Stop being Miss Inverse Snob, will ya? It doesn't wear well. Don't turn your nose down to success. If anything goes wrong with you and Blondie between now and post time, I'm seven digits away."

Before she had a chance to say anything, I closed the door behind her and took off.

Four-story walk-up MacGraw must have forgotten the seven digits. She never called. Did I read the script over and over again? You're damned right. And it still got a tear. If Elaine May were starring in it, forget the tears, it would have already been shelved. Here I am, head of a studio, certainly one of the biggest buyers in a town filled only with sellers. I'm Diamond Jim Brady offering gross percentages to people who don't deserve them, and I still can't get a nibble.

Bluhdorn was right. What kind of crazy business is this? I'll tell you. All eight actors whose ass I kissed to play the male lead in *Love Story* turned it down. Each went on to make his next film. Though I batted zero for eight, they did as well—each film was a disaster. Like Larry Peerce, half of the eight Barrymores made pictures that were barely released. Conversely, any one of the brilliant eight would have become "fuck you" rich making this "piece of shit." Oh, by the way, it was nominated for seven Academy Awards, including best actor and best actress.

On Paramount's official agenda, *Love Story* was one of fifteen pictures in pre-production. On Robert Evans's secret agenda, *Love Story,* a picture no one wanted to be connected with, was the one I knew would make it to the screen. I had an idea; I'll get some young, hot star, pay him gross from the first dollar, something he's never gotten. Greed will rule, put him up there with the big boys, a gross player. Even if they think the script stinks, their ten percenters will talk 'em into it.

Michael Douglas, Michael York, Michael Sarrazin, Jon Voight, the Bridges brothers—Beau and Jeff—Peter Fonda, Keith Carradine; all were offered a ten on the dollar. Eight batters—not a hit. They all turned it down.

A minor miracle! Arthur Hiller reluctantly acquiesced to direct my "Angel with a Very Dirty Face." His agent, Phil Gersh, persuaded him to take *Love Story* as a filler. He would squeeze it in between *The Out-of-Towners* and *Plaza Suite,* two other Paramount flicks.

My first bite and there was no way I'd let him off the hook. "Arthur, we'll push back *Plaza Suite* to accommodate your schedule."

There's no director in town more prolific than Hiller. If he ain't on the set, he ain't satisfied. Unfairly, Arthur has never been given his proper homage. Never been considered fashionable, though his batting average certainly makes him a slugger in any league. If it's the bottom line that counts, Hiller's record should make him a contender for the Hall of Fame. The filler, *Love Story,* made him a millionaire many, many times over. To me, hooking Hiller was akin to signing John Wayne, Clint Eastwood, Bob Redford, and Paul Newman to do a western for scale. My euphoria was short-lived.

Suddenly, one Wednesday, Ali remembered my seven digits. Not the charming lady who mesmerized me months ago at Grenouille in New York, but the angry with a capital *A* actress.

"The audacity—to sign a director I've never heard of without consulting me! It's my property. I'm doing the picture for slave wages. I'm living up to my option agreement. Have you *forgotten* the word 'courtesy'?"

"Listen here, Miss Grateful!"

Down went the phone.

Hyperventilating, I screamed through the door at my secretary to get Ben Benjamin, Ali's agent, on the phone. "Now! And if they don't know where he is, find him."

Ben, a gentleman of gentlemen, calmed my anger. His client, Mac-Graw, had no idea of the leprosy attached to her sudsy manuscript. By midnight, New York time, it was resolved that Ali would fly out Friday morning, arriving Friday afternoon, to look at Hiller's first cut of *The Out-of-Towners*. To me, this was a bellylaugh flick, from start to finish.

"He's good enough for Jack Lemmon and Sandy Dennis," I screamed at Ben. "He's good enough for Walter Matthau."

"Calm down, Bob, calm down."

"How the fuck can I calm down, Ben? What's this business coming to when I gotta audition a guy whose made a dozen hits for some fuckin' starlet?"

I called him back in an hour, but he was already in bed. "Cancel the whole fuckin' thing, will ya, Ben? I feel like Willy Loman trying to put this piece of shit together."

"Forget Ali, Bob, for me. Let her come out, show her Hiller's picture. Do it at your house. She won't be arriving till six and she's booked out the next morning at eight. If it doesn't work, cancel. I wouldn't blame you. She's really a good lady, Bob."

"Good. I don't know, Ben, but she's lucky. You're one of the few guys who could have pulled this chit."

The next morning I called Hiller's agent and Paramount Production. Naturally, I didn't tell Phil Gersh that I was auditioning Arthur Hiller's *The Out-of-Towners* for the starlet. Having all but made up my mind to cancel and wanting to protect myself, I told Phil that I might have to move up *Plaza Suite* to start production in November. I wanted to keep my word to Arthur, telling him I would accommodate his schedule to film *Plaza Suite*. Doing this protected me with a legal commitment on *Love Story* with Hiller. Then I called David Golden, *Love Story*'s production manager.

"Don't spend another dime. Not a telephone call on *Love Story*."

"We're prepped to go in eight weeks!"

"We may not be going for eight months. I'll know Monday. No more questions and, Dave, no more dollars. Got it?"

Picking Ali up in the lobby of the Beverly Hills Hotel, I drove her to my home and theater. Did it bug me? You bet . . . needing this starlet's nod of approval. Inwardly, I was hoping she'd not like Hiller so I could tell her she was on a one-way ticket east, her flick canceled. At least I'd finally get my nuts off with her.

"Miss Charming ain't gonna charm me tonight," I said to myself as I walked her through my front doors, out and around my pool to my projection room. Well, it didn't quite work out that way!

"I feel like I'm walking through my own private park in Paris," said Miss Crooked Tooth.

Prepared for her bullshit charm, it hardly made a ripple. Nor did I want to give her the satisfaction of the *plat de jour* house tour, which was my M.O. for almost any girl I'd ever met. My little gem of a palace was the greatest prop any guy could have, whether he be a billionaire or movie star. A true Garden of Eden—a "closer" to any lady who entered its gates. It had to be—a .333 hitter doesn't bat .900 by mistake.

"Fuck her and her snobbery," I said to myself, opening a bottle of champagne. "Let her look at the flick and get the fuck out," as heavenly Beluga caviar was served with baby potatoes and crème fraîche.

Arthur Hiller's audition was ready to roll. Well the screen never came down. Ah, but Miss Flower Child soon got wet, very wet, jumping into the egg-shaped pool, totally clothed, from shoes to headband. For a bohemian she sure as hell became comfortable very quickly living behind closed gates with two thousand rosebushes, surrounded by gardenias, daisies, and you name it. She was a flower child, all right, but now they were hers.

On day three of her "overnight" trip, Ali said, "If you think he's right, Evans, I don't have to look at the film. Who's going to play Oliver?"

Then I dropped it on her.

"Whoever you like has already turned it down. Whoever you half like has already turned it down. Whoever you hardly like has already turned it down."

Instead of being apologetic for her snot-nosed attitude, she giggled. "I knew it. Why do you think I jumped in the pool with my clothes on?"

That day, Phil Gersh got the nod that *Plaza Suite* was pushed back and *Love Story* was a go. Dave Golden, *Love Story*'s production manager, got a thumbs-up that he was back with the employed: "Get on to Boston, tie up the Harvard campus."

Back in L.A., though, we couldn't find Mr. Harvard. With no actor with any semblance of respectability wanting the gig, like it or not, we were left with only one choice—to test. Christopher Walken, David Birney, Ken Howard—you name him, we put him on the screen. Hoping that one plus one would equal eleven, Ali tested with all of them.

Tommy Tannenbaum, an agent pal of mine, even persuaded me to test Ryan O'Neal. I told him it was a waste of time. He told me he didn't want to lose a client.

"A favor, Evans, please."

"Don't forget the chit, Tommy," I let him know.

Who made the best test? Ryan O'Neal. Who did Arthur Hiller refuse to use? Ryan O'Neal.

"Evans, let's call a script a script. I'm doing it as a filler, I admit it. I don't have to move off the Paramount lot. I'm starting *Plaza Suite* at the end of the year and Ali made a great Brenda. Thought it would be fun working with her. If we use O'Neal, it's suicide. He just finished a five-year gig on 'Peyton Place'—a soap. We're not making the Bible here. Call it *Love Story* if you want, but it's still a soap. With Segal's dialogue, it will be 'Peyton Place' goes to Boston."

"Arthur, the kid made the best test."

"So what, it's perception. You can't afford it and I can't afford it. Let's use Chris Walken. He's a legitimate actor."

"That's the problem—he's an actor. O'Neal, like him or not, he's a reactor."

"O'Neal," said Arthur, "like him or not, I won't use him."

"Like it or not, Arthur, O'Neal's in the film."

The ball was now in Arthur's court. If I didn't fire him, he'd have to quit, which would mean he'd breached his contract and I wouldn't have to pay him. Knowing Phil Gersh, I took the gamble. Gersh would have had Hiller do the flick blindfolded not to lose the gig.

It was Friday morning, October 24, 1969. Ali and I climbed into our Mercedes two-seater and headed for the town hall in Riverside. Following in a limousine were our witnesses—my housekeeper, Tollie Mae; my butler, David Gilruth; my brother, Charles; and Peggy Morrison, a friend of Ali's from New York.

Wanting total secrecy, I'd instructed Bob Goodfreid, Paramount's publicity honcho, to be sure there was no press or associates, and no friends were to know. Bob arranged for us to get our marriage license in Riverside, then tie the knot in Palm Springs. It wasn't a good omen when, a few miles east of Riverside, the bottom of my Mercedes fell out. Everyone wanted to wait for AAA.

Grabbing Ali, I whispered in her ear, "Fuck the car! Let's get the show on the road."

Leaving the Mercedes right where it was, both of us snuck into the backseat of the limo and off we went.

There is nothing more personal than getting hitched. There's nothing *less* personal than getting hitched before hundreds of people, each one thinking it's not going to work anyway. The best would have been just me and Ali signing the license and sending it in. We did the next best: a two-dollar judge in Palm Springs and three witnesses. Afterward we uncorked Dom Perignon on the courthouse lawn, finishing off bottle after bottle, laughing and laughing.

A two-day honeymoon at Tony Owen and Donna Reed's home in Palm Springs and off we flew, ending what was to be the last of that ever-lovin' luxury—privacy. That night we flew with the *Love Story* group on the red-eye to New York. They continued on to Cambridge, Massachusetts, to begin principal photography in and around Harvard. I flew off to London, Paris, and Rome, not to look for my new fall wardrobe, but to put "the mountain's" fires out throughout the continent.

Tears streamed down her face.

"Love means never having to say you're sorry."

The camera held the close-up for a few seconds. "Cut!" yelled Arthur Hiller. "Ali," he said, "don't rush it. Be a little more halting. Take two!"

She did it again, then again. Take after take. Every time the tears were real. Every time she was more convincing.

"Cut!" said Hiller. "That's it. We've got it! Wonderful, Ali. You had *me* in tears."

She smothered me with kisses. "Evans, did you like it? The tears were for *you!*" My eyes swelled, knowing I was the luckiest man in the world.

The heat in Ali's second-rate hotel didn't work. The Celtics played their only bad game of the season in the Boston Garden. The bar where we shared an Irish coffee belonged in the slums of Dublin, yet that Thanksgiving weekend in Boston with Ali is what magic is all about. Letters upon letters followed. Every morning I would awaken, have breakfast and there waiting for me would be a handwritten letter of love from Miss Love Story.

"Erich, everyone thinks it's fluff. Write a novel. I'll get it published. It shouldn't take you longer than a week."

It took Erich Segal only a little more than a month to write *Love Story* the book. What took longer was to persuade a legitimate publisher to print it. Finally Gene Young, an editor at Harper and Row, offered to do it as a Valentine's Day throwaway, with a first printing of 6,000. That was like throwing it away before it had the chance to be a throwaway. I countered with an offer of $25,000 in promotion money if Harper would come out with 25,000 copies.

The throwaway became a runaway. Not only in America but all over the world, *Love Story* the book went to the top of the best-seller lists and stayed there all through 1970. When the film opened at Christmas, Erich Segal's 131-page novella was still number one on both the hardcover and paperback lists—something that's never happened before or since in motion picture history.

When *Love Story* the film moved locations from Cambridge to New York late in 1969, I flew to be with Ali. We spent our first Christmas and New Year's Eve at the Sherry-Netherland Hotel, ordering in the most romantic food in the world—chilled vodka with miniature baked potato shells stuffed with Beluga caviar, topped with crème fraîche. Though not realizing it at the time, it was by far the most romantic holiday of my life. Camelot was ours; at least I thought it was.

The only seeming friction was her prize possession Grounds, a Scottish terrier, her closest confidant and her Hope diamond. Her diamond, however, had a flaw—a crack in his bowels.

Loving animals, but never believing in indoor pets, it was tough to smile after opening the door to a suite that smelled more like a kennel than a boudoir. Army maneuvers were easier than getting from the bed to the door without needing a new pair of shoes. A small price to pay for the luxury of being with the most extraordinary woman of my life, who seemed to love me, by far, more than any other woman I had ever met. Her lethal embrace, her extraordinary affection, love, affirmation, fetching femininity, caress to family and friends, gave me an adrenaline I never thought I had, to break barriers I never thought could be broken. Few people ever touch Camelot in their lives. Was it a dream?

When *Love Story* wrapped in the middle of January, Ali moved back to Woodland, this time as Mrs. Evans. I was nice enough to give her one half of one closet. Her entire wardrobe consisted of scarves to use as turbans, embroidered tablecloths used for wraparound skirts, etc.—naturally, all second-, third-, and fourthhand. Yet, for years to come, her singular style fascinated the world; each year she was on the best dressed list. Style, unlike fashion, cannot be bought nor taught. You either have it or you don't.

Butler, chauffeur, personal maid, tennis pro, masseuse, cascading pool, and two thousand rosebushes surrounded my lady fair.

"This is all much too much for me, Evans."

Having lived through this line before, I laughed. "You'll get used to it."

We'd been home a week when her agent called. An offer, $100,000 net after taxes and agents' commissions, to lend her name to a thirty-second commercial for Love Beauty Cosmetics that would play only outside of America. She turned them down flat.

"Prostitute myself? No way."

"You're wrong, Ali. Think of your parents. Put the money away for them."

Adamant as her initial instincts were, I was equally adamant for her to bank the first big green that was ever offered to her. Finally acquiescing, for thirty seconds she was the Love Cosmetic Girl. The moment the 100 Gs arrived, both of us drove to City National Bank and deposited it, then went to the Bistro for lunch. We toasted the breaking of her virginity into the six-figure world. The interest each month would go to her parents. For laughs, our private phrase was "a dowry in reverse."

A Gulf + Western directors meeting was called to take place in my office—real Gunfight at the O.K. Corral time. Before it convened, I told my secretaries, "If Nixon calls, no interruptions. Clear?"

Then I opened the door to my room of gloom. The agenda was not what films to make, but what date the studio was to close. Everyone was suffering; all the majors were in the red. "Bluhdorn's Folly" was getting too much attention. Paramount was less than 5 percent of Gulf + Western's revenue, but was responsible for 95 percent of its publicity—all bad.

"We're in the oil and gas business and nobody knows it," said one of G+W's redneck directors. "It's girls, parties, premieres, movies; that's the business they think we're in. Even that would be okay, but not only have I not met a girl, I haven't been invited to one party, nor seen one movie. The only thing I get is flack."

"If we're gonna gamble, I'd rather go to Vegas," said another board member. "You only have the dice to deal with there."

Their held-back steam? Directed at only one person—me! The door opened; my secretary walked in, interrupting everyone. Is she out of her fuckin' mind? Before I could explode, a note was in my hand: "Grounds killed. Run over. Ali's out. Doesn't know yet."

While they're telling me they're rubbing out the studio, my wife's dog gets rubbed out. The little mutt was far more important to the survival of our marriage than the studio. I staggered over to Bluhdorn, showed him the note. Quickly, he thumbed me out. Driven back to my house in a trance, I was greeted by Tollie Mae.

"She ain't home, Mr. E. She's takin' some pictures with some long-haired weirdos. That dog of hers been dead over an hour."

I knew Tollie was getting her nuts off telling me. She "don't like no agin' hippie around, invadin' her territory," said Tollie.

A voice rang out. "Grounds . . . Grounds . . ."

Christ, Ali's home.

"Evans. What are you doing here? Did they fire you?"

"Grounds is dead."

She started to tremble, threw herself on the bed. I lay down next to her, cradling her in my arms.

An hour or two must have passed when the doorbell rang. There stood Charlie Bluhdorn. He was holding what looked like a little gray powder puff. It was a puppy. A brand-new Scottish terrier.

"This is for Ali."

"The starched collars?"

"They'll wait. Where's Ali?"

Like a delivery boy, there stood Mr. Tough Tycoon holding a little powder-puff puppy. Not waiting for me, he walked directly into the room where Ali was crying. The vision of seeing Charlie embrace Ali, handing this little puppy over to her, will stick in my memory till

Alzheimer's takes over. The studio crumbling, on the brink of bankruptcy, but who the fuck cared? There we sat watching our *Love Story* girl, tickling her new little powder-puff terrier.

"Where did you get the little mutt?" I asked him.

"From a kennel near Oxnard."

"Who'd you send?"

"Me. Who else could I trust?"

That's a man, no movie star, a real leading man.

Charlie, Stanley, and I talked the directors into a stay of execution on the condition that we run the production business from small offices wherever we could find them. The lot would become a rental facility for anyone who would pay the two bucks. A few weeks later, we found a suite of offices on Cañon Drive in Beverly Hills. It was barely big enough to accommodate a half dozen executives. From that little hole in the wall, not only did we become number one in the business, but the most historic successes in Paramount's history were conceived there, in a cubicle not fit for a barbershop.

Now the Gunfight at the O.K. Corral was taking place at Woodland. The stars weren't Kirk Douglas and Burt Lancaster, but the new Mrs. Evans and Mammy Tollie Mae.

"Sorry, Mr. E., but I'm not allowin' no agin' hippie cookin' in my kitchen."

Is she crazy, telling my new wife she can't come into the kitchen? She was, she meant it. It was either Tollie Mae or Ali. Till this day, I think Tollie Mae thought she'd win out.

A sad good-bye. Tollie Mae was a bachelor's lady no more.

"Bottom line—it's unreleasable."

Dinner was ready, our guests were there, I'd just arrived back from the studio having seen the first cut of our baby—a mongoloid. I promised myself I wouldn't, but I couldn't hold it back; I begged off on dinner, closed the door to my bedroom, and buried my face in a pillow.

Rushing in behind me, Ali put her hands through my hair. "Evans, you always exaggerate."

My face still in the pillow, I just shook my head, "Just two pretty faces, Ali. No plot, holes as big as the Boulder Dam." I turned over facing her. "It never fails, damn it. The fuckin' dailies always fool you. I'm sorry baby."

"You'll fix it, you always do." She smiled, kissed me. "That's why you're my Evans. You haven't slept more than ten hours all week. Get under the covers. I'll take care of your guests."

If I had one tenth the brains she thought I had, I'd have owned Paramount, not be working for it.

I jolted out of a deep sleep at three in the morning.

"Ali, I've got it. I've got it! I know how to fix it, but I don't have the bread, can't get another dime from G+W. I think they'd like me to fall on my ass. *Fuck!* How do I get some quick green?"

Ali's nude body embraced me as she whispered in my ear, "Who was the guy who told me 'when your back's against the wall, the impossible becomes possible'?"

As soon as I could, I got on the horn with Arthur Hiller; Dick Kratina, the cinematographer; his camera operator; and Ryan O'Neal. Three hours later we were all in my projection room at my home.

"We're on top of two mountains, fellas. One is living hell and the other is an oasis in the sky. There's just a hundred feet separating the two of them. How do we get from living hell to the oasis? We gotta try." I looked at my watch. "It's ten A.M. March 23. The bad news is that it ain't there. Now the good news is, it's there to be had. There's not a fuckin' dime in the budget. To make it worse, I can't let the suits know the deep shit we're in. Arthur, if they saw what we had on screen, you'd be shooting "Battery Park," not *Plaza Suite* next month."

A bit of color left the maestro's face.

"Ryan, if they offer you the third lead in a TV series, take it."

Looking to the other guys in the room, I continued. "Am I exaggerating? Uh-uh. It's an underplay. If we have to hijack the cameras, grow beards, get back to Boston, sneak in. We're missing silence, bike rides, car rides, running through the park together. The good part is it's all silent. We don't have to bring sound with us. The bad part is, not only do we not have money for plane fares, we can't let anybody—I mean anybody—know we're doing it. If the unions find out, they'll close the studio down. I'm gonna have my pal Gary Chazan buy the tickets on two different planes. The fares and hotels are on me, not on the company. Your agents can't know; if you trust your wives, you can tell them, but no one else. I'm putting my job on the line doing this. Not because I'm a martyr, not because my bride's in the film, but because we have a shot at grabbing the brass ring."

On separate planes they traveled, secretly they worked, together they conquered. This was no bullshit labor of love, rather selfish survival that turned into career explosions with gushers of green for everyone but me and Ali.

April 1 was one of the six days my Green Berets were secretly shooting away. It was also Ali's birthday. So not to blow their cover, I couldn't be with my bride to celebrate. Perverse, but it was the beginning of an M.O. that destroyed what was to be "forever." Whether it be a birthday, an anniversary, a holiday, or the birth of my kid, I was never there to share the extraordinary moments that make two people inseparable.

Ali and I spent a belated honeymoon at Tres Viedas in Acapulco— sun, swimming, sailing, and conceiving our only lasting production, Joshua. If only we'd taken more vacations.

A Man and a Woman, directed by the auteur Claude Lelouch, was possibly the only French film of its time that the entire world rushed to embrace. Few words were spoken. Silence, touch, and the brilliance of their score made for magical moments. Francis Lai was the genius behind the music. Taking his soundtrack, I temporarily mixed them to *Love Story*—and it was magic. But Francis Lai was unavailable.

No was never a word I accepted. My ace? A great friend, Alain Delon, who at the time was the number one star around the world (except in the U.S.). In France, he was close to God. Muscle? Schwarzenegger style. Poor Francis Lai. He had no choice—*Love Story* was now his to do.

Off Ali and I went to the Hotel du Cap in Antibes. She was pregnant, while I spent day after day working with Lai, thinking of the themes that could make *Love Story* an American *Man and a Woman.* He couldn't speak a word of English and I couldn't speak a word of French. The best way to work. The reluctant debutante won the Academy Award for his score. Not bad for a guy who didn't want to dance.

The fuckin' phone again. Luigi Lurasci, our top production honcho in Italy, was on the line about *The Red Tent,* a film Paramount was doing as a "Bluhdorn favor" (he was pals with its producer, Franco Cristaldi).

"We're in deep shit," Luigi said in broken English. "It could sink the company. It doesn't hold up. Can't cut it together. It's a mess. It makes no sense. Evans, we need you on the double. Tomorrow's too late."

I said to Ali, "Fuck 'em all, I'm not going. They fucked us on your birthday. They fucked us on my big four-oh. Instead of us celebrating it together, I was a carrier pigeon off to Rome tryin' to fix another Bluhdorn spaghetti western. Saint Peter couldn't have fixed that piece of shit. Well, I've had it—I'm tired of being called in to fix other people's mistakes. These fuckin' Italian hybrid flicks don't work in America. Never did, never will. It's one big jerk-off. Let some one else be the carrier pigeon. It's our first anniversary, baby, and we're celebrating it together. No half-assed flick is gonna rain on our parade."

Interrupting me, Ali said, "Shhh . . . Evans, you're the only one who can save it."

"It'll be a piece of shit either way."

"Uh-uh, give it the Evans touch. Do it for me."

"Instead of the head of a studio I feel like a Western Union delivery boy."

"You don't get it, Evans," kissing me all over my face. "Everyone knew you didn't want to make it. Now they're calling on you to save it. I'm so proud of you." Putting her finger to my lips, not letting me answer, "For me . . . please."

Awaiting me in Rome was a hand-painted sepia-colored, pictorial book. Inside were pressed daisies, poems, drawings, and quotes from Thoreau to Fitzgerald, a hundred pages lay between its covers. A romantic chronology of our first year together. A cherub was drawn on the last page, along with a circle in which was written: "Happy First Anniversary . . . My love forever . . . MacGroo."

Reading and rereading her written thoughts, I could only think what a lucky motherfucker I was. "Don't press your luck, Evans," I told myself. Yet, as every gambler does, pressing your luck is what it's all about.

Masochistically, fourteen hours day into night, for twelve straight days, there sat Mandrake trying to mold chicken salad from chicken-shit. Staving off a $15 million disaster, scene by scene I restructured the canvas. Who knows? With a little bit of luck, maybe it'll work. Get part of our investment back. (It eventually did! Its international receipts gave us our investment plus. I got a pat on the back.)

I was so fuckin' angry with myself for fucking up my priorities that I had to get my nuts off some way.

"Close down all European production," I announced. "It's a pain in the ass and a pain in the pocket." I had only one major scene to restructure when my assistant, Renzo, summoned me to the phone. "Tell 'em to call me back in two hours. I've got to make this drowning scene work."

Within five minutes the phone rang again. There was Renzo grabbing my arm. "Life or death, Roberto—*telephono.*"

It was my stockbroker, Stanley Garfinkle.

"What the fuck are you bothering me here for, Stanley?"

"Evans, you got a drought problem—cash."

"Is that all? Call me back in a couple of hours, will ya? I'm in the middle of reediting a scene that will save Sean Connery from drowning—"

"You're the one who's drowning. If I don't get $112,000 tomorrow by ten A.M., you're wiped out. Haven't you read the papers? It's the worst drop the market's had since 'twenty-nine."

I was too embarrassed to tell him I hadn't looked at a paper in more than a week.

"You schmuck. Why don't you have the brains of your brother? He doesn't own one stock on margin."

"Stanley, I don't have the bread. I'm cutting a picture. Can't it wait a few days?"

"By ten-oh-one tomorrow morning, without a check, you're worth zero."

"What the fuck am I supposed to do?"

"Ask Sean Connery. You're saving him from drowning."

There was one person I could call who had the money. My flower-child bride herself. She had 100 Gs in the bank, in cash. The first real hunk of green in her life. I can't, I can't ask her. What kind of fuckin' fraud you are you anyway, Evans? Chauffeurs, servants, private planes, sixteen-room palatial home and for an anniversary gift, I'm takin' her entire savings to pay a margin call.

Ya gotta do what ya gotta do. I picked up the phone and dialed my pregnant bride. She cut me off before I could even finish my story of woe.

"Bob, quickly, give me the name and address of where the money has to be. We can't afford to have it arrive there late."

Months later, Ali and I had the biggest fight of our relationship. I wrote a check to her for the money I borrowed. She tore it up. I wrote another. She tore it up.

Writing my third check, I looked at her. "If you don't take it and put it in the bank, I'm divorcing you. It ain't a joke; it's pride."

She believed me. She took it.

"There's a big problem, Evans. The board of directors want out. Get rid of Paramount, sell it, can't afford it. It's turning cash flow into a cash drought. They've had it. They want me out too, out of show business, get back to what I do best—making money, not movies."

The coldest November day in New York's memory was a perfect backdrop for commiserating with Charlie Bluhdorn. His spirits matched his complexion—green. He looked the way he felt—beaten.

"You don't deserve the heat, Charlie. Sell the fuckin' company." I got up, walked to the window. "They don't deserve you either."

I knew he was looking for a boost. He deserved it; he deserved more, but he never seemed to get it.

"Fuck 'em, Charlie. Stall. With your eyes closed you can buy another quarter. Give us one more shot at the table." No reaction. I walked over to the couch and for the first time took him by both arms and shook him.

"Charlie, that's all we need. We're gonna throw naturals with *Love Story.* Big green ones."

"You're crazy, Evans. You've always been crazy." Ah, but a smile. "I suppose that's why I love you. Your head, Evans, where is it? We need a miracle, not a movie."

Walking down Fifth Avenue toward the Sherry-Netherland, Charlie was somber.

"The board's already decided. They called an emergency meeting a week from tomorrow. Damage control. Protect the stock."

Walking through the revolving doors of the Sherry, I had a kamikaze flash. "Give me a half hour with the board, Charlie, a half hour."

Finally a laugh—a big one. "Evans, the one person they don't want to see is you."

"Yeah, that's why I want to see them. You better hope it works or you're gonna have to teach the crazy one the coffee business."

"You're crazy, Evans."

Giving him a good-bye embrace, "Yes, but crazy good. I've got one ace in my hand, Charlie—*Love Story*—gonna build a hand around it."

Charlie looked at me as if I was really crazy. *"Love Story,* ace, what are you talking about? I don't want to hear. You've caused me enough *tsuris."*

It wasn't good-bye time yet. Rather than go up the elevator to my suite, I took Charlie by the arm and continued through the revolving door back outside and stood under the awning.

"Who told me only losers take no for an answer?"

Shaking his head, Charlie couldn't help saying, "I knew I shouldn't have seen you today. It's up to Marty."

The next morning I was in Los Angeles. My first call was to Marty Davis. He'd already spoken with Bluhdorn. He seemed unfavorably disposed, but said he'd go over it with Stanley Jaffe. The next day Davis called me. He and Stanley had discussed it at great length. Colder than any turndown, he gave me an affirmative nod.

"You've got a half hour immediately following the luncheon, next Monday, two thirty, at the boardroom. Buy a one-way ticket."

Down went the phone. Why does everyone slam the phone in my ear?

Knowing his personality, his dry-ice affirmation was what I wanted. The more Marty liked something, the less he showed it. For the rest of the week Stanley and I planned a little show business surprise for our starch collared partners in zinc, oil, and gas. Peter Bart asked Mike Nichols for an afternoon of his time to film a presentation for his boss to deliver to the board of directors at Gulf + Western.

"Need you, Mike," said Peter. "We've got a lousy actor, but a helluva presenter."

Mike borrowed a set from "The Young Lawyers," a television series they were shooting at the studio. At last, I was working with a great director. Where were you ten years ago when I really needed you? Instead of spreading my legs for the collars, I'd be giving Beatty and Redford a run for their money. Without ever knowing it, Nichols saved Paramount from being buried. A belated thanks, Mike.

I spent the next few days editing what Mike had shot, interjecting various scenes from many pictures that were in production at the time. Fully aware that any product reel, no matter how tempting, would not change an already guilty verdict to innocent, I had another ace. Stanley and Marty wanted to know what I was preparing.

"Trust me," I told them. They didn't.

"Hey fellas, I've got less than a week before I'm thrown out. If it doesn't work, Marty, *you* can open the window."

"I will."

"If it works, will ya kiss me?"

Stanley burst out laughing. Marty again slammed the phone down in my ear. In an hour Stanley called back.

"You sure you know what you're doing?"

"Nope."

By Sunday at 6:00 P.M., I finished the last edit of Mike's footage and caught the red-eye into New York. No luggage, but a can of film under my arm. Not that Paramount was playing it tight, but the orders were clear—no hotel room for me. From a double-exposure corner suite at the Sherry to walking the streets and breakfast at the Plaza Hotel alone. At least they had nice johns downstairs, so I could wash up and make myself look presentable for the axe to fall.

When I entered the board of directors' anteroom, a secretary immediately got up and went into the boardroom. Out came Marty Davis with a warm embrace.

"Couldn't get a haircut, huh?" he said, shaking his head. "You look like a Woodstock reject." Without cracking a smile, "Charm your way out of this one." He opened the door. I walked in.

Before me sat sixteen of America's finest nonsmilers. Not one of them looked at me. Rather all sixteen looked through me.

"Gentlemen . . . I apologize for not being better dressed, but when you've got a one-way ticket and no hotel, it ain't that easy to keep up with the style of the room."

A laugh? Not a crack. Not even the white of a tooth in sight. Without a word, I slowly eyed everyone in the room. From under my arm I held up the film can.

"Call it a twenty-minute good-bye. Put it together last week. I asked Mr. Davis for permission to show it to you before I get out of your hair. Then I'll look for the longest, quietest beach I can."

Still not the white of a tooth. Maybe they left their dentures at home. The hanging judges, all sixteen of them, reluctantly adjourned to the small screening room adjacent to the board of directors' suite. Charlie, Marty, and Stanley were behind them. Quickly, I hopped into the projection booth and handed Al Lo Presti the reel.

"Give it a 'Hail Mary,' Alfonso, then give me one too. Look through the booth. When I sit, start it."

"You got it, boss."

The lights slowly went down, the curtains parted, and on the screen, a wood-paneled door opened. An extraordinarily large wood-paneled office. A tan well-groomed young man walks through the door, looks around the office, and then sits on top of a desk—me!

Good afternoon. My name is Robert Evans and I'm Senior Vice President of Paramount Pictures. My job at Paramount is to oversee our productions around the world. These past few years have been rough for Hollywood. We've made a lot of mistakes. Some people have learned from them and some people haven't. We have.

By the way, this is not my office. We tried to shoot it in my office. There was one problem—my office was too small to get even one camera in.

I was left with little choice, so I'm here at the studio borrowing a set from "The Young Lawyers" and that's where we are now. As a matter of fact, I don't even have an office at the studio anymore. Last year we packed up our gear, cut down our staff, tightened our belts, moved into small offices, little offices, in Beverly Hills. The money we spend is not going to be on extravagances. The money we spend is going to be on the screen. And speaking of the screen, well, that's the reason we're here today.

I'd like to have the opportunity to show you some of our product for next year. I'm going to show it to you in its roughest state. There are going to be disconnected scenes from several pictures. But I think it's going to give you a feeling of our trend for movies in the seventies.

We then gave the starched shirts a taste of Hollywood, unveiling carefully selected scenes from *Harold and Maude, A New Leaf, Plaza Suite,* and *The Conformist* for their eyes to feast upon.

Back to me. Mike's camera slowly panned to an extreme close-up. I gave the best and most *important* fuckin' performance of my acting career. Till this day, it still bugs me. Why didn't I meet Mike Nichols ten years earlier? "I could have been a contender."

But right now we're approaching Christmas and Paramount's Christmas gift to the world is . . . Love Story. Love Story opens all over America on Christmas Day. Love Story is a strange phenome-

non, it's the first time in motion picture history that a picture is being released while the book is still the number one book in the nation. I shouldn't say that. It's the number one book in the world. It's the first time in literary history that a book has been number one in the United States, France, England, Sweden, or for that matter whatever country the book has been published in. I think Love Story is going to start a new trend in movies; a trend toward the romantic, toward love, toward people, toward telling a story about how it feels rather than where it's at. I think Love Story is going to bring the people back to the theater in droves.

I think we at Paramount look at ourselves as trendsetters rather than trend followers. I could go for an hour and tell you about twenty or thirty projects that are in various stages of development and bore you with it. So I won't.

But I want to bring up one project, and that's The Godfather. I bring it up for several reasons—one, that it's starting production next month; two, that it's going to be our next Christmas's picture; and three, to bring up once the similarity between The Godfather and Love Story, which are the two biggest books of the last decade. Paramount owns them both.

(The camera now so close, my face fills the entire screen.)

But Paramount more than just owns them both. We didn't sit back in our plush chairs and write a check out for a million or a million and a half for the two most important books of this last decade. We developed both of these books. If it weren't for Paramount, the book Love Story would have never been written. If it weren't for Paramount, The Godfather would have never been written. Because we were in there in the beginning, spurring the writers on, working closely with them, to make these books the best-sellers they are . . . and the great movies we know they're going to be.

We at Paramount look at ourselves, not as passive backers of films, but as a creative force unto ourselves.

(Smiling at the camera now, I looked at my sixteen hanging judges as if we were all part of a big happy family.)

Gentlemen, one thing I promise you—Christmas of '69 will be very special throughout the world.

(With Mike's direction, I then took a long, thoughtful pause.)

Paramount's gift—Love Story—*will make it that. It's what life and love and Christmas is all about.*

(Another Nichols-rehearsed pause.)

Without you, Love Story *never would have been made. Without you,* The Godfather *would never have gotten to the screen there for the world to enjoy.*

(Looking now straight into the camera . . . silently counting . . . one . . . two . . . three . . .)

Thank you.

The screen went to black. The curtains closed. The lights heightened. Not a sound. A tap on my shoulder; it was Marty. "Wait in the boardroom."

Ten minutes later, Davis walked in. "Forget the haircut."

"Fired, huh?"

"Uh-uh. You're even a bigger fraud then I thought."

No kiss on the lips, but a hug. From Davis, that was more than an engagement ring, it was the gold band itself. Then a typical Davis zinger. "Evans, the beach, forget it. You don't need a tan. You need *mazel.*"

By thirty seconds I made the 5:00 TWA plane back to L.A. Landing, I rushed to the phone to call Stanley. His wife answered.

"Stanley is already asleep," she said.

"Awaken him please."

"Bob, you know Stanley."

"Please."

He picked up the phone. Was he angry that I awakened him? I don't think so. For five minutes the two of us laughed and laughed and laughed. He from a deep sleep, me from the airport. We never said a word, both of us hung up the phone at the same time laughing.

Back at Woodland, I realized that only twenty-four hours had passed since I had come and gone. But Paramount was now on the come, rather than gone.

By the time I arrived home, Ali was already asleep. Lying beside her in bed, I looked at her—then looked at her again. Incredible! Ripley wouldn't buy it. Here beside me was this flower child whose crooked-toothed smile on the screen was the one chance Paramount had for survival. The brilliant minds, sharpened pencils, international sales offices around the world, all bullshit. It came down to the power of a crooked-toothed smile.

Everything was building toward *Love Story*'s premiere in New York. The swell had begun. Ali was to be interviewed at length in New York by Mary Cronin for *Time* magazine's first cover of 1971. Ed Sullivan was setting aside the last segment of his show for Ali to sit on a chair, empty stage and all, to read poetry of Christmas, of love, of family. Every top magazine, TV show, and newspaper was desperate to have Ali MacGraw as their top story.

Her obstetrician told her that the seventh month of her pregnancy was the most dangerous. Too late to abort, too early for birth, and it is the month where it is far wiser to be cautious than cavalier.

How I remember his words: "If it were my child, especially with all the attendant pressures surrounding your life, Mrs. Evans, I would stay right at home."

Would you say my priorities were fucked up? I laughed at the doctor's caution.

"Ali, if I'd have listened to doctors, I'd have been under the knife three times by now and I'm still a virgin. Surgeons like to cut, lawyers like to litigate, and obstetricians like to scare the shit out of you."

"Evans, you're the boss."

Off to the Big Apple we went, Ali having no idea that four thousand jobs, including mine, were on hold awaiting the outcome of a crooked-toothed smile on the screen. What a smash she was on "The Ed Sullivan Show." Her poetry of Christmas love was music to the ears. Wherever we went we heard it over and over again. The next evening *Time*'s editor-in-chief, Henry Gruenwald, gave a most elite soirée for his cover girl of the year. How magical were the days and nights, especially sharing the feel of our little bambino kicking inside her tummy.

On December 16, 1970, *Love Story* had its world premiere at Loew's State in New York, opening nine days later on Christmas Day to spread love to every city in America. That rainy night, Ali and I slipped through the side door of the Sherry and into the limo. Outside Loew's State, an army of policemen went into assault position to keep the crowds away from her. For a woman who was seven months pregnant, it was terrifying.

The lights went down. Francis Lai's haunting piano and strings started up. Ryan O'Neal, alone and bereft in snowy Central Park, said in voice-over, "What can you say about a twenty-five-year-old girl who died?"

Only the title appeared—there were no further opening credits. During the first hour the silence was such that a single cough was an intrusion. Then seeping slowly through the theater, a most peculiar sound began. All I could see was white. Cocaine? No—Kleenex! By the time the end credits began to roll the entire theater was one white flag of surrender.

Stanley Jaffe arranged a small post-premiere party at the Hippopotamus Club. It wasn't really a party, it was a love feast. Everyone there felt just a bit closer to one another as Francis Lai's music from the film filled the room. Me, I felt like Casanova. The most extraordinary lady in the world on my arm and in her belly a little Evans to be.

At the bar, Ryan rushed over. "I know if it weren't for you I wouldn't have gotten the part. I owe you my career, pal." We embraced. With a glass of champagne, we toasted to it.

Ali's hand grabbed my arm. Her face ghostly. "I'm starting to hemorrhage, Evans."

With blood starting to stream down her legs, I rushed her into the waiting limo.

I told the driver, "Keep your hand on the horn, don't stop for lights and don't argue, you're covered." Within seven minutes we were in the emergency room of Doctors Hospital.

Suddenly, a night of triumph had turned into a night of terror. Though past midnight, my sister's obstetrician, Dr. Davids, raced to Ali's bedside. I paced the corridor, waiting, waiting, a half hour, an hour. A very sober doctor slowly approached me. Before he said a word, I began to cry.

"Ali will be OK"—his head down—"the baby, I don't know."

I started to shake, hyperventilate. The doctor grabbed me, and slapped me across the face, thinking I was possibly going into seizure. His voice low. "Snap out of it. You've got to be strong. Strong for her."

Instead, I fell apart. He had no way of knowing the self-contempt I harbored for not paying heed to her obstetrician. He found a room down the hall and gave me a sedative; it must have been a helluva strong one because it put me out for a couple of hours. The sun was coming up. I made it to the john, threw cold water over my face, looked at myself in the mirror, turned and put my fist through the wooden door. My hand was a pool of blood. Strange, I didn't even feel the pain.

The nurse came into my little cubicle. "Ali's awake now."

Wrapping a towel around my bleeding hand, I walked into her room. Immediately her eyes went to my hand. In typical MacGraw fashion.

"Get it caught in a phone booth?"

"Yeah!" That was all the time we had.

Two nurses immediately came in and wheeled her into the emergency room. Again the corridors became my pacing track. Dr. Davids approached me again. Again, no smile.

"Unless the bleeding stops, she's going to have to undergo a premature cesarean." He shook his head. "Seventh month, that's the tough one to get by."

Quickly the doctor disappeared into the emergency room. My secretary was there by now. Snapping back into reality.

"Call Ryan at the Warwick. Fill him in on Ali's condition. Tell him he'll have to cover for her at the premiere. Sumner Redstone, Paramount's biggest customer, is giving a charity premiere honoring Harvard University at his theater in Boston. Call Stanley, give him an update on Ali's condition." I quickly walked away, into the men's room and again burst into tears. Regaining my composure, I began to pace the corridor floor.

My secretary stopped me. "Mr. Evans, I just spoke with Mr. O'Neal. He said he won't go unless Ali goes."

Every attendants' head jumped up as I screamed out, "Is he crazy? Does he know the shape she's in? She could die!"

Her voice now quivering, "I told him that, Mr. Evans."

"Get him on the phone."

Thinking he misunderstood, I contained my temper. "Ryan, it's not good. Ali's in bad shape." I began to choke. "The kid may not make it." There was no reaction on the other end. "Cover for me, will ya?" I stuttered.

"If she goes, I go. Otherwise I stay."

For an instant, I thought it was the Devil himself paying me back. Less than twelve hours earlier the same guy was telling me how he owed his career to me.

"Ryan, maybe you didn't hear me right. Ali, she's in bad shape, real bad." I began to cry. "She could lose the baby. You hear me?"

"I heard you." He heard my crying as well. "If she doesn't go, I don't go, got it? Hey, I don't own any of the movie, but she does."

He never sent flowers. He never called to see if she or the baby survived.

The nurses were getting Ali ready for the cesarean when miraculously the bleeding stopped. This time I obeyed doctor's orders, and they were strict. Ali had to have complete bed rest. A day, a week, a month, bedpan and all, on her back until "pop goes the weasel."

When word got out of her near fatal mishap, the Sherry had to put another operator on just to fend off the calls. It seemed like half the world were on the call-sheets, but under *O* there was no O'Neal.

Love Story didn't open, it exploded, embracing great reviews from Vincent Canby of *The New York Times* and Charles Champlin of the *Los Angeles Times,* to *Time* magazine itself. Bluhdorn was so ecstatic over the notices, especially Canby's *New York Times* review, that he ordered it reprinted in its entirety in half of the newspapers around the country. What a come shot.

Like the Three Musketeers, Bluhdorn, Jaffe, and I drove, from theater to theater. We stood behind the last row. It was magic. By the final scene, the entire audience turned into one big Kleenex.

Christmas Eve now eight days away, I planned a bit of a surprise for my emotional mentor, the Austrian Horatio Alger. From 7:00 P.M. to 7:00 A.M., twelve hours a night for eight straight nights, Al Lo Presti and crew rearranged the venetian blinds on twelve floors of the new Gulf + Western building.

It was Christmas Eve. There was Ali lying in bed, back at the Sherry-Netherland. I invited Charlie over to join us for a toast of thanks. He arrived wearing a hand-me-down herringbone overcoat, looking like a refugee just released from Ellis Island. Quickly he walked into the bedroom where my pregnant lady lay in bed. Little did she know Charlie's Christmas kiss on the cheek was far from fatherly. He was kissing the cheek that saved "the mountain." Two ginger beers later, he got up to leave.

"I'll walk you home, boss."

Again, Charlie gave a kiss to his "flower-child savior" as she waited for a little Evans to pop. Excusing myself to the john, I rushed to the phone, directly dialing magic man Lo Presti, who was on standby anxiously awaiting.

"Count to a hundred, then pull the switch."

"You got it, boss."

Down the elevator and out the revolving doors we went. Snow falling heavily in our face, I pointed west to Charlie. Directly parallel, across the park, was the new Gulf + Western building, standing in the snow like no other building in the world. Twelve stories high, magically backlit, the venetian blinds lit up one third of the entire building with two words: "Love Story."

There he stood. The industrial magnate seeing Santa Claus for the first time. Tears began rolling down his face. He looked at me. Hardly audible he mumbled, "America. Imagine, twelve years ago I was walking the streets selling typewriters door to door. . . ." He threw his arms around me. "That's my building!"

Suddenly he was my son, not my boss. "It's the first real Christmas I've ever had, Evans."

"From me to you, Charlie." Then, pointing back to the building, I said, "Look. 'The Miracle on Fifty-ninth Street.' "

There we stood, tycoon and dreamer, two men standing on Fifty-ninth Street and Fifth Avenue, heavy snow all but covering us, living out what Christmas is all about.

On Christmas weekend, largely from young couples and families, *Love Story* grossed more than any film in history at that time. "It has only begun to bring in the money, but it has already altered the 'new' Hollywood beyond ready recognition," *Time* said in its January 11, 1971, cover story on Ali.

Pulling off the impossible is something you don't try twice. Not if you enjoy breathing. Was I riding high? You bet. Were my pockets still on empty? You bet. But who the fuck cared! No one was wealthier than Evans; I even smiled in my sleep, dreaming of those shocked faces, with their starched collars, of the boardroom stiffs. Sorry, fellas, one hit and you're back on top. That's show biz! Hate to tell ya, but there ain't gonna be no grave diggin'. Not at Paramount. Makin' magic for the livin' is our future. Got it? Hang on if you want or get outta my way. It's the 1970s and we're travelin' one way—straight to the top!

The doctor told Ali and me our bambino wasn't to hatch until mid-February. Now with the studio to run and plenty of problems with the casting of *The Godfather,* I rationalized to myself and Ali that it would be wise to spend a good part of January back at the studio protecting the new breath of freedom we were just granted.

Well, the doctors were a little off. Instead of holding Ali's hand as she was wheeled into the maternity ward in mid-January, I was in a casting session with Francis Coppola. Instead of watching my baby say hello to the world, I was letting Coppola know he was about to say good-bye to *The Godfather.* My brother, Charles, was awakened in the middle of the night and rushed my wife to the hospital, where, at 5:00 in the morning, little Joshua appeared. I missed what every man has told me is the highest high in a man's life.

Within twenty-four hours, I was looking into a room filled with incubators. Brought to the window was my little premature runt. After three days, the family snuck out the back exit of the hospital and up the back entrance of the Sherry-Netherland Hotel to avoid the mob of paparazzi. It would remain our temporary home until we moved back to Woodland in Beverly Hills.

The switchboard at the Sherry again had to put on an extra operator to screen calls. Like a schmuck, I picked up the one bad one. The voice on the other end made John Gotti sound like a soprano: "Take some advice. We don't want to break your pretty face, hurt your newborn. Get the fuck outta town. Don't shoot no movie about the family here. Got it?"

Never being scared of a threat, "Fuck you, mister. If you got any problems, take it up with the producer, Al Ruddy."

A silence. Slowly, "Listen carefully, motherfucker. I ain't gonna say it again. When you wanna kill a snake, pretty boy, there's only one way to do it—*you go for its head.*"

Click.

Enter Sidney Korshak.

We flew to London to meet the Queen Mother for the Royal Command Performance of *Love Story*. We checked into the Connaught with four hours to get ready. Ali, still a bit plump from Joshua's birth, had had her good friend Halston make a special dress. A simple black silk sheath that was supposed to enhance her new, temporary curves. When Ali put it on, there were two problems: her two breasts—each fell out one side of the dress. Great for a stripper, but not suitable for the royals.

We had forty-five minutes to get dressed and three choices to pick from—jeans and a T-shirt; the chambermaid's black dress with matching black shoes; or a secondhand, tie-dyed pantsuit, colored brown with white and yellow flowers, perfectly matched with black shoes and black gloves.

The limo was downstairs by now. If I showed one half my anger, Ali would burst into tears and wouldn't make it at all.

"You look beautiful, MacGroo. You'll start a new style," I said, as we nervously entered the limo.

Though it's protocol to wear gloves when you meet British royalty, I just couldn't do it to her. Better dirty fingernails than black gloves with a brown tie-dyed pantsuit.

In Leicester Square, the Queen Mum and Princess Margaret held their hands out for us and every other movie star in town before the premiere. Ali extended her bare fingers and turned on the charm. Nobody sniffed.

All of us stood in a receiving line as Lord Somebody introduced us, one by one, to Her Majesty and her younger daughter. It was a hell of a thrill, abruptly ending when the lovely princess shook my hand.

"Tony saw *Love Story* in New York." Tony was Lord Snowdon, her then husband. "Hated it."

"Fuck you too," I said to myself, smiling back.

Seated directly behind the Queen Mum, Princess Margaret, and entourage, I whispered to Ali as the lights went down, "A cashmere sweater, the old lady cops a tear."

The hankies were out, royal as they may have been, with the Queen Mum leading the sniffles. Broomstick Margaret even snuck out her little hanky.

Forget the Royal Command Performance—we never made it to bed. Both of us went back to the Connaught, changed clothes, only to return to the same theater, which was packed with a different audience. The flick was another premiere: the first closed-circuit, satellite telecast of a heavyweight championship bout, the first Muhammad Ali–Joe Frazier fight. Again, I cried. I lost a £2,000 bet.

Ali made every front-page headline the next morning—not for her performance in *Love Story*, but for her insult to the Queen Mother. There wasn't a snide British remark left out concerning Ali's fashion statement to the Queen Mum, ranging from "LOVE MEANS HAVING TO SAY YOU'RE SORRY" to "UNLIKE MUHAMMAD ALI, ALI MACGRAW LEFT HER GLOVES AT HOME."

On the plane back to the States the next morning, we read them all, laughing. But I wasn't laughing about that prick Halston fucking up Ali's night with his lousy tailoring. Almost maniacally, I insisted Ali show up at Halston's to personally confront him at 9:30 the next morning. Naturally, she obliged. At 9:45 the phone rang.

"Evans," Ali began, "I don't know what to say. . . ."

The next voice I heard was that of the effete Halston.

"I thought you were too sophisticated to be such a fool."

Who the fuck did he think he was talking to?

"Listen you motherf—"

Curtly, he stopped me. "Your wife, Mr. Evans, put the dress on backward."

Down went the phone and cut down was I as well.

A month later we were back in Europe, this time in Paris for *Love Story*'s French premiere. Madame Pompidou, wife of the French president, had organized the gala, a benefit for the Red Cross; it was the social event of the season.

Unfortunately, the site for the premiere was not a film theater, rather one used for concerts or plays. The projection and acoustics were all but unusable. Did the elite French care? Not at all. This was the theater; the rest was up to me.

After two days of a classical debate with the Gaelic bureaucrats, I was left with two choices: cancel the premiere (which the head of foreign distribution said would be a grave insult to the president of France) or put out an S.O.S. to my out-of-town French connection, Alain Delon, to aid me in my acoustic nightmare. My S.O.S. brought Delon to Paris within twenty-four hours. Together, we worked around the clock putting in new speakers, new projectors, and renting a new sound system for the night, all of which he personally obtained through his own muscle. At 3:00 P.M. on the day of the premiere, we were still hard at work on the finishing touches when I got a call from a George Craven—Mr. Front for the Pompidous. De Gaulle himself couldn't have been more definite: "Under no circumstance could Alain Delon attend the premiere."

What was this, a French joke? "Alain is my special guest," I said. "Without him there would have *been* no *Love Story*! Without Alain, Francis Lai wouldn't have taken my call."

"With Alain Delon, the Pompidous stay at home."

Then I got the lowdown. It seems that Alain was embroiled in *un grand scandale:* a murder no less involving the first family itself. The cast was not only all-star, but so explosive that it could very well topple the presidency.

The white-tie screening went off faultlessly, minus Alain Delon. Even the French succumbed. The super coolness of the French audience melted like ice cream on the beaches of St. Tropez. The night was beautiful. Romance filled the air. How proud my boss Bluhdorn and his French wife were. After all, it was their *Love Story* that brought the Mecca of France together. In her wildest dreams, Yvette had never thought her husband would be the center of attention in the city of Paris.

At the dinner afterward, the top society and political dignitaries of France sat at their place-carded tables. Violins faded into the background as a sixteen-piece orchestra began to play. After the first course was served, I casually walked over to the conductor and asked him if he would play the major theme to *Love Story* in five minutes.

Always a believer in fantasy and Cinderella, I made my request not capriciously but purposely. The moment the clock struck twelve, the conductor took his cue. I quickly slipped away to a side entrance. At the door stood the most handsome man in the world, white tie and all. Arm and arm we walked through the room. Suddenly, the buttering of a piece of bread could be heard. With me beside him, Alain walked directly to our table, took Ali by the hand, and asked her for the first dance. The star of *Love Story* rose and so did the Pompidous, entire entourage and all. As Alain and Ali danced, the president of France and his wife walked—walked out, that is.

For the next week Ali, Alain, and I went from theater to theater. It never failed. Even in so-called sophisticated Paris, boys and girls, men and women, walked out of *Love Story* arm in arm, misty eyed and mystically in love. For seven nights, we clocked one theater and, in particular, one guy who was there each night at the same time, but with a different girl. Naturally, each girl was crying as they walked out. So was he . . . every time. I wonder where they ended up. Forget Paris. Wherever we went, whether it be a café in Rome, an after-hours joint in Chicago, a calypso club in Jamaica, a mariachi bar in Mexico, a Spanish tavern in Barcelona, the melody of *Love Story* was played.

Men and women equally hungry for an all but lost emotion—*romance*—kept returning to *Love Story*. More than a film, it was an aphrodisiac, a phenomenon. A first in motion picture history, grossing more than a hundred times its cost.

Who would have thought that a $2 million reject, turned down by every studio in town, would not only awaken an all but dormant emotion but also alter an entire industry's thinking. A forgotten genre reborn. And just in time. Film attendance was at an all-time low. Was this the answer to bring audiences back to the theaters?

Lew Wasserman, then president of Universal, had his own judgment on *Love Story* in a January 11, 1971, interview with *Time:* "The audience that many companies felt was no longer there has been there all the time. I don't think the romantic interest went away. We went away."

Even more important, it accomplished a breakthrough. The American film started its ascension as the premiere film in every country in the world. Today, the American film stands alone as the only product manufactured in the U.S. that is number one in every country in the world. Excuse me, except for Coca-Cola. But that's bottled foreign.

In 1971, the reverence for the American film was far different than it is today. With rare exceptions, each country's own films dominated the local market—e.g., French-made films took the largest share of the grosses in France and the Italian film was number one in Italy. Why? Think of the foreign films that we Americans have all cringed watching, with out-of-synch dubbing and terrible dialogue delivered by bad actors. This was how our films came across in the foreign lands they played. The American film was then typically dubbed into four different languages—French, German, Italian, and Spanish. In each language, a new script would be written, actors picked to dub the voices, and directors hired to deliver the hybrid picture. It's hard to believe, but whether it be Clint Eastwood, Jack Nicholson, Dustin Hoffman, or Marlon Brando, no one in Italy or Spain had ever heard their voices.

Alain Delon, the man responsible for getting me Francis Lai for the score, was persistent on this point: "You like breaking barriers, Evans. Make *Love Story* a French movie—not a dubbed American film. Don't leave it to distribution to fuck it up. I'll get you the best French writers, actors, and directors, and it will be a French film, not an American film dubbed into French."

Alain's persistence caused the single biggest fight in my entire career at Paramount, going head to head with the top international distribution honchos. Fuck 'em—I put my ass on the line. What's the worst that could happen—I'd get fired? Instead of costing $18,000 to be dubbed into French, it cost $80,000. And I didn't stop there; I went all the way—German, Italian, and Spanish. Pissed? Did those European snobs want me to fall on my ass! Well, I ended up on my feet and it was the beginning of a new era of dominance. It is with that spirit I went to the studio each morning.

24

I met Henry Kissinger in the fall of 1970 at a dinner given for him by Joyce Haber and her husband, Doug Kramer, head of Paramount's television department. Ali was seated next to the President's national security adviser. I was at another table. Every time I looked over, she was laughing. Could this guy be that funny? He sure didn't look it.

Toward the end of the meal, he stood up and thanked his hosts, adding as he looked around the room, "One day I hope I, too, can get a tan." His timing was terrific.

Ali brought him over. "Henry, this is my husband."

She was already calling him Henry.

He gave her a smile. "You mean the king of Hollywood?"

I shook his hand. "You can make me king if you star in one of my pictures."

"I'm always open to negotiate. Which one?"

"The Godfather."

"For the lead?"

"No, the *consigliere.*"

"I'll have to speak with the President about it."

What charm. He didn't cut quite the same figure, but he was Cary Grant with a German accent.

The next day I had the chutzpah to invite him to lunch at Paramount. I never thought he'd accept.

Touring the studio, he seemed as awed as I would be on a personal tour of the White House. When I told him Walter Matthau was on the lot making *Plaza Suite* he said, "Do you think I could watch him do a scene?"

Maybe our friendship started that way—the recognition between two men that inside each of us was a little kid. It wasn't long before we were on the phone almost every day, three thousand miles apart. Surprise! It had nothing to do with girls.

It's been said many times before, but politics and show business really are two sides of the same coin. Particularly the kind of politics Henry and I were involved with. After all, as Henry frequently said, working for Richard Nixon wasn't too different from working for Charles Bluhdorn.

We'd laugh that both our phones were tapped, then shock the tappers. Henry would say, "The Israelis are really difficult to deal with, Robert."

"It's true, then. You're having sex with Golda Meir."

"Robert, I'm not *that* much of a patriot. Tell me, are Raquel's breasts for real?"

Two little kids. I don't think Henry could ever quite believe his sudden media celebrity, but nobody was ever better than Henry at playing out the courtship.

I believe it was Sunday morning, January 24, 1971, when I got a call from Henry in Palm Springs.

"Thanks for letting me know you're in town, pal."

His voice was solemn. "I didn't expect to be. I know you're busy,

Bob, but if you could spare the time I'd appreciate you're driving down here. Check into a hotel; call me when you arrive."

"Sure, Henry."

"Can you stay a day or two?"

"No problem."

Strange, he didn't invite me to stay with him. Henry was staying at the home of Leonard Firestone, the tire magnate. After checking into the Palm Springs Racquet Club, I called, Henry gave me the address of the Firestone home and told me to take a cab. Waiting for me at the Firestone compound were half of the Secret Service. Walking in, there was Henry, front and center, putting a finger to his mouth not to talk. We walked outside and onto the golf course.

"You're a good friend, Robert, to be here. I wouldn't have imposed on you if it weren't important."

"It's an honor, Henry."

He glanced back at the Firestone house. "It's all bugged, Robert. That's why we're on the eighteenth hole." Then, as if ordering a hot dog with mustard and sauerkraut, he continued, "A week from Wednesday I'm turning in my resignation."

"What?"

"I'm resigning."

"Why?"

"Why is not the question. I'm being told to."

As naïve as a kid in junior high, I blurted, "You're making history. You're the best thing they've got in the whole administration."

"That's the reason. Believe it or not," he said it with a laugh. "This little Jew boy is getting out of hand. I can't help it and they can't seem to contain it."

In the worst of times, he was telling me of the story of his demise with a sense of humor. *Now that's a great man!*

"Haldeman—giving him the benefit of the doubt," Henry continued, "he looks upon people of our persuasion with, to say the least, little kindness. The President . . . that's a different case." He laughed again. "I can't blame him. The more credit I get, the more he broods. Haig, he works for me, but does he like me? He rates right below Haldeman. The sad part of the whole thing is that the secretary of state, William Rogers, who's a very bright statesman, has a big problem with me—we are diametrically opposed on every international policy."

"What about Ehrlichman?" I asked.

"Bobby," he laughed, "whose side would you be on?" Now at the seventeenth hole, like a kid in kindergarten, he threw me a question. "Can you help me?"

The national security adviser to the President of the United States asking me for help? Maybe he *should* be fired.

"Me?" I began to laugh. "Why me, Henry? I know nothing about politics."

"Bob, you said it to me: 'Politics is nothing more than second-rate show business.'"

"It's a good line, Henry, but this ain't no joke. You've got the most brilliant statesmen in the world at your beck and call."

"That's why I'm calling on you. Whatever they advise, I've already thought of myself. Maybe you'll come up with the unexpected."

"Those are my words, Henry."

"I know. I copied them." He laughed.

We walked the golf course until the sun went down. I threw out suggestion after suggestion—from settling the war in Vietnam to making peace with Castro. Even if it were possible to do, it was impossible for Henry to achieve, for the simple reason he was confined to the United States.

"Why do you think I'm in Palm Springs talking to you?" He laughed. "It's getting dark. Go back to your hotel. Put on your thinking cap. Naturally, respect the confidence of the conversation. Come back tomorrow at ten and we'll continue walking the golf course. Let them call a cab for you; I don't trust the cars. And take a cab back in the morning."

Walking back to the Firestone estate, he whispered, "Don't forget. Tomorrow I'm down to nine days."

I didn't get two minutes' sleep the entire night. The only words I could say as I paced the floor were "The unexpected, the unexpected, the unexpected." I wrote down fifteen ideas to throw at him. We discussed all of them when we walked the golf course the next morning. From Walter Cronkite to Katharine Graham, idea after idea either had already been thought of or was impractical or unsympathetic to Henry's plight—until the last.

"This guy, Hugh Sidey from *Life*, he's also *Time*'s Washington bureau chief—he writes about you like you're the second coming of Christ. It's you who told me that from the President to a junior congressman, every Monday morning the first thing read is *Time, Newsweek,* and the *Washington Post.* Let's say, Hugh Sidey praised the brilliant insight of the President in picking Henry Kissinger, labeling it the most incisive appointment he's made since being elected president."

A dazed look from Henry.

"Sounds theatrical I know," I said, "but we're in the same business, pal."

In the spirit of confidentiality, I'm jumping ahead. February 4, 1972, *Life* appeared with a story written by guess who: Hugh Sidey. Its theme? Henry Kissinger and his historic influence on the presidency. The first no. 2 man who has ever wielded such power with such authority. Three days later, February 7, 1972, front and center on the desk of the President of the United States, every cabinet member, and all the senators and congressman was *Time* magazine. The cover? Henry Kissinger. The cover story?

PURSUIT OF PEACE AND POWER

Not conducted by Richard Nixon, but by his "triple, secret agent," Kissinger—on whose "diverse talents, energy, and intellect" the president had to rely.

In the middle of a furious argument with Francis Coppola, I was interrupted by a call from the White House.

"Robert, you can still call me at the same number."

We both laughed like kids.

Less than sixty days after Nixon's landslide reelection of 1972, I sat beside Henry in the Grand Ballroom of the Beverly Hilton Hotel. It was the American Film Institute's first Life Achievement Award. The recipient was John Ford, the crusty director of *Stagecoach, The Grapes of Wrath, Young Mr. Lincoln,* and *The Searchers,* the quintessential symbol of American conservatism in the most liberal of liberal community of the arts. President Nixon himself attended, as did Ehrlichman. Haldeman, a true Aryan, strutted by the tables not wishing to pay homage to liberal Hollywood.

Front and center was Henry's table. Beside him was not young Mr. Lincoln, but young Mr. Evans. Our table, contrary to the others of the White House hierarchy, was a glamorous one. I think Henry and I were the only two Republicans seated. Haldeman, Marine hair-cut and all, nodded a cursory greeting to Henry. No smile no hand-shake. His expression said it all. He wasn't looking to make new friends.

When Nixon stood to pay homage to Ford, the entire room, Demo-crats and Republicans, stood applauding their newly reelected Presi-dent. He and the First Lady received the longest, most enthusiastic, exhilarating applause that I've ever heard paid to anyone. It gave the entire room—and certainly me—a chill of patriotism to know that any American could be looked upon with such high esteem.

Within sixty days the scandal of Watergate had turned into a brush fire. The liberal media on the warpath made the American populace question rather than accept Nixon's legitimacy. His staunch cabinet now shaky, his own presidency in question. The order of the day in the White House was firing. His chief of staff, Haldeman—fired. Ehrlichman was about to get the axe as well. Nixon's historic breakthroughs now all but forgotten, the only one left—unscathed, no less—was the little Jew boy, Henry.

In May 1973, at Henry's insistence, I joined him at a White House dinner honoring West Germany's chancellor, Willy Brandt. Henry had asked me to arrive early so we could schmooze about some girl he had met.

A knock on the door. It was Ehrlichman. Why was he there? His office was now completely empty. He had come by to bid Henry good-bye. Henry shook his hand and wished him luck. No more Ehrlich-man.

Now we both started getting dressed for the black-tie state dinner. I was already dressed when Henry was having trouble with his tie. Fixing it right, he then put his jacket on. Smiling, he looked at me.

"You look like a male model, Bob."

I couldn't be that much of a liar—he didn't. He was at least twenty pounds overweight and if he added another two, the jacket button would have popped.

"Losing a few pounds wouldn't hurt."

"You won't tell anyone this, will you, Bob?"

"What?"

"I can't afford to." I began laughing. "It's true, between alimony, child support, and taxes, I can't afford to lose weight. I'd have to buy a new wardrobe and I don't have it in my budget."

"If I told this to anyone, Henry, they'd put me away."

"Me too, so don't tell it to anybody."

"What kind of world is this, Henry? My butler makes more money than you."

Then he whispered in my ear, "Come on, I want to show you something."

Like Huck Finn and Tom Sawyer, we snuck down the corridor into the sacred quarters of the Oval Office. It was empty. Henry knew the President and First Lady were getting attired for their grand entrance to honor their state guest. We Fred Astaired it through the Oval Office, passing the official desk of the President, toward a wood-paneled door. Henry opened it. *There we stood, the ambassador and the actor, right smack in the middle of the President's private john!* On the wall, within arm's length away was the President's private phone. There for his convenience, a hot button to each of his staff. Only one of the six buttons had a name below it; the others were all empty.

Our eyes met. Beaming, Henry pointed.

"I'm the only name left." A Kissinger laugh. "Remember Palm Springs . . . Bobby?"

25

"He's got something. Use him."

Couldn't understand the mumbling. "What did you say, Marlon?"

A long silence. "Pacino, he's a brooder."

"What?"

He didn't answer me; did he hang up? No, mumbling again.

"A brooder. He's my son . . . it's family. . . . His father . . . a brooder."

"I'm looking for an actor, not a brooder. He's tested three times, hasn't cut it."

"Nervous." Silence. More silence.

There was no one on the other end.

I shook my head. Did I dream it? I was asleep when I got the call? I hadn't heard from Brando since his agent, Robin French, rushed him to my New York office—ponytail and all—to pay homage. His mission? To cop the role of Don Corleone. Sonny Tufts, Troy Donahue, Tab Hunter, Fabian—put them all together—Marlon was colder.

Dino de Laurentiis burst into Bluhdorn's office.

"If Brando plays the Don, forget opening the film in Italy. They'll laugh him off the screen."

The orders from New York. "Will not finance Brando in title role. Do not respond. Case closed."

Brilliantly, Francis did a silent screen test of Marlon—that's all it took. With zero green in the till for a major star, it opened the door for Ponytail, who was desperate. For all the wrong reasons, a marriage was consummated. *Miracolo!* Two wrongs made a right. Marlon won the Academy Award, Paramount won the Bank of America Award and every other award as well.

Bluhdorn was right. "Crazy . . . This business is crazy!"

Concocting a bullshit philosophy that Italians, not Jews, must be the creative tissue to make a Mafia film work was what got the picture made.

The Godfather became the *numero uno* box-office champ of the world, breaking *The Sound of Music*'s record, and in six months did more business than *Gone With the Wind* in thirty-three years.

It drove Brando crazy. Why? When he originally signed to do the picture for scale, for cosmetics, we gave him a gross percentage. Small—but no one knew how small. A month before we started principal photography, his lawyer, Norman Gary, called.

"Bob, you must help me with Marlon. He's making your flick for scale and he can't pay his taxes, needs a hundred Gs. Can you help us? Put it against another commitment?"

"I'll get back to you, Norman."

Bluhdorn's face lit up.

"Give it to him. We don't want his next commitment. Get back his points. They're worth nothing anyways."

Bluhdorn's success didn't happen by mistake. In theory he was right. Marlon's gross percentage didn't kick in till $50 million in rentals. Only *Gone With the Wind* and *The Sound of Music* topped those numbers. Certainly, a Mafia film wouldn't come close.

Norman Gary bought it. For 100 Gs, Paramount took all of Marlon's gross points—eventually costing Marlon $11 million. He fired his lawyer, his agent, and everyone else close to him.

I lay in bed until the sun came up. Trying to decipher Brandon's disconnected word, "brooder," conjuring up thoughts of the two years that preceded his call.

It was an afternoon in the spring of 1968.

"Mr. Mario Puzo is here to see you."

Seeing him was strictly courtesy time. A favor to George Wieser: "He's a helluva writer, hungry, and writes your kind of shit, Evans."

As Puzo walked into my office two things stood out—a twelve-inch cigar and a stomach to match. Schmoozing about our mutual addiction (neither drugs nor girls, but gambling) created an immediate camaraderie.

Poor Mario, he had no wins to reminisce about. Without realizing it, he told me a story that was the key to his head. Only a brother gambler could have understood it.

"Been betting football twenty years, batting one for twenty. I followed the point spread that year till game time. There's always a couple of shoo-ins—no-brainers. I bet the other way. That's the fuckin' year I won."

"That's gamblin', pal . . ." Nothing more had to be said—we knew each other.

Mario belonged to a big club: Walter Matthau, Dickie Van Patten, and many more. All gamblers, all enjoying the same perverse sickness of losing. Do I understand it? No! But I also don't understand people enjoying pain.

From a rumpled manila envelope, he took out fifty or sixty even more rumpled pages.

"Thinkin' of writin' an inside story on the boys, The Organization—part real, part fiction. Callin' it *Mafia*. Name's never been used." He laughed. "Kefauver Committee branded it. You got yourself a real original. Could be good."

I eyed him. "In trouble?"

"Yeah, about ten Gs. They've been waitin' too long for it."

"You're covered, pal. I've just optioned *Mafia* for twelve five."

Mario's pudgy face broke out in a broad smile.

"Can we break out your Monte Cristos—celebrate?"

"Celebrate? . . . Survive! If you don't get that fuckin' fire hose out of your mouth, I'm gonna pass out."

Quickly palming a Monte Cristo from the humidor, he slowly smelled its aroma with the pleasure of a wine steward savoring the fragrance of a just opened bottle of 1932 Château Lafitte.

"Where do you get 'em from?"

"Vault town."

A Puzo double take.

"Zurich."

Forget the chair I held, the Monte was the key to his respect for me. Circumcising the tops with a wooden match, we lit up our heavenly smoke. He, the hustler—me, the shylock.

Again, for the wrong reasons, history was made. That's how *Mafia*—excuse me, *The Godfather* (we changed the title)—was born.

I looked at it as a gift, a chit. One gambler helping another gambler out of a heavy muscle jam.

A year and a half later, the jam turned into a novel. The novel turned into an explosion, instantly becoming the decade's number one runaway best-seller. For 10 Gs and change, I sat owning the rights to the Hope diamond of literature. There was one problem—timing. With all its international success, Paramount distribution didn't want to make the picture. No way, fuckers—not after *Funny Girl*.

"Sicilian mobster films don't play," was distribution's bottom line. When you bat zero, don't make another sucker bet. *The Brotherhood*, a perfect example . . . Kirk Douglas, an all-star cast, terrific reviews, no biz, not even a good first weekend.

Making matters worse, one director after another turned it down. Am I losing my fuckin' mind? Here I sit controlling the biggest book in the world; everyone congratulating me on my coup, yet my company won't make it and I can't find a fuckin' maestro to direct. Richard Brooks, Costa-Gavras, Elia Kazan, Arthur Penn turned it down. "Romanticizing the Mafia is immoral" was their single voice.

"Immoral? What about your agents? You deal with them every day."

I felt like a kid picking up a stone in the street that turns out to be an emerald, but you can't sell it because it's the wrong color that year.

The coup de main came when Hecht, Hill, Lancaster offered me a million-dollar profit on our minuscule investment. Burt Lancaster desperately wanted to play the title role. His production company was riding high and because it was for Burt, money was no object. Worse, Paramount was determined to sell it to them.

One evening, Peter Bart and I were pacing the floor.

"Is it Stanley, you, or me, Peter? One of us must need a shower. Between us, we can't get one director, not even a half-assed one to commit. Bluhdorn's right! This business is for lunatics!"

Peter, being the more analytical, said, "They're scared of it, Bob ... that simple. It's still a spaghetti gangster film. It's never worked yet."

"Get out the book that lists every picture made in the last twenty years. Mark each one that has to do with the Organization—*Black Hand, The Purple Gang*. Let's study them, see why they didn't work."

"It'll depress you more."

"Peter, I can't get more depressed. They talked me out of *Funny Girl*. It's not gonna happen again."

Distribution was right. Except for a B-picture or two—e.g., Rod Steiger in *Al Capone*—every film about Sicilians and organized crime had one thing in common—red ink.

"We've got a problem," Peter laughed.

"I don't believe in problems—I believe in solutions."

At two that morning, we found it. Outside of red ink, every one of the films shared another thing in common—they were written, directed, and produced by—and usually starred—Jews, not Sicilians. For example, *The Brotherhood* came out the year before, directed by Marty Ritt, starring Kirk Douglas, Susan Strasburg, and Luther Adler, and died.

"That's it, Peter. It may be bullshit, but it's the only defense we've got to get the picture made."

We stayed at the studio all night and called Stanley at 6:00 A.M., L.A. time. We all agreed to the party line: bullshit or not, there's a reason that this genre film never worked. It must be ethnic to the core—you must smell the spaghetti. That's what brought the magic to the novel—it was written by an Italian. The film's going to be the same.

There was one problem. In 1969 there wasn't a single Italian

American director with any credibility to be found.

"What about Francis Coppola?"

"Are you nuts, Peter? He's crazy!"

"Brilliant though," snapped Bart.

"That's your esoteric bullshit coming out. The guy's made three pictures: *You're a Big Boy Now*, artsy-fartsy . . . no business, *Finian's Rainbow*, a top Broadway musical he made into a disaster and *The Rain People*, which everyone rained on."

"It's Coppola or Lancaster," Peter shot back.

"There must be someone else. . . . There has to be." There wasn't. "Let me see if I can sell it to Stanley. He's going to blow a gasket on this one."

I was wrong. He didn't. Rather, he was pragmatic.

"He fits the party line, you'll smell the spaghetti."

Stanley blocked the Hecht, Hill, Lancaster deal, convincing the New York distribution honchos that I wasn't crazy. He explained why *The Godfather* would be a first. Reluctantly, they bought it.

There was one problem. Coppola didn't want to do it. He couldn't get a cartoon made in town, yet he didn't want to make *The Godfather*. To his credit, his convictions were strong in not wanting to immortalize the families that blackened his Italian heritage. Did he need a job? He owed more money around town than Nathan Detroit in *Guys and Dolls*.

Time was not on our side. Without an Italian director in place, the corporate hierarchy was more than anxious to embrace the Hecht, Hill, Lancaster deal. Here I am, on my knees begging this director who had made three features, all flops, to *please, please* put *The Godfather* on screen.

Three days of discussions later, Peter came into my office.

"Coppola will make the picture on one condition—that it's not a film about organized gangsters, but a family chronicle. A metaphor for capitalism in America."

"Fuck him and the horse he rode in on. Is he nuts?"

"Doesn't matter. He's Italian."

With fewer than forty-eight hours to make a decision—Hecht, Hill, Lancaster, or shake hands with the devil—Coppola was announced as *The Godfather*'s maestro.

Less than an hour later, Dick Zanuck, who was then head of Twentieth Century–Fox, was on the horn. "If you go with Coppola, you'll be testing for matador parts soon. Do it in *animation*—you've got a better chance." He laughed.

Minutes later, John Calley, at that time head of Warner Brothers, was on the horn. "Don't use him, Bob. Corporately, I shouldn't say it. His company owes us $600,000. Whatever money you pay him goes directly to us. Chalk this up as a chit for *Catch-22*." Calley had produced the Nichols film, which was far from a platinum success, for Paramount on my insistence.

Nevertheless, by default, Francis Coppola was handed the baton to orchestrate cinema history.

Auguste Rodin molding clay with his hands did not have the agility of Francis's brain when it came to seduction. Whether personal or professional, his persuasive powers made Elmer Gantry look like Don Knotts. Till this day, I doubt whether his own wife really knows who he is.

The casting of Michael Corleone became a cause célèbre between the two of us. He wanted an unknown actor—Al Pacino—and I wanted anyone but. Puzo's description of Michael in the book was diametric in every way to Pacino. Test after test was made—from the then unknown Bobby De Niro to every actor who had an O at the end of his name. Pacino tested three times, each worse than the last.

"Francis, the guy's no gangster; he's an actor."

"He's right for it, Bob."

"Not to me."

We were four weeks away from shooting an epic film in size, with a far from epic budget to produce it. "Six million and no more," were the orders from the high command. With the subject matter looked upon as a disease, all the money guys were looking to protect their losses, no less their asses. This meant that no actor in the film could be paid more than 35 Gs.

The war over casting the family Corleone was more volatile than the war the Corleone family fought on the screen. Brando's call tipped the scales. I then met with Coppola.

"You've got Pacino on one condition, Francis."

"What's that?"

"Jimmy Caan plays Sonny."

"Carmine Carridi's signed. He's right for the role. Anyway, Caan's a Jew—he's not Italian."

"Yeah, but he's not six five, he's five ten. This ain't Mutt and Jeff. This kid Pacino's five five, and that's in heels."

"I'm not using Caan."

"I'm not using Pacino."

Slam went the door. Ten minutes later, the door opened. "You win."

At 9:00 A.M. the next morning I was on the horn to Pacino's agent. "Your client's got the role."

"Sorry, Bob, it's forty-eight hours too late. We just closed a deal for him at Metro with Jim Aubrey, *The Gang That Couldn't Shoot Straight.*"

"Well, get him out of it. He wants this part more than air."

"Getting a pardon from a prison warden's easier than getting a favor from Aubrey."

"If Al finds out you didn't try, he'll dump you as his agent."

"So what? He's an actor. The Smiling Cobra—that's a different story, he runs a studio!"

"You owe it to your client. At least try."

"I owe it to my career. No way!"

I had no choice, so I called Aubrey. After all, we were friends— what did I have to lose? With the emotion of an IRS investigator, he turned me down. I picked up the phone again. This time a local call, dialing the Carlyle Hotel.

"Sidney Korshak, please."

"Yeah?"

"Sidney, it's Bobby."

"Yeah?"

"I need your help."

"Yeah?"

"There's an actor I want for the lead in *The Godfather.*"

"Yeah?"

"I can't get him."

"Yeah?"

"If I lose him, Coppola's gonna have my ass."

"Yeah?"

"Forty-eight hours ago he signed for the lead in a picture at Metro—*The Gang That Couldn't Shoot Straight.*"

"Yeah?"

"I called Aubrey, asked him if he could accommodate me, move his dates around."

"Yeah?"

"He told me to fuck off."

"Yeah?"

"Is there anything you can do about it?"

"Yeah."

"Really?"

"The actor, what's his name?"

"Pacino . . . Al Pacino."

"Who?"

"Al Pacino."

"Hold it will ya? Let me get a pencil. Spell it."

"Capital A, little l—that's his first name. Capitol P, little a, c-i-n-o."

"Who the fuck is he?"

"Don't rub it in will ya, Sidney. That's who the motherfucker wants."

"Where are ya?"

"At the New York office."

"Stay there."

Twenty minutes later my secretary buzzed. "Mr. Aubrey's on the phone, Mr. Evans."

"Jim?"

"You no-good motherfucker, cocksucker. I'll get you for this."

"What are you talking about?"

"You know fuckin' well what I'm talking about."

"Honestly, I don't."

The Cobra cut me off. "The midget's yours; you got him." Hanging the horn up in my ear.

Immediately I called Korshak.

"Yeah?"

"Sidney, it's Bobby."

"Yeah?"

"Aubrey just called."

"Yeah?"

"Pacino—I got him. What happened?"

"I called Kerkorian."

Kirk Kerkorian at the time was the sole owner of MGM. He never involved himself with the day-to-day running of the studio, a provision written in cement when Aubrey took the presidency. Kerkorian was totally involved in building his Las Vegas empire. The MGM

Grand was near completion, but he was going through a financial crunch as construction costs were considerably over budget.

"I told him Bobby needs some actor for *The Godfather,* that his schmuck Aubrey wouldn't let you have him. He tells me—get this, Bobby—'Sidney, I'd do anything for you, you know that, but my deal with Aubrey is he's got total control. It's Aubrey's call, I've got no say in it.' "

The operator interrupted. "Mr. Wasserman's on the phone, Mr. Korshak, says it's urgent."

"I'll call him back in ten."

"Well?"

"Well what?"

"What did he say?"

"Oh, I asked him if he wanted to finish building his hotel."

"Yeah?"

"He didn't answer, but he asked who the actor was. I told him. He never heard of the schmuck either. He got a pencil, asked me to spell it—'Capital A, punk l, capital P, punk a, c-i-n-o.' Then he says, 'Who the fuck is he?' 'How the fuck do I know. All I know, Bobby wants him.' "

"That was it?"

"That was it!"

His other phone rang. He didn't even say good-bye.

That's the inside, inside story of what eventually became—mind you, against my better judgment—possibly the greatest "sense of discovery" casting in cinema history.

I stayed in New York during the first week of shooting and then flew back to the Coast. Besides getting reacquainted with my wife and newborn kid, I had a dozen other films in various stages of production, not one without problems. One night, while I was having dinner in bed, my red phone went off. It was Al Ruddy, the producer assigned to oversee *The Godfather.*

"Evans, we've got a problem. The fuckin' guinea shoots a great scene."

"What's the problem?"

"It doesn't cut together."

"Put Aram on the phone."

Aram Avakian, the editor, got on the line. "Bob, shot by shot it looks great. Kubrick couldn't get better performances, but it cuts together like a Chinese jigsaw puzzle. We spent two days in the restaurant with Pacino, Sterling Hayden, and Al Lettieri. Each take was great, but nothing matches. The fucker doesn't know what continuity means."

Indigestion turned to heartburn. "Get the footage to me tonight."

"The sooner the better," Avakian agreed. "Every day the fucker shoots, it's burning money."

"Get it on the plane, if you have to bring it yourself, I want it at the studio tomorrow, clear? Put Jack Ballard on the phone."

Jack Ballard was the studio's eyes and ears on the film, reporting to me directly. Knowing his job was on the line, his critique of Coppola's incompetence was more severe than Avakian's.

Zanuck's and Calley's warnings flashed before me. Why the fuck didn't I listen? It's my fault and it's my fall. When your wife is lying in bed beside you, it's her natural reflex to ask "What's the problem?" Having ten to twenty pictures always in some stage of pre- or post-production, there's not a day you're not in the middle of a war. As much as Ali wanted to be a cushion to my daily batterings, her good intentions worked in reverse—it made me more tense, more abrupt. A loner is a loner is a loner is a loner.

The next day twelve reels arrived. Peter Zinner, an ace editor, and I spent the whole weekend in the editing room. The result—amazing. Francis's work—not just good . . . brilliant.

Sabotage wears many faces. This one I had never encountered. Sunday night I took the red-eye to New York. I didn't fire Francis. Instead I fired Aram Avakian and his coterie of production assistants, sent Jack Ballard back to the studio, and told Al Ruddy, the producer, that if I hadn't liked him as much as I did, he'd be fired too. In reality, it wasn't Ruddy's fault; without knowing it, he was the fall guy. Aram Avakian, an editor turned director, wanted, at all costs, to derail Francis, knowing that with Coppola out, he would have a good shot to take over. He almost succeeded. A keen eye and streetwise instincts prevented Francis from being an innocent victim of a well-conceived ruse.

Francis's nervous system during the weeks that followed were such that Charlie Bluhdorn himself became Francis's own godfather, going on the set every day to give Coppola the affirmation he so needed. Coming from Jaffe or myself, it would have mattered little, but from Charlie Bluhdorn, that was different. Not only was he the big boss, but when he was on, there was no one like him. The electricity of his embrace was possibly his most extraordinary asset.

Post-production began. From day one, the battles started. The conflict between Francis and me became so bitter that even Bluhdorn's persuasive mediation abilities were all but ineffective.

Post-production may sound like a technical word, but in actuality, it's the most important element in the anatomy of filmmaking. It's an art form unto itself that structures the arc of your story. Film, dialogue, sound, music, and effects are its five major tentacles. During the post-production process, each of these is structured and edited separately by highly talented artists, whose contribution is rarely appreciated or spoken of. Frame by frame with precision and skill, your canvas evolves its persona. Post-production is the key to film magic or film mediocrity. From it comes your completed canvas, which is presented for all the world to see and critique.

Whether it be the cinematography, writing, directing, or (for that matter) performances, all become pawns to those who control the magic of post-production.

"Dailies" is the operative word for time spent by the producer, director, cinematographer, actors (if they wish), and various department heads to examine and cull out the best of the previous day's filming. The director, being the captain of the ship, picks out his choices for the editor to assemble. With rare exception, the day-to-day viewing of dailies is a high—euphoric at times. Within a month after completion of principal photography, you are faced with an assemblage, and there for the first time you see the sum of all the film's parts as one. Without exception, your dream turns into a nightmare. The euphoria of watching the dailies abruptly turns to thoughts of suicide.

My first acting stint on film was opposite Jimmy Cagney. Day after day, the director, producer, cast, and crew would watch the dailies together. It was a new experience for me, watching everyone's enthusiasm for what had just been shot. What a high! I couldn't help but notice that Cagney was expressionless. Curiosity pressed.

"Mr. Cagney, pardon me for asking. We've all been watching dailies together for the past week. Me, I've been watching you. Everyone seems to be on cloud ten but you. Don't you like 'em?"

"You're new in this racket, kid. Dailies are like brides. How come there's so many beautiful brides . . . and ugly wives?" A Cagney wink, and off he strutted.

Francis and I had a perfect record; we didn't agree on anything—from editing to music and sound. The nine-month pain was worse than giving birth to Rosemary's baby. The pain also put my sciatic nerve on fire, ricocheting up and down my leg with the intensity of a burning sword.

Ali kept saying, "It's only a movie, it's only a movie."

She was right, but my priorities were too fucked up to pay heed.

David Gilruth, my butler, wheeled me into one of Paramount's projection rooms for the unveiling of Francis's cut of *The Godfather*. In the theater sat Francis with his quadrille of assistants and editors, (film, sound, and music), plus the rest of his production team. Also present was Al Ruddy, the film's producer. Peter Bart and I were representing the studio. Before the picture started, Coppola introduced me to Robert Towne, who then was Hollywood's top script doctor. Francis had brought him in to write Brando's death scene.

I was feeling like a cartoon character having various hands turn me over from one orthopedic bed to another. This had been my M.O. for over a month—from bedroom, to home screening room, to Paramount's screening room, to a bed on wheels, going from sound stage to sound stage, there I was, the "sciatic kid." The victim of a pain that makes a thousand toothaches a kiss to build a dream on.

The film was to open in four months—Paramount's Christmas gift to the world. The lights went down; the picture started. Two hours and six minutes later, the screen turned to black and the room began to fill with light.

Pain does not make you more charming. "David, wheel me back to my office. Francis, I want to speak with you—*alone.*" The pain was now throbbing more in my head than my back as I impatiently waited for Francis. A half hour later the Prince arrived. "You're late," I growled.

"Couldn't help it. All my boys are telling me the picture's great. Don't touch it."

"The picture stinks. Got it? 'The Untouchables' is better. You shot a great film. Where the fuck is it—in the kitchen with your spaghetti? It sure ain't on the screen. Where's the family, the heart, the feeling—left in the kitchen too?"

Francis glared. "Al, Fred, Greg, Walter—they think it's my best work."

"What the fuck do I care what they think! It stinks!"

"Let's get Towne's opinion," said Francis.

"He's your friend, not mine. But he doesn't get a weekly paycheck. Bring him in."

To Francis's shock, Towne agreed with virtually every criticism I vented regarding the underwhelming result to an overwhelming canvas.

I limped over to him. "Schmuck! You shortchanged yourself. What studio head tells a director to make a picture longer? Only a nut like me. You shot a saga, and you turned in a trailer. Now give me a movie."

The next morning, I told the New York honchos that the picture could not be ready for Christmas. I didn't need a phone to hear their screams. Coppola, of course, was on their side.

"You've got it for Christmas. Evans is crazy. He wants to change everything," shrieked Coppola. "Hear this. He wants me to make it longer."

When the opening of a high-profile film is postponed, it brings with it an immediate stink, spelling "suicide" to the world of exhibition. What was thought of as an anticipated event now became the buzz of a potential white elephant.

"This guy, Evans, must be on acid making the picture longer" was the crux of the exhibitor's uproar. "Even if the picture's better, who gives a shit? How are we going to get turnover, sell popcorn?" was the unanimous cry.

The order came down—unalterable in its dictate: "Evans, the picture is to be ready for Christmas."

"I quit." I meant it, too.

Pain gives off strange vibes. You just don't give a shit.

A year before, they would have booted me out on my ass. But *Love Story* had saved Paramount. I was their fair-haired boy. If I couldn't press my instinct now, I might as well go back to acting.

"Evans, you're killing the morale of the company," screeched Bluhdorn.

"Fuck 'em, Charlie. They're only as good as the product they have to sell, and what we've got now ain't good enough. No, that's not fair. I've bent over too many times on this flick to take gaff from any of your suits. I'll bottom-line it to you—it's 'The Untouchables' in 70mm. The fat fuck shot a great film, but it ain't on the screen. It's either in his kitchen or on the cutting room floor. Is it more important to make Christmas or have a shot at making it great? If you want *Paint Your Wagon,* you've got it. Let the robots in sales bring big numbers in on that. The Monday after it opens, watch them run for the hills."

"Everyone in distribution's seen it," Bluhdorn snapped back. "They all think you're wrong."

"Really."

Here's where an acting career comes in handy.

"Charlie, think of that Sunday afternoon I forced you out of your bath. 'We've got *Funny Girl,*' I said. God, you were excited. It was you and I against the rest of the Paramount world. You said to me then, 'You're right, Evans. I agree with you. But you haven't been in the seat long enough to back you against the entire company.' I've made my bones, Charlie. I've been in the seat long enough. Open for Christmas and take me off your Christmas bonus list. I won't be here." I put the phone down.

Through the industry, word spread like leprosy: *"Godfather—a bomb!"*

With his bearish looks, great smile, and operatic manner, Francis had more bravado than P. T. Barnum. At the core, however, he was a scared, prepubescent kid. One day, leaving the editing rooms at Goldwyn Studios, Francis angrily muttered, "You're making this picture so long, Evans, half the people will be asleep before it's over."

"Just keep adding texture, Francis."

"Evans, you're ruining the picture!"

"You don't know what you've got, Francis. Give me the whole nine yards. We've got a shot at being remembered."

"I'm tired of listening to your hype, Evans."

"Fuck you! We got a shot to break fifty million in America alone, if you don't compromise."

"Are you on LSD? Only *Gone With the Wind* and *Sound of Music* hit those numbers."

"Yeah, and we will too, if you don't fuck it up."

"And you'll buy me a Mercedes, too, if it does, huh?"

"You're damn right I will."

The day *The Godfather* passed $50 million, Francis bought a Mercedes 600, the most expensive on the market. The bill wasn't sent to Paramount, but personally to Robert Evans.

The Hollywood Foreign Press Association had voted Ali "World Film Favorite." The annual Golden Globes Awards presentation was a televised dinner scheduled for a Sunday night in mid-January 1972. It dovetailed with Ali taking off the next morning to start *The Getaway* in El Paso, Texas. It was to be our last night together. I wanted it to be festive.

At three that afternoon Francis and his ass-kissing quartet arrived in my projection room. For hours we went at it. Finally Ali pulled me out of the fray.

"We have to leave, Evans, please. We're supposed to be there in a half hour—"

I cut her off. "I got a crisis with this motherfucker. You'll have to go without me. Your presentation is last. I'll get there before, I promise."

Angry with myself for allowing *The Godfather* again to fuck up my life with my lady fair, I went back to the projection room.

"Let me make it real clear, Francis. It's my way or no way."

"What's that supposed to mean?"

"It means that if it ain't my way, you're off the picture. Could I be more clear?"

Up he got, as did his quartet and on to the tennis court they went. I was so pissed that this one film was screwing up my whole life that I was hoping he would take me up on my threat and walk. He didn't.

When he returned, he said, with disdain written clearly across his face, "Okay, it's your way."

The tension of the day put my sciatic nerve on full-speed pain. Trying to dress myself for the black-tie affair, I managed to put my black tie on, but I couldn't bend over to put on the black socks. Pulling my pants lower, I rationalized, who'll notice anyway. Lying in the backseat, I was driven to the Beverly Hilton, hoping against hope I wouldn't have a stroke and take the spotlight from Ali.

Arriving in the ballroom, I made my way to her table. Seeing me approach, she jumped up, far more concerned over my crisis than her award.

"How did it go?"

"My way."

"That's my Evans."

I made it just in time. Charlton Heston was center stage in a celebrity-packed ballroom talking of Ali's meteoric rise.

"In three years," said Heston, "Ali MacGraw has gone from being the Most Promising Newcomer of the Year, to the Best Actress of the Year, to the World Film Favorite of the Year."

With that, came a standing ovation. The only one who couldn't stand was me. She bent down to kiss me.

I whispered in her ear, "Do the unexpected. Just say 'Thank you very much, now I'm making my getaway' and walk off."

I waited for the one-liner. It never came.

On the way home I asked her, "How come you didn't use the getaway line?"

She just smiled.

I had won the battle, but dear Francis had won the war. *The Godfather* propelled him to legendary status—the maestro of the decade. However, because it was a studio-produced film, not a package deal, Paramount controlled 84 of the 100 points—unheard-of in today's world of film. The bottom line was that its profits back to the company had to be the most lucrative amount in cinema history.

Me? I was half crippled. Did I get a bonus? No. Did I get a raise? No. A kiss from Bluhdorn? Yes. But not one from Ali. Instead she dumped me, because *The Godfather* was my obsession, not hers. And my one and only son, Joshua? He too would be lost, to be seen only two weekends a month.

26

The combination of Bluhdorn, Jaffe, and me was too perfect. If I were jealous, which I'm not, I would have resented the relationship between my boss and his new twenty-nine-year-old president—that's how nuts Charlie was about Stanley. Stanley felt the same about Charlie. How could things go wrong? Over a woman, that's how.

Charlie liked to think of himself as a talent scout, always complaining, "Evans, why don't you have more beautiful girls under contract like the old days? There's no glamour anymore in this business!"

One day over lunch, at the Bistro, Charlie met a girl named Joanna Cameron. He thought she could be the next Natalie Wood. No one enjoyed the vicarious thrill of sense of discovery more than Charlie. What better example of that than me, or for that matter, Jaffe?

Stanley and I were casting *Star Spangled Girl,* one of Doc Simon's less memorable efforts. No major female star in town wanted to touch it.

"Why not Joanna Cameron?" said Charlie.

"We're running this company," Stanley exploded. "Stay out of casting!"

"Hey, Stanley, he's chairman of the board."

"You said it, I didn't, it's beneath him."

What Stanley didn't understand was that nothing was beneath Charlie. His closest friend was Owen, his chauffeur. For him, finding the next Natalie Wood was a bigger turn-on than finding his next company to gobble.

Unlike me, both Stanley and Charlie were confrontational; that Friday, they locked horns. Stanley told Charlie to stay out of our ballpark. *We* were running Paramount. The last thing we needed was capricious casting ideas. Stanley got so angry, he slammed down the phone before Charlie could even get in his screams.

"Hey, Stanley, this is no way to end the week. Call him back . . . settle the goddamn thing . . . friendly style."

I was talking to the wrong guy. I've never met anyone more intransigent when it comes to principle. Later that night, Charlie called me.

"Please, Bob, speak to Stanley. He's like a son. But I would never let my son talk to me that way. Call him. I can't. Tell him to apologize."

"No problem, Charlie." Wrong again, Evans. Jaffe was one strange cat.

"The film business to Bluhdorn is an avocation; to us, it's *life.*" said the twenty-nine-year-old. "I'm not testing this bimbo."

"Hey, it's his store too. Fuck it! Who gives a shit?"

"I do."

What balls! Not even thirty and he wouldn't say "I'm sorry," to the chairman of the board. For the next forty-eight hours my shuttle diplomacy bombed. The last thing Charlie wanted was to fire him, but

Stanley refused to say two words. Imagine, two fuckin' words: "I'm sorry."

Three days passed, Charlie gave me the bad news. He was left no choice, he had to fire Stanley. If he didn't, he'd lose face to the fifteen thousand people working for him.

"Make Stanley a terrific production deal. I want him here forever."

I did. From *The Bad News Bears* alone, Stanley's first picture as an independent producer, he made more money than he would have made as president of Paramount in five years. Me? I lost the best partner I ever had. Who could we get to replace him? Not me. I didn't want to move to New York—I didn't even want to work in an office. All I wanted was to make pictures. It came down to two candidates: Young and Rubicam's Steve Frankfurt, whose advertising vision catapulted a throwaway flick, *Goodbye, Columbus,* into a blockbuster hit. A year earlier he had saved our ass on *Rosemary's Baby,* a flick on the then taboo subject witchcraft that no one knew how to sell. A minute to post time and Frankfurt saves the day with the slogan "Pray for Rosemary's Baby"—only one line, but it turned a doubtful entry into Paramount's largest grossing picture of the year. No mistake he was labeled Madison Avenue's Creative Godfather.

Second choice was Frank Yablans, the tenacious, tough, no-nonsense lightning rod who was running Paramount's sales. Within three years, Yablans had worked his way up from assistant sales manager to head of distribution. He was a dynamo who knew the size and shape of every movie house in the country. Frank wore his ambition on his sleeve. As he would later tell *Time* magazine, "It's easy to be humble if you were born a prince. I came from a ghetto." The son of a Brooklyn taxi driver, a guy whose first job was plucking chickens, Frank had more chutzpah by mistake than anyone had on purpose. Balls? Jimmy Hoffa took a backseat.

We had to make a quick decision.

"Do you think Yablans is too crazy?"

"No, Charlie, too hungry! Remember Christmas?"

The previous Christmas Day, Frank and I had been going over the box-office returns on *Love Story.* The only place it wasn't breaking records was Washington, D.C. On the spot, Frank called his district sales manager, ordered him to leave his family feast and drive around Washington to check the theaters. An hour later the poor guy called back. He'd found a theater where the exhibitor was charging only a dollar a matinee. Yablans screamed, "Get him on the phone!"

"Frank, I can't. He just came out of intensive care—cardiac arrest."

"What hospital is he in?" A minute later Frank had his victim on the horn. "You're denigrating *Love Story*! I don't want to hear excuses. If you don't take action immediately and rectify the situation, I'm gonna open the picture in two theaters across the street! Merry Christmas."

By sundown the exhibitor had gone back into intensive care, but the price of a tear, in his theater, had gone up.

"Can you live with him?"

Cocky Evans: "Sure I can."

"Then put Yablans in as president. . . . I'll buy Young and Rubicam. We'll have 'em both."

27

Beside my bed was Ali's wedding gift to me: a leather-bound book containing F. Scott Fitzgerald's short story "Winter Dreams," each word calligraphed by Ali herself. Its postscript: *"24 October 1969. Forever."*

My wedding gift to her was Daisy Buchanan.

She was a Fitzgerald freak, constantly reciting *The Great Gatsby* from memory. Paramount had filmed Fitzgerald's novel twice, and had failed twice. The rights had reverted to the author's daughter,

Scottie Lanahan Smith, who said she never again wanted to see her father's masterpiece as a movie. Sam Spiegel, Ray Stark, Sydney Pollack, and Robert Redford were among the many trying to change her mind.

There's no motive stronger than wanting to surprise the lady you love. Her only fantasy since childhood was to play Gatsby's femme fatale, Daisy Buchanan.

Again cutting to the chase, the impossible became the possible. I got the rights from Fitzgerald's daughter and Daisy was Ali's to play. When I surprised her with the news, she smothered me with kisses and whispered, "Evans, you really *are* Gatsby."

Who could be more chic than Truman Capote to write the screenplay? He was desperate to do it. "I know just the way to bring all that purple prose to the screen!" he cooed.

On weekend nights, Ali and I ran a film festival for the toughest audience in town. Among the mainstays were Warren, Dustin, Jack, Roman, Mike Nichols, Cary Grant, Fred Astaire, Roman Polanski, Sue Mengers and her husband, director Jean-Claude Tramont.

Sue was the first woman superagent in town. She had signed Ali and Ryan before *Love Story;* her clients ranged from Streisand to Gene Hackman. Her manner was outrageous, her tongue more lethal funny than Don Rickles at his best; but her caring and loyalty unmatched. Soon Mengela became our closest friend.

Although I was fond of the two Charlies in my life, both became the bane of our marriage. Charlie, my boss, had a nightly ritual. Before going to sleep in New York, he would take a bath, climb into bed, and call me. Any other time would have been okay, but his bedtime was my dinnertime. Uncannily, he always called just as I was about to put food in my mouth. It didn't matter whether we were having guests or a romantic tray for two in bed. I was the man who never finished dinner.

My brother, Charlie, was a different story. More my fault than his, as I never confronted it. Wherever we traveled, he was always with us—London, Paris, Monte Carlo, Acapulco, you name it. I know Ali didn't invite him.

One day after we'd made love, she jumped into the shower. As usual, I quickly got on the horn to my brother. Toweling off, she snidely laughed, "Filling him in?"

The Hotel du Cap was the arc of our marriage. For three years, each July, we paid homage to the rock on the Riviera.

Our first summer, glorious. Ali, three months pregnant. My brother? Sure, he was with us. Was Ali pissed? Sure, she was. Days later, my brother took off for Sardinia. It was the first day Ali could lie nude in our cabana. Enjoying the sun and silence, she rolled on top of me.

"Miss him already, huh?"

The next night we went to the opening of Jimmy's in Monte Carlo. Joining us was David Niven and his wife, Hjordis, and Dustin and Anne Hoffman. In full splendor, the Eurotrash were out in all their glory. For the first time, Ali was beginning to feel like we were really Mr. and Mrs.

Two nights later, Dino de Laurentiis threw us a bash at Le Pirate, a crazy beachfront restaurant, where naked pirates climbed the netting and the maitre d' smashed wine bottles against the rocks.

"Evans, it's starting to feel so good," Ali whispered.

"The baby?"

"No . . . us."

It was! My back was even feeling romantic. No tension, no pain.

The following summer, there we were again. What a year! The best production of our lives opened: Joshua! Demanding were the twelve months, but "good demanding." For the three months preceding our visit, all we could think about was "Oh! To be on the rock again."

The Hoffmans must have felt the same. They, too, were there. Together we strolled through the streets of Eze, Beaulieu, or Villefranche, devouring succulent cuisine at some local bistro. It's the closest one comes to heaven. Making bets, we'd stop people on the street, humming the melody of "Mrs. Robinson" from *The Graduate*, finishing with *Love Story*'s melodic theme, and then asking which tune they recognized. Competitiveness was the core to discover which of the two was more memorable. Mighty close: both the Evanses and Hoffmans claimed victory.

Gianni Agnelli was not only the wealthiest and most influential man in Italy, but certainly the most charming and debonair, with looks even more dashing than his wealth. To say he had big eyes for Ali would be an understatement. Gianni was a longtime pal and being in his company was an aphrodisiac in itself.

One afternoon, he brought his sailboat and docked it by the rock on Cap d'Antibes. He swam in to join us at our cabana. After an hour of sun, the three of us dived into the Mediterranean and stroked it back to his sailboat where lunch was waiting. The film *Indecent Proposal*? Forget it. Gianni would have turned over all of Fiat to get Ali. An Italian is an Italian, is an Italian is an Italian . . . *tutto italiano!* After a marvelous pasta lunch which Gianni personally prepared, we bid him *au revoir* and back to the rock we swam, laughing about Gianni's single-focused attention.

Siesta time it was, but it wasn't. Once back in our high-ceilinged boudoir, it took only a quick glance in the mirror to see a lump on Ali's cheek grow into the size of a golf ball. Who gets mumps in their thirties? Ali did. As a kid, mumps are not dangerous. As an adult, it's a different story. There are lots of chefs on the Côte d'Azur, but medical specialists on mumps are not that easy to find. Half of them didn't even know what the mumps were.

The local French doctor, who had never even seen mumps before, said, "Mumps can be very contagious. If you have children, stay away until it's totally gone."

In short, till the infection cleared her system, no going back to L.A. for Mrs. Evans.

The phone rang, S.O.S.—big trouble on *The Godfather,* "need you back here on the double." Decision time. Stay with my sick wife or fly back to troubled waters? Troubled waters got the nod.

In the spirit of that bravado, the house of marital bliss came tumbling down by July 1972, though back at Hotel du Cap, we were dealing from a different deck—save-the-marriage time. On to the rock flew Sidney Korshak, my *consigliere,* for one purpose and one purpose only—to keep our rocky marriage from falling into the sea. Each day Sidney would sit with Ali for hours, trying to persuade her to make the marriage work. Convincing? Momentarily.

The following July, the Evanses didn't make du Cap. How could we? Mrs. Evans had a different last name.

28

"My ole lady, we've split. Feel like I'm back in the streets. Don't know where to park my bones."

"Let's grab a burger at the Bistro, talk about it."

"How 'bout the Hamlet."

"The Bistro—we can walk there."

"I look like a bum."

He may have, but so what? McQueen was the hottest male star in the world, the perfect Hollywood cowboy, skintight T-shirt and jeans, not hand-me-down, but tailored to order.

Me, I wanted to talk about *The Getaway,* a heist film written by Walter Hill that the new boy-wonder director Peter Bogdanovich was directing for Paramount. *The Getaway* was the furthest thing from Steve's mind. His ole lady, Nellie, was all he could talk about. Steve was not a happy camper. Always a romantic, I felt for the guy. He seemed totally lost, with no place to go.

"Sunday I've got a tennis marathon at the house," I told him. "But forget the tennis; your dance card will be filled with new talent for a year."

"Sure I ain't imposin'?"

"Imposing? If you're a no-show, I'm not making the flick. Got it?"

A good-bye laugh. "Yeah, see ya."

The players were all male; the watchers all female. McQueen seemed a bit uncomfortable. Between sets, I rushed into the house and found Ali busy pressing flowers.

"Come out!" I demanded. "Meet McQueen, make him feel at home."

"In an hour . . . look how beautiful the daisies are pressed in the book."

"Fuck the daisies, McQueen could be Gatsby."

Capote's script was due within a week. Nicholson and Beatty were my first two choices. Ironically, only a few years earlier Warren wanted to buy the rights and produce *Gatsby* himself, but not star in it.

"The only one to play Gatsby," he said to me, "is you."

"You prick. Now that I'm on top, you want me to fall back on my ass?"

"Wrong. You're the only Gatsby I know. Play yourself; that's all you gotta do. I'll line-read you if I have to."

Neither Nicholson nor Beatty were interested, feeling Ali was wrong for the part.

"Right for the part of Jordan, but not Daisy," both of them echoed.

"And fuck you too!" was my answer back.

In early December the script arrived. Truman and his companion, an air-conditioner repairman from Palm Springs, came over for dinner. Bruce never said a word all night while Truman had Ali and me in stitches with the story of how he had "improved" Fitzgerald's "illiterate masterpiece."

I kept thinking, He better have. I'm in for $300,000, against the strong objections of Bluhdorn and Yablans—neither of whom wanted a third *Gatsby*.

But, as it turned out, Truman's script was *Ada* revisited.

"Maybe *I'm* illiterate, Ali, but I don't know what the fuck I'm reading. It's a miscarriage." A terrible downer to blurt out.

Trying to turn a negative to a positive, I continued, "Fuck *Gatsby*. Make *The Getaway* with McQueen. Together, you'll make it the hottest picture of the year."

"Bob, drop it. Who's gonna buy me as a vagrant on the run?"

"It's not written in granite. *Casablanca* had seventeen rewrites."

"What about *Gatsby*?"

"Fitzgerald ain't easy to lick. You'll end up being a character actress before we get a script. We're back at the starting gate without a jockey."

"Playing Daisy is the only thing I wanna do."

"Hey, let's be realistic. You've been off the screen for two years. If we're lucky, it'll take another year to get a shooting script on *Gatsby*. Personally I don't think we'll ever get one. Fitzgerald writes essences. Not one of his books has worked on screen."

"My Evans will make it work."

"I haven't yet. Use *Getaway* as a filler. At least you'll be in action."

"I'm not like you. I don't want to be in action. I want to be here. You can hardly walk."

Paying little heed to her vibes, I took on Peter Bogdanovich.

"If Ali were Helen Hayes, she couldn't get away with it. It's written for Cybill." Cybill Shepherd at the time was Peter's lady.

"If the Bible can be rewritten, so can *The Getaway*."

"Great! We'll make her a runaway from Wellesley in her Mercedes convertible."

"Bottom line, Peter, McQueen and MacGraw together is blockbuster time. That's the business I'm in."

"You stick to your business, I'll stick to mine. No Cybill; no Bogdanovich."

Good-bye, Peter. Hello, Sam Peckinpah.

Helping me out of the bathtub, Ali began massaging my lower back. "I'm not leaving, Evans. Your whole back's in spasm. I'm worried. Get someone else to play the Texas floozy."

A Jewish mother was the one thing I didn't want. Alone, not having to answer to anyone, was my Utopian thought.

The phone rang. It was agent Freddie Fields, who headed First Artists, a production company started by McQueen, Paul Newman, Barbra Streisand, Dustin Hoffman, and Sidney Poitier.

"Steve doesn't think Ali's right for the part. He'd rather go with Tuesday Weld or Katharine Ross."

"Freddie, Ali's *perfect* for the part. Have him come over for dinner."

Steve, Ali, and I were in the middle of dinner when I excused myself. "I've got a script to read. You guys get to know each other."

The next day Ali and I flew to Acapulco for a rest. Some rest. My host, Melchor Perusquia, gave me a phone with a two-hundred-foot extension cord that went from his house, down the cliff to the beach. Before I had a chance to dive into the sea, five calls had come in. It rang again.

It was Sue Mengers. "Bobbee . . . Steve wants a yes or a no from Ali."

"You talk to her. I'm tired of trying to convince her."

For twenty minutes Ali stood firm with Sue. The only thing that interested her was playing Daisy.

"Stop talking Daisy! Talk reality. It's never gonna happen anyway." I grabbed the phone from her hand. "Sue, she's doing *The Getaway*. That's it. Let's hear the deal, and it better be good."

Hanging up, I looked at Ali. Whatever was in her eyes, it sure wasn't love.

Twenty minutes later, the beach phone rang again. It was Freddie Fields. Steve wanted to meet with Ali before giving his final okay.

I ran to the ocean where Ali was swimming. "McQueen wants to meet you in L.A."

"But we're flying to New York tomorrow for Christmas!"

"You fly to L.A. I'll fly to New York."

Glaring at me, "Is this really what you want me to do?"

"Yes!" A wave hit me and knocked me over, as well it should have.

Three days later, after flying back to L.A., to meet with McQueen, she joined me at the Sherry-Netherland in New York, different, distant. Did I pay heed? Of course not.

Angrily, she John Hancocked to do the film. Once Ali signed, Freddie Fields proceeded to give me a spiked steel dildo up my ass. With premeditated complicity, he loopholed Paramount's control of the now hot McQueen/MacGraw *Getaway,* sliding it into his own First Artists Company, which he personally controlled. Nice guy, huh? Bluhdorn and Yablans were justifiably furious.

"Get Ali out. Freddie Fuckface Fields ain't gonna fuck Frank Yablans," he yelled. Frank was tough. He was also right. Me, I made the dumbest decision of my life.

"Ali's doing the picture. That's it, Frank."

It all but cost me my partnership with Frank and my friendship with Charlie. No gray in this altercation. Black and white, they were right; I was wrong. Worse, both of them thought I was losing it. Again, they were right. I was—losing my wife, that is. Were my priorities fucked? What do you say about a guy who wants to get rid of his wife so he can be free to fight full-time with his director? Coppola was my primary thought, not Ali. Pure joy for Prince Coppola—making my life miserable. But no way was he going to slide something by me. Every hour of every day, I was on him like a cheap glove. Not once thinking of taking two days off to visit my wife on location, the very lady who had begged me not to be away from her for more than two weeks at a time. She was now shooting love scenes in El Paso with one of the world's most attractive men. I never gave it a second thought.

How could she fuck around on me?

Two months passed. At last I was going to see my wife. Fly to see her? No! She was flying to see me, be on my arm for the opening of *The Godfather.* My ego was so enormous that I never picked up the slightest vibe that her head and heart were thousands of miles away. Worse, I was also the last to find out. That memorable evening, to me and the thousands surrounding us, no two people looked more in love. A picture tells a thousand words. Stop reading and find the picture of the two of us dancing. That was the night. Ask yourself, how can a man ever read a woman? A man who thinks he can is a man who knows nothing.

A month later I was in Paris working with Danny Goldman, Paramount's head of foreign distribution, choosing top writers, directors, and actors to translate Paramount's gusher, *The Godfather,* into French, Italian, German, and Spanish. I had just convinced Louis Malle, one of France's premier directors, to helm the French version. I was on cloud nine, knowing his unique talent could translate an American *The Godfather* into *Le Parrain.*

Not a hybrid, rather a French film made in France. An expensive coup, paying Malle 100 Gs for a French version only.

"Sheer lunacy," distribution barked.

"A cheap buy," I answered.

Le Parrain became the highest grossing American film in French cinema history. Bursting with enthusiasm, I dialed El Paso to tell Ali of my coup.

"Sorry, Mr. Evans," said the operator, "no answer."

"Ring the nanny's room."

Missy, Joshua's nurse, picked up. "Ali's not here, Mr. Evans. She should be in shortly. I'll tell her to call you."

"Any time tonight, Missy."

Jumping up in a cold sweat, from a bad dream, I called El Paso again. No Ali. I laid back on the pillow. "Nah," I said to myself, "it couldn't be."

The phone rang at eight. It wasn't Ali—it was a wake-up call. I called El Paso before breakfast. Awaking Missy.

"Where the hell is Ali?" Silence. I knew she was covering.

I flew to Rome for the Italian dubbing of *The Godfather*. The moment I reached the Hassler Hotel, I called El Paso where it was now five in the morning. Ali's room-extension rang and rang.

"Sorry, no answer." squeaked the operator.

"Ring the nanny's room."

"Where's Ali?"

"I don't know, Mr. Evans."

I knew. And I knew she knew. Suddenly the Italian *Godfather* wasn't so urgent. I took a car to Cinecettà, where Alain Delon was shooting a film.

"It's a location fuck, that's all," shrugged Delon. "Happens all the time. When she comes home everything will be fine." Why couldn't *I* be French?

Later that afternoon, I connected.

"Where the hell have you been?"

"I fell asleep in my dressing room."

"You're lying!"

"You're right."

"You're with McQueen, aren't you?"

Silence. "Yes."

"I'm leaving for El Paso."

"Forget it! You missed the plane months ago."

I left Rome that night.

Missy and Joshua were at the airport to greet me—no Ali. I was checked into a hotel twenty miles out of town, just over the border in Mexico. Holding back my tears, I played with my son for the next few hours. Ali arrived at nine that evening.

When you ask too many questions, you get answers you don't want to hear. Alain was wrong—it wasn't a location fuck, it was full-blown, madly-in-love time. Ali's affair with McQueen had been going on for months. The last thing she wanted was to spend the night with me, but she did. It ain't a good feeling being kissed with a passion you've never felt before—none.

The next evening, she didn't return to my border hideout, but Sam Peckinpah did. "We're old pros, Bob. The situation stinks, but I've gotta finish the picture. As long as you're in town, McQueen's a no-show."

"Fuck him and the horse he rode in on. What about Ali?"

"Bad shape. Her eyes are like two balloons; can't stop crying."

"I ain't leaving. I'm going over to see Ali, now."

"Bob, don't."

"Fuck you too, Sam. I hired you to direct the film, not direct me. I've been laid, parlayed, and relaid by fuckin' Freddie Fields. Now his client, McQueen, is fucking me in the ass. Well the fuckin' is over. If there's gonna be any fuckin', it's gonna be me doin' it."

I sped into town, ran up the stairs of Ali's hotel, and banged on the door.

"I need time to think, Evans. Please, please, leave. Let me finish the picture and get home—for Josh's sake."

Women's tears always seem to work. On the plane back to L.A., I checked my watch. "How could I be so fucking dumb? It's an hour and forty minute flight and I never once took it till infidelity got me off my ass."

The fracas in El Paso became immediate fodder for the press. Instantly, the affair was common knowledge. One of my first calls was from Henry Kissinger.

"If I can be of any help, Bob . . ."

"Thanks, Henry, but it's too late."

"Do you want it to work?"

"Sure, but it's useless."

"If I can negotiate with the North Vietnamese, I think I can smooth the way with Ali."

"Henry, you know countries, you don't know women. When it's over, it's over."

A few days before *The Getaway* was to wrap, Ali called, said she was sending Josh and Missy home first. She was going off to the springs to thaw out and think.

How exciting it was seeing Joshua arrive back at Woodland. Five days later, Ali too arrived back in L.A., not to come home to Woodland but to go away and commiserate with herself. Paranoid and nontrusting, I sent my loyal friend, Gary Chazan, a true original whose bite is even tougher than his bark, to check out my questionable lady's arrival.

"I'm lookin' at the two of 'em. They're waiting for their luggage. . . . Should I break his fuckin' head?"

"Not yet. If they get into the same car, ram 'em. Get him out of the car . . . do what feels worst."

"Got it."

"He's a black belt, Gary, could be tough."

"He's a fuckin' actor." Laughing out loud.

A few hours later, Gary called back. "They took separate cars. He headed into the city. I followed her all the way to the hot springs. She just checked in. Want me to hang out and see if he shows?"

"Leave it."

That weekend was both my brother's birthday and Mother's Day. I rented a weekend house in Palm Springs for me, Charles, Joshua, and the nanny.

Ali called.

"It's so good to be away from everybody. How's Joshua? Is he all right? Is he happy being home? Evans, please come and pick me up. I miss you."

Maybe Alain was right.

"Bobbeee . . ." a long Mengela giggle, then in a half whisper, "McQueen just huffed out of my office, slammed the door in my face," another giggle, "told him, I'm trying to convince Ali to stay with my Bobbie. It's a good thing I'm hot!"

Memorial Day weekend, Sue Mengers, her husband, Jean-Claude, Ali, and I went to Palm Springs. Sue couldn't have cared less about losing Ali as a client. She wanted her back with me. Sue was my Kissinger—peace was just around the corner. But behind closed doors Ali and I weren't even holding hands.

I never asked her where she was during the day—I was afraid to find out. Coming home from the studio one day, I was surprised to see Sue and Ali in the living room having a fierce argument. Sue waved me away.

The next day I found out that Freddie the Fraud had given Steve the key to his beach house. Why? To fuck my wife. Nice guy, huh?

I began to tremble. That no good lying piece of shit. Just the year before I'd saved Freddie's ass. His wife Polly Bergen owned a cosmetics firm, Oil-of-the-Turtle. Freddie had heard Bluhdorn might be interested in buying into the cosmetics business and had asked me to intercede on his and Polly's behalf. I knew Freddie had once lied to Charlie—a cardinal sin in Bluhdorn's book. I told Freddie there was no way I could get them together.

"Freddie, you know Charlie's feelings toward you."

"Please, Bob."

Charlie was in a meeting with the top executives of one of his many companies, Associate Investment. I broke in.

"Charlie, I know you've been looking to buy a cosmetics company—"

Bluhdorn exploded, "Hold it! Does it have to do with Freddie Fields?"

Knowing how to get to him, down on my knees I went, hands up, as if I were talking to God. "Please, Charlie, do it for me?"

Charlie slowly panned the other eight men in the room, loving every second of the drama. "These people from Hollywood! I told you they're crazy. They're all crazy! See what I have to put up with? I won't see Freddie, Evans,"

Still on my knees looking up.

"It's important Charlie, for me." Relishing the drama for his cohorts to laugh at.

"Is Polly with him?"

I shook my head yes.

"Have her here tonight at eight P.M.—alone!"

Within seventy-two hours, for a high seven-figure amount, Gulf + Western was now the proud owner of Oil-of-the-Turtle. A year later "the turtle" drowned. For years, there wasn't a week that passed where Bluhdorn didn't throw my bended-knee plea in my face. Did Freddie appreciate it? Sure, he went out of his way to give Steve McQueen the key to his beach house, to fuck my wife.

Click, the fence went up. Click, the fence went down, all $186,000 of it, a hydraulic fence disappearing four feet into a brick slab on a click. Click it again, it automatically rose four feet above the ground, tightly surrounding my egg-shaped pool. A first in its design, it was there for Joshua's protection. There was one problem. Joshua wasn't there; he was with Ali.

Did it haunt me? Well, let's just say I became a total recluse, sitting alone by the pool, night after night, pressing the button, watching the fence go up, go down, up, down. Hard as people tried, no one could break my spell. Those around me were getting concerned that I was flipping out. It didn't bother me; I was in my own world. Days turned into weeks, weeks into months. The hottest new bachelor in town couldn't bring himself to go to a dinner party, much less to look at a woman. My pleasure was fulfilled by the click-click of the fence going up and down.

In the end, I had no say about it—Sidney Korshak ordered the fence taken out. He was right; it was a crutch that kept me with the past. No matter how hard it hurts, you've got to trudge ahead. Stand still—you'll only get older.

Success breeds strange bedfellows. Sharing history was the key that attracted Coppola to take over where Truman Capote left off and adapt Fitzgerald's *Gatsby* for the screen. Quite a coup, since he had just won the Academy Award for writing *The Godfather*. Waiting anxiously in the bull pen was Jack Clayton, one of England's finest maestros, set to direct. The impossible became possible. In three months, Coppola delivered a screenplay that really worked. Full speed ahead was the dictate. Paramount now filled a big hole in their release schedule—*Gatsby* would be the Christmas picture.

From Sue Mengers and Ray Stark to Eileen Ford in New York, everyone extended themselves to find Miss Right for the now reclusive bachelor. No matter how right Miss Right was, in my eyes she would still be Miss Wrong. Call it wallowing in your misery, but never once did I leave the gates of my Woodland hideaway.

A howling bark so eerie that I jumped from my bed, through the front door and out to the driveway. Was it a wolf? Uh-uh, a tall, lanky hunk of lady with a humongous white German shepherd.

"You're at the wrong place."

"If I'm at the wrong place, I'll leave," a throaty voice answered, as she turned to leave down the long winding driveway. "Big mistake, Evans."

"Hey, who the hell are you?"

Doing an about-face, she said, "Chiles. Lois Chiles."

Still not understanding, "Yeah?"

"I'm doing a film with Ray Stark."

"One of Ray's jokes, huh?"

"I've never been a joke. Sydney Pollack is directing me: *The Way We Were*. It's Ray's. He must be a good friend. He gave me orders to break your spell."

Ray wasn't Hollywood's top producer by mistake. He was right, she was the only who could have. She did.

Moxie? This dame put the word to shame. In two days she moved in, lock, stock, and barrel. She had met Jack Clayton months before in New York. Jack told her that she'd make an interesting Jordan, the second female lead in *The Great Gatsby*. Being a cocksman, he must have told a hundred others the same. Heifetz's finesse at the fiddle paled compared to Lois's finesse with me. It wasn't difficult, I was an open wound.

"If Ali's not playing Daisy," she'd sigh, "why, I'd just *love* to test for it."

Schmuck that I was, I thought she dug me. Fuckin' *Gatsby* was a double-edged sword. My desire to make it was now totally lost. Coppola's script, Clayton set to direct, Redford desperate to sign on as Gatsby.

To Bluhdorn, Yablans, and me, Freddie Fields eeled, "I'm making it up to you, fellas. . . . How's this for casting: McQueen and MacGraw together for nothing? Wants to do it as a gift for his ole lady."

Bluhdorn panted, "Both of them together, for nothing? Freddie, I don't like you, but I could kiss you."

Guns were drawn.

"No way, Charlie. Forget it!"

"Are you crazy, Evans? *Gatsby* with the two of them? And a Coppola script. Paramount'll have the biggest picture of the year."

"I don't care if it doubles *The Godfather*. I'm not going through any more hell. It's them or me."

The chairman stopped cold in his tracks, his trigger cocked, his glasses off, silently squinting.

"It's your call, Charlie."

Two minutes of silence from Bluhdorn. Never did his eyes leave mine.

"No. It's your call, Evans."

Moments like this stay with you forever.

The casting of Daisy Buchanan got more press than the search for Scarlett O'Hara. Every major actress wanted the part. Like Scarlett O'Hara, no matter how big the star, they all had to lower themselves to be tested. Not one actress refused. One morning I opened a letter and a pressed daisy fell out; the note read, "May I be your Daisy. Love, Mia."

We narrowed the list of Daisys down to Mia Farrow, Faye Dunaway, Candice Bergen, Katharine Ross, and guess who? Texas moxie herself.

A few days before Christmas, I flew to New York, where the tests were being shot. Forty-eight hours later, the duel was to start, no holds barred. The setting? Gulf + Western's screening room. The gunslingers: David Merrick, the film's producer; his hired gun, Alan DeLynn; Jack Clayton; Frank Yablans; Robert Evans; Charles Bluhdorn. All our pieces were cocked. Making the first move, I stood up.

"Gentlemen, I'm setting the rules. We're going to look at all the tests, then the order of critique will start with Mr. Clayton, followed by Mr. Merrick, then Mr. DeLynn, myself, Mr. Yablans, and last Mr. Bluhdorn. It's my only dictate. When the tests are over, everyone can take their best shot. Let's roll 'em."

Close to an hour later the curtains closed, the lights came up.

"They're all marvelous," said Jack Clayton, "but only Mia has the right vulnerability. She's spent her whole life being a butterfly. She's the most haunting—"

Merrick didn't let Clayton finish.

"They all stink! What are we playing games for? There's only one person who can play Daisy—Ali MacGraw. It was bought for her, and we get McQueen as a bonus. Am I losing my mind? Why are we watching the minors, when we've got the biggest male and female star on a silver platter for nothing?" Fiercely eyeing me, he continued, "Let's start being professional, Mr. Evans."

His flunky, DeLynn, stood up. "I totally agree with David."

Silence is a wonderful weapon. They could have screamed their fuckin' lungs out, I held the ace. The 250-pound cleaning woman who scrubs toilets would play Daisy before Ali got the part. Bluhdorn's not the type of guy to go back on his word. Did he love me? Sure. But that didn't figure in his rationale. McQueen and MacGraw were just a single feature. I represented twenty to forty pictures and he fuckin' well knew I'd walk. Holding aces, I was somewhat professorial.

"Candy Bergen has a regal quality . . . a breeding—"

Yablans quickly interrupted. "She's wrong!"

Merrick's voice cut through, "They're all wrong! It's MacGraw. Let's get down to reality!"

Then Uncle Charlie jumped in. "Hold it! Hold it! It's too important a decision. Let's look at the tests again."

Bluhdorn's timing personified his success. The room darkened, the curtains opened again, and again the tests began, Mia's the first to run. On her last line Bluhdorn stood up.

"Jack, I have to agree. Mia Farrow has a certain vulnerability, a *mystical* quality."

"You're right," I authoritatively echoed, "absolutely right. She has that hint of spoiled arrogance—"

Apoplectic, Merrick jumped to his feet screaming, "Is everybody crazy? We have Ali MacGraw and Steve McQueen working for nothing. And we're ending up with *Mia Farrow?*"

"I agree with David," seconded his stooge, DeLynn.

Now Yablans growled, "You're goddamn right he's right! Is this a movie company or a lonely hearts club we're running? I'd like to know, so I can tell my wife what business I'm in."

It was tough biting my tongue, but I did. Because Yablans was right again.

Cutting everyone down to size, Chairman Bluhdorn interrupted, "Ali MacGraw is not doing the picture. Is that clear? Paramount owns the rights. Is that clear? If anyone wants to walk, have a Merry Christmas. Is that clear? Mr. Clayton is right. The best Daisy is Mia Farrow."

Suddenly a hush prevailed. Bluhdorn didn't make his bones being just another pretty face.

"Thank you, Mr. Bluhdorn," said Clayton. "Let's talk about the part of Jordan. May I suggest Lois Chiles? She has a wonderful throaty voice, a certain . . . masculinity."

"I've had enough of this shit!" Yablans interrupted. "Evans's wives! Evans's girlfriends! Are we running a brothel or a movie company?"

"Hey, Frank, hold it! *I* didn't suggest Lois Chiles for anything," I said. "It's the director who wants her, not me!"

"The only reason the broad got tested is because she spread her legs for you!"

Bluhdorn jumped up. "Apologize to Bob, Frank!"

Yablans apologize? He walked out. He was right!

"Jack," said Charlie, "you want Lois Chiles for Jordan Baker?"

"Yes."

"Okay, settled. Now can I leave for my Christmas vacation?"

"Lois, I've got a Merry Christmas for you. Get your ass up here real quick!"

She was at the Carlyle in twenty minutes. If I ever felt like a mogul it was then.

"You got the part of Jordan, Lois. Congratulations."

She pulled away as I bent over to kiss her.

Her voice was one I'd never heard before. "Jordan? You're telling me I'm *Jordan*? I want Daisy, do you hear me? I want *Daisy*!"

From seductress to witch in a blink. Shocked? Yeah.

"Thanks, kid, you just put me through college, you got the part. You earned it." I walked to the door, opened it. "Now get the fuck out!"

She didn't get it. "But we're leaving for Acapulco tomorrow. . . ."

Cutting her off with the warmth of an iceberg, "You're lucky the elevator's near. Listen real close. I'm a memory. Got it! If we're in the same room, you don't see me. Got it! Now get the fuck outta my life. Got it!"

29

I'd been kissed enough. Bluhdorn's Golden Boy now wanted some gold of his own. In 1966 when I started with Charlie, there were eight major companies. Paramount was ninth. In 1971, we ascended to number one and were only getting stronger. By that time, I had charmed Lucille Ball into selling her Desilu Studios, which she had bought from RKO, adjacent to Paramount. Their film library came with it as well—"I Love Lucy" and "The Untouchables" being two of the many. Not bad, huh? The price wasn't bad either. A fire sale couldn't have gotten it for less.

Whether it be fortuitous or not, Charlie's Golden Boy was delivering results, not weather reports. Our relationship was indeed strange. Akin to husband and wife—he the man, me the woman. Lover Bluhdorn wanted his lady to live well, but not too well. Never wanting me to earn big green—to become independent or have "fuck you" money. No different than husbands are to wives.

I've never had a girlfriend nor wife who was more jealous than Charlie of any affection I showed toward others. He was even jealous of my affections to the other Charlie in life—my brother. For better or worse, that's where I stood in Bluhdorn's heart and mind. While others in my very position were compensated times three, and not bringing in results, Charlie never even gave me a bonus. Not for *Love Story* or *The Godfather*. For that matter, not for Desilu, which was beyond the call of duty, and happened only because of my close relationship with Lucille Ball. It was a billion-dollar gobble for a ten-million-dollar check. Not a bad meal, huh? But not a crumb was left over for schmuck Evans.

Forget being kissed, I was being fucked! My brother Charlie, an astute businessman, kept prodding me to confront my boss Charlie.

"You're borrowing money from me to pay taxes while you're building his empire into megabillions. Doesn't make sense to me. Schmuck, they're keeping you in the closet when it comes to green. Wake up. Your head's in the clouds."

It came to a head when my direct involvement was responsible for Charlie's gobbling up the prize package of the decade, Simon & Schuster. The price? Eleven million dollars. Its worth today? North of three billion. Marty Davis was covered when Bluhdorn, through Davis's ingenuity, purchased Paramount at a bargain-basement price. What about me? *What about nothing!*

Locking horns with Charlie on financial matters was akin to my challenging Pete Sampras at Wimbledon. He had more shrewdness in his toenail than I had in my whole body. Without question, my years at Paramount were the quintessential good-news and bad-news situation. The good news: the entire candy store was mine to run; Charlie rubber-stamped my every dictate. The bad: "Keep 'im broke; it keeps 'im around."

I was a big man in the industry, living in a big home, with a big problem—I couldn't afford to pay my taxes. It wasn't by mistake—Bluhdorn wanted it that way.

While I was living rich, everyone around me was getting rich. Irving Thalberg had received a percentage of every film made under the MGM banner. With that in mind, I sent for my heavy artillery, Sidney Korshak, and asked him to have a powwow with Bluhdorn.

"My contract's up. I've been throwing sevens too long and I'm still behind the eight ball."

"I'll take care of it and quick," answered Korshak. "You're gonna get gross. I don't care if it's just one percent on every film Paramount makes. Charlie'll go for it," he laughed. "It's still only futures—nothing retroactive. The prick still doesn't have to write out a check."

Korshak may have been known as the Myth, but he was no myth to Charlie. His proposal was turned down flatter than Twiggy's chest. Bluhdorn wasn't smart, he was brilliant—one of the very few I've met who genuinely deserve the adjective. He knew my weak link—ego—and pressed it, knowing it far overshadowed my greed.

"I want Bob to make history," Bluhdorn told Korshak. "He can make one picture a year, for five years, under his own banner, Robert Evans Productions, and still remain head of Paramount. The last person to have that was Darryl Zanuck, thirty years ago. Paramount and Evans will be fifty-fifty partners, with third parties coming off the top. If the picture's a hit, he'll make big money. But he'll do more. He'll break a barrier that can't be done in Hollywood today and I want him to do that. I want to be proud of him."

Korshak was a negotiator, not an entertainment attorney. He presented Bluhdorn's deal and, like Simple Simon, I fell for it—hook, line, and sinker. Bluhdorn was quick to get the contracts drawn and signed. For the next five years I'd be Paramount's head of production, with no bonus and no raise, but a great announcement in the trades and *New York Times*. At the height of my career, with the toughest lawyer in America, I ended up with a kiss but no cigar.

The first production of the Robert Evans Productions had its origins over dinner with Bob Towne. Having just read Capote's disastrous script of *Gatsby,* I'd asked the best script doctor in the business to meet me for dinner at Dominique's. Before I could get into *Gatsby,* Towne began telling me about an original screenplay he was working on.

"It's about how Los Angeles became a boomtown—incest and water. It's set in the thirties. A second-rate shamus gets eighty-sixed by a mysterious broad. Instead of solving a case for her, he's the pigeon. I'm writing it for Nicholson."

"Sounds perfect for Irish. What's it called?"

"*Chinatown.*"

"What's that got to do with it? You mean it's set in Chinatown?"

"No. *Chinatown* is a state of mind—Jake Gittes's fucked-up state of mind."

"I see," I said, not seeing it at all.

Towne was a script doctor who didn't have enough money to get new soles for his shoes. Yet at the time, his integrity was such that he turned down $175,000 for *Gatsby* to *schreibe Chinatown* for $25,000. After an hour of his telling me the story, I understood it less, but how could I turn down the top script doctor in town when he's willing to work for scale plus change? Whatever he lacked in prosperity, he made up for in industry panache, and I wanted to be A list all the way on the first flick bearing my banner.

Six months later, Towne delivered his first draft. No one understood it—especially me. Just like the title, it was pure Chinese. The more Towne tried to explain, the more frustrating the exercise. I couldn't take it.

"Don't explain it, Bob. *Write* it."

From Frank Yablans to Norman Whiteman (head of distribution) to Gary Chazan (who had become my assistant), all echoed: "Don't make this your first picture. The only place it'll be seen is in your projection room."

One afternoon, Frank and Gary cornered me in my office.

"It's your call, Evans," Yablans said. "If you want to make it, you've got my okay. But you're here alone with Gary and me. Don't bullshit us. Do you understand the fuckin' script?"

I couldn't lie. "Nope."

"Don't feel bad about it. No one else does either. Don't make it, please. I don't want you to fall on your ass the first time out."

Gary interrupted. "Frank's right, Evans. See if you can lock up *The Gambler* as your first picture."

With my leg throbbing from sciatic pain, my thumb in my mouth like a newborn sucking a bottle, I paced before them. I knew I had Nicholson locked, and, even though I didn't understand the script, I knew Towne was a great writer. I felt like a blind gambler wanting to throw back to back sevens.

"*Chinatown*'s my picture, fellas. That's it."

"With everything at your disposal, Evans, you pick this piece of shit," Yablans chided. "It's fuckin' suicide, but what the fuck do I know? I used to pluck chickens. It's your ass. You've done crazier things before. It's yours, kid." Then he hugged me, his head still shaking in dismay.

"Polanski from London, Mr. Evans."

"Roman, I've got two houses for you to look at. I think you'll like them both."

"I can't come for two weeks."

"The script's a fuckin' mess, Roman. I need you here yesterday."

"I've got to go to Poland, Bob, for Passover."

"Fuck Passover, Roman. If you don't get here, we're never going to get into shape. I'll have Passover at my house."

A first: I'd never held a Passover seder in my home. I didn't know what to serve, but if it took matzos to get the maestro to America, matzos it was.

Jack was already set for the film. Six months earlier, he had finished *The Last Detail,* written by Bob Towne. Nicholson and Towne were as close as two guys could be. Towne, the son of a very wealthy realtor in Los Angeles, and Jack, the vagabond with an earth-shaking smile, whose leading-man status had not yet been revealed.

Because Jack was always playing character roles, *Chinatown* was his first stab at being a romantic lead. My money was on the Irishman. That's why I wanted to make the picture. The devilish wink of his eye lit up the screen. His devastating smile shook not only the rafters but the limbs of most every woman I knew. His cracked voice did the rest. In person, he was a room-rocker; on screen, he was just himself—a screen-rocker. It's hard to fathom, but at the time, I was alone at Paramount in my belief that the Irishman had a billion-dollar presence. To them, everything about *Chinatown,* from Roman Polanski (who hadn't made a hit since *Rosemary's Baby*) to the script *no one understood* and the leading man and woman, was an "Evans jerk-off."

"Pal," said the Irishman, sitting across from me in the projection room, "do you understand the pages?"

I dumbed it, not answering.

"If you do, explain them to me. Roman's parking here tomorrow. Maybe he'll understand them." He picked up the script. "Could Towne have written it in Polish for the Polchick?"

Polanski blew into town, but *really* blew when he read the script. Yet his resolve was decisive: "I'll fix it, I'll fix it. Have I disappointed you yet?"

Feverishly, Roman got into the screenplay with Bob and the fights started. Not unlike Coppola and myself, there wasn't one nuance in the entire screenplay they agreed on.

Meanwhile, a Chinese acupuncturist had been summoned from Paris to be the thirty-eighth person to work on my sciatic problem. He was taking out the hairlike needles (which hurt like hell by the way) when an urgent call was put through from Polanski.

"What's the emergency, Roman?"

"Bob, tomorrow."

"Yeah."

"Don't tell me you forgot."

"What?"

"Passover. Is everything arranged?"

Passover? I didn't even know when Passover was.

"You forgot, didn't you?" Roman snickered. "And you're my producer! It's like a Polish movie. I've got a script I don't understand and a producer who's flirting with senility!"

"When is Passover?"

"Tomorrow."

"Starts at sundown, huh?"

"It does in Poland."

"Okay, Polchick. Be here at sundown tomorrow and don't forget, wear a tie."

Punctually at sundown, dressed in suit, shirt, and tie, Roman arrived. Greeting him were Anne and Kirk Douglas; Carol and Walter Matthau and their son, Charlie; Audrey and Billy Wilder; Sue Mengers and her husband, Jean-Claude Tramont; the fetching beauties Leigh Taylor-Young and Joanna Cameron; and sporting a yarmulke, Warren Beatty. From the drawing room, we adjourned to the dining room, where my butler and two servants proceeded to serve a Passover meal authentic enough to get the nod from Golda Meir. Only half of the guests at the table were Jewish in faith, but in spirit, it was as festive as joining a kibbutz betrothal.

Star-fuck I did. Who gets Kirk Douglas to be the rabbi? Not dubbed, either; in perfect Hebrew, Spartacus himself recited aloud the prayers. This hunk of Viking male was a better rabbi than actor.

Down to the last detail, the evening was perfect. Young Charlie Matthau, at that time no older than ten or eleven, was there to answer
"the four questions" from Rabbi Douglas. Without a youth present,
that touching moment would have been lost. Out came the camera
and I took dozens of pictures of the evening.

When Roman had hung the phone up thirty hours earlier, I was
determined to take him at his sarcastic word and show him what a
producer really is. First step was to ask Sidney Korshak to call the
Hillcrest Country Club and get the head chef to prepare what constitutes the perfect Passover feast. One call from Korshak and the chef
was at my home the next day with plates, silverware, every condi-
ment imaginable (including red horseradish), prayer books, and two
educated waiters who knew how to serve what at the right time.

My snobbish butler, David, didn't know the difference between
gefilte fish and bluefish. If he did, he pretended not to. But he did
look very patrician at the door, black tie and all, greeting my Passover guests.

Thank you, Sidney. I don't think anyone else in town could have
delivered Hillcrest on wheels (and by the way, in deference to Sidney, totally gratis). A myth is a myth, is a myth, is a myth.

Roman left that night whispering to himself, "Now *that's* a producer, that's a producer, that's a producer."

Me, I kept studying the Polaroids, thinking to myself, Is Warren
Beatty really Jewish, is Warren Beatty really Jewish, is Warren
Beatty really Jewish?

30

Jane Fonda was everybody's first choice to play opposite Jack. There was one problem—Fonda was hedging, not sure she wanted to play the part. Understandably, she didn't understand the script. Concurrently giving me heartburn was Sue Mengers, Faye Dunaway's agent. She pushed her client on me to the point of blackmail. Thank you, Sue—Dunaway's singular mystery on screen was among the best casting choices of my career. Making her deal, however, was another story.

"Bobbee, I need an offer by the end of business, Friday. Otherwise, I'm closing a deal with Arthur Penn for my Faye to star in *Night Moves*."

"Sue, I'll get back to you tomorrow. Now leave me alone."

I immediately called Roman. "I know Jane's one, two, and three on your list. She's playing cute with us, Roman. Get her to say yes or tell her to fuck off. Otherwise, I lose Dunaway."

"I don't want her anyway. The script's tough enough to understand. I don't need her *mishegoss.*"

"Then settle with Fonda tonight. You've romanced her enough; it's time to make love. Tonight, Roman!"

Fuck her he didn't. Fucked he got. Fonda didn't want to play. My first call the next morning was to Sue.

"Sorry, Sue, but the studio wants to go with Jane. You and me talking now. I still want Faye. She's more mysterious. That's what the part's all about. But what can I do?"

Hooked by the bait. "Plenty! It's your picture. If you want my Faye, tell them all to take a flying fuck."

"Easy for you to say, Mengela."

"Convince Nicholson that Dunaway's more interesting. Then call Bluhdorn, tell him to back you." A giggle. "Then drop it on the fuckers. It's Dunaway or no way!"

"It won't work. Bluhdorn wants Fonda too. Hey, I've got an idea. It's a long shot: *dinero* . . . not Bobby De Niro . . . dinero *dinero.*"

With the instinct of a jungle cat, Sue got the message *quickly*.

"Okay, what's the deal?"

"Don't give me your sarcastic shit, Mengela. I'm trying to make something work that no one wants."

Sharper than a Vegas pit boss, her voice now two octaves lower, "What's the deal, prick?"

"Fifty thou—"

The phone slammed in my ear before I could finish. I waited for her to call back. She knew I was waiting. She didn't call. I'm still the buyer though. She's the seller.

Finally, Mengela made the first move. She had no choice.

"Bobbee . . . you don't want Mengela to lose a client, do you? You know what a prima donna she is. If I mention numbers even close to that, she'll fire me. They're all crazy."

"Mengela, tell Dunaway I'm doing this for you, not for her. You know it. I know it. And she knows it . . . she's colder than Baskin-Robbins."

"Arthur Penn doesn't think so, Bobbeee. Remember *Bonnie and Clyde, The Thomas Crown Affair—*"

I interrupted her role call. "Remember *Doc . . . The Deadly Trap . . . Oklahoma Crude?* Three in a row. For a dame, I don't care who she is, three strikes in a row and you're out. Sue, listen real careful. I love ya. The only shot we have is bargain-basement time. I've got a weak link I can play on. They want John Huston to play old man Mulwray. There ain't no money in the budget for it. That's my hook. Got it?"

"Got it, prick," hanging the phone up in my ear.

Again, I waited for her call back. She knew I was waiting. It was her call to make—she had no choice. It was now past 7:00 P.M., I poured myself a scotch, patiently waiting for the phone to ring. It did.

"Bobbeee?"

"Mengela."

"We'll take it."

"I think it could be too late. You should have gotten back to me sooner. Let me get on the horn and try to stop the deal with Fonda."

"You prick, you no-good bastard. First you make my client spread her legs, then you tell us 'I'll get back to you'? You son of a—" Slam went the phone in my ear.

At eight the next morning I called Sue. "I've had a tough night with Roman, Sue. He's scared shitless that Dunaway will be difficult to work with. Thank God, Jack was there, he helped me convince him. Tell Faye she's got the part."

Like a Sotheby's auctioneer, "Closed?" said Mengela.

"Closed," I said. "Do I at least get a thank you?" I got a giggle.

"Bobbeee . . ."

"Yeah?"

"I fibbed." Another giggle. "There was no part in *Night Moves* for Faye." Mengela was getting off. Her giggling nonstop.

I held the phone, until lack of oxygen made her stop.

"Mengela?"

Hardly able to catch her breath, "What?"

"Fonda passed."

I lost the hearing in my left ear from the slam of the phone.

Roman: intense, focused, punctual. Towne: lethargic, scattered, perpetually late. Two brutal months of preparations with Roman not knowing whom to kill first; Towne or Hira, Town's white, shaggy and shedding, giant hunk of a sheepdog.

"Hira, Hira," Roman moaned. "Wherever I go there's hair. I'm scratching where I shouldn't. His script stinks, his dog smells. I should have stayed in Paris. Wherever I go, there's dog shit."

On September 28, 1973, World War III started—*Chinatown*'s first day of principal photography. The tension so tight, not a word, not even hello, was uttered between its creators. Nicholson was getting his nuts off, his smile on full, sucking up the lunacy of his pals' mutual disdain.

Autocratic Roman barred Towne not only from the set, but even from seeing the dailies. As referee, I now had to watch dailies with Roman at the studio and again with Bob at home.

"The Polack can't interpret English," Towne said.

Poor guy; he only had two ears to vent his anger—mine. Worse for Roman than Towne was Dunaway. Was she difficult? No, "impossible," said the maestro. A perfectionist. "Silk stockings were a must to be part of being a lady in the thirties," she declared. Didn't matter to her that in the seventies they were nowhere to be found. She insisted, and we searched until they were found. Hurrah for you, dear Faye. Roman didn't share my feelings.

"Tell me, it's true," Roman said. "You're paying me back for Passover. Dunaway's a menace. Towne's a mess. Up there someone's telling me, 'Schmuck, you should've spent Passover in Poland.'"

It was a hair that broke the camel's back. Dunaway dressed to the nines—hat, veil, and all—confronting her newfound shamus, Nicholson in a clandestine rendezvous at a posh thirties L.A. restaurant. The scene demanded sparks to fly. Sparks did fly, but not on the screen. Through the camera, Roman saw a wire of a hair reeling up from Dunaway's veil. He went over and plucked it to save the shot—instead of thanks, he got a smack across the face.

"Touch me again, I'll call in my troops!" screamed Dunaway in full theatrical fury.

The set closed down. A summit was called. Sue Mengers was out of town, so agency boss Freddie Fields took on the challenge.

"Forget Polanski, he's crazy. I'll give you Mark Rydell—he'll make a picture out of this mess."

"Fuck you, Freddie. Polanski's my choice, Dunaway's my star. I'll handle it."

First to Dunaway. "The two scenes you've shot—spellbinding!" Dunaway was hardly impressed. Then came an offer hard to refuse: "An Oscar nod or a Rolls Corniche—one of the two I personally guarantee is yours."

By then Coppola's Mercedes was a legend. How could she refuse? Melt she did. Then I went to Roman.

"What you're getting from Dunaway makes Svengali look like a peasant."

A balk . . . a shout . . . a Polish moan of despair.

"An Oscar nod, or a Rolls Corniche," I offered. "Without one, the other is yours courtesy of yours truly."

A Polanski look. A Polanski laugh.

"Make it a Bentley and you can bring Dunaway back to the set."

Luckily for me, they were both nominated for Oscars, and everything else you could name.

Chinatown's last scene brought with it the heavy luggage of deep dispute and fence-straddling second guesses.

"Ruinous . . . immoral," said Towne. "It is not the story that I told."

Roman saw it another way, the evil way, the unexpected. "It's what 'memorable' is all about," he said.

"Demented," Towne fought back.

"That's right," I said. "That's why Roman will get his way."

Till this day, Towne vents his anger toward me. How *could* I have sided with Roman? Poor Robert, for all his *schreien* he copped his one and only Oscar for his "fucked up" *Chinatown.* Subjectivity rarely allows the artist the proper perspective he needs to judge the merits of his work. An overview is needed, showing your canvas for the objective eye to critique. Call it by its proper name: *previewing.* This area, by far, is the biggest bone of contention that I have with the industry today.

With production costs inflated and the price tag for television advertising obscene, the final product is not left to the opinion of its maker, nor for that matter to the audience, but to "invitees."

If you are invited to my home for dinner and the roast beef is served cold and dry, you don't complain since you are a guest. If roast beef is served the very same way in a fine restaurant, back to the kitchen it goes. Why? When you pay the two bucks, your opinion matters. No different in film. Shopping malls are canvased, invitees are picked. If you hate the film, you don't walk out; if you love the film, you don't stand and applaud. In days of old (or days of mine), we'd test the response in the theaters. Many a time, the audience would stand and shout, "we want out," or stand and shout, "we want more." Today, that emotion is no longer there, only the invitee numbers telling us about how our film fared. It's called the age of marketing. In reality, it is the age of despair.

The first preview of *Chinatown,* in San Luis Obispo, was a disaster. By the time the lights came up, half the audience had walked out, scratching their heads. Roman and I felt the only way to save the picture was to give it a new sound—eerie, haunting, mysterious—"a lonely horn." It took only eight days of Jerry Goldsmith brilliance to accomplish the impossible, a solo trumpet played against strings. His theme was so erotic and eerie that magically *Chinatown* became mesmerizing.

When the lights came up the next time we previewed it, the same silence was there, but the audience was transfixed.

Chinatown had a gala screening at the Directors Guild. Everyone in town was there. When the film was over and the final credits began to role, there was no applause, but no one stood up to leave. It was more eerie than the film itself. The curtains closed; the lights came up. Still not a murmur. I was sure it was a bomb. I was reassured of my assurance when Rona Barrett, the gossip columnist of the day, passed me and gave me a nod of despair: "How could you make this picture?"

Sue Mengers was more blunt. "What kind of *mishegoss* is this?"

Next was my old pal, Freddie Fields, unable to hold back his smile. "Sorry, kid," he waved to me.

Nine months later, *Chinatown* was honored with eleven Academy Award nominations. The film was a six-to-five favorite with the Los Vegas odds for a clean sweep. The reason it was swept under, instead of over, was because of me; it was the only picture of the five that a studio head personally produced. When one sits in the catbird seat, for every one yes you give, there are a hundred nos. Unlike the other four producers, my nos had alienated a preponderance of voters.

It would be my last year to helm "the mountain" and that year brought Paramount forty-three Academy Award nominations— more than any other studio had received in a single year since the beginning of the Academy. That's wasn't good enough for me. I wanted to accomplish the impossible—run a studio and have my own picture win the Academy Award, then resign and go into independent production. Well, it didn't quite work out that way. Bulls and bears end up in comfort, pigs in the gutter. I was a pig, and that's where I ended up. Instead of resigning as head of Paramount three months earlier and being out there with the rest of the folk, I had to be a first. In doing so, I not only fucked myself, I fucked the others nominated for the film. Many of whom deserved to win but, because of the backlash against Mr. Big Shot, they were swept under the carpet with me.

Since the *Chinatown* crew went in as overwhelming favorites, the bookies cleaned up. Of the three Paramount films nominated for best picture—*Chinatown, The Godfather Part II,* and *The Conversation*—*Chinatown* was nominated in the most categories (eleven), but ended up with only one Oscar—best screenplay.

One of the conditions Francis Coppola had insisted on in agreeing to make *Godfather II* was total control. He certainly didn't want the likes of me around again. Its first preview, however, at the Coronet Theater in San Francisco, was a disaster, and he suddenly became collaborative. Paul Hagar, Paramount's super post-production man, and I were invited into Francis's inner sanctum to restructure his Sicilian fiasco.

"It's your night," the maestro now said, as we stood together in back of the Dorothy Chandler Pavilion before the ceremonies started.

"No, Francis, it's yours."

My pal Beatty, who had never before graced the Oscar telecast as a presenter, had offered to present the best picture award; he wanted to announce my name in front of the world as producer of the best picture of the year. There I sat, front row, with my brother as my date, watching Beatty open the envelope for the world to hear. A subliminal look, an unnoticeable wince—I was the first to know the Oscar was not mine to take.

Smile and all, Beatty announced the winner: "Francis Ford Coppola, *The Godfather Part II.*"

It was mine too, but by proxy only. To Roman's chagrin, the one Oscar for *Chinatown* went to Shakespeare himself, Robert Towne.

Post-showtime, Prince Machiavelli graciously approached me.

"I've lost all the joy of winning. Again I forgot to thank you."

He ain't called the Prince for nothin'.

"If you ever want to get rid of Evans at a party, just light up a joint," cracked Polanski.

Though I was in my forties, the entire drug era passed me by without notice. It wasn't my scene; I barely even drank.

Nineteen seventy-four ended with a platinum bang: a new five-year contract with Paramount. No raise in green, but here I was the only head of a studio with my own production company, with the calling card of *Chinatown* as my first at-bat. Envied by the outside world, but how little they knew.

Continuing sciatica left me throbbing with pain too weary to even touch the taste of success. From the Mayo Clinic to every half- and full-assed specialist in the country, the consensus was unanimous—operate. Surgery would mean having to learn to walk again, but there was no assurance that the pain would not come back in full force. I passed and continued searching for something to numb the pain.

Lying beside me, a Hollywood princess. "Is it me?" she asked. "The pain can't be that bad."

"It is."

"It's the third night we've shared. It must be me."

With that, I gave it my best. Valiant, but no cigar—instead, a searing pain from my back down to my leg. In a cold sweat, I turned on my side to catch my breath. She snuggled close.

"Don't even try."

Wearing only a necklace, she handed it to me. A gold cylinder dropped from its chain. Unscrewing the top, she whispered to me, "Take a sniff—a sniff of life."

"Is it what I think it is?"

"It'll help."

"Uh-uh, not for me."

"For me?" she cooed.

My first experience into the world of white.

Did it help my back? No. Did it help my nose? No. Did it fuck up my career? More than that—*it fucked up my life.*

With Ali and Joshua no longer at Woodland, I was overseeing fifteen to twenty pictures a year, working eighteen hours a day, seven days a week—much of the time from hospital beds set up at home.

There's nothing more debilitating and draining than constant pain. There's nothing more false and destructive than artificial energy. Keeping your motor on high eighteen hours a day, which I was doing, commuting from one editing room to another. What started out as a fuck drug all but ruined my life of fucking. Cocaine being one of the "caine" brothers—Novocain, Xylocaine, procaine. It's a cold bunch of guys; they're all freezers. Dentists use Novocain before they drill you to freeze the surrounding nerves. Like his brother, cocaine freezes the nerve as well. The wrong one. A snort of brother coke stops the rush of blood from brain to tool. Coming up short is your cock. Coming up long is dialogue and energy.

Hooked? How could I be. Every time a new woman entered my world, or my life, or my bed, I immediately stopped with the straw. Not because I didn't enjoy it, rather the freeze prevented me from performing in the sack. There was one problem; almost every new lady I met was using the stuff. Not being the most self-disciplined person, it wasn't long before I was using it again. Soon I started to peter out. And there went the relationship.

Cocaine loosens the tongue and softens the weewee. Soon you forget you have one. I remember taking a well-known German actress to Acapulco. Lying in bed one evening—snorting—she began showing me pictures of various castles she owned in Europe.

"Old family, huh?"

"No, rich business. I'm an international courier."

"Of art?"

"No, of drugs."

"You're putting me on."

She wasn't. She proceeded to describe her incredibly lucrative double life.

"You've made enough money. Why don't you get out?"

"They'd kill me."

My friend and associate Gary Chazan was with us in Mexico. Later that night I told him the story. He looked at me as if I were Macauley Culkin.

"Get her the fuck out. Now!"

"We're getting along great."

"Are your brains in your ass? She's history! Got it?"

The next afternoon my lady fair flew out of Acapulco, and out of my life forever.

A decade later, another lady would enter my life. Gary was gone, and I was still Macauley Culkin.

Chinatown's success was a double-edged sword. "What about *our* films?" complained Paramount's other producers. "Evans shouldn't be allowed to run productions and make his own pictures."

"Bob," said Bluhdorn, "it's just not working. Why did you have to make *Chinatown*? Couldn't you have made an ordinary picture?"

"What are you trying to tell me, Charlie?"

"Go back and just run Paramount."

"I'll think about it, Charlie."

"Evans, don't give me more problems. Stick to running the company."

In love, in health, in life, it takes but one bad night to destroy a thousand good ones . . . and so it did.

Yablans, Bluhdorn, and I strolled over to the Coronet Theater in New York where *Chinatown* was playing. The line was around the block. We listened to the conversations of the audience as they exited the theater. The awe of their reactions to what they had just viewed was somewhat akin to the second coming of Christ. To Bluhdorn and Yablans, it wasn't just a minor but a major miracle. Why? Neither of them yet understood the film.

On to Pietro's Steakhouse to celebrate. Frank, who had the shyness of P. T. Barnum and the balls of Goliath, abruptly ended his career at Paramount.

"Charlie," he toasted, "there are the haves and have-nots, and Evans and I are the have-nots. Paramount reached the heights of Mt. Everest and we're two schmucks without so much as a rope to climb it."

The celebration turned into an altercation. Frank hung himself with the rope he said he didn't have; it was over for him before dessert arrived. For defending him, I was paid back with Bluhdorn's perversity. A corporate shake-up. Yablans was out. Barry Diller was in. Too bad for Frank—there was no brighter guy, no harder worker. He thought he was a throwback to the old movie tyrants of yesteryear—the Mayers, the Warners, the Cohns. There was a slight difference. Those guys owned the candy store, Frank didn't. He was expendable as toilet paper. The pedestal that he sat on was not high enough for him to put the wrong people's noses out of joint.

Enter Barry Diller, who epitomized the new breed of Hollywood bosses: pragmatic, insightful, and more focused on the future than on the process. Barry set the mold. Mike Eisner, Jeff Katzenberg, Bob Daly, John Peters, Peter Guber, Frank Mancuso were to follow.

Not unlike the tennis pros of old—for instance, Alex Olmedo, a Wimbledon winner, who went on to servitude as a Beverly Hills tennis pro—Yablans and I were the last not to touch the brass ring. Following Olmedo, Jimmy Connors came onto the scene, breaking barriers, bringing the brass ring of green to championship tennis (Connors and all the champions to follow became multimillionaires). Diller and Eisner, like Jimmy Connors, broke the financial barrier of top honcho executives.

Yablans was rough and tough. Diller, smooth and lethal. Oh, and throw in a little brilliance to boot. The day after he was appointed corporate head of Paramount, Barry flew out to California to meet with me. Over breakfast at the Bel-Air Hotel, I let Barry know he could count on me to make it a good partnership.

"Robert, let's get something straight. We're good friends, we're confidants, but we're not partners. You work for me. Is that clear?"

This was coming from the guy who but two years before, as a television executive, had raced to the airport in Acapulco to pick up couriered *Godfather* reviews and rush them back to me. Yet, he was right. The catbird seat was his and it was not to be shared. There could only be one boss.

"No one can ever say you lack candor, Barry. It hurts, but I respect it. It's your candy store! Now, can I go out and just make pictures, try to make a living?"

Diller laughed. "Fine, Robert, but we never want you to leave Paramount. I'll construct a producing deal that'll make you happy. I expect you to stay on for six months as head of the studio, at least to fill me in on who my enemies are."

Across the banner of both trade papers, the *Los Angeles Times, The New York Times,* and many entertainment pages across the world, the headlines trumpeted, "MOGUL EVANS TURNS INDE-

PENDENT WITH HISTORIC DEAL." Never running short of being
in the headlines, take it from me: big headlines do not make for big
pockets.

It didn't take long for me to get a taste of my new deal. On a handshake, I had already given Yablans half my points on *Chinatown*—
it's called stay-alive money. Now that he was gone, Bluhdorn wanted
Frank's share. Charlie, Barry, and I met for dinner.

"Charlie, they're my points."

"You gave them to Frank and I'm taking them from Frank."

"They're a pimple on your ass, Charlie. I need them to pay my
taxes!"

"You gave them to Frank. They belong to Gulf + Western!"

"God damn it, they don't. They're mine. It was an oral agreement,
a handshake, stay-alive time. Now Frank's gone. It's in my contract,
they're mine."

"You're right. Legally they're yours. There's also a closet in your
office. Do you want to be in it?"

Listening to the coldness of his words, I couldn't help but think
love has many faces—some of them ugly.

My lips quivered, hands shook, heart pounded, all but cracking
through my chest.

"Your butler's a homosexual," said Steve McQueen, on the other
end of the phone. "Your surroundings, the way you live, is not the
environment that's right for Joshua. We're a family unit. For
Joshua's sake, I intend to change his name to McQueen . . . have full
control . . . see that he's brought up properly."

"Are you finished?"

"Not quite," said McQueen. "Bill Thompson is preparing custody
papers."

"Good. Take your best shot, motherfucker. One of us, pal, only one
of us, is going to come out in one piece."

A call to godfather Korshak. A clandestine meeting with the
toughest Irishman attorney west of Chicago—Arthur Crowley.

"No problem, but it's gonna cost two hundred big ones, maybe
more. Is it a problem?"

"Put in my left and right arm if that's the price."

A steel-eyed look. "We'll set a meeting here at my home, two weeks from today, with his mouthpiece. This actor punk's gonna get a second asshole."

Two weeks to the day, a meeting was called; I arrived an hour early by request. Before me lay a dossier almost a foot in height.

"You got off cheap," Crowley said. "It came in for less than a hundred and fifty."

"What?" I asked.

Holding up his bible, he explained, "This, you schmuck! Your actor friend . . . his passport to oblivion."

"What's in it?"

"None of your business."

The doorbell rang. In walked lawyer Thompson, with his client Macho McQueen.

A quick whisper from Crowley. "You're holding four aces, kid. Sit back, relax, and watch the show."

The most bizarre meeting of my bizarre life began unfolding before me.

Smiling, Crowley cordially asked McQueen and Thompson if they would like a drink. Both shook their head no. Then looking to me.

"Sure, a scotch would be fine."

With the casualness of hosting a cocktail party, he walked to the bar and fixed me a scotch. Then he eyed Thompson.

"Bill, before we start, could we have a word outside alone?"

The two walked out by the pool, leaving McQueen and me alone. Awkward? Not for me; after all, Crowley told me I was holding aces. I hope they ain't deuces.

"Have a beer, pal?" I asked McQueen. A double take? No, a triple take.

Both lawyers walked back into the room. Thompson's color had changed from redneck to albino white.

"Steve, I've got to speak to you outside." Nonplussed, McQueen looked up. "Now!" said Thompson.

Within minutes, hired gun and Macho McQueen walked back into the room.

"We're leaving," said Thompson, giving Crowley a curt good-bye. They began to walk out. I jumped in.

"Hold it, Macho, the meeting ain't over."

Macho turned.

"The kid, what's his name?"

Hardily audible, "Josh."

"Josh who?"

He mumbled.

"Speak up, Macho, don't hear ya."

Macho wasn't up to being dressed down.

"Josh Evans," he blurted, quickly turning to walk out.

"Hold it, Macho, I ain't finished." He swung around, a time bomb ready to explode. "From now on, Macho, it's Mister Evans, got it?"

Get it he did, like it he didn't. From that moment on, Macho McQueen addressed Joshua's father as Mister Evans.

Sitting on the couch hysterically laughing were Nicholson and Hoffman. Maybe it was their laugh that got my goat, but I was on fire. I was on the phone with New York's chief of protocol, Mr. Angela Biddle Duke.

"Give me the rock, Mr. Protocol—no problem. But NBC, ABC, and CBS are going to be there tonight. Ever since you stole Manhattan from the Indians for forty-eight bucks, you haven't been straight with anyone. That's why the city is on its ass. The rock's fine, pal, and read about it tomorrow." This time, it was me slamming the phone down.

Tears of laughter were now coming from my royal actor pals. "Funny, huh?" I said. "I'll bet you each a suit that by four this afternoon, his royal highness will be on his knees begging me to take the key."

The phone rang. The royal voice.

"We must have been disconnected."

"No, I hung up."

"We're in a crisis now, Mr. Evans. Two weeks ago President Sadat of Egypt was the key's recipient. The Jewish population protested so vehemently, we were left with little choice. We rescinded the presentation. Even the powers to be in Washington couldn't change the mayor's mind. It wasn't their problem. The emotions in the city were such that presenting the key could have ignited a revolt. I think it a bit cavalier, a slap in the face, as it's been only two weeks, to present the key to the city to someone else, not even a head of state."

"I didn't ask for the key. It was offered to me. Give me the rock,

Mr. Protocol, it's okay, no problem. But get ready to get one back in the morning." Down went the phone again.

Black comedy always gets to the Irishman. Shaking his head, "The rock, pal, the rock. Whatcha gonna do with a rock, break a window?" His wicked smile egging me on.

"No. Double the bet, Irish. The key will be mine by four."

Again the phone rang. This time it wasn't the royal voice, instead a very worried one, Mr. Walter Wood, the head of New York City's film commission.

"Bob, we're in a very tough spot here."

I cut him off quickly. "Stay out of it, Walter. Just repeat my message: 'The rock will be fine.' "

"But you threatened—"

"Walter, just stay out of it," slamming the phone in his ear.

An hour passed. Again, the ring of the phone.

"Bob," said Film Commissioner Wood. "We've called an emergency meeting at Gracie Mansion. That's how serious the problem is. Reconsider, will you?"

"There's nothing to reconsider, Walter. Tell the boys at Gracie Mansion that I'll be honored to accept their rock. Oh, get a pencil. Write this down. I want you to tell 'em something else. Ready? Tell 'em I'll take the rock, but I'm gonna clean their clock like it's never been cleaned before."

Down went the phone. Down went Nicholson in hysterics. Down went Hoffman with a pen, writing down the expression. It was one he had never heard.

The clock struck three . . . the phone rang too: damn it, the key was mine; I would have enjoyed the rock more.

During the past decade, I had brought more film production to the Big Apple than any film honcho since World War II. In the fall of '75 the Big Apple's finances were in even worse shape than mine. New York was flat-assed broke—worse, deep in the red. But it would have been even redder without Paramount's infusion of business.

Hardly the worst reason for making me the first guy in flicks to be the recipient of the key.

Neither his royal highness, Sir Anthony Biddle Duke, nor the mayor, Abe Beame, made an appearance at the Americana Hotel ballroom that night. They weren't missed! To name but a few of the rainbow that flanked me on the dais: from Secretary of State Henry

Kissinger, his Lordship Laurence Olivier, frick and frack, Dustin and Jack, many a beauty—Faye Dunaway, Raquel Welch, Jennifer O'Neill, Marthe Keller, to Shirley MacLaine. Wow, writers galore: Alan Jay Lerner, Bill Goldman, Pete Hamill, Bob Towne, and on and on and on.

And toasts aplenty. When my pal Kissinger, who flew in from Washington especially for the night, stood up to speak, he was greeted with a standing ovation. As it subsided, Kissinger started:

I am extremely jealous that someone managed to get the key to the city this week. I wouldn't feel too badly, Bob, if the mayor didn't come to present it himself. I know what it takes to get the mayor anywhere.

But, if I can borrow the key, I will give it to our current state guest on loan, when he comes through Washington again. I am extremely self-conscious when I speak before a group as talented as this. Especially since I know a good percentage of you are trying to get my accent straight, so you can imitate me. . . .

I have not worked with Bob Evans. I know nothing about the film business and I don't have to be here. I am here because Bob is a very good friend of mine, with a great capacity of warmth and friendship. In good times and difficult times. And in my job, one meets many people who are interested in power and many people who have something that has to be accomplished politically. But Bob has been a friend. When neither of us could do anything in the world for the other—except human relationship. So I wanted to express my appreciation for being able to share this evening with him and all of you. It has been said that a friend is somebody with whom it is possible to be silent. That's exactly what I am going to do now. Thank you very much. . . . (Another standing ovation)

Breaking two barriers in one year ain't bad: the first recipient in my industry of New York's key, and the first adjunct professor of the arts in Ivy League history. Not a bullshit Honorary Professor either, but a full-fledged one; a member of the faculty, cap, gown, and all. Though my credentials fell a bit short—never receiving a high school diploma—it didn't matter. Call me by my rightful name: Professor Robert Evans of Brown University.

How did it happen? Months and months of prodding through more red tape than a new tax bill. Why? Professor Von Nostrand, the university's dean of English, pleaded to the affirmative action committee that I was the only one who could fulfill the university's criteria, enabling the English department to introduce a needed credited course to their curriculum—"The Anatomy of Film." My compensation? Zero. Begrudgingly, the high llamas of the Ivy League acquiesced.

Not unlike a president, governor, senator, or ambassador, *once a professor, always a professor.* Forget getting letters till this day from students addressed to Professor Robert Evans. How about suggesting to a young beauty that she tell her folks she was dating an Ivy League professor, not a Hollywood producer?

"Send 'em a picture if you want, I've got plenty of 'em—cap, gown, and all . . . it ain't no lie."

If only my mom and pop could have seen their black sheep Bobby in cap and gown, an Ivy League Professor. Wherever they are, I hope they found out.

Brown was a coed university, with hundreds of many hungry young ladies yearning to discover "the magic of Hollywood," rather than the magic of medieval art. I swore to myself that I'd play it straight . . . no more alley cat time. "You're a professor—don't forget it," I kept telling myself. It worked. For three years, Professor Evans was beyond reproach.

In March 1979, Liv Ullmann—a great actress, a great lady, and my lady as well—joined me at my university as a contributor to my monthly seminar, discussing in detail Ingmar Bergman's *Autumn Sonata,* which Liv had completed the year before. Her co-star was Ingrid Bergman, in her last picture. At the time, Liv was rehearsing to open in the Broadway musical *I Remember Mama.* Although it was inconvenient to shuttle back and forth between Rhode Island and Broadway, she was always there for me.

Putting her into a cab bound for the airport for her flight back to New York, I whispered, "See you at midnight, Norway."

Kissing me good-bye, she replied, "Leave early, darling. . . . New York's so cold."

While she was on the plane, I was in an important faculty meeting, discussing new plans for a new theater for Brown's new prominence in the Ivy League. Suddenly, it was blizzard time in Rhode Island—not a tropical state. By nine that evening, the airport, town, and even the gas stations closed, as did our faculty meeting. Not easy getting back home, with chained wheels, at five miles an hour. The dean of English kindly trudged me to the nearest hotel—a Howard Johnson manor.

"Made reservations for the first plane out. Sorry you're stuck, but that's Rhode Island. Get a good night's sleep, professor."

Entering my cubicle room, I quickly unzipped my fly, desperate to take a piss, but the ring of the phone interrupted. It had to be a mistake, no one knew I was there.

"Yeah?"

"Professor Evans?"

"Yeah?"

"Ann Smith." (In the spirit of chivalry, a pseudonym.)

"Yeah?"

"You don't remember, do you?"

"No."

"Tonight at the faculty meeting, the redhead, the one who brought you over the danish."

Remember? Fuckin' A I did!

"How'd you know I was here?"

A fetching giggle. "Never underestimate a lady."

"I don't."

"I'm studying theater. Opening Monday at the Providence Playhouse, doing Chekhov's *Three Sisters.*"

"That's a big bite."

"A fun one." she cooed.

What the fuck is she calling for?

"When the semester's over, I'm coming to Los Angeles to stay with my cousin."

Ah . . . she wants to see the studio.

"Wonderful. Call me at Paramount. I'll arrange a tour for you and your cousin, take you to lunch at the commissary."

No response. What the fuck's going on? Finally . . .

"Professor . . . *what are you doing now?*"

Cupping the phone with my hand. No fuckin' way! You're a Professor. Don't go back on your word. Play it straight. She can't get here anyway—can't see two feet in front of you. Fuck it!

"Room 536 . . . *get here quick!*"

An alley cat is an alley cat is an alley cat is an alley cat.

31

"I will not use him. It's that simple, Bob. I want an actor in his twenties."

John Schlesinger, whose *Midnight Cowboy* was one of the best pictures I had ever seen, was adamant and rightfully so. The role called for a twenty-four-year-old. Yet I insisted Dustin Hoffman play the Marathon Man.

A dentist solved the age problem by building a bridge across Dustin's six front teeth, making them a quarter of an inch longer. Enlarging them subliminally erases a good five years. Strangely, the older you get the larger your nose, the longer your ears, the shorter your teeth.

The making of *Marathon Man* provided my career's most treasured casting in Sir Laurence Olivier. Olivier had not worked much in recent years, outside of cameo parts in films such as *The Seven Per Cent Solution*. I investigated and found out that it was impossible to use Olivier for more than a week's work at a time. Why? He was uninsurable, his body riddled with cancer. "Uninsurable" means that if an actor dies or becomes incapacitated during production, insurance does not cover the loss. As brilliant an actor as he was, not only was he unemployable, but destitute to the point of not being able to afford sending his son to college. Richard Zimbert, head of Paramount business affairs, told me to forget the thought of Olivier. "Vegas wouldn't cover him at a hundred to one."

I tasted it—the high drama. My good friends Merle Oberon and David Niven arranged for me to meet with the House of Lords. Off to England I went. Billy Graham couldn't have been more persuasive. Members of the House of Lords persuaded Lloyd's of London to bend. Begrudgingly they gave me the impossible—six weeks of insurance.

Olivier arrived in New York, frail, hardly able to clothe himself. Miracle time, *Song of Bernadette* revisited. But this was no movie— this was the real thing; the only actual miracle I'd ever witnessed. With practically every organ in his body infected with cancer—remission! Spirit overcame illness, and Olivier was reborn to continue on for thirteen more years making film history.

Possibly the most emotional embrace of my life was his simple whisper to me: "I'm here because of you, dear Robert. I never believed in miracles—I was wrong."

Olivier and Hoffman, the most virtuoso actors of their generations. A rhapsody of opposites, however. Olivier depending on the written word, the text. Hoffman, the organic, transferring himself into the character itself. Playing a compulsive runner, just for a take he'd run a mile to be out of breath.

"You can't fake being out of breath, Bob—it has to be real," said organic Hoffman.

In a scene where the killers all but drown him in a bathtub, Dustin rehearsed by holding his head underwater until he almost drowned himself—ending up in the hospital with an oxygen tank.

At least on Dustin's part, there was great unspoken competition between the two. On the set they were enormously respectful of each other, but occasionally the surface cracked. "Why don't you just *act?*" Olivier would say after Dustin kept everyone waiting an hour while he analyzed whether he should or should not take off his shirt.

It was a turn-on to Dustin that his filmography would now include playing opposite the great Olivier in his good-bye scene, before going to greater heights—heaven. Sorry Dustin, it didn't quite work out that way. Whenever I asked Hoffman how he liked acting with Olivier, he'd always say, "He's marvelous in the theater."

Olivier stayed in my guest cottage for several weeks. He was playing a monster, a Nazi dentist who had drilled gold out of Jewish prisoners' teeth before their trip to the furnace and was now forced to leave his hideaway in the Uruguay jungles and chance a trip to New York to retrieve his hidden wealth of diamonds. While Olivier was preparing for the scene in which he was to torture Hoffman with the tools of his profession, he told me he had found the missing link to his character.

"The gardener, dear boy, in front of the window, cutting the roses, the care he took pruning each branch. The delicacy of his touch. That is how I shall torture Dustin."

"Larry, I don't get it."

"Not condescending to who I'm playing. For the character himself doesn't look upon his torture as wrong. The dental tools I use . . . I savor. The hurt they inflict, that's my pleasure. No different than one who savors his gun, his knife to inflict wounds. They don't look upon themselves as doing anything wrong. Nor shall I."

He had finally found the core to the character, one that made his portrayal quietly, chillingly evil. So mesmerizing his evil, his performance captured most every award around the world; his lordship lived to accept them all. When production of *Marathon Man* moved to L.A., Olivier was the star everyone wanted to meet.

One evening I gave a dinner to celebrate the rebirth of a beautiful lady I was seeing, who had months earlier survived a suicide attempt. It was the first birthday of her new life, and I invited Dustin and Anne Hoffman, Warren Beatty and Jack Nicholson with their dates, and among others, Cary Grant, Douglas Fairbanks, Jr., Alain Delon, and my house guest, Lord Olivier, to celebrate it.

After dinner all of us adjourned to the projection room for dessert.

When the cake with a single candle was brought in, Olivier gave a moving speech about the preciousness of life and the miracle of being reborn. Everybody reached for their hankies. Then I stood up.

"Larry, you ain't a lord for nothing. I've arranged for you to critique four scenes from four films. All four were done approximately at the same time twenty years ago. After you view them, your lordship, I ask of you one favor. Pick the one actor of the four who had the best chance to become the next big star."

Perplexed? You bet. Not only Larry, but the entire room. The lights dimmed. The curtains closed. The screen went down.

The first image was that of a pockmarked, rodentlike Dustin Hoffman, speaking out of synch in some terrible French-Italian co-production—his first film. Everyone roared but Marathon Man Hoffman.

"How did you get this, Evans? There's only one print and I own it!" Dustin screeched.

"There ain't nothin' I don't have on you, kid. Don't forget it."

I pressed the intercom. "Next."

The image was not a film. Rather a segment of a half-hour TV sitcom. Dwayne Hickman the actor, "Dobie Gillis" the TV show. Into frame walked his pompadoured rival. Who was it? Looked familiar. Could that be Warren? It sure as hell was. Did he get laughs? More than anything he's ever done in his whole career. The only one who didn't laugh was him.

Nudging me. "How'd you get this, you prick?"

"Easy. The guys who had the film wanted me to do it. They must really like you."

Pressing the intercom again, "Next please."

A choirboy's face filled the screen. A high-pitched voice echoed through a house. It was *The Cry Baby Killer*—a two-day Roger Corman quickie. The choirboy was sure as hell no choirboy. It was the Irishman himself, Nicholson. Laughs? Before or since, never louder.

"Thanks, pal," eagle-eyed the Irishman.

Pressing down on the intercom once again, "Last scene now, thank you."

There on the screen was Ava Gardner. This was no TV sitcom, two-day horror film, or hybrid-dubbed piece of celluloid. This was the most alluring star of cinema, she gazing into the eyes of her young matador—yeah me. It got the biggest laugh of all. The lights came up.

"Total candor your lordship: who of the four would you have picked to end up a star?"

He stood, looking at all his victims.

"Dear boy, who do we all work for?"

Whether it be a restaurant, an industry function, or a party, the word spread so fast of *Black Sunday*'s explosion on the screen that the phrase "bigger than *Jaws*" became boring to hear. The advance buzz was so loud that everyone offered to buy my points; finally, three Lebanese met my price. $6.8 million in cash for my 38 points of ownership. With negotiations all but closed, the morning mail arrived with a letter from Bernie Myerson, president of Loew's Theaters. Though everyone spouted *Black Sunday* as being the successor to *Jaws,* Myerson's written prediction was tantamount to a nod from Don Corleone in *The Godfather*.

"That *Black Sunday* will definitely outgross *Jaws*." Changing my mind.

I told my secretary to get my lawyer, Ken Ziffrin, on the phone.

"Kenny, I ain't sellin'. Zanuck and Brown made over twenty big ones from *Jaws* and I own more points than both of them together. Fuck it, the dice rolls with *Black Sunday*."

"It's too big a gamble, Evans, you can't afford it. Grab the money and run. You're a lucky Jew, don't be a dumb one."

"Sorry, Kenny, I'm going for it. I want to be a rich one."

Kenny was right, I was a dumb one. Did *Black Sunday* do more than *Jaws*? It didn't do more than *my* jaw. Reviews? Better than good! Enough to take a two-page ad in both the *New York* and *Los Angeles Times* listing sixty rave reviews from coast to coast.

John Frankenheimer, the helmsman of *Black Sunday,* possibly more than any other director I've worked with, knew how to execute an almost impossible logistic feat. First he got permission from the NFL; then the Orange Bowl in Miami, where the Super Bowl was taking place; then shooting the actual Super Bowl itself (Pittsburgh vs. Dallas). He then coerced Goodyear into allowing us to use their blimp as the "heavy" in the picture; managed a cast of thousands upon thousands; and unraveled a story so extraordinarily realistic that it worked against us, evoking a passion that all but cost us our lives, literally and figuratively.

To this day, it seems hard to believe that the entire canvas cost less than $8 million to put on the screen. Only Frankenheimer could have done it. Its production scope makes *Jurassic Park* look like a back lot flick. If made today, its cost would tilt the $100 million mark.

Why didn't I receive Myerson's letter a week later? The points I didn't sell weren't worth enough to cover a coach ticket to Miami. Even worse, forget the money I didn't make, the controversy of its subject matter caused an uproar that personally cost me a fortune. Why? Telling another terrorist story was not good enough. I had to go a step further, expose the gray area, tell both sides of the complex story, including what had made the film's leading antagonist, played by Marthe Keller, join the Black September terrorist movement.

Blazing across the front page of the leading Jewish newspaper, *The B'nai B'rith Messenger,* was the headline "ROBERT EVANS, HITLERITE." Immediately, notices were put up in Jewish-owned stores throughout the country calling for a boycott of the film. That was a gardenia compared to its flip side. The Red Army of Japan threatened to blow up every theater around the world that exhibited *Black Sunday.* To them, it was sacrilegious to the plight of the Arab people. I had to hire three shifts of guards, twenty-four hours a day for six months, at a cost of $2,800 a day to protect my home and family from extremist reprisals.

Jaws? A blimp ain't no fish—just hot air.

It was only a year earlier. Raquel Welch whispered in my ear, "It's my first Super Bowl game," as we sat on the fifty-yard line with eleven cameras covering Robert Shaw running across the entire field in pursuit of a deadly terrorist.

"Only you, Evans, could have a cast of fifty thousand."

"Yeah, and not pay scale."

The crowd went wild. Terry Bradshaw had just thrown a touch-down pass and Pittsburgh was ahead. The only one who didn't stand was me. I was worried whether we got the shot of Robert Shaw, be-cause the NFL would only let us do it once. Continually checking the results of our eleven-camera crew, I must have been a pain in the ass climbing over the CBS sportscasting trio of Brent Musburger, Irv Cross, and America's sweetheart, Phyllis George, while they play-by-played the Pittsburgh Pirates/Dallas Cowboy duel. Unfortu-nately for them, we shared the same row, only eight seats apart.

When the next Super Bowl rolled around, Brent, Irv, and Phyllis play-by-played it again, the only difference was that Phyllis had a new last name—Evans. Months earlier Ed Hookstratten, Phyllis's business manager and mentor, had given a bash at his Bel Air home. Warren Beatty and I were Hookstratten's two choices to be Phyllis's blind date for the evening. Working harder for the gig, I got the part. Not a kiss good-night, but it didn't matter. It was me, rather than Warren, whose foot was in the door to America's sweetheart.

If ever the title fit the person, Miss America fit Phyllis George. She had all the glamour in the world but she was still the wholesome, small-town girl from Denton, Texas. Phyllis had become the first woman sportscaster on a national level. The Texas-size smile on CBS between Brent Musburger and Irv Cross, she was the first Miss America since Bess Myerson to become a household name. Her dimples were so deep that a scoop of rocky road ice cream could fit in each one. She was the real thing—America's sweetheart.

A month later, we bumped into each other on Rodeo Drive. Chance meeting—lunch for two. From that moment, we never left each other until she became the fourth Mrs. Evans.

There was one problem in our bond of Mr. and Mrs.: she was Miss America and I wasn't Mr. America. Her first marriage—my fourth. Her marital bliss: a white picket fence, church on Sunday, the Bel Air Country Club. I never belonged to a club; I didn't want to move; my place of worship is my home, not a church; and I didn't want more children. Would you say we had much in common? She wanted a church wedding. I wanted to exchange vows on the high cliff overlooking Acapulco watching divers jump into the sea below.

We compromised. A private morning wedding under the old sycamore tree at my home. Then off to Acapulco to watch the divers.

Shortly after our marriage, *Los Angeles Magazine* did a story on Phyllis. There she was on the cover, her smile aglow, her dimples deep, a football under her arm. The caption read: "What happens when a country girl turned Miss America hits it big in TV sports and hooks up with Hollywood's most notorious Prince Charming?"

Disaster, that's what. Everything Phyllis wanted was right. But she couldn't fight the biggest mismatch of the decade. When being interviewed on national television, smiling Phyllis cooed, "I know I'm not the first Mrs. Evans, but I'm definitely the last."

Poor Phyllis, she was in for one hell of a surprise. Square? Let's just say she made Mary Tyler Moore look like Madonna.

I can't think of a bad thing to say about Phyllis. On every level she was the girl a guy wants to bring home to mother. But my mother was dead and ego was what motivated my perversity in wanting to make Miss America Mrs. Evans. I couldn't understand what she saw in me. I was everything she was not. She was everything I would have liked to have been. My goal was to clean up my act, and she was the inspiration. But, damn it, it's true that you can't teach an old dog new tricks, and I was one hell of an old dog. The more I told her I was wrong for her, the more she wanted to prove it would work.

I planned a scenario that would ensure a split, giving her the dignity of her leaving me, not me her. It was the first of my four marriages where the cause of the breakup was not infidelity (and that's only because I never got caught!). Rather, filmmaking was my "mistress."

My biggest surprise of the entire relationship was her mother calling me, pleading, "What did Phyllis do wrong? I know it's her fault."

My persuasive best was needed to convince her that Phyllis's only fault was in choosing me.

In 1985, *Only the Best,* a pictorial coffee-table book celebrating the greatest gifts of the twentieth century, was published; one page features, "Phyllis George to Bob Evans." Its text:

Wedding presents are an age-old custom, but how often does one hear of a divorce present? Among her many talents, anchorperson and former Miss America Phyllis George is an accomplished pianist. She had always wanted an early Steinway, and shortly after marrying Hollywood producer Bob Evans she found the piano of her dreams. The beautiful instrument was made in 1872, its glossy frame carved entirely of rosewood.

The piano was part of an estate, and so it was some time before it arrived in the Evans living room. The Evanses were thrilled to see that it fit into the room as if made for it.

The marriage lasted less than a year, but when the piano's ardent possessor started to pack up her treasure, she changed her mind. "It is too beautiful here," she said, "I can't take it from you; it is yours."

How can you meet a better dame? Beautiful, earns twice your bread, needs nothing from you but love returned; and not only did I blow it, but I myself set it up for it to happen. Worse even, with no remorse.

Less than a month after Phyllis and I split, the McQueens became MacGraw and McQueen. Less than an hour after that news broke, my old pal Beatty was on the horn.

"Your ole lady, she's free. Do you mind if I call her?"

I couldn't believe his words.

"Warren, she ain't my ole lady, hasn't been for five years. Why are you asking me? It ain't my call."

A rare Beatty stammer, "Well, I just felt I should."

"Why?"

"I don't know, it just felt like the right thing to do."

"You do the right thing?"

We both laughed.

"For some reason, she's still your ole lady."

"Then don't call her," I said. "It ain't fair to her. If you weren't living with Keaton, she'd be the best thing that could ever happen to you. She's too good a dame to hurt for the sake of a notch. You've asked me, so I'm telling you—pass."

Before I could take a piss, the phone rang again. This time it was the wicked smile himself on the horn.

"Whaddaya think, Keed?" Nicholson drawled. "Now that your ole lady's free, is it worth a dial?"

"She ain't my 'ole lady,' she's McQueen's. Why are you calling me?"

"Well, it don't feel right without your nod. Don't ask why. I don't know."

"Call her if you want, but you're with Toots [Anjelica Huston], Irish, and Ali's too vulnerable for you to play it shady. Got it?"

"Got it!" said the Irishman.

The difference was, one called and called, and the other passed. Who do you think called? Who do you think passed? Let's just say, Nicholson called another lass.

Before Warren got hitched to Annette Bening (who is one sensational lady), for years he had been terribly orthodox when it came to hitting on a pal's lady: *never on Sunday*. Ahhh . . . but Monday through Saturday was different. Then it was a religious experience. No wonder he's called "the pro" by his friends (or those who think they are).

Until his marriage, Warren stood alone as the single most competitive person I've ever known. His obsession in life was to be *first—*

first with the new hot girl in town, preferably model or starlet; first to be shown the new hot screenplay, the new hot role, or for that matter the new hot anything—as long as it was *new and hot.*

The quickest way for a girl to get to Warren's heart was for him to discover that I was seeing her. For many years, we shared the same doctor, Lee Siegel. The good doctor told me the one way he'd get Warren's blood pressure on high was to egg him on. "Hate to tell you, Warren. Evans has got the edge. You're about equal in quantity, but he's about three points higher in *quality!*" Did it bother Warren? Poor Lee lost a patient.

During the four decades of friendship we've shared, neither of us has broken an unwritten law. That of not discussing whom we've been with. Though brothers-in-law many a time, we never questioned who our in-laws were. The only way we'd find out was through the girls themselves. Why is it girls talk more freely than men today?

Though a terrific pianist, Warren considers his fingers far more agile when it comes to the telephone, himself the Horowitz of the dial tone. He candidly admitted in a *Rolling Stone* cover story that his singular greatest talent was his virtuoso speed-of-the-Touch-Tone.

Can you imagine his outrage when I nonchalantly threw him the curve that my kid Joshua could "out-touch" him? Cracking Warren's veneer ain't no easy feat.

"Your kid," he wailed, "I'll wipe him off the street."

"No chance. He's got the edge, the kid's in his teens, Nimble doesn't come with age, pal!"

"Nimble? Fuck you! What about Horowitz? He was in his eighties!"

"Yeah, but could Borg get a set off Becker? No way."

That did it. Beatty blew his cool. A first. "Where's the fuckin' runt?"

"Here."

"I'm coming right down."

Warren Beatty rushing down the mountain to take on my kid? He must be putting me on. He wasn't it! Suddenly it was *Gunfight at the O.K. Corral.* Instead of the Old West, it was my projection room. Instead of two hardened gunslingers testing their Smith and Wessons, two Beverly Hills nimble finger-slingers were preparing for their dial-off. On the count of three, it was quick-dial time. Facing each other, each warrior dialed the same number from a different phone.

The one who lived was the one who got the voice on the other end.

By Western standards, Warren should be four years dead by now. But it's Hollywood and he's still on every A list in town. Did it bother him? It wasn't his shyness that kept him from talking to my kid for more than a year.

How do you spell fashionable? W-A-R-R-E-N B-E-A-T-T-Y. From his first film till today, Warren remains the quintessential Hollywood movie star. He defies the bottom line, in an industry where the bottom line is the only line. He has remained for more than thirty years, without missing one, front and center on every studio's A+ list.

Our offices were across the lawn from each other at Paramount. He had completed *Heaven Can Wait* and it was soon to open. Always seeking opinions, he wanted mine. He asked me if I would drop by his office for a moment. Walking in, I was surprised to see Norton Simon, who at the time was one of America's primo art connoisseurs. Before I had a chance to say hello, Warren took a life-size board and turned it around. There before us was a picture of him in sweatpants, shirt, and sneakers. Heavenly wings adorned his back.

"Like it? It's the poster for the film."

Studiously critiquing it, Norton looked up.

"Striking! No . . . extraordinary. Too good for a film ad," he laughed.

I didn't answer. A quick Beatty look.

"Well?"

"It's okay." I nodded.

"Okay?"

"Yeah, okay."

"That's all—okay!

"Yeah."

"Fuck you! I know why you don't like it." He laughed. "I'm better looking."

"Uh-uh . . . no *cojones*." Pointing to the poster. "Your sweatpants, there ain't no crease. Looks like you're sporting a pussy."

Did it bother him? Within two minutes the entire hierarchy at Paramount knew of his dissatisfaction—no, call it anger. Playing insulted to the hilt, he cared little that all the artwork had been completed and was ready to be shipped. Coolly, he insisted that every ad, every poster be scrapped. Did he get his way? That's what Warren Beatty is all about. Poor Paramount, to satisfy Beatty's manhood they were left with no choice but to redo the film's entire advertising campaign. The cost? North of a half a million. By far the most expensive *crotch retouch* in cinema history.

"David Geffen calling Mr. Evans," said the Carlyle Hotel operator.

"Put him through."

"Bob, could I join you this morning? I'm dying to meet him."

"Sure, but we've got a lot to get through today. Calvin's doing Ali's entire wardrobe for the film."

It was a Sunday morning in May 1978. Calvin Klein was kind enough to personally outfit Ali's character for her lead role in my new production, *Players*. Ali and I picked David up on our way to West Thirty-eighth Street. Introducing David to Calvin Klein made me feel like Streisand's *Hello, Dolly!* matchmaker. They must have gotten along—I haven't heard from either since.

Ali and I had only three days in New York, before taking off to London. Both of us were staying at the Carlyle. Unfortunately for me, in separate rooms. In secrecy, I called my very close friends David and Helen Gurley Brown. I whisked over to see them and begged for Helen's help. I hoped, since she was Ali's close friend, that she could persuade Ali to give us a second chance.

"It'll work. I know it will this time."

With me present, Helen called Ali, asking her to come over for a visit. She'd be there in an hour. I was as excited as a twelve-year-old boy going out on his first date. David suggested we take a long walk.

"Leave it to Helen—if she can't make it work, no one can."

The two of us walked for hours, a stop at O'Neal's for a beer . . . then through Central Park.

"Bob, if Helen pulls it off, can you be faithful?" asked Professor Brown. It didn't take long to answer.

"Nope."

I got the longest triple take of my life. It didn't matter anyway. Helen didn't succeed. Ali had minus zero interest in rekindling anything.

Several months earlier, Michael Eisner had laughed: "You'll get Wimbledon like I'll take over Disney."

I got Wimbledon. He took over Disney. I ended up in the red. He ended up the *numero uno* honcho of the business.

If I could get Goodyear to give me their blimp as the "heavy" and the NFL to allow me to shoot the Super Bowl as a backdrop to terrorism for *Black Sunday,* why not Wimbledon for *Players*? To Wimbledon's board of governors; the tournament's royal patron herself, Princess Anne; and all the members of the most prestigious bastion of not only tennis, but any sport there is to play, there I was evoking the magic of film to chronicle Wimbledon in perpetuity. It must have worked.

Now all I needed was a script. There was a far bigger problem. When the picture finished shooting, I still didn't have one. Arnold Schulman talked a good script but wrote a terrible one. Many years later, Ivan Lendl approached me in St. Maarten, congratulating me on *Players;* it was the most realistic sports film he had ever seen, so realistic that he'd watched it eleven times. Lendl was right: never had a sport been transformed to screen drama with more authenticity than *Players,* but the story surrounding it was as weak as the action was authentic.

Players involved an older woman and a hustler kid tennis pro, she the inspiration to the kid going straight and ascending to the top. Ali was my first choice to play the mysterious beauty leading a double life, a lady of high social standing and a girl of the streets kept by an older man who controlled the strings, purse and all. Ali at that time was at an all-time low, ready to walk into the ocean one way. Not only was she the mother of my only son, but she was perfect for the role and—like it or not (and I didn't)—her presence still made my heart skip a beat.

The actor cast as her young *amour* had to be a tennis pro as well, so there weren't many contenders. Dean Martin's son, Dino, got the nod. Robert Redford handsome, ranked 150th in the world of tennis, with a terrific personality, he was, I thought, a sure bet for stardom. *Players* opened—and didn't play.

"ROBERT EVANS' REVENGE ON ALI MACGRAW" headlined the *New York Post*'s review. That said it all. The critics didn't review the film, rather they editorialized it. The script may have had more holes in it than a tennis racket, but the reality of a sport brought to the screen was worthy of respect, no matter how minor, but certainly not harbored resentment. It was *Love Story* ten years later. The critics . . . well, they just had a field day. They didn't want us to get away with it again.

"Fuck him! He shaves his beard off or I shut down the picture today. Got it?"

"Calm down, Evans, will you?"

"Michael, I've had it. Last night we had dinner at the Palm in Houston. Three people came over and asked for my autograph, not his. And he's supposed to be the biggest star in the world?"

Within twenty-four hours, Michael Eisner, Barry Diller, and Don Simpson joined me in Houston. It was June 29, 1979, my birthday.

"Fellas, you gotta back me. Travolta's hiding behind his beard because he's got a little scratch above his lip. A fuckin' cat bit it. His cleft, his smile, made him a star. Now I get him with a beard. He looks like an Italian butcher."

"What does Jim think?" asked Eisner, referring to director James Bridges.

"He likes it. So does Travolta's whole coterie. He's got more of an entourage than the President. I'm not taking any orders from any starlet who's just become a star. Travolta's working for me, I'm not working for him. That's why you overpay me."

"How many scenes have you shot with Travolta?" asked Eisner.

"Too many—about six. We're coming up to where Travolta applies for a job at a factory. It's the perfect place for the boss to say 'we don't hire guys with beards.' "

The projector was turned on. We looked at John Travolta in a beard. The next day the biggest star in the world shaved his beard off.

Then, till the end of the picture, the biggest star in the world refused to talk to me. Did I care? Did you? The producer is always the enemy. The stronger the producer the bigger the enemy.

Developed from an *Esquire* article by Aaron Latham about the Texas blue-collar scene around Gilley's, the world's biggest roadhouse, *Urban Cowboy* was now a $12 million blast on film, starring John Travolta, the Tom Cruise of the 1970s. Located near Houston in the town of Pasadena, Gilley's was where 7,000 people a night could do everything from playing pinball to riding a mechanical bull, to drinking themselves into a quickie in the nearest trailer. It was 100 percent prime redneck; the girls at Gilley's were tougher than any linebacker for the Chicago Bears. One of them, Milly, held the record for taking on 168 guys riding the bull in one week. By the time the picture was over, she'd lost the title to another lovely.

When Irving Azoff, the record producer who controlled the rights, showed me Latham's article, I was immediately turned on. Here was a slice of Americana that had never been put on film before. From fashion to dance and slang, it had the potential to be a trendsetter. With no star, no script, and ten minutes with Eisner, a $12 million budget was put on "go" for *Urban Cowboy* to start dancing on film.

Jim Bridges was set to direct. Travolta had already signed to do *American Gigolo,* but was desperate to go western. Good-bye, *Gigolo.* Hello, *Cowboy.* At the time, anything John wanted, John got.

For the tough-cookie female lead—a real star-making part—we were looking for a new face. We interviewed thousands of girls and tested hundreds. It came down to two unknowns: Michelle Pfeiffer and Debra Winger. We shot the deciding test at Gilley's. Michelle and Debra were both born for bucking the mechanical bull, but Winger won out. Why? Because I wanted Pfeiffer.

The summer of 1979 registered as the hottest and wettest in Houston history. To pick up clear dialogue, we had to turn off the air-conditioning in Gilley's. Everyone passed out but the bull. Tempers were hotter than the weather. And I took most of the heat.

Grit was the issue. Travolta, Bridges, and company wanted *Grease* in chaps. I wanted *Saturday Night Fever,* raunchy ranch style.

Did I still need energy-fuel from cocaine? Can't deny it. But compared to the users I met in Houston, I was a cub scout. On a half dozen nights I hobnobbed with the so-called cream of Texas society. I never saw anything like it. In Hollywood one did cocaine in the john. Down there they put it out like popcorn, in platinum bowls.

When *Urban Cowboy* finished shooting, Travolta threw the wrap party—lunch at his ranch. My invitation must have been sent to the "mechanical bull."

"I want it, Barry."

"Evans, if you want it, it's yours," said Diller.

It was the opening night of *Annie* in New York. The spirit it evoked was infectious, euphoric, for everyone from eight to eighty.

"Barry, we're gonna give Charlie the musical he's always wanted."

"You've already got a yes. I'll be on it first thing tomorrow."

Diller gave me the yes, but Ray Stark outbid him. *Annie* was sold for double-digit millions—the highest price paid for a Broadway musical. Redheads don't come cheap.

Never being a cartoon reader or watcher, I mistakenly pressed the wrong channel. Staring me in the face was this one-eyed cornpipe sailor. Stealing my philosophy:

> *I yam what I yam,*
> *That's all what I yam.*

That's it! Popeye, you're growing taller—straight up to the 70 mm screen. Spread the gospel, sailor, "The celebration of the individual."

Getting Jules Feiffer, the sophisticated cartoonist, playwright and screenwriter, to write the script, along with Hal Ashby to direct and Dustin Hoffman to star, exploded every possible emotion I'd ever held back.

Losing a doubles match with Guillermo Vilas, the world's number one player, as my partner, was by no means a high, when I was interrupted by an emergency call. It was Jules Feiffer. Hardly audible, I'd never heard anybody sound more distraught.

"I've had the worst day of my life. . . ."

"Jules, what the hell's the matter?"

Between groaning, he told me that Dustin had thrown him out.

"What are you talking about?"

"He kept me waiting two whole days. By the time the little fuck gave me an audience, I was drunk. . . ."

"Sober up. I'll straighten it out."

Ashby and I flew to New York.

"Give Feiffer a second chance," I asked Dustin. "His ideas for *Popeye* are brilliant."

Dustin wouldn't listen. It was Jules or him.

Putting my cards on the table. "I'm going with Feiffer."

"You're telling me you don't want me to do the picture?"

"Nope, I'm telling you that *I'm the producer,* I want Feiffer as the writer, he's spent a year on it."

"Get the fuck out of here!"

The next day, Liv Ullmann had invited me to a private screening—very private, just her and me—of her new Bergman picture. We were walking down Madison when we bumped into Courtney Sale, who would later marry Warner Brothers mogul Steve Ross. She was on her way to Dustin's town house on Seventy-fourth Street with bagels and lox for breakfast.

"Join us, Bob, will you?"

"Not a good idea," I told her. "Dustin and I had a beef. Let it cool."

Liv pushed me, laughing, "You sound like two little boys fighting. Let's go, Bob."

"Don't think it's a good idea."

"Even if I want to meet him?"—taking my hand and kissing it— "That's no way to treat a lady."

Good chance to say no, huh? I should have.

It ended up being one of the most disturbing encounters of my life. For an hour, Dustin and Liv talked about doing things for "the love of art." It bugged me. I knew all too well that when it came to making the deal, Dustin was more concerned with green than art.

Whatever I said set it off. The veins in Dustin's neck turned purple, his whole body started shaking like an epileptic's. The obscenities he shouted at me were nuclear. No Bergman film had a scene to match this—it was a miracle that Liv and I made it out of there in one piece.

Now outside, Liv was terribly concerned. "Maybe he's having a stroke, should I go back up?"

He and I didn't speak for a long time. When we did, as in all love affairs, the heat was over. Good-bye, Dustin; hello, Robin.

"What do you think, Michael?"

Eisner jumped in. "He's great on 'Mork and Mindy.' Do you think he can carry a film?"

"Who can? All I know, he *is* Popeye, not a *Jewish* Popeye."

Within weeks, Robin Williams was Popeye the Sailor Man come to life.

Set too was my composer, the offbeat Harry Nilsson. Hal Ashby had gone on to another film and I had no director. Feiffer's comedic script emphasized social corruption. Director after director turned it down, claiming it was too complicated.

I suggested Bob Altman. Paramount had distributed *Nashville*, his masterpiece, but people in the corporate suite went white when I mentioned his name.

"He's uncontrollable," they said. "We can't deal with his irreverence."

"Fellas," I said, "that's what the story is about—irreverence."

Reluctantly, Diller and Eisner okayed Altman.

Altman, Feiffer, Williams, Nilsson, me—somehow I'd ended up

with a surfeit of irreverence. Paramount was so worried, they hedged their bets by selling off half the picture to the Walt Disney Company. The two studios would split the cost of production. Paramount would distribute *Popeye* in America, Disney in the rest of the world.

It was the first time that ultraprotective, ultraconservative Disney had ever allowed its name to be shared—and the first time they'd ever let a name like Eisner appear in one of their press releases. Little did they imagine that only a few years later the name "Eisner" was it, at the Big D, no less followed by a Katzenberg.

I hadn't just hired Robert Altman, I had hired his whole troupe. Altman's company, Lion's Gate, was like a commune. From the grip to the costume designer to the editor, they all had one loyalty—to guru Altman. Again I was the outsider.

Everything about *Popeye* was topsy-turvy. Summer was the ideal time to shoot, but it was already the fall of 1979. If we put it off nine months we'd lose Robin Williams to "Mork and Mindy." Christmas 1980 was the ideal release date for a film with big family appeal. To make that, we would have to start shooting in January. But Popeye's Sweethaven is a rickety New England seacoast village. New England in January? We would have to build Sweethaven from scratch, and it couldn't be done in the tropics.

On paper, the Mediterranean island of Malta met all the criteria: sunny weather from January to May, rocky terrain, and a huge water tank where we could shoot miniatures, which had been built by the government to attract filmmakers.

I flew to Malta with Altman and the talented production designer, Wolf Kroeger. Greeting us was the head of the local film commission, all his surrogates, and Miss Malta, who must have come in last in the Miss Universe contest. On a scale of one to ten, she was at best a two. Nine months later, leaving Malta, she grew in beauty to a full eleven. Another month in Malta, she would have been Mrs. Evans. That best describes Malta.

Between October and the New Year, we cast the rest of the film. For Popeye's girlfriend, Olive Oyl, Altman wanted loony, the studio wanted loopy. Loony was Shelley Duvall, the airhead heroine of Altman's *Thieves Like Us* and *Three Women*. Loopy was Gilda Radner, the hot young comedienne of "Saturday Night Live." I sided with Altman, but to appease Diller and Eisner I flew to New York to see

Radner in her one-woman Broadway show. She was terrific, but her Olive Oyl would have been strictly kosher.

Shelley Duvall's next film was Stanley Kubrick's *The Shining* with Jack Nicholson. I saw it. I lied, telling Diller and Eisner that Duvall would be the big screen's next Lucille Ball. It was the best white lie I ever told. Till the Sun Never Rises, I'll look upon Shelley's Olive Oyl as classic.

By January the rest of the cast was set and Wolf Kroeger had built most of Sweethaven, a three-quarter-size fishing village that remains the most magical set I've ever seen. Knowing there were no customs in Malta, I headed for the rock, packing everything I needed into two steamer trunks—including substances I shouldn't have needed. Everyone's luggage arrived but mine. I wouldn't have worried if my name hadn't been on the tags.

Upon arrival, Altman and I had an audience with Malta's prime minister, Dominic Mintoff. Six months earlier, on "60 Minutes," this Marxist potentate had told Mike Wallace what a terrible country the United States was and what a terrific fellow his friend Libya's Colonel Qaddafi was. At his residence we weren't ushered into the reception room, we were taken down to the sea.

There we stood, watching the prime minister, who must have been at least sixty at the time. He was at least twenty feet out in the freezing Mediterranean sea tossing a medicine ball back and forth to a young aide standing on dry land.

It was a feat an Olympic athlete would have a tough time duplicating. Did he know we were watching? You're damn right! It's what little guys do to prove their power.

All I could think of was the last American film shot in Malta, *Midnight Express,* about an American sent to a Turkish prison for having drugs in his suitcase. If he'd been tortured for marijuana, I would get the chair.

Once the prime minister put on his robe, I got the courage to ask for a favor.

"My luggage apparently got lost between Rome and Malta."

"I'll try."

His tone said it all: it was the last thing he cared to do.

"Prime Minister," I lied, "in my luggage I have a personal letter from Dr. Kissinger to you."

"Henry Kissinger?"

"Yes, sir."

"A letter from *him* to me?"

"Yes, sir."

"Why are *you* carrying it?"

"He happens to be a very close friend of mine."

Immediately, he rattled off an S.O.S. for my luggage.

The next day, Altman and I were back at the residence, lunching with Mintoff, when two military guards came in and whispered something in their boss's ear.

"We have found your luggage, Mr. Evans," said the prime minister. "It was in Ecuador. It is arriving at three o'clock. Shall I have it delivered here?"

"I would appreciate it if you could have it delivered to the hotel."

He nodded. "Please send Mr. Kissinger's letter to me immediately."

"Of course."

The luggage was there when I got back from lunch. Two guards stood by, waiting for the letter.

"Gentlemen," I said, "after I unpack I will deliver the letter to the prime minister in person."

The moment I saw the car disappear, I headed to the airport and took the first plane out; luckily, it was going to Paris. I hung at the airport to catch the first jet to New York, where I called Altman.

"If Mintoff asks for me, tell him I've been called back on a family emergency."

"What happened?"

"No letter, that's what."

He laughed. But it was no laughing matter.

"Henry, I need you."

"I thought you were in Malta."

"I'm at the Carlyle."

"The last time you said that I ended up at *The Godfather.*"

"I need you real bad."

We met in the lobby of his apartment building, the River House.

"I can't do it, Bob. I can't have my name on a letter to Mintoff. He's one of Qaddafi's closest allies."

"Henry, you've got to."

"Can I write it in German?"

"It's not a joke."

"Bob, how could you be so naïve?"

"I'm sorry, Henry. I feel like an idiot, but without this letter they could close the picture down."

Rationalizing that omission is not lying, I told Henry half of my dilemma, the good half. Knowing, if he had any inkling of the "bad" half, not only would he not have written the letter, but he never would have spoken to me again.

"Could Nancy write it?"

"Don't make it harder, Henry. Please . . . please."

Up in his apartment he wrote a letter in longhand to Mintoff, saying that any help the prime minister could extend to his friend would be greatly appreciated. He signed it.

"Do you *have* to give it to him?"

"Yes."

32

Tragedy is part of life: how very few escape its touch. It's not tragedy itself, but the degree of it that counts. A family destroyed before your very eyes, within a flash—that's tragedy with a capital *T*.

It struck my brother in January 1975. An inferno swept through the home of his ex-wife, Frances, and his daughters, Melissa and Elizabeth, killing them all—sparing only his son, Charles, Jr. My brother was on the phone with Frances when she began screaming. Charles raced to her house to find it in cinders, Frances and his two beautiful daughters, age ten and eleven, burned to a crisp. Crash! *A haunted life.*

A captain of industry, a dashing raconteur, a charmer of charmers, a ladies man, a man's man, a lost man.

Tragedy brought us closer, until another tragedy all but destroyed decades of envied love.

It was the last week in April of 1980. I picked Charlie up at LAX and we limousined it to Palm Springs. It had been five years since my brother's horrific trauma and by ritual, every couple of months we'd long-weekend it together alone. Laugh, cry, reminisce, talk about the past, the future—you name it, we shared it.

Ten days earlier, I had been S.O.S'd back to the States from Malta by Michael Eisner.

"Travolta's been in the editing room every night with Jim Bridges. Don't like what I hear."

"Can't leave, Michael. If we get one more day of rain, that's it. *Popeye*'s Sweethaven is in the sea."

"It's your call, Evans. If we change the name to *Urban Cowgirl,* don't blame Paramount."

Thirty flying hours later, I was back at the studio, watching Travolta as our Urban Cowboy.

"Eisner's right. Where's the fuckin' raunch, the sweat, the dancin'? There's no heat! It's all been shot. Now I'm lookin' at a fuckin' ballet."

"We don't have to be exploitative," bristled director Bridges. "John's the biggest star in the world."

"Oh really! Get this straight, Mr. Director; the grit, the raunch, the down and dirty go back in. I'm lookin' for *Saturday Night Fever* goes West, not *The Red Shoes.*"

He got it, but he didn't get it all in. When director and star lock together, you can win a battle, but the war? Forget it. The editing room floor, not the theaters, ended up with the heat.

Urban Cowboy's double-album soundtrack was pure platinum. *Urban Cowboy,* the film, was sterling silver. A summer hit, but certainly no platinum blockbuster.

I took a weekend furlough from battle, Charlie flew out from New York. The two of us lazed around Marvin Davis's pool in Palm Springs . . . played tennis, swam, laughed.

Successful as Charles had been in his quest for wealth, he was that lost in his quest for happiness. Tragedy haunted his every day. Business kept him alive and his was booming. Whatever Charlie touched, gushed. From clothing tycoon to real estate baron, within a decade, ain't luck, *it's brilliance.*

On our drive down to the Springs, Charlie told me he was in final negotiations to sell half his real estate holdings to a Dutch bank for close to $100 million. Not bad for a guy whose only previous real estate experience was buying an apartment. Was he excited about it? No, when your life's in shambles, dollar signs come in a distant third.

"Take a fling, try something new. Hey! Make a flick, with your brights, you'll win an Academy Award."

Charlie didn't say no.

"Read something last week, gave me belly laughs. Buddy Hackett sent it over. It's been around for years, but funny is funny, the title's even funny—*Would I Lie to You?* George Hamilton is dyin' to do it. He'd be good for it too. It's about an actor who can't get a gig, so he dresses in drag, and as a broad he never stops working. I'd make it myself, but if you want it, it's yours. Take a shot, for twenty-five Gs you can option it."

Charlie took the shot, bought the rights. A month later, Dustin Hoffman, who was preparing a film about Renee Richards, the male tennis pro who had a sex change, then played the female tennis circuit, read *Would I Lie to You?* He canceled the Renee Richards story. Good-bye, George; hello, Dustin. Good-bye, *Would I Lie to You?*; hello, *Tootsie.* Was I surprised? Not at all, it was Charlie all the way. A winner is a winner is a winner is a winner.

Me? I was flying high too. For the first time I had gross points from the first dollar on two of Paramount's biggest pictures of the year—*Urban Cowboy* and *Popeye.*

"Can't make your kinda bread, Charlie, but Hollywood rich ain't bad either. It's my shot at 'fuck you' green. The only way I can fuck up is by gettin' sick, not protecting my back. Flicks ain't real estate, Charlie, I've got to fight for every frame."

Sick? A week from that very day, I didn't get sick, I got *very* sick, terminally sick.

Charlie went back to New York, and I returned to the studio fighting the Bridges-Travolta combine for more grit in the saddle of *Urban Cowboy.*

A call from my brother: "Ilana called."

"Ilana who?"

Brothers in life, brothers on film. French movie idol Alain Delon during one of his many stays at my home.

A bad night! Batted only one for six. Commiserating with sister, Alice, and brother, Charles, at the Governor's ball following the Academy Awards in 1971. Nominated for six, Love Story copped a lonely one—Francis Lai for Best Original Score.

While guesting at my home in Beverly Hills, the good Doctor Kissinger met my son, Joshua, for the first time.

His new title didn't change his old habits. Now Secretary of State, dear Henry Kissinger still resided at my home whenever he visited Los Angeles. Lucky me!

At the starting gate of a trip to hell and back! Signing Francis Coppola to direct Mario Puzo's best-selling novel, The Godfather.

ANY MAN WHO SAYS HE CAN READ A WOMAN'S THOUGHTS IS A MAN WHO KNOWS NOTHING.

Receiving my Ph.D. degree on how little I know. My wife Ali and I dancing as one at the post-premiere bash of The Godfather. *Was she madly in love? You bet! But not with me. Did I know it? Would you?*

By far the best actress I've ever met! Ali hated every moment of the night! Kissinger didn't.

Al Pacino and Jimmy Caan both "made their bones" that night, exploding into stardom.

Happy 100th Birthday, dear Adolph! Zucker, that is. From around the world they flew to cheer Paramount's and Hollywood's founder. From left to right: Alfred Hitchcock, Frank Yablans, Bob Hope, Charlie Bluhdorn, and me. Seated is the birthday boy himself, Adolph Zucker.

Kirk Douglas winning the Academy Award. In Hebrew, that is. For his brilliant, authentic portrayal of a rabbi reciting the holy prayers at a Passover suprise feast for Roman Polanski. (Left to right) Seated: Walter Matthau with son, Charlie, Rabbi Douglas, Leigh Taylor Young. Standing middle row: Carol Matthau, Anne Douglas, Joanna Cameron, Sue Mengers, and half of Billy Wilder. Standing back row: Warren Beatty, Roman Polanski, myself, and Jean-Claude Tramont.

Is Warren Beatty really Jewish?

Laughing up a storm with Jack Nicholson over Roman Polanski's daily frustration with writer Bob Towne during the filming of Chinatown.

With my favorite lady, Sue Mengers, and my star, Faye Dunaway, greeting the audience after the first showing of Chinatown.

A clean sweep for Chinatown at the Golden Globes. Catherine Deneuve presenting me with the Globe Award for Chinatown as best picture.

Not tonight kid. At the Academy Awards it was a clean sweep, but this time under the rug. Chinatown, nominated for eleven awards, copped but one. Best Original Screenplay. Bob Towne, Jack Nicholson, and I arriving at the awards.

"Damnit! Again, I forgot to thank you," apologized Prince Francis Coppola after he won the Oscar for Godfather II.... **Sure!!**

If only mom and pop could see me now—their black sheep son—a full-blown Ivy League professor.

Laughing it up with Charlie Bluhdorn and Frank Yablans the night I was presented with the key to the City of New York.

To the world he was Lord Laurence Olivier. To all his pals, Larry, who celebrated his eighty-sixth birthday at my home. It was the best bash of the year.

The quintessential example of a picture telling a thousand words. It sure in hell summed up my relationship with Dustin Hoffman.

"Just act, dear boy," quipped an impatient Olivier as Hoffman relentlessly searched for his character's motivation in the climactic final scene of Marathon Man.

With Raquel Welch watching Super Bowl Ten. While eleven cameras were simultaneously shooting footage for my film Black Sunday.

With Marie Sophie Pierson, my fair lady that year, attending Henry Kissinger's fiftieth-birthday party at the Harmony Club in New York.

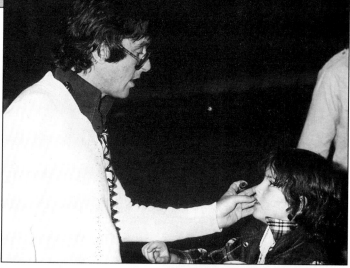

Celebrating my son, Joshua's, eighth birthday while shooting Players *in Las Vegas.*

Barry Diller, Jane and Michael Eisner paid director Robert Altman and myself a surprise visit while filming Popeye *in Malta.*

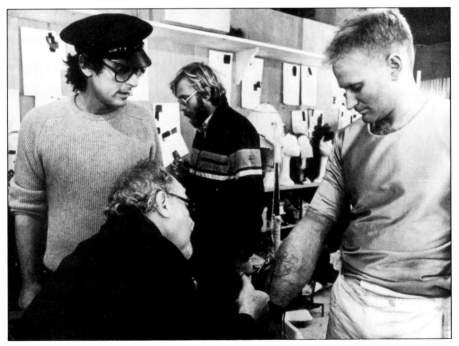

Watching a desperate Robert Altman mold Robin Williams's arm into that of Popeye.

Two Bobs, surrounded by two beauties. Cathy Lee Crosby, Evans, Hope, and Cheryl Tiegs all singing "Get High on Yourself."

The camaraderie—totally posed. The reality—fierce competitors were Richard Zanuck, William Niles, Charlton Heston, and me as Cosmopolitan's camera clicked a quick shot for their article on Star Power on Hollywood's Exclusive Tennis Courts.

(Courtesy Elyse Lewin)

Going nose to nose with Jack Nicholson as we brought in 1985 together.

THE 'COTTON CLUB' MOVIE ROLLING ALONG

Photo by Ralph C

"Clockwise: Robert Evans, producer/director of The Cotton Club; *George Kaufman, president of Kaufman Astoria Studios; Michael W. Proscia, international vice president of the International Alliance of Theatrical Stage Employees and Moving Picture Operators of the United States and Canada (IATSE); Michael W. Proscia (IATSE); Ralph Cooper II, consultant to Robert Evans. Actresses Marilyn Matthews and Desiree Davis flank Producer Robert Evans as he greets Big Red's entertainment editor, Don Thomas, following a press conference announcing that New York City will be the site for the filming of the motion picture* Cotton Club. *The announcement was made by George Kaufman, Milton Forman, chief consultant of Kaufman/Astoria Studios, and Robert Evans, who said, 'I look upon the* Cotton Club *motion picture as a complete integrated venture. Hopefully its success will introduce a new pattern of employment for the Black artists and technicians. Integration is today, and today is where people are, and that's where the* Cotton Club *motion picture is.'"*

Birthday-feasting the family Coppola at Elaine's in New York. Thirty-six hours later, Francis barred me from the set of Cotton Club. *Was it the pasta? No way, it was too good!*

Celebrating the opening of Stanley Jaffe's new flick Racing with the Moon *were from left to right: the producer himself, Stanley Jaffe, Frank Yablans, a very tanned Evans, a very successful Michael Eisner.*

A quick hello and good-bye to Sharon Stone while shooting Sliver *in New York.*

A rarity! A quiet moment alone with my son, Joshua.
(Courtesy Alice Springs)

Love is better the second time around! Back with brother Charles sailing the Caribbean together.

"Ilana Garcia, the shirtmaker. She's found pure white silk shirts."

"You're kidding?"

"Sealed," said Charlie. "There's a catch, we gotta buy five. They're wholesale—four thousand each."

"Wholesale? Cedars pays twenty-four bucks a shirt."

"That's Cedars, Ilana tells me seventy-five hundred is a bargain. It's ten thousand and up, that's if you can get it. Get this, she boasts, Mick Jagger would do a concert in Yankee Stadium for zip for this order."

Would you say the world of toot was crazy in the 1970s?

"She'll hold 'em for only twenty-four hours."

Pharmaceutical cocaine was mythical. Manufactured by only one company in America, Merck, it was obtainable to the outside world only by heist. So mythical was its allure that it became the DEA's most effective bait to entrap schmuck buyers. That was us. I'd met Ilana just twice, while on business in New York, and it wasn't to take her to the theater. Charlie knew her well, from the social scene around town.

Twenty-four hours later, Charlie was on the horn.

"What do I tell her? She's called twice."

"Let's buy it, we'll split it three ways, Mike, you, and me." Mike Shure was our brother-in-law.

"You're sure?" Charlie asked.

"Yeah, why not? We'll vault it. Just make sure it's kosher. This ain't no kibbitz, be real careful."

"Careful . . . I'm not like you. Who's more cautious than me?"

"Yeah, but this sounds too good, and that's bad. Charlie, promise me you're nowhere near when the deal goes down. Get a schmuck delivery guy from the Stage Deli, your chauffeur, or anyone to pick it up, but not you, promise?"

"Promise."

The deal was to go down on Friday. All that day there was no word from my brother. At 7:45 that evening, I was going out the door, on my way to pick up my kid for dinner, when my houseman hailed me.

"A Miss Garcia on the phone, says it's urgent."

Leaving the motor on, I rushed to the phone.

"Yeah?"

A scared, stuttering Ilana. "Where's Charles? I'm worried about him."

"I don't know, haven't heard from him all day."

"He was supposed to be here for the transaction. Does he have the money?"

"How the hell do I know? I'll try to find him. Where can I call you?"

She hung up. I was scared shitless. I called Joshua, said I'd be a little late. Then called my brother's apartment, his beach house, my sister's apartment, her country house. An eerie no answer. Instead of picking my kid up for dinner, I opened the door to hell.

Minutes later, the phone rang, it was Charles.

"Bob, Mike and I have been arrested, we were set up, just left the DEA office."

"Arrested? What are you talking about? Ilana just called me asking for you."

"What? She was arrested too. That means she was calling you from the DEA's office. I was there, saw her on the phone."

"She asked me where you were, I told her I didn't know. What the fuck's going on, Charlie?"

"At five thirty this afternoon, Mike and I were in my office, two guys walked in."

"Did you know them?"

"No, but they said they had what I ordered, so I let 'em in. I locked the door, they took out the bottles, I took out the cash, and they took out the handcuffs."

"I don't believe what I'm hearing. You're telling me you let two total strangers into your office and you hand them nineteen Gs. Are you fuckin' nuts!"

The Charles Evans I knew pre-1975 wouldn't open his door to a stranger even if he wanted to sell him a winning lottery ticket. Now he's shaking hands with a stranger holding a potential fifteen-year prison term—this can't be!

"Don't worry, Bob, you aren't in any trouble. I told them you had nothing to do with it."

"You mentioned my name?"

"This Hall guy, the arresting officer, I talked him out of making us spend the night in jail."

"Charles, how did my name get into it?"

"I suppose Ilana must have said something—"

"Yeah. But I wasn't *there!* Don't you understand? They want to involve me—to get ink!"

"What do you mean, 'ink'?"

"Publicity!"

"Bob, you're not going to be involved, I promise."

It was a promise he had already broken. The first call on Saturday was from my brother's attorney, Charles Ballon.

"Speak to no one," he said. "I think I can make this whole thing disappear."

"You think! What's my involvement?"

"Don't know, just keep your mouth shut."

I did.

Saturday night, I flew up to San Jose for the first preview of *Urban Cowboy*. John Travolta *was not* the biggest star in the world, since—even with a full week of advertising the preview—the theater was only half full. Did anyone think it was *Saturday Night Fever*? No, but I had a 102 degree fever, sweating out the stacked deck awaiting me three thousand miles away.

Good-bye, Malta—hello, New York, and the beginning of the end. The end of respectability, the end of being a role model, the end of acceptance, the end of many a dream—one being the recipient of the Academy's Irving Thalberg Award, which I had been told was to be mine that year. The one award I wanted more than any in my life.

Far more important, it was the beginning of the end of a family together. The beginning of the end of a forty-year love affair with my brother, and the beginning of a blackening cloud that would haunt me till the day I die; the cloud far blacker because *it did not have to happen.*

Seven digits separated the second half of my life from one of pride, to one of disgrace. One call to my mentor Korshak, and my lack of involvement would have disappeared faster than paper burns.

"You can't bring in Korshak," harped Ballon, my brother, and my brother-in-law. "He's too highly profiled."

"Bullshit! He's been my mentor for twenty years."

A firm no was the unholy three's dictate. Till the day I die, I'll never forgive myself for allowing my own family to rape me of my constitutional rights. How could I have been so fuckin' dumb? Ballon was my brother's attorney, protecting him—not me.

Until that moment, my record didn't bear a traffic ticket. Then, within a blink, I went from legend to leper. Worse, it was someone's else's blink.

"All your brother had to do was keep his fuckin' trap shut. If

Charles didn't have diarrhea of the mouth tryin' to talk his way out of spending the night in jail, the name Bob Evans would never have come into play."

These venomous words were spewing daily from the lips of dear brother-in-law, Mike. Calling Charlie everything from a rat fink to a coward. Rather than confront my brother with my pent-up anger, I let it fester. This was a cardinal error. Expressed emotions, rather than muted, open the door to dialogue and understanding. Confrontation is a weakness in my persona; it led to a decade of darkness between my brother and myself.

The incidents that followed exposed a Mike I never knew, confirming my doubts over the veracity of his diatribe against Charles.

(In 1983, my brother-in-law Mike *again censored* my rights. He intercepted a six-page hand-written letter that was addressed to my sister, Alice, marked "personal and confidential." He refused her the right to open its seal and read it.)

That did it! Censor me once, shame on you, censor me twice, shame on me. I've never spoken to him since. Sadly, with it went the decades of love I had shared with my sister.

Ballon's distinguished law firm represented my brother; a junior G-man fresh from the prosecuting office was picked to be my mouthpiece. Mind you, Korshak, my lawyer for twenty years, whom I was forbidden to counsel with, could have settled my bustless bust with a two-minute phone call. Ah . . . but for this new legal eagle, it was a big-time case, with big ink to boot.

I was back in Malta overseeing *Popeye*. On the Friday of Memorial Day weekend, 1980, I was awakened from a deep sleep by my new counsel. He was in shock. The government had decided to throw the book at me—the whole unabridged one: fifteen felony counts, starting with distribution and on and on.

"Tell it to me again."

He did.

"The entire charge has no validity," spouted my choirboy attorney.

"You schmuck! The validity is *ink*. Got it?"

"You've lost me."

"John Martin, the new D.A., is using my carcass to make a name for himself. Now do you get it?"

My Kafkaesque entrapment was a secret to all on the rock. I owed it to Bob Altman to fill him in on the horrible dilemma facing me.

"Keep cool. Keep it under wraps. Stall, stall, stall." Bob embraced me. "Nothing is gonna happen."

I couldn't share my worst fear with Altman: that if anything did happen, Prime Minister Mintoff, the anti-American cocksucker, with Qaddafi's backing, could release Kissinger's laudatory introduction—a letter dear Henry begged and begged not to write—to the world. Not only would it disgrace one of my closest friends and America's most prestigious statesman, but I'd be America's new Benedict Arnold.

From the rock I took the longest plane ride of my life, landing at JFK that Sunday. My brother was there to meet me and drove me back to his apartment. Charles was friendly with New York Senator Jacob Javits, who had recommended the presidential appointment of John Martin as federal prosecuting attorney for the Southern District of New York.

Though it was a holiday weekend, Charlie miraculously tracked Javits down at a country club in Long Island. The senator was kind enough to drive back to the city to meet us at my brother's apartment. Charles told Javits the story.

I interjected. "I'm not concerned for myself, senator, as much as I am for Henry Kissinger. He did me a great favor, against his better judgment; he wrote a letter of introduction to Prime Minister Mintoff on my behalf. The effects of Martin's far-fetched indictment against me could not only be ruinous to Henry, but an embarrassment for our country."

Charlie interrupted, "Jack, there must be something you can do."

Javits's face went red with anger. "Absolutely not." He then pointed at me. "Your deportment is shameful."

"But I didn't—"

He cut me off. "I don't wish to hear any more. I'm leaving." Turning back to me, he added, "Call Henry immediately. Warn him." Not giving my brother a second glance, he stared through me. "I'm ashamed of you." Then he slammed the door behind him.

I did not take the senator's advice. I was too ashamed, too scared to call Kissinger. I had too much respect for him, too much disdain for myself. There I stood knowing that my actions could tarnish a man who for a decade had been one of my closest friends, one whom I'd stop a bullet for; but now I'd left him naked to take one. For the next decade, I purposely refused his embrace, never telling him why.

Only once, at Lowell Guiness's 1985 New Year's Eve party in Acapulco, did we exchange words. Seeing Kissinger across a very
crowded room, I had turned the other way. Without asking me, Denise Beaumont, the lady I was with, walked to Kissinger's side, took
him by his arm, and brought him over to me. Our eyes met.

"Bobby, why haven't you returned my calls?"

Kissing him on the cheek, I said, "Because I love you, Henry. Don't
ask any more questions. Happy New Year."

Six more years would pass before another word was said between
us. Thus I lost a friendship I cherished as dearly as any in my life.

The indictment was scheduled to be handed down June 11, 1980.
Pleading that our attorneys had not had sufficient time to prepare
our case, we got a stay of execution until July 31. I cried with joy. It
was more than a stay; as long as lips stayed sealed, *Popeye* and crew
would not have to jump the rock.

"Let me call Korshak, please!" I begged.

"We'll tape your mouth" were the words of the unholy three.

Bad news travels fast. The buzz that something was awry spread
west.

Korshak called. "I hear you're in trouble. What's going on?"

Intimidated so by the three wise men, I did the unthinkable: I lied
to my lifelong protector. "Nothing's wrong," I mumbled.

"If I find out different, I'll break your head," he barked back.

As I turned fifty at the end of June, instead of basking in the glory
of achievements past, I was a rat cornered, my carcass lay naked for
the locust's ink. My fiftieth birthday present? A lie detector test. On
a Saturday morning I found myself in one of life's more demeaning
positions—fingers wired as I answered yes or no to a dozen questions
concerning the felony counts. No was my answer to every question. I
didn't know it at the time, but my every move was being watched by
a dozen people behind a two-way mirror. A polygraph expert had
been flown in from Denver especially for the test. Rarely does the
expert evoke absolute innocence, rather some degree of equivocation.
Call it self-protection, but not this time. The conclusion: *total truth.*

It didn't matter. Unfortunately, the name Evans with the given
name of Bob, blasts whomever the accuser may be to prominence.
Whether it be slight or fright it happened to me before, and it sure in
hell has happened to me since. It's called INK, in bold letters, usually
in red, taking first billing over the masthead of the newspaper itself.

Knowing this outrage was soon to blow sky-high, I was faced with the intolerable pain of bringing it to the attention of my mentor, friend, and boss, Charlie Bluhdorn. Silently, he listened as I unraveled the entire nightmare. He asked for all the legal documents, and any and every paper that had to do with the case concerning any of the three defendants. The following Sunday, I received a call from him to drive to his home in Connecticut to review what could be a catastrophic situation. From early afternoon through late evening, we carefully evaluated each allegation.

Was Bluhdorn angry? Foaming at the mouth! Not about the deed I was being charged with, but about the stupidity of not involving the man himself, my protector, Mr. K. Taking off his glasses, Bluhdorn looked at me in silence, squinting. He walked over, our noses almost touching. "You dumb idiot, Korshak could settle this sitting on the toilet. The entire legal staff of Simpson, Thatcher reviewed each and every charge. Do you know their opinion? Guilty of usage, that's it. You may be crazy, but you're not insane. You can't plead guilty— you're innocent. If you do, it's over—not for your brother, or brother-in-law, but for *you*. You're not a private citizen, chopped liver is what they'll make out of you. I'm not asking, I'm demanding that you change your plea to innocent. It's the truth. If you don't, I'll never forgive you."

He never did. Neither did Korshak. Gone now were the sacred embrace of Kissinger, Korshak, and Bluhdorn, three of the five fingers that made my life singular. Never to return again.

On July 31, 1980, before Judge Vincent Broderick, Charles, Mike, and I pleaded guilty to the misdemeanor charge of cocaine possession. Brought up to the DEA office by two of their toughest, I was fingerprinted, photographed, and arrested. For the sake of anonymity, the pricks snuck me out the back door, knowing the press corp were there waiting in full. No movie star ever had more flashbulbs go off in his face. Throwing myself into the backseat of the car and onto the floor, I thought it was a nightmare. It was, but it wasn't a dream, it was for real, and it was only the beginning.

From New York to Los Angeles, above the name of the papers themselves, headlines blared:

PRODUCER BOB EVANS PLEADS GUILTY TO COKE BUST.

FILM MOGUL EVANS PLEADS GUILTY TO COCAINE BUST.

BOB EVANS, TWO OTHERS, PLEAD GUILTY TO COCAINE

BUST. And on and on they read from Los Angeles to Istanbul.

Is it possible to be busted when you're three thousand miles away from the bust? Mae West's measurements never spread that distance.

On the morning of October 7, 1980, Judge Broderick was more than fair in his sentencing. *Newsweek* magazine reported:

> *The judge could have thrown him in jail for a year, but instead Hollywood producer Robert Evans* (Love Story, The Godfather) *got a year's probation. In a Manhattan federal court, Evans, his brother Charles, and brother-in-law Michael Shure pleaded guilty to possession of three ounces of cocaine. The court deferred judgment and ordered Evans to use his program for young people. That could mean only one thing—a movie. After a year, if the probation is not violated, the charges will be expunged, the case dismissed.*

Rather than cop a plea, let me quote from Aljean Harmetz, the chief *New York Times* entertainment writer:

> *Charles Evans and Michael Shure purchased five ounces of cocaine for $19,000 from undercover narcotics agents in New York on May 2.*
>
> *Although Robert Evans was 3,000 miles away in California at the time of the sale, he pleaded guilty on July 31, in New York to possession of cocaine.*

Bluhdorn's prediction was on the nose. Like a plague, front-page headlines blasted out, such as JUDGE GIVES EVANS ONE YEAR TO PRODUCE *(New York Post);* FILMMAKER EVANS OFFERED CHANCE TO CLEAR DRUG RECORD *(Los Angeles Times);* and JUDGE ORDERS PRODUCER ROBERT EVANS TO DEVELOP YOUTH ANTI-DRUG PROJECT *(New York Daily News).*

When I arrived back in Los Angeles, Greg Bautzer, my longtime friend, mentor, and marriage broker to Bluhdorn, was waiting for me at home. Hours earlier he had read the headlines. Before I could bring in my luggage, he grabbed my arm.

"How did Korshak let you get into this mess?"

"I didn't call him."

He didn't believe me.

"Don't try to protect him."

I cut him off.

"You've got it wrong, Greg. I didn't let him protect *me*."

His face reddened, his nostrils widened.

"*You didn't bring in Korshak?* I'm not hearing right. Do you know who his closest friend is? A top guy at the DEA. They go back more than thirty years. Went to college together, Schmuck!"

Holding back steam was not a Bautzer trait. Pointing his finger right in my face, he ranted.

"Eight months ago, two brothers, both performers [he told me who], were appearing at Anaheim. A broad called the police, told them her ex was pocketing an ounce of cocaine. Right smack in the middle of their show the police busted in, took them offstage, cuffed both of them. The broad was right—one of the brothers was pocketing it. They took him to Anaheim jail. They allowed him one call. It was to Korshak. Twenty minutes later he was out and the big man hardly knew him. And *you* didn't call him?"

I shook my head no.

He grabbed both my shoulders, shook me. "Don't zipper your mouth to me. I've got too big an investment in you—I was the one who introduced you to Bluhdorn . . . to Paramount. Give it to me straight."

"My brother wouldn't let me."

"Your brother? What the fuck does he have to do with it? You're dirty in usage—that's it! Even I know that. Don't bullshit me, I know you too well, your brother can't bully you."

I didn't answer.

"Tell me I'm right."

Again I didn't answer. Greg knew then it was true: I had danced to my brother's music.

"And you're the guy who made Paramount number one."

He stormed out. I ran into my bedroom, crying uncontrollably until the sun came up the next day.

Paramount, the company I'd saved from the graveyard, gave a statement to the press concerning my new infamy:

Evans is not an employee of Paramount and has not been an employee of Paramount for four years. He is an independent contractor producing pictures for us.

Suddenly the media coined a new middle name for me, Bob "Cocaine" Evans. Nothing travels faster than raunchy gossip. Going to dinner was a hassle, as was taking a piss. Going to the john was taboo in public. If I did, gossip would spread like a brushfire. "He was tooting, not peeing." By necessity, my home became my sanctuary more and more.

Popeye was Paramount's Christmas entry. A few days before its New York opening, Bob Altman was sitting in Elaine's restaurant with his agent, Sam Cohn, when Roy Scheider, Richard Dreyfuss, and a young lady walked over to say hello.

The lady was introduced to Altman, who looked up and asked her, "Are you the columnist with the *Daily News*?"

"Yes," she smiled.

Altman stood, a carafe of red wine in hand, and then slowly poured the entire pitcher on her head. Suddenly she was a redhead with a red face, wearing a red dress, red stockings, and red shoes.

"Been reading your column for the past month, my dear. 'Cocaine' Evans is my partner! Next time call him Bob."

Elaine's was abuzz. Altman . . . he couldn't care less. Gotta love a guy with them *cojones*. Altman's drenching the fourth estate in red wine far from helped *Popeye*'s reviews. But who the fuck cared.

Popeye's spinach filled my pockets with green, his muscles bulged bigger around the world than they did in America. No blockbuster, but no black eye, *Popeye* ended up as the fifth largest grossing cartoon character brought to the big screen.

Vincent Canby called *Urban Cowboy* the best American film of the year when it opened and it opened big. The residual income from the flick, and from the 6 million albums at seventeen bucks a pop, helped me survive a decade of unemployment. During the entire gold rush of the 1980s Diamond Jim Evans didn't earn a single buckaroo.

May 2, 1980! What a difference a day makes.

Charles and I differ in our opinions concerning my legal guilt. Though it was his hand caught in the cookie jar, it was me who said, "Let's buy it, put it in the vault." But it was he who broke his promise— *no personal contact.* The most expensive broken promise of my life.

Who's right? Who's wrong? Who knows? It's conjecture.

What's not conjecture, they were caught, I was not.

What's not conjecture is that my own family denied me my inalienable constitutional rights of counsel. What's not conjecture is that my brother's and brother-in-law's names faded into the background, while mine became part of drug folklore. What's not conjecture is that they went from rich to richer as I went from famous to infamous. What's not conjecture: they thrived, I starved. They traveled five star, I traveled from in-law to outlaw. While they granded, I was branded Bob Cocaine Evans. What's not conjecture: like the misdemeanor itself, the incident was erased from their future forever. Yet no matter what my accomplishments, the second paragraph of my obituary is already chiseled in granite: "In 1980 Robert Evans pleaded guilty to a cocaine bust." It doesn't matter that I was *never busted.* It doesn't matter that I was totally exonerated by Judge Broderick, or that the misdemeanor was erased from my record. What does matter is that it will never be erased from that second paragraph.

I've been guilty of many things in my life. But my arm ain't three thousand miles long.

In the spirit of love . . . Forgive? Sure! . . .

Forget? Yeah, with senility. . . .

Judge Broderick's dictate was to produce a thirty-second anti-drug message that would be aired within the year as a public service commercial on television. If it was accomplished, not only would we be exonerated, but the charges against us would be erased from our records.

Imagine, a court dictate ended up making television history.

My sister, Alice, excited Steve Karmen, the composer of the "I Love New York" campaign to come up with an anti-drug lyric targeted at America's youth. He created the lyric "Get high on yourself." The response was more than high, it was explosive.

My brother, Charles, was to pay the cost of making the commercial. I was to make it happen.

What started out as a month's endeavor ended up taking a year and a half of my life. Why? Our sixty-second commercial became the embryo that ignited the largest anti-drug media blitz in television history.

Getting our foot in the door to get the commercial produced, however, was another story.

I realized scare tactics hadn't worked, so "Get High on Yourself" had a different message, accentuating the positive. But why should anyone help me spread the spirit? It was a penance cure, not a cure for heart disease, AIDS, or cancer.

"Who's gonna show? Why should they?" Everyone laughed.

Luckily, Cathy Lee Crosby came to my aid. Her never-ending enthusiasm helped make it all happen. Her vision was to corral a huge assemblage of celebrated peer images, intertwine them with street kids of every color—united as one voice, they would blast out in song "Get High on Yourself."

I said it. Everyone said it. It's impossible! *Nothing is impossible. It happened!*

Bob Hope, Paul Newman, Muhammad Ali, Magic Johnson. . . . Cheryl Tiegs, Carol Burnett, Kate Jackson. . . . Ninety-three international celebrities were asked to contribute their time and effort. Ninety-three out of ninety-three showed.

"I'm the wrong guy to tell 'Tinseltown has no loyalty.' "

Two weeks after we shot our sixty-second commercial, Bob Hope saw my first cut of it. Impressed? Immediately he picked up the phone and called the White House wanting to speak to the President himself, Ronald Reagan.

Within seventy-two hours, Cathy Lee Crosby and myself, joined by Brad and Susan O'Leary (whose influence in D.C. carried much weight), were ushered to the White House. There we showed the "Get High on Yourself" commercial to America's first lady, Nancy Reagan. Strange, huh? My penance lyric gave the first lady the hook she needed to perpetuate a new cause: "Just say no to drugs" became hers.

Brad O'Leary then carried the ball. Within two weeks, every important media giant was aware of the White House's enthusiasm of a new positive spirit toward kids.

Were we hot? No, historic.

What started out as a public service message became the core of NBC's new fall season. The Sunday before Bob Hope kicked off the

first of NBC's fall specials on "Get High on Yourself," Brandon Tartikoff, the network's entertainment president, commented to anchor-
woman Sue Simmons:

> *This is a historic event, even for network television, to devote an
> entire week for the purpose of focusing on a single subject and gearing
> all the programming toward that. . . . We're not only doing the prime-
> time playing of those public service messages, but we have the
> "Today" and "Tomorrow" shows participating, . . . and also the radio
> division of NBC will be doing an audio version of "Get High on Your-
> self" all week long. . . .*
>
> *I think there might have been . . . skepticism when Bob Evans did
> his term of sentence, which was to produce these public service mes-
> sages. . . . What has sort of emanated from all this is far beyond his
> commitment or promise to any judges. He has been up for ninety-six
> hours editing this special; even as we speak they're putting in final
> pieces and everything. It is a giant effort and he has literally pushed
> back his movie projects one year to devote himself to this. And I think
> if people knew that, that sort of skepticism would disappear because it
> is very altruistic on his part to make this happen. . . .*
>
> *What happened was I went over on a Sunday afternoon to take a
> look at this public service message. . . . Usually in television people
> come to you with ideas to do shows and they always want to do more
> than what you're willing to give them. In the case of "Get High on
> Yourself," I preempted them by starting first after I saw the spot. I
> said, "If what you're looking for is a special, I don't think that does
> justice to what you're about here." This is a very important and cru-
> cial situation in this country, which is youth and drugs. And a spe-
> cial, I mean, you know, George Burns does a special, or Lynda Carter
> does a special. I said I would love to see if my management would give
> me the whole week on NBC, to use the power of what networks have,
> which is so rarely used for these purposes, and see if we can put a dent
> into this problem.*

Only three weeks earlier, on a blistering Sunday night in the middle of August 1981, I was interrupted by a pale Brandon Tartikoff.
The heat was not bothering me, since I was into my forty-eighth hour
in an air-conditioned studio at Compact Video. I was desperately trying to structure an hour-long special that was scheduled to follow

Bob Hope's upcoming one. This was not an easy task—I had no writers, no story, no script, only spirit. Brandon, whose boss was Grant Tinker, asked me to hold everything up. He sure looked worried as we both walked into a private room.

"NBC's Head of News Bill Small called Grant Tinker tonight, Grant called me. Take a deep breath, Evans. From an unimpeachable source, Small has found out that you are going to be set up."

My face paled too. "What do you mean 'set up'?"

"Small doesn't know, but someone out there is trying to discredit the show—what we're trying to get across. Could be one of the other two networks. We're getting more covers on your Sunday special than we've had in years. Both *Newsweek* and *Time* are covering it too. They'd love to see us fall on our asses. Could also be the big guys in the drug business. Could also be the DEA."

"What?"

"NBC is gonna accomplish more in a year than all their agencies together have done in twenty. There's more featherbedding in the DEA than in the Pentagon. Wake your butler up, have him come over now. I'll wait till he gets here."

At three that morning, David Gilruth, my butler, Brandon Tartikoff and I planned damage control to its extreme. NBC wanted to protect their own ass; in doing so, they also had to protect mine. If the tip was accurate, they'd be the laughingstock of the media, and I'd be the next Benedict Arnold.

Tartikoff explained that setting me up for a fall would be easy to do. "A kilo of cocaine over your fence, then a raid."

For the next three weeks, three guards and three dogs surrounded my home. The guards were patrolled twenty-four hours a day, seven days a week.

No one—not even the boy delivering groceries or the mail—got close to my fences. Woodland was sealed tight. Two bodyguards flanked me wherever I went. A trip out for a hot dog at Pinks was a big deal. I couldn't put the mustard on—they did, and only then did I eat it.

With guards protecting us, we moved from Compact to Pacific Video to finish the show. There I stayed, an inpatient for the ten days until "Get High on Yourself" aired. Why is it easier doing something bad than something good? The morning after "Get High on Yourself" aired, the dogs, guards, everything disappeared—all except for an

NBC invoice, billing me for $47,000—the network's damage control expenditures.

From around the country, NBC's phone lines were on overload, congratulating them on their breakthrough programming. At lunch the next day, I showed a glowing Brandon Tartikoff the bill NBC had sent me. Studying it carefully, he looked up, smiled, and burned it.

Once branded, always branded. Good is soon forgotten, and you become fair game to a new breed of journalism, its guise—investigative reporting. In truth, it's a cover for celebrity journalism, building innuendos and half-truths into fact.

I'm thinking of the Saturday morning when I was about to leave for Palm Springs when my butler buzzed.

"Mr. Ross on the phone."

Without asking which Mr. Ross (I knew many), I picked up the horn.

"Steve?"

"No, Brian."

"Who?"

"Brian Ross."

"Do I know you?"

"No, but I know you. Tonight at six P.M. on NBC national, my story is the headline of the news: 'Bob Evans, the link putting DeLorean in the clink.' A government informant . . . a plea bargain for his own coke deal."

John DeLorean, the churchgoing friend of my ex-wife Phyllis, had been arrested in a coke sting bust.

"Is this a joke? DeLorean . . . I've only met him once . . . four years ago. What's your number, pal? I want to call you back."

Quickly he rattled off his number at the NBC offices. For all I know, this guy could be a nut case. I dialed the main switchboard at NBC. He checked out: not a nut case, but the real thing—NBC's chief investigative reporter.

"What do you want from me?" I asked.

"A statement."

"You've got the wrong Evans, Mr. Ross. I know nothing about DeLorean except that he goes to church on Sunday."

"Mr. Evans, I'm not asking you to deny the charge. We have proof. You met in Newport. Don't deny it . . . it's a fact."

"I've never been to Newport. Wouldn't know how to get there if I tried."

"Is that all you have to say?"

"No. Your facts are wrong. You can't air this, it will ruin my life—"

He cut me off. "Is that all you've got to say?"

"No, I beg you to wait till Monday. Give me a chance to prove—"

Cutting me off again, "Listen in at six." Down went the phone.

The news department stands alone in a television network's hierarchy. From the President of the United States to the president of the network, by dictate, no one fucks with the news. That's the power of the fourth estate. It took me but a half hour to discover that Ross was NBC's golden boy of investigative reporting. Despite the fact that his "scoop" had not one iota of truth, once it was aired, I'd be ashamed to walk into any room anywhere.

In my eyes, a rat fink is no less repugnant than a murderer or child molester.

Whom can I call for help? In less than five hours the guillotine drops. A flash. I dialed Ed Hookstratten, my ex-wife Phyllis's manager, at home.

"Hookstratten residence," said a voice.

"May I speak to Mr. Hookstratten please . . . it's urgent."

"Mr. Hookstratten doesn't live here anymore."

"This is his home, isn't it?"

"Yes, but the Hookstrattens are separated."

"But it's Saturday. Where can I find him? It's really life or death."

Down went the other end.

When I dialed his office, his service picked up. I told the operator, five hundred bucks if she could track him down: he was "America's most wanted" to me.

Money talks. "It's a deal. If he's around, I'll get him."

Within ten, Hookstratten was on the phone. Without catching a breath, I told him my plight. The Hook, as he's known by all, was the television industry's biggest news and sports manager, representing everyone from Tom Brokaw to Jessica Savitch. He knew I was a sacrificial lamb, since the one time I met John DeLorean was with the Hook, and Ed knew we had never seen each other since.

"Stay by the phone—I'll get back to you."

A half hour later, Hook: "Just got off with Brokaw. He's got no involvement or control over weekend news. I asked him who is in control, that I am witness to Evans's innocence. If untruth goes out on the air, with the knowledge of the truth, Evans will sue the network and win.

"Hook, what can I say, let me keep trying.

"Brokaw just off the horn, tells me I should get to Jessica Savitch quick. She's my client too. Weekend news is her bailiwick, it's her lead story." Savitch was calling on the other phone—he hung up in my ear.

Twenty minutes later, not one fingernail was left, I picked it up on one ring.

"Don't know yet, we're far from home, Ross's story is already on the wire service to their five O-and-Os," Hook said, referring to the five "owned-and-operated" stations that NBC itself controls. "It's the headline scoop. I'm calling each of them and threatening them the same way I've just threatened Brokaw and Savitch. Go to church . . . Hope for the best."

No president, whether it be corporate or state, no king, queen, or pope could have pulled off what the Hook did for me.

A postscript: in his hunger for sensationalism, NBC's so-called ace investigative reporter, Brian Ross, made a slight miscalculation. Three weeks later, the government informant in the DeLorean case was uncovered. His name: *Richard* Evans. Strange, a doctor can be sued for malpractice, and a lawyer disbarred. The esteemed profession of journalism should also have a code of ethics.

To you, dear Hook—you are one ballsy guy! Very few would have gone those extra nine yards, sacrifice his own position to help another. I owe you a big one!

33

Pete Sampras, Steffie Graf, Michael Chang, Boris Becker, tennis legends all, yet none belong in *The Guinness Book of Records,* I do! No player in tennis history has played forty-one sets of tennis with Jimmy Connors as his doubles partner . . . and lost all of them.

"Let's just stay pals, Evans." Connors half smiled. "No more partners, huh?"

In May 1981, the cover of *Cosmopolitan* carried the line "Star power on Hollywood's exclusive tennis courts. How the rich and famous play the game." Inside a story by William Murray read:

The action court these days, according to Forrest Stewart and others in the know, is at Bob Evans's place in Coldwater Canyon. Nobody would think of playing a set there just for the fun of it. It's not uncommon for the host and his guests—among whom, as regulars, are Jack Nicholson, screenwriter Robert Towne, Dustin Hoffman and Robert Duvall—to bet up to a thousand dollars a set.

The match I have come to think of as quintessentially Hollywood took place on the private court of Bob Evans, the Paramount producer. It pitted Evans and his brother, Charles, against Ted Kennedy and his good friend John Tunney. With a number of celebrities, including Warren Beatty and Jack Nicholson, looking on, heckling, and making small side bets as to the outcome, the Evans boys won the first two sets handily. At this point a TV producer named Wendell Niles, Jr., himself an A player, offered to bet a thousand dollars that the Evanses would not win the third set. The bet was taken and other sizable wagers were made, after which Kennedy, grinning broadly, removed the back brace he'd been wearing under his shirt and really began to pounce. The play wasn't even close, as he and Tunney massacred the Evanses, 6–2 "It was the sweetest money I ever won," the hustling Niles crowed later.

Called the hustle center, my court became Bobby Riggs's home away from home. Preparing for his 1973 match against Billie Jean King at the Houston Astrodome, he practiced against every top player in Southern California. Bobby, who was then fifty-five, called it practice; in reality it was pocket money. The offer was the same to all from eighteen to forty: $500 a set, giving the challenger two games and service. The old hustler hopped around the court for three months and didn't lose a match, except one—to Gary Chazan. Better players than Gary lost to Riggs, but none had Gary's heart to win. Riggs was so pissed that he refused to play Gary a double-or-nothing set and said he had to be at an early dinner.

His match with Billie Jean King was so heralded that it was aired on CBS at 9:00 P.M. It stands alone as the only occasion when professional tennis has been aired during prime time on network television (and that includes the finals at Wimbledon). The Astrodome was completely sold out for the match, which had little to do with tennis and much to do with the battle of the sexes.

After Bobby picked up his last $500 before leaving for Houston, I walked him out to his car, wishing him luck.

"Your hospitality been real sportin', Evans." His finger went to his lips. "Between you and me . . ."

"Yeah?"

"Beg, borrow, steal, put every C note you got on the ole man." Putting his arm behind him, his hand flat to his back, he came closer and whispered. "Could put a nail through it . . . still beat her with one hand." Laughing, he got into his car. "Don't tell no one, the odds are getting out of hand. No surprise, it's the sucker bet of the year."

Two weeks later, Riggs lost in straight sets, 6–2, 6–3. I lost the biggest bet of my life—he probably won the biggest of his going the other way. A hustler is a hustler is a hustler is a hustler.

Late-night talk-show hosts have one thing in common—sore losers. One day on the courts, Merv Griffin thought he was a shoo-in against me.

"A hundred-dollar check to the winner," he chuckled.

An hour later he signed his autograph to a hundred-dollar check.

Two years later, I was a guest on his show. As I waited in the green room, one of his assistants came over.

"Merv would like you not to mention the tennis match."

Standing backstage, I heard his glowing introduction and walked to the chair beside him. I sat, casually mentioning . . .

"Remember the hundred-dollar check you signed, Merv? The time I beat you at tennis? Framed it."

Quickly his head turned, pointing for a commercial.

In L.A., "Let's play tennis" is tantamount to New York's "Let's have lunch."

For years Johnny Carson and I threatened a match. Finally we had to face the day. I won the flip, so my court was the turf. Saturday morning, 9:00 A.M., my intercom buzzed. "Mr. Carson's arrived."

I had forgotten all about it, having just called it a night three hours earlier. If it wasn't Johnny Carson, I would give the guy a G just to leave. My head throbbed so, my butler had to put my socks and sneakers on. A quick jug of orange juice, a quick number three Tylenol, and off I went, "double visioning" it to the court.

Johnny was in the midst of his stretching exercises, limbering his limbs with the focus of Boris Becker. A large cup of black coffee and onto the court we went, starting to rally. Every ball he hit looked like three. I didn't hit one ball back. Poor Johnny, he'd driven all the way from Malibu to play with a guy who couldn't hold his racket up. Ready now to start the set, I excused myself, took a quick piss and two more Tylenol. The first 16 points of the set, I didn't hit one ball over the net. Within two minutes it was 3–love for Carson. An hour and a half later, a tortured Carson was on the wrong side of a two-set match: 4–6, 3–6. His disgust was difficult to hide.

"Shouldn't have played . . . back's killing me."

Monday morning, his wife Joanna called me.

"What happened Saturday, Bob?"

"Nothing. Why?"

"The strangest thing: Johnny came home, I asked him how the tennis was, he slammed the door, hasn't spoken to me since."

Dustin Hoffman had the form, strokes, and agility of a minor-league McEnroe. Jack Nicholson and I were gutter players. Fifty sets later, Dustin was on the short end of winning two out of fifty, blaming it on bad calls, bad light, bad back, bad racket, you name it, bad everything.

For my next birthday, four guys carried a ten-foot-high made-to-order Wimbledon referee chair onto my tennis court. A present from Hoffman, yes—but a hint as well. When Dustin next came over, a ref made the calls. Twenty sets later, he hadn't done too bad—he won once. No wonder he doesn't play here anymore.

Take it from an old tennis bum, my court has hosted many a player, many a watcher. Many switched partners, both on and off the court. Tennis anyone?

34

A high school dropout knows what an actor, a writer, or a director is, yet a Rhodes scholar has no idea what a producer is.

Generalizing a producer as a fat, bald guy who sits in a back room, smokes a cigar, hustles, extorts—name it, he'll do it, *anything*, to get his flick made.

Really? Then why is it that David O. Selznick, Sam Goldwyn, Darryl Zanuck—producers all—are chronicled in greater depth than any actor, director, or writer?

I'll tell you why. It's the producer whose vision (which he then shares with others) eventually ends up on the screen. He's the one who hires the writer and director. When a director hires a producer, you're in deep shit. A director needs a boss, not a yes man.

As Paramount's production chief, my biggest financial loss was creating the Directors Company. The industry's top three helmsmen—Coppola, William Friedkin, and Peter Bogdanovich—shared ownership with Paramount, with total autonomy. The result? Total disaster!

Contrary to popular belief, legit producers never have to raise a dime. The major studios are hungry to write a check for exciting new material. None want financial partners. If they roll the dice, they want to cover the bet themselves.

Legit producers are few, a dying breed. There are many "cocktail party" producers. (By a recent census, they outnumber the police.) Dilettante, agent, photographer, lawyer, hustler, deal maker, playboy, financier, starlet's husband—all fraudulently carry the moniker "producer." None of these guys have the vaguest notion of budget, casting, pre-production, production, post-production, final edit, final theater selection, advertising, marketing, and collecting the "dough-re-mi." Those are just a few of the many facets a legit producer is responsible for.

Speaking to the ladies: If you're ever approached with the line "You ought to be in pictures, I'm a producer," tell the guy to fuck off. He's a fraud, and the pictures he wants to put you in don't play in theaters. "You ought to be in pictures" just ain't the M.O. of a legit producer. Quote me if you want.

An actor gives twelve weeks to a flick; a director, at most a year; a producer, rarely less than three to five. If the flick's a hit, the dance card of both director and actor is filled for years. Not so for the producer. "What can you do for me today?" is his life. Damnit! Rodney Dangerfield's right again: I don't get no respect.

Each film has its own life, though all share a connective tissue. Success has many fathers, while failure is quickly orphaned.

The guilds, both directors and writers, both have a single purpose: to protect their membership and to offer it a podium. They are counterproductive at times and care little who pays the tab. On the other hand, the Producers Guild has no purpose. Reminiscent of the eight Arab nations—never united.

The arrogance of possessive credit, a Directors Guild dictate, is repugnant in its posture. Politically, bleeding liberals all, yet shamefully autocratic when it comes to sharing a collaborative effort.

"Sam Schwartz," a fledgling director, gets his big break in the big time—*the big screen*. Ray Stark, a prolific, professional producer, takes the gamble. Throughout production, his vast experience umbrellas the new kid on the block's inexperience. Yet, by Guild dictate, it's "A Sam Schwartz Film." . . . Ray Stark who?

Success or failure, each film carries its own drama, villains, heroes, contributors. More often than not, the intrigue behind the camera is far more textured than what's on the screen.

The Godfather is a telling example. Principal photography had been completed. There was one problem, we didn't have an ending: it was never written, shot, or structured. Mayhem plenty—many of the principal characters were knifed, shot, or strangled, but that ain't an ending. Peter Zinner, one of the film's two editors, took the task upon himself. He choreographed mayhem with religion, intercut murder with the baptism of Michael Corleone's newborn child. He saved the day—he saved our ass!

Now, decades later, it's still up there with the most memorable climaxes in cinema. Not godfathered by its director or producer, but by a faceless wonder. Coppola went on to become the decade's maestro, Evans its boy genius . . . but Peter Zinner—who? Oh! He silently disappeared, looking for a new gig—saving another producer's or director's ass.

Is it the director's picture? Damn right! But it's also the actors', writer's, editor's, cinematographer's, composer's, and producer's. *Filmmaking is a collaborative effort.*

Is it not worthy of investigation by the legitimate critic to uncover the contributions before writing their critique in granite? It's called doing your homework.

The Directors and Writers Guilds annually throw a bash honoring their own, singling out one as the best. But not the Producers Guild. What's wrong with us? We've got tuxedos, we wanna show off and be named "best," win The Willy Loman Award.

35

"It's not *Godfather,* Evans," angrily thrusting his finger at me. "I've had it! You do it or I do it. Evans stays, Coppola goes."

Intrigue, anger, blackmail, deceit, pussy galore, macho grandstanding, back stabbing, and threats to life and career plagued the five-year making (and near unmaking) of *The Cotton Club.* The treacheries involved were so bizarre that *The Godfather* and *Scarface* combined pale by comparison. I can only tell some of the story—not wanting my life insurance canceled.

On December 12, 1980, the making of *The Cotton Club* was announced. From New York (the *New York Times:* " 'POPEYE' PRODUCER EVANS' NEXT TRY IS MAKING 'THE COTTON CLUB' ") to Hong Kong (the *Free Standard:* "BLOCKBUSTER MOVIE-MAKER ROBERT EVANS TO DO A FILM ABOUT A HUNK OF HISTORY—'THE COTTON CLUB.' "), it made entertainment headlines around the world.

Jim Haskin's pictorial history of the Cotton Club was the embryo. Its carrier was George Wieser, the guy who brought me *The Detective* and *The Godfather.* The club's canvas was Harlem at its nasty best—the 1920s and 1930s. Its distinction, breaking barriers for great black talent to be seen and heard. Its hypocrisy, that, although located in the middle of Harlem, it carried the edict, "No colored allowed—whites only." Its celebrity . . . in order to gain entrance, you had to be one. "Goin' uptown" was in. Awe them "coffee and creamers," hear them voices—Duke Ellington, "Cab" Calloway, Lena Horne—watch them dancin' toes of Bill "Bojangles" Robinson.

The long-legged showgirls known as coffee and creamers made thirty-five bucks a week, but were all decked out. Mink coats, luxurious apartments, limousines—they had it and more.

Located between midtown Manhattan and the Bronx, Harlem was open territory. Open to anything and everything, from the numbers racket to bootlegging. You name it, it was open. Every crooked nose from Lucky Luciano to Dutch Schultz wanted in.

A fuckin' natural! Violence, sex, music, I'm holdin' *The Godfather* with music. Look out, eighties—here I come!

We completed the poster before the first word was written. Against a background of mayhem and dancing, it read: "The Cotton Club: its violence startled the nation, its music startled the world."

As I presented the poster to more than a hundred international buyers at the 1982 Cannes Film Festival, I showboated, "If you don't like the poster, don't buy the film."

"Who's in the film?" asked a man in the back.

"Who was in *The Godfather?*"

Two hours later and $8 million richer, the *Cotton Club* poster—with no story, no script, no cast—raised more in foreign pre-sales than any finished flick at the festival. I said to myself, "Raise another twelve mil and I'll be completely independent, own it, be the Selznick of the eighties." I was going to be an owner for the first time, as well as a director. The first frame of the film was already embedded in my thoughts: "To you, Pop, wherever you are . . . Bobby." If not for Pop, I'd never have tasted Harlem in the 1930s.

If it was going to be *The Godfather* with music, who better to write it than my pal Puzo? No cheap buy Mario: now a million-dollar ticket.

Like a scene out of a cheap flick, Melissa Prophet, an actress who appeared in my film *Players,* was on the horn. Her then mentor was Adnan Khashoggi, labeled the richest man in the world. Las Vegas was his temporary habitat. Investing in films, his temporary whim.

Purred Melissa, "AK and Robert Evans, what better combination?"

Familiar with Arab mentality, I purred back. "Not interested, leaving for New York, closing a deal with Ricklis."

Menachem Ricklis was also a millionaire many times over. A Jew no less, but so what, I didn't even know him.

Within the hour an anxious Melissa was back on the horn. "AK would like you to stop in Vegas before meeting Ricklis."

It worked.

"Call you back."

"Call me back?" Melissa said. "Are you crazy! He's the biggest spender in the world, and you're calling *me* back?"

"Okay, okay. Have his plane pick me up, wait for me in Vegas, fly me to New York."

"You are crazy."

"No, I'm Evans."

"No, you're a fuckin' prima donna."

Four hours later, I arrived in Vegas on Khashoggi's private jet. Another of his fleet, a custom-built Boeing 727, was waiting to fly me east. There I met the infamous Khashoggi, toga and all. He was not a bedouin, but rather the charmer of charmers. "A double seduction," Melissa coined it later.

"Like to gamble?" He smiled.

"Like to breathe?" Smiling back.

A hundred feet down the corridor from his suite, a door opened into a private casino. There were blackjack, roulette, baccarat, and crap tables, with croupiers behind each; it was all dreamlike. With entourage and Melissa surrounding him, AK cutely dimpled. "Your choice."

Korshak's heavy stick, twenty years earlier prompted:

"Let's pick up the dice."

Suddenly a stack of fifty $1,000 chips was before me. Gamblin' hundreds was more my style, but it was his turf, his game. Not showing weakness, I casually cylindered the fifty into five stacks of ten. The chips? No gift—a trap. He knew it. He knew I knew it too. He wanted me owing.

Twenty minutes later and forty-eight chips blown, another fifty chips were stacked before me. Khashoggi picked up the dice, put a hundred thousand on the line, and threw a nine. Then, pressing the odds, he backed the line with another hundred, covering every number from four to ten—10 Gs on each. Shaking the ivories, he let 'em roll; up turned a four and a three. It's called crapping out! Within the blink of an eye, a quarter of a million was wiped from the green felt.

Stepping on an ant couldn't have bothered him less.

No wonder they give him his own casino!

Not me, now deep into my second stack, I was plenty bothered. Picking up the old ivories, I prayed to God—my God, not Allah. He heard me. For more than twenty minutes, "them ivories" went my way to the tune of a hundred and fifty big ones.

"Let's have dinner."

"You're quitting?"

"No, I'm hungry."

Khashoggi, pinching me on the cheek as if I were a Miss Universe, said, "Pay Puzo the million. You're a winner. There aren't many. We'll make good partners."

My million-dollar crap shoot!

For months, Puzo and I collaborated on *Cotton Club*'s written canvas. It was 1982, my fuckin' luck! Interest rates broke an all-time high—22 ½ percent. Financing anything was near impossible. Funding a virgin director's flick, lunacy. AK's brother, Essam, certainly thought that. He strongly objected to his brother's caprice. With Arabic purpose, systematically he cut my deal south. When the contracts were finally drawn, $12 million was set to be turned over to *Cotton Club*'s production till. Adding the eight I had already raised from foreign sales, I was home free. My ass was covered and for the first time I'd be able to do my venture my way. No cast approvals, no script changes, no interference—total control.

The closing was set. At breakfast at Essam's home in Beverly Hills, the brothers Khashoggi sat, surrounded by their financial advisers and lawyers. Sitting there as well was my *consigliere*, Ken Ziffrin, who had represented me for more than a decade. No one negotiates with slicker innuendo than Khashoggi. While lamb and eggs were being served, Essam threw another condition into the hopper. He wanted *my house* to be put in as collateral against overages.

Was I hot? No, on fire. I turned to his dimpled brother. "It's over, AK. I'm outta here."

He looked up smiling. "What's the matter, Bobby?"

"It started out you and me. Now it's Essam, you, and me. I don't like your brother. *And I don't like being Arabed down.*"

"Bobby, we're just negotiating."

"Yeah, sure! Before it's over, I'll be owing you. My house, my kid, you'll have it all. You guys are too smart for this country bumpkin."

"Sit down, Bobby. We can work it out," smiled Khashoggi.

"Uh-uh, AK, let's stay friends, huh? Share laughs, ladies, hangouts—you name it, we'll share it. But this way I keep my kid." A nod to ashen-faced Ziffrin. "We're outta here, Ken."

Walking us to the front door, AK pinched my cheek.

"I'm always here, Bobby. The door is never closed"—kissing me on the cheek—"you'll come back. They all do."

"Thanks, Santa."

Once the door closed behind us, Ziffrin's face shook with anger.

"Are you outta your fuckin' mind? Interest rates at 22½ percent and you're turning down twelve mil?"

"Hold it, pal. If you don't treat me with the same respect I treat myself, take your shingle and shove it!"

"Don't get it, do you? You're certifiable. I'm firing *you!*"

He was right—I was certifiable. Walking out on 12 big ones when you're directing your first flick!

Luckily, Melissa Prophet's resilience brought three other backers to my doorstep. Ed and Fred Doumani and Victor Sayyah from Vegas promptly paid back Khashoggi the money he advanced to Puzo. Khashoggi demanded 25 percent interest on his two-month investment. An Arab is an Arab is an Arab is an Arab.

Months later, in December 1983, when *The Cotton Club* was in the midst of principal photography, I was interviewed by the *Los Angeles Times*:

Evans said, "All the money for Cotton Club *is coming from Ed and Fred Doumani (and partner Sayyah). Every dollar. They stood up for this film when other guys wouldn't. They did it without a contract, just on the shake of a hand. My own family wouldn't do that."*

Now that *The Cotton Club* was fully OPM (Other People's Money) financed, industry heat was hot to distribute the suddenly celebrated flick. It mattered little that I was a virgin director, insisting on final cut (final everything!), plus big gross percentages. The magnet of OPM had more allure than an all-star cast. Paramount was first to knock.

Bluhdorn, Diller, Eisner, and Mancuso all wanted in, so they threw a big bonus into the pot—Richard Gere. Hot off *An Officer and a Gentleman,* he was the male flavor of the year. Gere's deal was signed before Paramount's deal closed. At last! The eighties were starting to look good. Richard Pryor was set to co-star, but the dollars didn't work. Hello, Gregory Hines.

My luggage was packed and I was airport bound to close the *Cotton Club* deal with Paramount's Frank Mancuso in New York when the phone rang. It was Stan Kamen, head of William Morris, a close, personal pal for decades. Never an agent, always a friend.

"Just got off the horn with Bill Bernstein at Orion. They want *Cotton Club* more than air."

"I'm off to New York to close with Paramount."

Stan whispered, "This call is between you and me, promise? Paramount, I can't afford to lose. Orion, I don't give a shit about. But fuck 'em, Bob. Fuck 'em all—*you're fully financed!* To Paramount it gives you a slight edge. Orion—that's different. You're Christ revisited—you name it, you'll get it."

With no cash in the bank, I'd be sophomoric not to at least listen. For others I'd made hundreds of millions. For myself, nothing. Anyway, I owed it to the guys putting up the bread; it's their money on the line. The deal that gets their money back first is the deal to make. Canceling my flight, I met with Bill Bernstein, Orion's chief business honcho.

Unlike Paramount, Orion's mainstay was distribution. Helping to finance their flow of product, their M.O. was pre-selling foreign theatrical rights and domestic ancillaries. HBO alone was then coming up with 30 percent of the budget on each Orion film, guaranteeing the cable network a steady flow of feature flicks.

Paramount's M.O. was diametric. The studio was a full-blown production/distribution empire, with big pockets and *mucho* cash to spend. Their business was producing and financing films, not pre-selling territories, not pre-selling anything. Paramount didn't pay on delivery, rather from day one. Their distribution organization was proud, powerful, arrogant, and rightfully so—they collected close to fifty cents on the retail dollar (Orion was lucky to collect thirty). Orion passively waited for product to be finished before viewing it. Conversely, Paramount assiduously critiqued each day's dailies. Paramount didn't need your money. Orion desperately did. A big-budget blockbuster, fully OPM financed, would be a coup of coups for Orion.

In that spirit, Bernstein ingeniously structured a deal that covered Orion distribution's ass, and covered mine with "fuck you" money for the rest of my life. Equally important, I had *total creative freedom.*

Within two hours a deal was structured, an offer I couldn't refuse. Looking through Orion's deal memo, Stan Kamen shook his head in awe.

"It's the richest deal I've ever seen. Congratulations!"

Paramount, my home studio, which was still renting a car for me, had the right to counter. Their chief business honcho, Richard Zimbert, didn't believe Orion's offer; he must have thought I was stoned.

"If you're trying to hustle a richer deal, it won't work." Testing my veracity, "Send the deal over. If your numbers check out, the car we rent for you is yours to keep. If they don't, you pick up the rental. Deal?"

"Deal!"

My rented Jag became mine to keep. The most expensive bet I ever won.

Gere and I hit it off great. He moved into my guest cottage, stayed for five months. When Los Angeles hosted buyers from Hong Kong to Barcelona during American Film Week, each night in my projection room, Gere and I did a horse-and-pony show. A buyer is a buyer is a buyer is a buyer. Together, we let the Diamond Jim buyers know what they were getting: Gable and Tracy, a buddy flick, great music, plenty of shoot-'em-up, great dancing, plenty of man and woman stuff. You name it. They were gettin' it. Our act down so pat, we could've taken it on the road . . . yeah, but still no script.

With $20 million in the till, I tried the impossible—getting concessions in order to shoot in New York. The New York unions were suffering 40 percent unemployment. The impossible worked. The front page of *Variety* on Wednesday, February 23, 1983, announced the news:

N.Y UNIONS CRIMP WORK HOURS TO LURE PIX— EVANS "CLUB" KICKS OFF "EXPERIMENT"

Breaking a sixty-year-old standing contract provision and taking a cue from the crafts in Europe who have benefited from a runaway production plight in the U.S., the Gotham-based picture locals have agreed to a shorter workday for the Robert Evans production of Cotton Club.

Instead of a twelve-hour workday starting at 7 A.M. and including obligatory overtime and a lunch break, crew for Evans $20,000,000 period piece will toil for eight hours from 11 A.M. to 7 P.M., and instead of breaking for lunch would partake in a continuous buffet set up when time allows.

At a crowded press conference Wednesday, where Orion Pictures chairman Arthur Krim confirmed that his company will distribute Cotton Club *next year, Evans revealed that the unprecedented concession induced him to shoot the Harlem Jazz Era–themed pic in New York instead of running off to London where he said he easily could work within budget.*

"I have $20,000,000 to make this picture," Evans told the Hotel Carlyle press session. "Anything more than that and they're going to take my house away." He estimated his contract with the eight N.Y. craft unions will enable him to make a $30,000,000 or $40,000,000 picture for $20,000,000.

New York desperately wanted *The Cotton Club* made in the Big Apple. Everyone on cooperation-plus. George Kaufman's Astoria Studios housed the production. Milton Foreman worked closely with the eight craft unions and watched every dime spent. I made him associate producer. My first choice for each key backfield player gave me thumbs-up. It's never happened before, it's never happened since. Hey, maybe it's true: what goes around comes around. All were on board, protecting a maestro to be, his budget, his vision.

Cinematographer John Alonzo: "You got me. Fuck my other commitment. I owe it to ya. Made my bones on *Chinatown,* didn't I?"

Richard Sylbert, *numero uno* production designer, snob: "You want me? You've got me. How can I say no? You're the guy who made me Paramount's production chief."

To have a great eye, great savvy, and great ear for music is rare. All qualities fit producer Dyson Lovell. "Waited twenty years to work with you. When do I start?"

Ready to rock 'n' roll, my all-star backfield was now in place.

Pre-production was now officially on go. Richard Sylbert started construction at Astoria Studios. Jerry Wexler signed on to supervise music. Milton Foreman all but lived at Astoria, checking the price of each nail, each piece of wood. The clock was now ticking at $200,000 a day.

Puzo turned in his third draft. Gere and Sylbert cornered me: "Still not there, needs a fresh eye."

Scripts are never written, rather rewritten, rewritten, and rewritten. On a hunch, I called Coppola in Napa Valley.

"Who's the best script doctor I can get? Need a quick rewrite."

"Me."

"Thanks, but I called for advice, not your pen. Can't afford it."

"How's nothing sound? Get the script to me by tomorrow, we'll speak over the weekend."

Five days later:

"Needs major surgery. Don't panic, I've got the key. Can you fly up to Frisco?"

"When?"

"Tomorrow. Have Gere, Hines, and Lovell come up too. Give us a few hours alone first, see if we agree. Then we'll present it to them. We'll start at ten. Have them here by three. Cook dinner at the house. Stay the night."

Gere and Dyson were munching a salad when I broke the news of Coppola's involvement on the script. Gere's face lit up; Dyson's didn't.

Later Dyson told me, "Gere's gonna do everything he can to get Coppola. Not just to write, but to *direct* the film."

"Come on, Dyson. We're working great together."

"Don't have a clue, do you, to an actor's head?" laughed Dyson.

There I was in hilly Frisco, watching Francis smoke a joint. Just smelling it got me stoned. With chalk in hand, the Prince stood before a huge blackboard.

"Rosencrantz and Guildenstern, Harlem style. The rise and fall of *The Cotton Club* through the eyes of two minor characters."

He brilliantly and meticulously chalked an entirely new *Cotton Club* canvas. Hours later, when Gere, Hines, and Lovell arrived, Coppola repeated his performance. That evening at Coppola's Napa estate was love-feast time!

The next morning, Gere, Hines, Lovell, and I flew back to L.A. Gere cornered me.

"He's a fuckin' genius. We finally got a handle on it. Never thought it would happen. If I were you, Evans, I'd get on my knees, beg him to direct. That's if you want *The Godfather* with music. You said it, I didn't. Now you've got a chance. 'Evans, Coppola, Puzo,' not bad, huh? And you own it all!"

Did Dyson know his cat!

Coppola's favor soon turned into a quarter-million-dollar pen job. The Doumanis and Victor Sayyah bristled.

"We like what we've got, sex, shoot-'em-up, music. What the fuck do we gotta bring someone else in? Fuck him and his quarter of a mil."

They were right, but they didn't have to deal with the fragile egos that come with the turf in making a film. That's the producer's head-ache. It was their money and no was their answer. Telling them about the shaking stage my *Cotton Club* was on wouldn't have been smart. My shrinking pockets personally forked over the $250,000 to Coppola.

After six weeks of breathless waiting, Francis's holy pages arrived, bearing no resemblance to his bullshit hype. My backers went nuts. My nuts went shrinking.

"Fuck Coppola—the old script's great," barked the partners three.

It was too late. Francis had already Elmer Gantryed the cast. Puzo's million-dollar script was now a piece of shit. My backers' smiles were fading too. My pockets also fading, I forked over *another* quarter of a mil for a Coppola look-see.

"Put what you chalked on the blackboard on paper, not this Harlem Renaissance shit. It's my two bucks, it's what I want. Nothing more, nothing less. Blackboard only."

Weeks later, his second draft was now near finished. Gere, Hines,

Dyson and I visited Napa again, Richard continually nudging me: "Convince him to direct."

The clock was still ticking. Each day at another 200 Gs. What was originally a gift was now a $500,000 dent in my quickly shrinking pockets . . . and still no script. Instead of breakin' his fuckin' jaw, I kneed it, begging him to take over the reigns, direct the flick.

"You'll make it great. Me—I don't know."

Charlie Bluhdorn was right: this business is fuckin' crazy, the people in it even crazier. Here I am on my knees begging a guy who delivered a piece-of-shit script to take over everything. They should have put me away. Why didn't they? Life would have been so much easier.

Days later, he finally accepted, but on one condition.

"It's your picture, Evans, I'm just there to help."

With that, the first royal nail was hammered in my coffin.

The cast, crew all on salary, and the investors were already in the Big Apple. At Astoria Studios a start date was being set.

Coppola was now the director. Me, his Siamese twin. Together we worked closely on cast, music, costumes, production design . . . still no script.

Burdened with the enormous responsibility of an imminent start date, Coppola cried for help in the form of a ten-day script polish from Pulitzer Prize winner William Kennedy.

The investors roared. "Is he nuts? Between Puzo and Coppola we've forked over a million and a half, ten Gs a fuckin' page, now you tell us nothin' on them? What kinda fuckin' business is this?"

"A fuckin' business. What can I tell you?"

"Don't like it," said the three.

"Don't blame you," said the fading producer.

Coppola's request granted, Kennedy was brought in for a ten day "heavy green" polish. Ten weeks later he was still writing, still collecting heavy green. When the flick finished shooting, he was still writing. . . . Couldn't have been *The Cotton Club,* that flick's finished . . . still no script.

For a cover story that ran in *New York* magazine on May 7, 1984, Michael Daly interviewed a number of the cast and crew, including Bob Hoskins, who played Owney Madden:

"I gained twenty pounds waiting around for something to happen. You sort of sit around and eat and drink and philosophize, and sud-

*denly you've forgotten what you do for a living. Then somebody says,
'You're on the set,' and you say, 'What do you mean I'm on?'"*

*And when an actor was finally summoned, there was a panicked
rush to freshen the makeup and shake off the dullness that came from
waiting. Hoskins often hurried onto the set with no clear idea of what
Coppola wanted. He says "He would just toss things out in the air
. . . I could never figure Francis out at all. I just did what he told me.
It's into Aladdin's cave with him.*

Ted Koppel devoted the entire December 9, 1984, "Nightline" to
the making and near unmaking of *The Cotton Club*. Maurice Hines,
who played the brother of his real sibling, Gregory, told Koppel:

*If I forgot a line or forgot the structure, because all our scenes were
improvised, Gregory and I improvised. Francis kept saying, make it
real. . . . And if I forgot, I would sort of like grope. And he loved it. I
said, "Francis, I'm messing up here." He said, "But you're groping in
character."*

Back to the last Monday in June 1983, still no script, still no start
date, $5 million down the drain, and the clock ticking away at 200 Gs
a day. My financiers' smiles had long disappeared. Coppola summoned the department heads, the three investors, and me to his office at Astoria Studios. With his wife Ellie beside him, he slowly
panned each and every one before him. He knew the moment was
right, the next nail was ready to be hammered in my coffin. Suddenly
he thrust his finger in my face.

"It's not *The Godfather*, Evans. I've had it! Fed up with you. Tired
of your second guessing. Tired of everything about you. The family's
packed, we're outta here. You do it or I do it. You stay, I leave."

Shocked? I thought I was hallucinating. Thirty-six hours earlier,
I'd feasted his entire family at Elaine's for his son's birthday. How
could a guy I plucked from near obscurity to superstardom vent this
vitriolic hatred? No mistake about it—this was an ingeniously conceived, ten-year-festering come shot, a royal fucking from Prince Machiavelli himself.

The guys from Vegas were in no mood for creative flack; leaving
town was a better bet than testing their sympathy. Not wanting my
life insurance canceled, I had no choice but to spread my legs. The

Prince knew it, I knew it. Perfect timing, your highness. Siberia bound, I shrunk from boss to dwarf.

If only I signed the distribution deal at Paramount, the private financiers would have been covered. Then, had there been any flack from the Prince, his asshole would be the only place he'd be able to talk from. But *if* is a big word—instead I was at Orion. No ifs, ands, or buts, it was the beginning of the longest nightmare of my life.

Wicked Francis had convinced his virgin backers that a completion bond was a waste of money: "Don't blow 5 percent on completion insurance. It's an interior film, no weather problems. Made *Rumble Fish* at half this budget. Fuck spending a mil on insurance, have a good time with it. With twenty mil, it's a shoo-in. If I bring it in below, will you throw in a bonus and fly my family back to Napa?"

I begged them not to listen, they didn't hear. The Prince's wand had already spelled its magic. The 20 mil? Erase it—write in 48 instead.

August 28, 1983, principal photography commenced . . . still no script.

William Kennedy also spoke to Michael Daly of *New York* magazine:

"It was like writing on deadline all the time," Kennedy says. "And nobody but Francis and me really knew what was the future of this script." At one point, Kennedy went to Albany to attend to some personal matters. As Kennedy was leaving his house to fly back to New York, an assistant called from the studio and said that Coppola needed a new scene immediately. Kennedy wrote while his wife drove him to the airport. Just before boarding the plane, he stopped at a pay phone.

"I called it in, and Francis shot it," Kennedy says.

As new pages came in, the script supervisor, B. J. Bjorkman, struggled to shuffle them into what had already been written. She says, "Every time there's a new draft, the pages are a different color, and finally you get such a spectrum of colors that you're going, 'Are these the new pink or the old pink?' "

Starting a flick minus a script is tantamount to waiting for an accident to happen. When it happens in a major studio, they send in the troops. The only troops here were the three investors, and Coppola got them to think they were Selznick, Thalberg, and Zanuck combined. Forget me, I was quarantined to what was commonly called the "crisis center," a town house originally rented to be my home and office during production. Now there were more guys walking in and out of there seven days a week than at any brothel in town. Except at ours, there were no girls made, just threats. As the numbers escalated, the threats did too. I could fill a book of quotes that would be a best-seller in every jail in America.

Robert Osborne, veteran film critic, newscaster, and ace Hollywood reporter on L.A.'s Channel 11 news had this to say one night:

I have interviewed several people involved in the day-by-day shooting of The Cotton Club. *The word that all of them used most consistently was "waste"—waste of time, waste of shots, waste of money. Over one million dollars, for example, was spent just on extras for a single nightclub sequence, because of insufficient preparations. This is their interpretation, not mine, on the part of Coppola. Other accusations include nepotism, also drugs. One cast member told me, "There was so much coke on the set, you couldn't believe it."*

Thank heaven for small favors: they couldn't blame me for that. Quarantined to the crisis center, I was not allowed on the set.

Harsher winds were in the air. Call it running out of money. Midway through principal photography, Francis's onerous contract was still not signed. Miffed, he hopped off to Paris, a million-dollar-a-day vacation, paid for by the Doumanis. This forced them to capitulate to every contractual demand Coppola's henchmen put before them. Angry? No, quiet—dangerously quiet.

Joey Cusumano, no professor he. In a story in the August 1983 issue of *Life* magazine on the U.S. government's war against organized crime, he was referred to as "Joseph Cusumano, 47, reputed mob lieutenant." But who cared? He was now riding shotgun playing producer, and getting credit as such in trade ads and eventually on the screen. No hood, but producer he, and an uninvited roommate at the crisis center. By now every bed was taken, many a night by guys I didn't know or didn't want to know.

It got worse. My great backfield? Francis fired Dyson Lovell, fired John Alonzo, fired Milton Foreman. Dick Sylbert? He was desperate for the axe, but he didn't get fired—not because Coppola didn't want to, but because Coppola's longtime collaborator and buddy Dean Tavoularis was unavailable, busy on another flick. Sylbert later told "Entertainment Tonight" that *The Cotton Club* "was like this vampire. And you figured every night when it went back into its coffin, somebody would stick a stake in its heart and it would never rise up again. And every day it got out of its coffin and came to work." Poor Dick couldn't escape the vampire.

Another veteran whom Ted Koppel of "Nightline" interviewed was choreographer Henry LeTang: "I said, 'Francis, I take the day off, you go berserk, you fire everybody, I say what the hell is going on?' He said, 'The only people that's going to stay on this movie are you and Gregory Hines. The rest of them—out! I don't want to have seen them.' Real demonstrative person."

Costs were skyrocketing, so heavy muscle ordered me to bring in extra green. I'd already given up my entire salary. In all good conscience I couldn't go to someone I knew and ask them to invest in a flick with no script, no direction, no ending. But the boys weren't interested in weather reports. "We're borrowin' against your house." I could have said no, but if I did, I probably would never see it again anyway. The shylocks who had forked over $3.5 million to my now distraught partners literally owned my house, lock, stock, and barrel. When an outstanding $46,000 insurance claim was finally settled, they cashed the check, not me. The roof kept leaking, and my insurance policy got canceled. How could it get worse? It did . . . still no script. Fuck the script, what about breathing? Not an easy feat.

Orion finally had to funnel $15 million to keep the skyrocketing *Cotton Club* shooting. In the process, the Doumanis were laid, parlayed, and relaid. Before the Doumanis would collect a dime in profit, the picture would have to outgross *The Godfather*. It didn't.

Orion couldn't care less how good the picture was. Their only interest was recouping their $15 million. If the film was half finished, it would still be released for Christmas.

Payroll was every Friday. Orion's weekly $2 million advance had already been spent on other excesses as each week the bills mounted and mounted. There was nothing left in the coffers to make the next payroll.

"We need two million by Friday," growled my new pal, Cusumano. "Get it." Why he didn't heist a bank I'll never know, but get it he meant. No kibitzer Cusumano, he was more comfortable holding a

.38 than a Steadycam. Orion's next drop-off wouldn't be until the following Thursday, far too late to make that Friday's payroll. Not making it would shut the picture down. To reopen it a bond would have to be put in place. Forget the money for the bond, we didn't have it for payroll. Muscle forced me to confront anyone I knew for a quick loan with guaranteed payback. In desperation, I met with four men. Each of them was many millions richer as a result of my talent, each knew the money was guaranteed by Orion (with papers to prove it). Each turned me down, each for his own reason.

I had one last shot to survive. Not the picture—*life*. Biting my tongue, I doorbelled a lady whom I had done well for, although not nearly as well as I had for the four men. I had opened a door for her, and once the door opened, it was her talent that made her millions. Before I could finish my first sentence, she interrupted, "How much do you need?" I told her. "Sure you don't need more?" She wrote the check. It was deposited the next morning, saving the flick from closing down. Five days later I hand-delivered the $2 million, whereupon she said, "If you need it for reserve, keep it. Pay me back later."

What can you say? A lady is a lady is a lady is a lady.

Denise Beaumont, a girl I had been seeing in Los Angeles, flew to New York with her four-year-old daughter to hold my hand. With inventive maneuvering, I made room for them to stay for two weeks at the crisis center. Her ex-husband paid her a visit, spending two days with his kid. He pulled Denise aside.

"Give Evans any excuse, get the hell out of here quick. The guy's eight-to-five to live it another week. I'm not asking, I'm telling you. Get the hell out."

I didn't die. He did.

The picture was winding down . . . still no script. No money left in the Doumanis' pockets, no house for Evans to go home to, no more money from Orion either. As Coppola sucked the blood out of everyone, I realized I coined the wrong nickname: Dracula was more fitting than Prince Machiavelli. It must have been, he made the film eight years later. For Dracula he didn't need a script, he could have phoned it in.

Near jingle-bell time of 1983. Francis telegrammed me his Christmas cheer. I read it. Did it bother me?

Telegram

11A059(1235)(1-0076730347)PD 12/13/83 1234
ICS IPMMVIO MVN
03611 12-13 1132A CST MVIL
ICS IPM31TI
4-016751S347 12/13/83
ICS IPMMTZZ CSP
  2127060360 TDMT ASTORIA NY 132 12-13 1223P EST

PMS ROBERT EVANS RPT DLY MGM, DLR
234 EAST 61 ST
NEW YORK NY 10021

DEAR BOB EVANS,
I'VE BEEN A REAL GENTLEMAN REGARDING YOUR CLAIMS OF
INVOLVEMENT ON *THE GODFATHER.* I'VE NEVER TALKED
ABOUT YOUR THROWING OUT THE NINO ROTA MUSIC, YOUR
BARRING THE CASTING OF PACINO AND BRANDO, ETC. BUT
CONTINUALLY YOUR STUPID BLABBING ABOUT CUTTING *THE
GODFATHER* COMES BACK TO ME AND ANGERS ME FOR ITS
RIDICULOUS POMPOSITY.

```
MAILGRAM SERVICE CENTER
MIDDLETOWN, VA. 22645
14AM
```

```
1-010357A348 12/14/83 ICS IPMNXNB NYAC
0020 MGM TI NEWYORK NY 100 12-14 83 115P EST
```

```
ROBERT EVANS
17 EAST 66 ST
NEW YORK NY 10021
```

```
FOLLOWING IS CONFIRMATION COPY OF TEXT OF TELEGRAM
SENT 12-14-83 TO FRANCIS FORD COPPOLA
SHERRY NETHERLAND HOTEL
781 FIFTH AVENUE AT 59TH ST
NEW YORK, N.Y.
```

```
DEAR FRANCIS,
   THANK YOU FOR YOUR CHARMING CABLE. I CANNOT
IMAGINE WHAT PROMPTED THIS VENOMOUS DIATRIBE.
   I AM BOTH ANNOYED AND EXASPERATED BY YOUR
FALLACIOUS ACCUSATIONS, WHEN ALL I DO IS PRAISE YOUR
EXTRAORDINARY TALENTS AS A FILMMAKER.
   CONVERSELY, YOUR BEHAVIOR TOWARDS ME GLARINGLY
LACKS ANY IOTA OF CONCERN, HONESTY OR INTEGRITY. I
AM AFFRONTED BY YOUR GALL IN DARING TO SEND THIS
MACHIAVELLIAN EPISTLE. THE CONTENT OF WHICH IS NOT
ONLY LUDICROUS, BUT TOTALLY MISREPRESENTS THE TRUTH.
I CAN NOT CONCEIVE WHAT MOTIVATED YOUR MALICIOUS
THOUGHTS, BUT IF THEY ARE A REFLECTION OF YOUR
HOSTILITY, I BEAR GREAT SYMPATHY AND CONCERN FOR
YOUR APPARENT [ILLEGIBLE] BEHAVIOR. HOWEVER, DEAR
FRANCIS, DO NOT MISTAKE MY KINDNESS FOR WEAKNESS.
ROBERT EVANS
```

```
14:01 EST
```

```
MGMCOMP
```

TO REPLY BY MAILGRAM MESSAGE, SEE REVERSE SIDE FOR WESTERN UNION'S TOLL-FREE PHONE
NUMBERS

Apparently Coppola didn't take too kindly to my response. Word spread quicker than any of the flick's dance steps that he went berserk, bashing his hand through his desk.

Another excerpt from the "Entertainment Tonight" report on the film:

The rocky horror show continued for eighty-seven days, then the filming was finally finished. Post-production began smoothly enough here in the Cotton Club *offices until yet another monster reared its ugly head. Robert Evans, banished from the set by director Francis Ford Coppola, went before a court of law to gain control of the movie. A federal judge ruled that Evans should be treated as a general partner, even though he had no money in the movie. And the Coppola camp, with Barry Osborne in charge, won control of the film's editing process.*

David vs. Goliath 1983. Alone I stood strong, taking on Orion, the Doumanis, and Francis Coppola.

The Doumanis brought suits against me, charging that, since the film's escalating $50 million budget was a result of my mismanagement, I shouldn't be allowed to continue as the film's producer. What they really desperately wanted was to remove me from my position as general partner. They didn't want me controlling the books. The triumvirate was so certain of winning with $48 million vs. zero on their side, they forgot one thing: doing your homework. I did. A historic victory. With no money invested, I gave the triumvirate a second asshole. The kid stayed in the picture. With my triumph came barter time, the general partnership was my ticket to the Doumanis paying the two bucks, releasing Woodland back to its rightful owner.

The circuslike trial with its surprise knockout-punch victory, caused mucho media interest. More important, it illustrates, through the verbatim quotes, the difference between man and man.

Walking down the stairs of the federal courthouse, Channel 11's Larry Atteberry asked me, "Do you think the picture will be a success despite all these problems?"

"Francis's work on it is brilliant. And I hope we'll be working together. We've fought together many times, only it wasn't in court. I just hope we have the same luck as we had in *The Godfather.*"

Catching Coppola, Atteberry had a question for him. "What you were saying, that Evans would second-guess you if he were back in command.

"That's his middle name . . . that's what he does all these years."

Coppola had taken the stand earlier to defend the Doumanis and assert that "Evans caused chaos." He had never experienced anything like this before, he stated.

How do you cause chaos when you're barred from the set? Unquestionably the chaos was deeply lodged in Francis's cerebellum. Yet I wouldn't dignify his malicious diatribe. Publicly, I continued defending him and the brilliant work he had done on *The Cotton Club*.

Through good times, friendship comes easy. But when you have to weather grit, threats, and disasters, coming out friends is what true friendship is all about. Today both Ed and Fred Doumani and Victor Sayyah remain my close friends.

On October 1, 1984, Orion had its first preview of *The Cotton Club* in San Jose. Though I wasn't invited, I was there, stared at as if I were a leper. Two hours later when the curtains closed and my blood pressure was way up, I grabbed the Doumanis. "Come back to the hotel with me, please."

Their heads between their legs. Full depression time.

"Fellas, it can be saved. There's a great picture there, but it's not on the screen—it's on Coppola's cutting room floor. The guy went double budget and gave us half a picture. He took eleven musical numbers out—the most important one, 'Stormy Weather,' cost over a million to shoot. The fucker didn't put it in. He's made a collage out of an era."

The Doumanis now knew they'd been Elmer Gantryed by the Prince. I felt bad about it; whatever our fights, our arguments, I was the one who brought them in. Forget the fact that I had no points, no involvement. I wanted to help.

Like two prepubescent kids they looked up. "What should we do?"

From the darkness of night till the midday sun, I wrote a letter to Coppola, pouring my heart out to the maestro. Problems are easy to criticize, but solutions don't come easy. Thirty-one pages of solutions, and fourteen hours later, I signed off.

Starting with the opening credits, I enthusiastically expressed how our original vision—*The Godfather* with music—could evolve into reality.

If the "Making of *The Cotton Club*" were a book rather than a chapter, I'd insist by contract that this entire critique be part of the text. For good reason hyperbole comes easy; the critique's text, however, pinpoints the importance of what is commonly thought of as a nondescript profession—producer. What follows here is the cover letter and the first paragraph of the thirty-one-page critique, which exemplifies the spirit in which the entire document was written:

October 1, 1984

Dear Francis:

Many years ago Moss Hart told me that relationships in our business are built on such strange personal emotions that they become three-sided: your side, my side, and the truth. . . .

With this in mind and putting all personal feelings aside, what you are about to read bears greater consequence to our lives and careers than any decisions we have ever fought over or agreed to in the past. . . .

By now, you must know I have no personal financial involvement in The Cotton Club. *If the picture does ten dollars or three hundred million it bears no effect on my bank account. It does on yours, however. My involvement now is totally one of pride, professionalism, moral obligation to the investors, and from a selfish point of view to our audiences who are anxiously awaiting your vision of the Cotton Club era. When Francis Coppola takes on a subject matter which combines the richness of the roaring Twenties, the Depression that followed, and interweaves as the foreground the struggle, birth, and sense of discovery to the world of the black entertainer and the greatness of his music, one expects an event. Anything less leaves you open to a backlash both from the audiences and the critics. Your pictorial investigation of it has been shot in the best Coppola fashion. And what are we left with? Montage followed by montage followed by montage followed by montage. What a cheat—to you as a storyteller . . . to you as a director . . . and to the audiences who expect more than MTV when they pay their five dollars. . . .*

You have shot, and brilliantly so, an "era film." What we are left with, however, is a slick flick that is only somewhat entertaining. If Phil Karlson made The Cotton Club *and it cost twenty million dollars, you could get away with it, but Francis Coppola's name is*

*on it instead, immediately making the audiences and critics
anticipate something magical. . . . Phil Karlson would not have had
the brilliance of film that you have shot, but unfortunately much of
that film is presently on the floor and not on the screen.*

*The picture has been shown twice. The consensus of the cards
more than evidences what I'm saying. This is not Orion patronizing
you, whose sole interest is to get the picture for Christmas. This is
me telling you cold, hard facts that will affect your future even more
than mine. There have been six pictures previewed that are being
released for Christmas. Our picture has had the lowest audience
ratings of the six. If it went out for bidding today, we would get
theaters—not the ones we want, and certainly not the terms we
want. This I know for a fact. I have spoken to two of the biggest
exhibitors in the country. They already know the disappointing
reaction to the film. And their hard-ons have become very soft. And
these are friends, Francis—close friends. For Orion it is fine. With
their deal they will get their money out if you delivered them a
postage stamp. Believe me, Francis, their entire concern is to get
their money out. For the Doumanis it means bankruptcy. They will
never see one dime from the film. The renegotiation of the Orion
deal gives Orion all first monies and leaves the Doumanis holding
the bag. The only hope they have is that* The Cotton Club *is a
smash—a big one. In its present form it is not, Francis. It is
lackluster, not blockbuster. Let us not be ostriches. The audiences
have told us. The exhibitors have told us. Bad word spreads quicker
than good. . . .*

Am I negative on The Cotton Club? *I most emphatically wish to
express to you I am not. I would be less than candid, however, not to
say that I am worried. Very worried. And terribly frustrated by not
being used to my fullest abilities at this pivotal moment to help
make* The Cotton Club *the smash it can be. It is your film, Francis,
not mine. [But] not having communication at this very pivotal
moment is very counterproductive. My god, Francis, if Gromyko
and Reagan can meet and have an exchange of dialogue, why can't
we? You owe it to yourself—if no one else—to put personal feelings
aside. Use me. Use my objectivity, which you cannot have at this
moment, being so closely attached to the film. Francis, you are
shortchanging yourself, and badly. I state to you unequivocally that
there is a great film here. I know it. I see it. A film that can be*

remembered. Unfortunately and understandably, you are running scared, not sure of what you have. You are taking shortcuts and by doing so you are irreparably damaging your canvas. Allowing The Cotton Club *to fall into the category of just another movie. Don't run scared, Francis. Go all the way. Give them a show. Give them the Coppola texture that is now on the floor. There is brilliance there. The longer and more textured the piece, the shorter it will play. Again, what better example is there than* Godfather I? *If I didn't think it were there I would certainly not be this passionate in my plea to you.*

With my feelings expressed the best I can, I will now be specific as to what I think will make the difference between a slick flick, which we now have and which could be open to terrible criticism, vs. what I know is there—a critically acclaimed blockbuster, which has the opportunity of being long remembered. . . .

Evans

Critique

Credits: I think the credits that were on the film before which were handwritten on black had simplicity and style. The credits as they are now open the picture with the wrong note—they are a title company's jerk-off and more importantly they are most difficult to read. The simplicity of the other credits is far more you, and for that matter me, than the Deco credits presently on the film. Don't let some half-assed artist sway you into being overly fashionable. Style and simplicity always overshadow and outlast fashion.

Reading and rereading the pages, suddenly smiles crossed the Doumanis' faces, a first in months.

"What's in the letter, has it all been shot?"

"And more."

Like kids in a candy store, "We could have a winner!"

Holding the thirty-one pages in his hand, Ed spoke out. "Leaving now, driving up to Napa, delivering this by hand. Francis better listen, I'm gonna stand watchin' him read it."

With forty million of green on the line, Ed would have driven to Hong Kong. Napa was no short drive. At high speed six hours. For the first time the brothers saw light from darkness.

Twenty-eight hours later, the three of us sat together commiserating. After twelve hours of driving to and from and five hours patiently waiting for his highness to grant him an audience, he read the thirty-one pages. Ed related Francis's reaction to us.

"He would rather see the picture do three hundred thousand and not three hundred million than have Evans get credit for being the saving grace."

That December 8, *The Cotton Club* had its gala premiere in New York. The Prince purposely ignored my every written word, and the finished cut didn't include one of my suggestions. It had hardly changed from that first underwhelming preview in San Jose. *Cotton Club* the film, unlike Harlem's club, was not the talk of the town— any town. Somber would best describe its audience reaction. Somber as well best described its box-office results. Royalty always gets covered. Prince Machiavelli royally fucked all. He collected millions.

Film critic Ken Turran put it most succinctly when asked by Ted Koppel on "Nightline" what he thought about *The Cotton Club.*

I think that there's no coherent story there just for openers. It really feels to me as if the film was thrown together, as if Coppola didn't want to put in the work that goes in before, didn't want to have a coherent script, didn't want to take the trouble to do that. He wanted the exhilaration of when you get on the set, which can be very exhilarating to be a general in front of all those people. But I think you can't just wing the movie. Movies have to be thought out ahead of time. They have to have, as The Godfather *did, a book with a very solid plotline. You just can't make it up as you go along.*

What did I learn from this failure, this disaster, this five-year nightmare? A fat fuckin' *nothing!* To say you "fucked up but learned from it" is bullshit, a cop-out. You can learn from a mistake. A mistake done twice is not a mistake, it's called *failure.*

At an early age, a man of great wisdom gave me the key to making it.

"You learn from success, kid—not failure. If you've only touched it once, a term paper, a temp job, hitting a homer, dissect it. Was it timing, focus, homework? Get to the core. Find out the whys, the hows. That's the key. Use it . . . go with it, don't be afraid. When you get your shot, then you'll be ready. Success ain't easy, kid, but the more you taste it, the easier it gets. No different with failure." The wise man smiled. "The more you taste it, the more you get it." Putting his finger to his lips, "Shhh . . . Don't spread it. It's tough enough out there. Keep it to yourself."

36

Nicholson and I were lying on my bed one Friday night, watching the closed-circuit Hagler–Leonard fight. That day, Frank Yablans, then president of MGM, offered me $2 million to produce Roman Polanski's *The Pirate*. Was $2 million an inflated price? Times five it was. But it was also conditional. I was the key he needed to get Nicholson to commit to the picture. Did I need the $2 million? After *Cotton Club,* twenty bucks would help.

Come the eighth round, Nicholson was finally bending toward

going to sea with Polanski. Not that he wanted to, but he knew how much the two mil meant to his "notorious" pal. By the twelfth round, we both came to the same conclusion. Fuck it. Who wants to spend a year in Tunisia? Instead, let's make the sequel to *Chinatown: The Two Jakes*. The fight now over, we called Towne at home, asked him to meet us at three the next afternoon in my projection room.

For six years, Towne had structured in his mind the second part of a trilogy in the growth of Los Angeles, so he was euphoric when Jack and I said, "Let's put it on go." While the core of *Chinatown* was water (the dearth of it) and the discovery that old money was holding back its usage, *The Two Jakes* was boomtown. It would be set postwar, 1947, when real estate and oil were competing like two fighters in the ring for the control of the city's future. It was really Christian vs. Jew—oil being the Christian, real estate being the Jew.

Like *Chinatown*, *The Two Jakes* was half drama, half reality. The story of the two Jakes takes us into the late forties, with Jake Gittes looking for Evelyn Mulwray's lost, incest-conceived daughter. Jake's search would involve him in a double murder and pit him against the older man she was now married to—the heavy of the piece. His name, too, was Jake. The character was a combination of Lou Towne, Mark Taper, and every other entrepreneurial Jew responsible for changing the face of the City of Angels to that of a thriving metropolis.

Nicholson and Towne pulled the rug out from under me that day in the projection room. The only way they'd go forward on the project was if I played the other Jake.

"Lookin' to put in the last nail, huh? I'm fighting for my life . . . and you guys want me to go back into makeup. That'll go over real big, now they'll know I'm nuts. Both of ya: Go fuck yourself!"

A wicked smile, "Trust the Irishman, Keed." Eyebrow on crocked, "You'll cop the fuckin' Oscar. You don't need no words. Our noses, you and me—profile, eyein' each other, it'll knock 'em on their ass. You'll be a fuckin' movie star again!"

Picking up the phone, Irish dialed Barry Diller.

"It's Jake, here with the Beener and the Keed. The three of us wanna give you *The Two Jakes* on a platinum platter. We'll work for scale, make the flick for ten mil, keep the budget down. You can't afford payin' us, we're worth too much, we'll be partners, huh? No lawyer-agent bullshit. Just us and you—a one-page memo. You know why I wanna do it? Nose to nose on the screen, the Irishman and the Keed don't need no dialogue." Barry couldn't be taking the call seriously. "One thing the Irishman ain't, Barry, is dumb. Evans and Nicholson's noses touchin'—it's 'fuck you' money time. That's why you've got my smile for nothing."

The phone went down, his eyebrow up. "We're in makeup, Keed, we're goin' eye to eye."

The executive suite's game of musical chairs, indigenous to the "new" Hollywood, soon propelled Diller to the chairmanship of Fox; Eisner became the chairman of Disney. Replacing Diller at Paramount was Frank Mancuso, who was previously head of marketing and distribution. Frank was, and to this day remains, family. Our careers span back several decades, and I was thrilled that my pal was now head honcho of "the mountain." Ned Tanen, a top producer and extraordinarily bright studio executive, took over for Eisner. To celebrate his elevated position, Mancuso toasted *The Two Jakes* as his big flick for Christmas 1986. Martin Davis—the *numero uno* cheese of Gulf + Western, who controlled Paramount—made a rare appearance at the studio. A luncheon was given in his honor. Surprisingly, I was seated by his side. Beatty, Nicholson, and Harrison Ford were also at our table.

I'm thinking to myself, What am I doing here?

Marty gave me the answer: "You've always been an actor, Evans. How else could you have gotten away with being such a fraud?"

Did he say it in jest? I was afraid to ask. I still don't know.

"Make this work, Evans, and you'll be a hero," said Davis. "When you get the above the line working for scale and are really partners with the studio, that's where the future lies. If the picture works, everyone gets rich. The above the line get real rich. If it flops, none of us go to the poor house. It gives us a chance then to make double the amount of films. More people will be working. I'm proud of ya."

Wow, did I feel good that day. Call it "welcome back to the fold."

Getting a script from Robert Towne is akin to closing a deal with the Japanese (it took him eight years to finish writing *Shampoo*). To have the picture ready for the following Christmas, we had to start shooting that spring, which meant I needed Shakespeare to turn over his script in two months. He was madly in love and engaged to marry a ravishing Italian beauty, and she wanted the wedding of the year.

"Dear Robert," I said, "finish the script, and I'll throw the wedding of her dreams."

In October 1985, 180 people sat under the shade of the old sycamore. Robert and Louisa had declared their vows. Towne's best man was Pat Riley.

His present to me was the script of *The Two Jakes*. Great businessman I am, the wedding was not in the budget. Dom Perignon or Cristal was not good enough; a special Italian champagne was imported. At $200 a bottle, it set the tone for the party.

Robert didn't quite keep up to his end of the bargain, because the script was 80 percent complete. (Now, almost a decade later, it remains 80 percent complete!) A month later, I heard Bob was pissed that I didn't give him a wedding gift. Maybe I skimped on the party; it only cost me over 100 Gs.

Towne was writing and directing, Nicholson and myself starring and producing. "We get equal billing, Keed. I'll take first billing in my racket, you take first in yours. Okay with you, Keed?"

What other guy would insist on giving equal billing above the title to an actor who hadn't made a picture in twenty-five years?

The film was to commence principal photography Tuesday May 6, 1986. The Sunday before, Frank Mancuso was throwing a party for the cast, crew, and studio honchos, toasting the launching of his first production as chief. By now, *Chinatown* was cinema folklore; everyone in distribution was panting for its sequel. Maybe the black cloud hovering over me for five years will open, and I'll see a bit of sunshine again.

Friday afternoon, four days before shooting, Bob Towne—who just six months earlier had referred to me in the preface to his leatherbound, limited-edition *Chinatown* screenplay as "one who in memory and in life remains a standard for every kind of human generosity and one I have yet to see matched in this town"—paid me a visit.

Silently, he sat in a chair, his eyes to the floor, rabbinical in thought. With a verbal baseball bat, he gave me a full swing to the balls. "Bob, you should drop out of the cast. I haven't had enough time to rehearse you."

I know the feeling of being shocked. I'm a pro at it. But Towne's words were a new sensation . . . an electric shock.

"Robert, the picture starts in four days. Are you crazy? Forget

Evans the actor. Evans the producer won't accept it. Who the fuck are we goin' to use in my place?"

"I don't know."

The wounds of *The Cotton Club* were still open; I couldn't afford another catastrophe.

"What about Nicholson? Did you tell him?"

"I just left him."

"What did he say?"

Not looking at me, "It's okay with him."

Quickly I reached for the phone and seven-digited my co-star.

"Jack, I'm here with Towne. What the fuck's going on?"

"You tell me."

"Uh-uh . . . you tell me."

"Is Towne there with you?"

"Yeah."

"Get your ass up here . . . now! Alone!"

"What about—"

He cut me off. "Fuck him. Just get up here."

Without a look at Towne, I raced out of the house, up to Mulholland. There stood Jack.

"I've got some pain in the ass . . . hemorrhoids. Don't need another one. Why ya backin' out?"

"Backin' out? Towne tells me he doesn't want me in it and that you said fine."

"You're makin' my head hurt as much as my *ass!* Get him on the horn. . . . Listen, Beener, Evans is playin' Berman or I ain't playing' Gittes. You left your game in the locker room, huh?"

Slamming the phone down, he looked up. "Towne tells me you don't want to play a Jew?" Both of us burst out laughing. Jack had to stop—his ass hurt too much.

"What about Shakespeare?"

"Fuck 'im."

The next day Jack was rushed to the hospital with severe hemorrhoid problems. Though his pain was excruciating, his resolve on the Keed remained adamant.

That night, an altercation ensued between Shakespeare, the Irishman, and the Keed that lasted till 4:00 A.M. Monday morning. Poor Irish: his pain was such that he couldn't sit, lie, or stand, but his resolve was intransigent. Meanwhile, Towne ranted on how I would ruin his prose.

"Hey, Bob, I didn't ask you to do it, you insisted."

Nicholson hit it on the nose. Towne left his game in the locker room. Who better to blame it on than me? A guy who hadn't been in front of the camera for more than a quarter of a century.

Being the victim, I had the least to say of the three. Watching them, I couldn't help but think the difference between loyalty and loyalty. At three in the morning, I awakened my new counsel, Alan Schwartz. Poor Alan had been my lawyer for a year now, and we hadn't been able to put two weeks together without a problem. This was a big one. The picture was to start in thirty-six hours or be canceled.

Driving me from Mulholland back to my home, Alan begged: "Please, Bob, you can't afford it, back away."

Neither of us slept that night. Till the sun came up in the morning we discussed our options; there weren't any. Again my back was to the wall.

The phone rang—it was the Irishman.

"The Beener's goin' down to see the honchos at Paramount, tell 'em he don't want cha. Sure you haven't slept, but stand strong. My asshole's killin' me. Don't know how, but I'll get down there, be with you. The Keed's gonna be in the picture, got it?"

The bombardment started. Mancuso had his ass on the line, *The Two Jakes* being his first gig as head honcho. He left the studio and rushed up to my home, Ned Tanen right behind.

"Bob," said Frank. "You're family. We're like brothers. I beg you to drop out. You can't afford to throw snake eyes. Not again."

Tanen and Alan Schwartz quickly agreed. Nicholson's plea rung in my head.

"If it's okay with Jack, it's okay with me, gentlemen."

"What's his number?" asked Frank. His face was pale as Jack gave him the score.

"He's coming down," said Frank. "Says he can't put his pants on, he's got such pain in his ass. But he's coming down and he's fighting mad. Ned, you know what he told me? 'Without the Keed, you ain't got the Irishman.'" Mancuso was stunned! "What the fuck did you get us into here, Evans?"

Tanen, Mancuso, Schwartz, and I stood there. The four of us thought the same thing at the same time: the guy's jinxed (meaning *me*). I have to be—wherever I park my hat, there's a snake under it.

"We need this picture real bad," said Frank. "Please, I beg of you, don't blow it."

"What have I done?"

Both Tanen and Mancuso shook their heads and took a walk outside around the tree, leaving Schwartz and myself alone in the projection room.

Alan shrugged his shoulders. "I never thought I'd have a client too hot to handle—I was wrong."

Like Hopalong Cassidy, in limped Nicholson. Within half an hour, it was resolved. Tanen and Mancuso embraced me. I was the second Jake. By dictate, not necessarily by desire. Ahhh . . . act three had yet to begin.

Three hours later, around my circular oak table sat Ned Tanen; Frank Mancuso; Robert Towne with his attorney, Bert Fields; Jack Nicholson with his attorney, Ken Kleinberg; and Alan Schwartz and me. Heated? No, on fire.

The phone rang. It was for Ned Tanen. Urgent. Quickly, Tanen picked it up. His hands began to shake. His lips quivered. His ex-wife had just committed suicide. His two little daughters had just discovered their mommy's body. A nightmare? Worse. Quickly he left.

Mancuso wanted to reconvene the next day. Towne refused. Three hours later, with every insult imaginable thrown at me by my dear friend, Robert, Jack stood up.

"Listen, Beener. With Evans, I take nothin'. Is that clear? Without him, I want my six mil against fifteen percent of the gross. Is that clear?"

Picking up a piece of paper from the table, he grabbed a red Magic Marker, he filled the 8-×-10 white sheet with a big 2, then next to it, he then spelled out seven letters M-I-L-L-I-O-N.

"From me to you, for your cockamamie script, I'm payin' you two big ones for an eighty-percent job. I'll get it back from first proceeds. If you wanna direct, I ain't gonna stand in your way. We're supposed to start tomorrow. Too many guys here have their ass on the line. Hey! The Kid stays in the picture. Clear?"

It wasn't.

Needing the $2 million more than Mike Tyson needed a good lawyer, Towne couldn't take being out-machoed by Irish. *The Two Jakes* circa 1985 never got made.

That ended the first half of the eighties. The good half.

37

Barry Diller hosted a political get-together for Michael Dukakis. At the time, Dukakis was one of the many hungry hopefuls looking to get the nod to head the Democratic ticket down the line in 1988. A Barry Diller bash gets out all of Tinseltown—everybody who was anybody was there.

I was cornered by Swifty Lazar, who goggled me. "Only Diller gets you out, huh? Two weeks from Saturday I'm giving a dinner for Deborah Kerr and her husband, Peter Viertel. You and Peter go back to the ole Zanuck days, don't you?"

Shaking my head yes.

"Then this one you're coming to. I know I'm just an agent, not head of a studio, but no 'out of town' excuses this time."

"An agent? You're the biggest star here, Swifty. Can't think of an evening I look forward to more."

A double goggle take from mighty Swifty. Then he rushed off to meet the evening's new Democratic hopeless.

The first order of business the next morning was to RSVP. Poor Swifty had no idea that he made me an invitation I "couldn't refuse."

Quickly scanning Swifty's living room, Ray Stark quipped "A-plus all the way! Not a civilian in the joint."

Except for myself and a few other renegades, the crème de la crème of the establishment was there in full attire. Eight candlelit tables filled the dining room–patio area. Swifty, his wife, Mary, Deborah, and Peter each hosted a table. For supposed sentimental reasons, I was one of the lucky to be seated at the Viertel table, my date, Sue Mengers, at my side. On the other side sat Nicholson with his lady, Anjelica Huston. Completing the rest of the table were Fran and Ray Stark, Felicia and Jack Lemmon, and Carol and Walter Matthau.

When dessert was served, I rose, clicking my glass. "May I make a toast to our guest of honor?"

It was the first—no, the only—toast of the evening. Mengers winced, "Veh iz meer . . ." Surely thinking I was stoned, but she was wrong. I was determined!

"A toast to you, dear Peter, the only man I've ever met who shrunk me from six to three feet in less than thirty seconds."

My eyes slowly panned the room.

"It's true! Thirty years ago, I met our guest of honor in Morelia, Mexico. Me, a half-assed actor picked to play the bullfighter in *The Sun Also Rises*. Peter was Hemingway's choice to write the screenplay. Remember, Peter? You invited me over to your bungalow to meet you. I knocked at your door, you opened it, you looked at me, just looked. Then, you began laughing. 'You play Pedro Romero? Uh-uh, not in my film.' Then you slammed the door right smack in my face."

Picking up my glass.

"To you, dear Peter, the single most intimidating man I've ever met."

Nervous laughter filled the room. Viertel *wasn't laughing*. He immediately stood.

"Bob, let's face it, you were all wrong. We needed the real thing for the part, a bullfighter, not a—"

Interrupting Viertel, Nicholson jumped up.

"Yeah, Peter, but the Keed got all the reviews. Ain't it the truth?" he roared.

The room roared too. Viertel's face turned the color of his wine. My toast? Well, I don't think it went over too well with the Lazars. I was never invited back, even for a fund-raiser.

Lew Wasserman, the patriarch of our industry, invited me to be one of the select group of forty to celebrate his fortieth wedding anniversary to his wife, Eddie, at their home. Quite an honor!

What a difference a decade makes. Ten years later, when the Wassermans celebrated their fiftieth anniversary on the back lot of Lew's studio, Universal Pictures, fifteen hundred people were invited. They must have lost my number, I wasn't one of them.

The Harmony Club in New York hosted four hundred luminaries, who flew in from around the world to celebrate Henry Kissinger's fiftieth birthday; I was Tinseltown's only invitee. It was table and place card only. Me? I was seated at Henry's table; only one seat separated us.

Ten years later, the same club, with the same aplomb, the same luminaries, toasted Henry's sixtieth. Damn it! This time my place card wasn't at his table, it wasn't at any table. How could it be? I wasn't invited.

Hurt? Not really. If I were him, I wouldn't invite me either. Sliding from famous to infamous is not a person who fit the Kissinger agenda of the 1980s and 1990s. I understood it, I respected it.

Love lost between man and man is no different than love lost between man and woman: when it's over—it's over. Yet the decade of memories we shared will stay with me forever.

The flip side.

It was the day of Academy Awards for 1987. Jack Nicholson was nominated for his performance in *Ironweed*.

Two nights earlier, the two of us finished off a bottle of Cristal at his Mulholland home. We talked about everything and nothing. One thing we did conclude, this wasn't his year to cop the Oscar.

Six hours before the big night was to start, my butler drove up to Nicholson's home. His mission? To personally deliver to Jack a locked, leather satchel with the key to open it. Inside, it was filled to the brim with stacks of enlarged one-hundred-dollar bills. On top was a note: "Yeah, you're a long shot tonight, Irish, but fuck it! By mistake, you're gonna cop more awards than any actor in film history. Money talks, and my money is on you."

I was out of breath, in the middle of a tennis workout with my pal and tennis pro, Darryl Goldman. An urgent call interrupted our match.

"The green, is it real?" heckled Nicholson.

Both of us burst out laughing.

"As real as my tennis game."

"Tell Darryl to let you off easy. Hit the shower, will ya, put on your blacks. You're my date tonight for the awards."

"Your date?"

"Yeah, was goin' alone, there was no one I wanted to walk in with. Lookin' at them stacks of green, I'm thinkin', who's a better arm-piece to walk in with than you, Notorious."

These words were coming from the most respected film star in the world, inviting me—at the time an industry leper—to be his arm piece at the Academy Awards!

My immediate reaction was no. "Not up for it, Irish."

"Then get up for it. Let all of 'em see us nose to nose. Can't hurt, Keed."

"Can I call you back?"

"Call me back! We gotta be there in three hours, doors close at five thirty."

"I'll call you right back, promise."

Hanging up the phone, Darryl looked at me.

"Are you nuts? He's inviting you to be his date for the Academy Awards and you say no."

In a cold sweat, I stood there, desperate not to go.

"It's tough to understand, Daryl, but the last time we went to the awards together, I was top guy in town."

I called Sue Mengers for her opinion. She quickly cut me off: "If you don't go, never call me again."

I dialed Irish.

"You got me, on two conditions."

"Yeah."

"You gotta pick me up. Have a bottle of Cristal in the backseat."

"Yeah, what else?"

"You can't try to fuck me. It's our first date!"

Irish kept each promise, and the reluctant debutante enjoyed the best night of his dark decade.

From our klieg-lit entrance and throughout the entire evening, arm and arm we were. In his inimitable style, Nicholson made it clear for all to see that Evans is back, and Irish is with him all the way. Suddenly, people began taking my calls.

38

The last time I was in downtown Los Angeles was for the Academy Awards—the biggest night in Hollywood. Lights, limousines, stars. This time, it was a different story. Rather than the evening lights, it was the morning breeze. Rather than a limousine, I arrived in a nondescript car, hoping not to be recognized. My lawyer, Robert Shapiro, had arranged for my arrival as a witness. We had special permission to drive underneath to the judge's entrance. A friend of Shapiro, a judge, was there to meet us and take us up to a private elevator. I stepped out of the elevator and looked Shapiro straight in the eye.

"I can't do this, I can't take the fifth. I'm going to testify."

Grabbing my arm, my lawyer said, "If you do, I leave!" His eyes were as cold as his words. Did I pay heed? You bet I did.

Our attempts to avoid television cameras? Forget it! Heading down the long corridor to Division 30 of the Criminal Courts Building, it was Academy Award time revisited. Lights, cameras, action. Instead of an acceptance speech, words that I'd never thought I'd utter were going to come from my mouth: "On the advice of counsel, I respectfully refuse to answer any questions based on my constitutional privilege under the Fifth Amendment."

Eight long years before I was staying at Francis Coppola's Napa Valley estate. Richard Gere, Gregory Hines, Dyson Lovell, Coppola, and I were behind closed doors. Coppola's just finished second-draft script of *The Cotton Club* was being read aloud by Gere and Hines to make comments and changes on. A knock at the door. Sofia, Francis's daughter, came in and whispered in my ear. "An urgent call, Mr. Evans."

"Damn it. Sorry, fellas." I ran to the main house, rushed to the phone.

It was Greg Bautzer, still bristling from my 1980 coke bust.

"I've been hearing rumblings I don't like."

"About me?"

"Why do you think I'm callin'? This guy Radin, do you know him?"

"Yeah, why?"

"He's missing, that's why. And your name's involved."

"He's not up here, I swear. Now can I go back to rehearsal?"

"Rehearsal? I stepped out of a meeting with Kirk Kerkorian to make this call. It's no joke. You can't afford another 1980."

"Greg, how do I know where the guy is?"

"Bob, it doesn't matter. If I hear it, others do too. Protect yourself, take no chances, you can't afford more bad press. I've already put in a call to Robert Shapiro, he's the best criminal attorney in town. Don't leave the phone, and keep your fingers crossed that he's available."

"Greg, I hardly know this guy Radin. Where do I fit in?"

"Your name is Bob Evans, that's where it fits in," hanging the phone up in my ear.

I wanted to get back to rehearsal, but I didn't want to piss off Bautzer, not again. The phone rang. *My life changed.*

"You don't know me, and I don't know you, but I know a lot about you."

For the next thirty minutes I told this new voice in my life, Robert Shapiro, everything that I remembered.

"It doesn't ring true, Mr. Evans, you're too bright, too successful, I don't believe one word you've told me.

"You and I are going to have a long talk. Innocent or guilty isn't the point. Lawyer-client confidentiality is. Forget me, any lawyer you deal with needs the confidentiality of truth."

"Mr. Shapiro, I haven't told you one lie!"

He began to laugh. "If I played back to a jury the conversation we've just had, they'd laugh me out of court."

"I don't know why, I've told you the truth. Can it wait four, five days? I'll be finished with rehearsal."

Another laugh . . . not a good one.

"Four, or five days. You needed someone yesterday, this is not 'Entertainment Tonight,' Mr. Evans. You're lucky my wife's a fan of yours. If you can't fly down, I'll fly up. Be in San Francisco early tonight, meet me at the Mark Hopkins, eight P.M."

At three o'clock the next morning, after being examined and cross-examined with more harshness than Bobby Kennedy at his best, my new *consigliere* took a break (a cup of tea, two Bufferins, a cold towel), then sat staring, not at me, just staring.

"Do you know what I learned these last seven hours? You're the single dumbest man I've ever met. How could someone who's known all over the world, made history, be so fucking stupid?"

No one had ever talked to me that way before.

"A guy who can't read or write has more smarts than you. You're not guilty, you're plain fuckin' dumb innocent. Do you need help? You don't know how bad. Let me be the one to lose sleep over it. The more you sleep, the less you'll talk. Your mouth is more dangerous than an accident ready to happen. The only thing I demand is that you tell me everything, no matter how much it hurts. If you don't, you're the one who's going to lose."

"No problem, Mr. Shapiro. I've got nothing to hold back."

"From now on, it's not Shapiro, it's the two Bobs."

During the next days, I filled him in on every detail I remembered regarding Roy Radin. How I was looking to put together a motion picture company, to raise enough money privately to finance my own films and own the negative (the most valuable asset in Hollywood). How I was receptive to meeting rich people outside the industry, people who were captivated by the mystique of film. How my house became a revolving door from the wealthy to the entrepreneurial and the hustler—you name it, they all came in and out. How a chauffeur from Ascot Limousine, a company I half owned, told me about the new customer he was driving night and day, a wealthy divorcee from Texas looking to get into the film business.

"Who recommended her?"
"Oh, the Morrison family, the largest stockholders in General Motors, split their time between Bel Air, Grosse Point, and Palm Beach—top of the line. This lady I'm driving is good friends with them."
"What's her name?"
"Jacobs, Laynie Jacobs."
"How old?"
" 'Bout thirty-five, real looker—your type, Mr. E. Would you like to meet her?"

Wealthy? Divorcee? Midthirties? Real attractive? Fuck films . . . don't have one of her kind on my dance card. Can't show up with a twenty-one-year-old starlet at a serious dinner.

Two days later, escorted by our matchmaker chauffeur, we met. She was a real looker. Knowing that no lady is going to put fifty mil into the picture business, I wanted to get business over with quick.

"I need a minimum of fifty million dollars to start the company I've structured."

Southern drawl and all, her response was just as I had thought. "Five or ten million was closer to what I was thinking of."

"That's a lot of money. I'd be careful who you meet. This town is full of talkers lookin' for a way to take a lady like you. I'm giving you good advice; don't put any money in films."

"I do know someone who has that kind of money. Has access to it. Good friends with the Rothschilds. With your name he could raise it on the phone. Lives in New York." A Southern laugh. "He'd come by bus to meet you."

"We're talking about a lot of money, Miss Jacobs."

Battin' her Southern belle eyelashes, "Call me Laynie. You should meet him."

"No rush."

Forget flicks! My head was into more creative play.

"Mind if I ask him to fly out?"

"Mind if I fix you a drink?"

"Rum and coke'll be just fine. Let's have him fly out . . . gotta Southern hunch. His name's Roy Radin."

We clicked glasses and toasted to her Southern hunch.

Having met many Laynies throughout my life, I didn't need legal counsel, but that's where it ended. When it came to business, knowing half of me is a twelve-year-old, I always protected myself with a Korshak. For the first time since I began shaving, I was without counsel—Ken Ziffrin had just fired me weeks earlier. My M.O. had always been the same—whether it was a realtor, a financier, or an investment banker, credentials were reviewed by my legal eagles. Roy Radin's credentials wouldn't have gotten him through Paramount's front gate. Good timing, huh?

Shapiro listened patiently, to everything I told him. It was obvious the prosecution was showboating, trying to connect Radin's disappearance with *The Cotton Club*. There was never a deal between us or a dollar exchanged; there was a handshake, that's all, to fund a company that never came into existence.

Four people had been accused of the so-called Cotton Club murder, which had become one of the most highly publicized murder cases in Los Angeles history. Now the jury foreman announced the verdict. Laynie Jacobs-Greenberger (as she was then called): guilty. Of murder in the second degree, and kidnapping for the purpose of murder with great bodily harm. A crime carrying life without possibility of parole. Metzer, Marti, and Lowe—guilty. Metzer—first-degree murder. Marti—first-degree murder. Lowe—murder in the second degree. The jury would now begin to deliberate on the death penalty for Marti and Metzer for their role in the murder of Roy Radin.

Roy Radin's death would normally not rate any interest in Los Angeles. At the time there were seventeen other first-degree murder cases in trial. However, because I had met with Radin and Jacobs and drawn up contracts to have Radin finance a motion picture company, I gave the case headline value; the names Robert Evans and *The Cotton Club* still sell newspapers.

Everything about this movie was a nightmare: the shooting schedule, the unions, the script, and the director, my dear friend, Mr. Coppola. With my personal need to pay attention to every aspect of the picture, I was totally drained, working around the clock, answering a hundred phone calls a day.

During *Cotton Club*'s production in New York, a celebrated movie star was in town promoting her film. We went to Elaine's for dinner and then back to my brownstone. It was the first time in more than a month I had the luxury of spending time alone with a woman. Knowing that my dream of *The Cotton Club* was about to become a reality, I looked at her.

"You've never had better timing. You have no idea how much being here tonight with me means."

It was after midnight. By habit I shut my phones off at midnight unless I'm expecting a specific call, since any call coming in after midnight is never a good one.

Rubbing my back, giving me a caressing massage, she saw the blinking light.

"The light's blinking."

"Fuck it . . . don't stop."

She continued her massage south. The light was still blinking.

"Pick the phone up, please. The constant blinking makes me nervous. It may be important."

"It can wait till morning."

"Please?"

A bit pissed, reluctantly I grabbed the phone. "Yeah?"

"It's Shapiro. Roy Radin is dead. He's been found in a deserted canyon near Lancaster."

I lay there in shock, totally stunned, as if I had been poisoned. Before I could even ask a question, I heard words I will never forget.

"Evans, it's no longer a missing-persons case. It's a murder case."

From that point on, I would always get an emptiness every time I picked up the phone and heard Shapiro's voice on the other end. He told me that the police would be calling, that they'd want to talk to me, and that we would sit with them while I told them the absolute truth. Although I believed him, I didn't sleep the rest of the night.

I had already talked to the police about three weeks before, when a missing-persons report had been filed by Radin's family. Shapiro and I had met with Glen Souza, who was the head of the Los Angeles Police Department's missing-persons bureau. Souza told Shapiro how a lawyer had come out from Miami to meet with him in response to his request to talk to Laynie Jacobs. The lawyer traveled five and a half hours in each direction, only to sit with Souza and tell him that he was Laynie's lawyer and had nothing to say.

Souza also gave Shapiro some information regarding Roy Radin's background. He outlined the story of a drug rip-off involving hundreds of thousands of dollars. It was the first time that I had heard that Laynie Jacobs was married to a major drug dealer. He spoke of Radin's large usage of cocaine.

The Radin family had hired a private investigator named John O'Grady, who called Shapiro seeking information about his missing client. O'Grady outlined his theory of the case to Bob. He told Bob about Jonathan Lawson—Radin's secretary. O'Grady reported that Lawson saw Radin leave in a limousine that was headed for La Scala restaurant in Beverly Hills. He was being picked up by Laynie Jacobs. Radin had sensed something was wrong because he asked a former actor, Demond Wilson, to follow him with a gun. But, in the bumper-to-bumper traffic on Sunset, Wilson lost sight of the limousine.

O'Grady discovered a man by the name of Tally Rogers, who had previously been convicted of a narcotics offense. He was a known drug dealer who had brought two hundred kilos of cocaine to the West Coast through Laynie. She discovered that those drugs were missing and unpaid for, and that Radin was the suspected culprit. O'Grady concluded that Roy Radin died as a result of a payback for this drug rip-off.

As in many a murder case, the law protects the perpetrator. The government has to build a solid case before they have a chance to indict and then win. That procedure is too expensive to go through without a strong prosecutorial belief of victory. Both politically and financially, the albatross of a hung jury, a mistrial, or an outright loss is a career-breaker to the underpaid prosecutors endeavoring to make their way up the ladder of success.

As the years passed, I paid little attention to the machinations of the government's investigation of the murder, I had to believe they didn't have enough evidence to build a case, indict, and win. As Joan Didion reported in the September 4, 1989, issue of *The New Yorker:*

*Around Division 47 of Los Angeles Municipal Court, the down-
town courtroom where this spring and summer a preliminary hearing was held to determine whether the charges brought in the 1983
murder of a thirty-three-year-old road-show promoter named Roy
Alexander Radin should be dismissed or the defendants should be
bound over to superior court for arraignment and trial. . . . "Everybody's working this one," a reporter covering the trial said one morning as we stood waiting to get patted down at the entrance to the
courtroom, a security measure prompted in part by a telephoned
bomb threat, and encouraged by the general wish of everyone involved
to make this a noticeable case. "Major money," he added. . . .*

*The almost febrile interest in this case derived not from the princi-
pals but from what was essentially a cameo role, played by Robert
Evans. . . .*

*Not only was Robert Evans not "on trial" in Division 47 but what
was going on there was not a trial—only a preliminary hearing, intended to determine whether the state had sufficient evidence and
cause to prosecute those charged, who did not include Evans. . . .*

"Mr. Radin was an obstacle to further negotiation involving The
Cotton Club," *the prosecuting attorney had argued in conclusion.
"The deal could not go through until specific issues such as percentages were worked out. It was at that time that [Laynie Jacobs-] Greenberger had the motive to murder Mr. Radin."*

*I was struck by this as a final argument, because it seemed to sug-
gest an entire case based on the notion that an interest in an entirely
hypothetical share of the entirely hypothetical profits from an entirely
hypothetical motion picture (at the time Roy Radin was killed,* The
Cotton Club *had an advertising poster but no shooting script and no
money and no cast and no start date) was money in the bank. All that
had stood between [Laynie] Greenberger and Fat City, as the prosecutor saw it, was boilerplate, a matter of seeing that "percentages were
worked out." . . .*

*The detectives were keeping in touch with motion-picture produ-
cers, car phone to car phone, sketching in connecting lines not appar-
ent in the courtroom. "This friend of mine in the sheriff's office laid it
out for me three years ago," one producer told me. "The deal was, 'This
is all about drugs, Bob Evans is involved, we're going to get him.'"*

*Here we had the rough line for several quite different stories, but it
would have been hard not to notice that each of them depended for its
dramatic thrust on the presence of Robert Evans.*

Unfortunately for me, Didion was right. The night before I was to appear in the Criminal Courts Building of Los Angeles, I couldn't sleep. I was in turmoil about the words that Shapiro said I must speak. I had searched for every alternative and consulted with friends and leading lawyers about my forthcoming appearance. Deep down I knew that I would be following Shapiro's advice. But the decision was one of the most difficult I would ever have to make.

Shapiro had had chilling words of caution. "It's possible, but very unlikely, that the judge will not let you exercise your privilege under the Fifth Amendment," he said. "If that happens, the judge could find you in contempt of court if you refuse to answer any questions."

He warned me further that the penalty for contempt could be an immediate jail sentence. I was stunned to learn that by following my lawyer's advice, I might end up in jail! Shapiro then assured me that he was preparing for that possibility by drawing up a writ of habeas corpus; basically, he explained, if I were jailed, he would go to a higher court with it and get me released pending the review of the judge's ruling. However, Shapiro did caution me that since it was Friday, if the case dragged on until the afternoon, there might be a problem because of the weekend.

There I was, a witness for events that took place eight years before. Now I was worried about ending up in jail. I couldn't believe this was happening to me, nor could I believe it could happen to anyone.

So there would be no surprises, Shapiro sent a letter to the district attorney (and thereafter released it to the press), indicating that I would follow his advice. I would not testify because the district attorney stated I had not been cleared as a suspect. Until the time that the D.A. had adequate information to clear me, Shapiro indicated, he would not change his opinion.

In criminal cases, the prosecution's first witness is known as the leadoff. It is usually the most compelling witness who would outline the most important elements of the case. *I* was the leadoff witness. Shapiro couldn't believe the D.A. would call me. He felt this was being done to call attention to the case and make it more newsworthy, and he was absolutely right. When I appeared in court there was not an empty seat. All the vultures were there: the producers and would-be producers of miniseries and TV shows; the book writers looking for an angle; the newspaper reporters and magazine writers of the world press. People began to refer to it as "the Evans Case."

Although I knew I would not be testifying to anything, my heart felt like it was coming out of my skin. I sat in what lawyers describe as the hardest chair in the world.

The prosecutor rose and approached the podium as the clerk stated, "State and spell you first and last name."

"Robert Evans. R-o-b-e-r-t E-v-a-n-s."

"What is your occupation?" Cohn, the prosecutor, queried.

Shapiro gave me the nod. "Based on the advice of counsel, I respectfully refuse to answer that question. I exercise my privilege under the Fifth Amendment of the United States Constitution."

The prosecutor raised his voice in an angry tone and told the judge such questions did not call for any information which could possibly incriminate me, and that he vehemently objected and asked the court to order that I answer the question. The judge reserved the ruling and asked the prosecutor to continue.

"Did you know a man by the name of Roy Radin?"

I repeated the same answer.

"Do you know a woman by the name of Laynie Jacobs?"

Again the same response from me. The prosecutor continued with what seemed to be an endless line of questions to which I gave the same answer. Shapiro interrupted and said that this was unnecessary and unwarranted and that he would advise me—and I would follow his advice—to exercise my rights not to testify.

Judge Patti Jo McKay then made her decision. "I require you to answer those questions. I cannot see how they could possibly tend to incriminate you."

The blood ran out of my body. I started to quiver inside. Here it comes. I'm going to jail. I can't believe this!

Shapiro seemed calm and confident. He looked at the judge and firmly said, "May I see you in your chambers, your honor? I have an offer of proof to make."

What the hell is going on? I thought. Fifteen minutes later Shapiro walked out with a smile on his face. I breathed a sigh of relief.

Shapiro later told me that he was direct and to the point with the judge. "Your honor," he said, "there is no question in my mind that the statements made in answer to any of these questions, based on the previous public statements of the prosecutor and the police, could possibly tend to incriminate my client. That is the only test. However, if I make a disclosure to you, judge, of what those factors are, it would require you to declare a conflict of interest and remove yourself from hearing this case. I, therefore, respectfully request you transfer this matter to another court for an independent hearing of the issue with Mr. Evans's privilege under the Fifth Amendment."

The judge was now put in the awkward position of either having to hear Shapiro and run the risk of not being able to continue with the case, or sending the matter out. Since most judges relish high-profile media cases, the outcome Shapiro expected took place.

Judge McKay returned to the bench and stated, "This case is in recess until further notice."

The courtroom sounded like an aviary. "What happened? What's going on? What can you tell us?" was coming out of every mouth from every direction.

Shapiro told me to remain calm and that he was very optimistic about the outcome. I walked with him, and he took me to another courtroom where I was allowed to stay in the chambers of another judge he knew; finally he came back and reported that the ruling was in my favor. Shapiro had shown this second judge a notebook of all the case's press clippings over the last eight years. Just about every article told the same story and included a version of the line that had been haunting me for years: "Bob Evans has not been cleared as a suspect by the district attorney's office."

"That simple statement caused the judge to rule in our favor," Shapiro said. The D.A. had inadvertently, with those few words, put himself in a position where he could not get my testimony. Even though he said in open court, "Bob Evans is merely a witness in this case," these past statements came back to haunt him.

I thought that would be the end of it, but I was wrong. I walked down the hallway into an elevator, with the press running behind. The cameras were flashing, the reporters demanding I answer questions. The elevator doors closed and we proceeded downstairs to our previously arranged location. We were inconspicuously slipped into a nondescript car and returned to the sanctuary of my home.

I still did not fully comprehend what had taken place. Shapiro calmly described everything and said, "This is the end of it. Evans, you will never have to testify or say a word about *The Cotton Club*,

Roy Radin, and Laynie Jacobs-Greenberger again."

The preliminary hearing continued for approximately four months. After the first few days, the spectator section began to dwindle. At the end of the hearing, Judge McKay ruled that she had a strong suspicion the defendants were guilty of the charge of murder, and ordered them to stand trial. This was carried as a two-paragraph story on the back page of the Metro section of the *Los Angeles Times*.

During the months between the arraignment and the beginning of the trial, Shapiro was contacted by just about every attorney in the case. They all wanted to talk to me and all wanted me to testify as a witness for them. Apparently, each felt I had something to offer that would benefit their case. Shapiro remained firm in the idea that I should not talk to anyone and I continued to follow his advice.

About a month before the trial, Shapiro received a call from the prosecutor saying they wanted to subpoena me as a witness. My lawyer ended up having the same conversation he had with the prosecutors over the past year and a half played out again. The prosecutors asserted that Evans would be nothing more than a witness, and there was no reason that I shouldn't talk to them and testify. Shapiro reiterated that he was very conservative in his approach as an attorney and that under no circumstances would allow me to testify until the time the prosecutors had determined that I was, in their words, "cleared as a suspect."

What were they looking for? Why were they doing this to me? What purpose did it serve? Certainly all the evidence in the reports pointed to the fact that the overwhelming theme of the murder case was a narcotics rip-off and payback—not the making of *The Cotton Club*. Why were they persisting? Shapiro remained convinced that it was because my name ensured media attention.

During one meeting, the prosecutor yelled at Shapiro. "These are rough and tough people. These are dope dealers and murderers. I know Evans is scared. He has every reason to be. But we know that Laynie Jacobs told your client, Robert Evans, that Roy Radin was killed, and she no longer had to worry about him! Laynie told him she did it. Laynie told him she did it. There is no other reasonable explanation!"

Shapiro listened patiently and told prosecutor Cohn, "You know Evans had nothing to do with this. You are destroying this man by putting so much pressure on him. This case had nothing to do with *The Cotton Club*. There was no deal or money. If you check with any-one in Hollywood, the chances of making money on any such project for outside investors are slim at best. To insinuate, with no money changing hands, and just the handshake agreement between people interested in funding a company that never came into existence, was not supported by any facts."

They would go on and on with the same theme for four months.

Cohn, unyielding: "If he has nothing to hide, why doesn't he talk to us?"

Shapiro's response was "If he's only a witness, come out and say he is."

They went round and round battling like two fighters in a ring. Sometimes losing their tempers, other times talking in civilized tones. But the result was always the same. "Why wouldn't Evans say that Laynie Jacobs told him she killed Roy Radin?"

And always Shapiro repeating, "Because she never did."

That was the standstill. Neither side willing to bend one inch. Ul-timately, I would have to suffer the consequences. I certainly would not testify and lie simply to satisfy the prosecution's theory. On the other hand, if I didn't I would face the logical public conclusion: that if I hadn't done something wrong, why wasn't I testifying?

Shapiro responded to the district attorney's subpoena for me to testify by filing a motion to quash. In lay terms, this means that the subpoena was not properly issued, that I had no testimony to offer, and therefore I should not be required to even come to court. He filed an extensive brief quoting legal precedent that supported our posi-tion. It was up to Judge Curtis Rappe, a former high-ranking federal prosecutor trying his first case, to make the ruling.

At the hearing, Shapiro walked back into chambers and I could see that look in his eye—he had prevailed once again. The judge ruled that the privilege to take the Fifth did exist, that it would be redundant for me to testify and redundant for me to come to the witness stand. It would serve no purpose whatsoever. Then, I finally heard the words that I had been waiting for—for eight years.

"Evans, this matter now has to be placed behind you," Shapiro told me. "You will not be called as a witness. You will not have to testify for any side in this case. Further, you should never discuss this case with anyone. Why? Because somewhere, sometime, some place, there may be some prosecutor or detective who feels something said, even in jest, might have some significance. Remember, Evans, the statute of limitations never runs out in a case like this."

All the defendants were convicted. Me? Not only was I not convicted, but I was never charged with a crime . . . anything! But I was punished. Punished by innuendos, lies, character assassination, and nightmares that jolted me out of bed in a cold sweat. Punished by disgrace for something I had nothing to do with, something that I had nothing to be ashamed of. Punished by a lifetime of silence. Until the day I die, I am not allowed to discuss the case without consulting with my attorney, Robert Shapiro. The pages you have just read met with his approval.

Only after the verdicts were in did *Vanity Fair* publish an article, stating that Roy Radin's murder had *nothing to do* with *The Cotton Club*. It was a simple case of drugs and murder.

Radin's death caused me eight years of *living death*. Justice? Well I'm still here. Wounded? Sure, but you gotta go on . . . stay in the picture.

A nightmare is a nightmare is a nightmare is a nightmare. But with it came a sense of discovery—call it *human relationship*. In a hotel room in San Francisco I met Robert Shapiro, a man who became my counsel, rabbi, father confessor, friend, and brother. His services priceless, yet never once a bill. I've asked him many a time, "Bob, what's the number, what do I owe you? I'm no charity case." It never fails, he just looks at me and smiles.

39

Doors closed on me quietly. Calls made were not returned. Book after book, script after script were submitted. No one ever said yes—they didn't even say no.

Though still ensconced in the prime offices at Paramount, I may as well have been the Shadow. *Popeye* and *Urban Cowboy* hit the screens in 1980. Seven years later, the only product Evans delivered to "the mountain" was embarrassment. Respectful of my past legend, I always got smiles and nods, yet not one discussion led to more than a discussion.

Ending whatever I had left of a legacy to be, my good friend Bob Towne hammered the final nail into my coffin. Now, from legend to leper, I sat alone, the phone not ringing, not an agent submitting.

It was 1987 and Paramount was celebrating its seventy-fifth anniversary. Twenty years earlier, it was me who put my ass on the line, begging to keep the studio from being sold to the cemetery behind us. Now a momentous anniversary picture was to be taken. Close to a hundred actors, actresses, directors, producers, and studio chieftains would gather to pose for this historic shot. It was eerie watching the photographers snap away, less than fifty feet from my office window.

Ali MacGraw, my ex-wife, was among the stars in the shot, no one belonging in it more than she. *Love Story*—in reality, her child—had kept Paramount alive. Without its success, "the mountain" would have crumbled into anonymity—sold off by its parent company or erased from its ledgers to save further embarrassment. Ali came to my office.

"Evans, hurry, you're late."

"I'm not . . . Wasn't invited."

Bewildered? Shocked!

"You should be front and center!"

"Comes with the turf, kid," I said, wiping her eyes with a Kleenex. "Now go out there and give 'em the MacGraw smile."

For the next hour, there I sat glued to the window. Thinking, thinking, thinking . . . If not for me, graves rather than sound stages would have filled the shot. Once king of "the mountain," now I was not even allowed to climb it.

A few weeks later, I was informed by memo that the studio was terminating my auto and health insurance.

A month passed and Richard Zimbert, head honcho of business affairs, paid me a rare visit.

"We go back too long, Evans. It's not me talkin', it's the orders I've been given. The truth? No one at Paramount wants to do business with you."

"Been expecting it. When it's over it's over."

"The office, Bob, we need a date."

"Is ninety days okay, Dick?"

"Sure."

Quick pat on the shoulder, a quicker exit.

My twenty-year home had been pulled from under me. From behind the gates of Paramount, I was now behind the gates of Woodland. What was once my home, my oasis, my one retreat from the outside world, was now a lobby. During the sixties and seventies, every hour of every day was spent with writers, directors, actors—fantasies came true. Now, in the eighties, I was spending every hour of every day with fund-raisers, so-called entrepreneurs, film financiers, and international consortiums. Individuals with big pockets, small pockets, no pockets, continually coming through my home, all supposedly desperate to be in business with me. Yet bullshit rather than money talked. Weeks turned into months, months into a year. I felt akin to a new girl in town, dating a different guy Friday, Saturday, and Sunday—but no one calls on Monday.

It was gold-rush time, the decade that made millionaires into billionaires. "Entertainment" was handed a new moniker—"communications"—legitimatizing a business once thought of as "fickle flicks" into a high-profiled, profitable industry, its future painted in gold and rightfully so.

The American film is the only product we manufacture that is number one in every country around the globe. It's the only thing the Japanese can't knock off, duplicate, or make better. Billions rather than millions became the purchase ticket for a Hollywood studio, so thirsty were our competitor-friends to become members of the elusive club the American film.

Texas and Evans shared one thing: the cash boom of the eighties left us both with a cash drought. While the decade flourished, we both fell from grace. Texas is oil, Hollywood is film. With earthquake force, the price of oil barreled south. With equal tremor, Evans's career in flicks followed right behind.

In 1982 *Forbes* magazine featured four of the wealthiest bachelors in Texas. Oil being oil, naturally they were deep in it. Through an intermediary (a choreographer, no less), a big powwow with these guys and eight other Texan oilmen was arranged at my Paramount office; they were all interested in investing in a finely honed business plan that partnered them with Paramount and me. The twelve fat cats arrived in three private jets and spent Friday at Paramount, reviewing, structuring, and restructuring a multifaceted plan. By Saturday afternoon we had consummated a $75 million co-ventured entity. At last a bit of sunshine. The eighties were starting to look

good. It was celebration time! A quick invite—but a great turnout!
Two hundred candles hung from the ole sycamore, caviar by the kilo,
Cristal champagne by the case, many a toast, many an embrace.

Monday morning, all twelve boarded their jets and flew back to
their ranches. As their planes landed, it was earthquake time, Texas
style. Oil fell out of the barrels, with no buyers to catch its flow. It
was 1929 revisited for them there oil guys, as it was for most of
Texas. My twelve partners ran for cover? Could be—they haven't
resurfaced yet.

Texas was my state of the eighties. Another intermediary (no
choreographer this time, but a distinguished merchant banker)
introduced me to a thirty-four-year-old dynamo, a self-made half-
billionaire. Young, vital, perceptive, he flipped to be in flicks. Were
my pockets empty? Naturally. Did I play my hand strong? Naturally.
Talking film with Evans meant doing it on his turf. I wasn't lazy, but
I knew as I drove him through those gates of Paramount that they—
not I—became the seducer. This mini-mogul kid was relentless,
never tiring. For four days and nights we went at it, naturally surrounded by our legal eagles. On Friday at noon, a deal was consummated and contracts signed. Checks drawn to the tune of twelve
million big ones. Were the checks good? Better than government
bonds. Partners now, we embraced. He jetted off to Houston. I cavi-
ared and crème fraîched it, celebrating my biggest night of the eighties until I watched the sun come up in the morning. A 7:00 A.M. ring
of the phone. My throbbing head pounded. Shut if off? Pick it up?
Fuck it, I'll pick it up—fucked I got.

Flying back to Houston on his private jet, my thirty-four-year-old
dynamo had a heart attack, his first. He didn't need another one—he
died.

My contemporaries—Barry Diller, Michael Eisner, Stanley Jaffe,
Martin Davis, Jeff Katzenberg, Frank Mancuso, and Doug Kramer—
shared three things: each ascended to become a captain of the industry; each at one time in his career was in awe of the much haloed
Robert Evans; each looked upon him as a role model and each out-
roled his model.

Jealous? Never, ain't my style. Respectful? You bet! Success is one
thing, continued success another, it doesn't happen by mistake. My
hat's off to all of them!

Each month below-the-belt punches were hitting me—lower and

harder, from all directions. My character, persona, and professional abilities were now lost. Festered anger overshadowed creative thoughts. It was a cop-out. The more it festered the more intransigent I became. Soon my life's closest relationship eroded, until we were no longer brothers. Its resolve? Actual disownership. Where did the fault lie? *With me.* Intransigence—whether it be a nation's or a person's—makes it all but impossible to find a solution.

In reality, the problem wasn't my brother, rather the effects of public disgrace, the effects of drugs, and the effects of continued failure never before experienced that all but shriveled me into obscurity. Then lightning struck, *bad lightning.*

40

May 21, 1989.

Nine minutes before midnight . . . from behind the bars of my cell-like room, I watched the elevators carefully. One of the four doors opened. I made my dash . . . hospital gown and all. The guy behind the desk tried to stop me. It was too late. The doors closed. But damn it, I was on the wrong elevator—one that stopped on every floor, five to be exact. The elevator hit the main floor. Two male attendants approached.

"Mr. Lombardo, you're not allowed to leave the facility unless you're in the company of an attendant."

My throbbing paranoia was such that I had committed myself under the alias of "Lombardo," shielding me from any further media damage.

"May I go out front?" I asked them. "A friend of mine has driven down to see me."

Reluctantly, they escorted me through the revolving doors, leading me out to the carport of the mental-health ward—in reality, a loony bin—Scripps Memorial Hospital, a few miles north of San Diego.

Waiting for me in a limo was my personal chauffeur from Ascot Limousine. What the guards didn't know was that hours before I had snuck out of my cell-like room to a public phone in the ward, called my limo service—collect—and instructed them to have John Paul, my personal driver, come down—"on the double, wait for me as long as necessary and ready himself for a quick getaway."

With a guard on either side, I whispered to John Paul, "Come back tomorrow at noon on the dot, and wait! It may be an hour, a day, a week, keep your motor running. Got it?"

If I weren't his boss, he would have committed me himself! He must have thought I was crazy as I smiled, turned, and walked back to my cell block accompanied by my two escorts.

Two days earlier I had committed myself to prevent the possibility of suicide. I was put behind bars and stripped of all my belongings. The claustrophobia alone shot my blood pressure up over the 200 mark. Sure in hell not wanting a D.O.A. on their hands, the nurses kept shoving sedatives down my throat, trying to calm me. I had made a horrible mistake, with no way out.

The next afternoon, as the attendants were all busy checking in their new victims, I cautiously eyed the bank of elevators, waiting, waiting. . . . I'm off! The express elevator opened. I made my second dash. Wham! The doors closed. I made it! I made it! Flashing through my paranoid head: no one in a hospital gown is allowed on the main floor. *I'll stand out like a leper!* The elevator doors opened. I took off. Two goons picked up on me immediately. Edwin Moses couldn't have made it faster through the doors. An arm's length behind, the posse was reaching out.

John Paul better be there.

He was, a good hundred feet away, in the carport. Tasting me, one of the goons grabbed for my hospital gown. Though I was older than the two of them put together, they came in second and third. I slammed the car door behind them, hardly able to catch my breath. "Move it!"

Only three months earlier, subliminally masochistic, I rid myself of the last bastion left of my dignity—I sold Woodland. The effect was such that I all but lost the will to function. Nightmares were telling me I would never leave there alive. I begged the new owner, a wealthy French industrialist named Tony Murray, for more time. What had been my Garden of Eden for close to a quarter of a century was mine no more. Even more painful was that I was now a tenant in my own home, paying $25,000 a month for the privilege. Could I afford it? Not by a long shot.

As we drove north toward L.A., trying to settle my shattered nerves, I grabbed a tiny bottle of J&B, opened it, gulped it down. "Back to Woodland," I said to John Paul. Putting up the divider, I turned on the television set, nervously flipping the channels. Can't be, it's me: "Tonight, for the first time, 'A Current Affair' will uncover the real story of Bob Evans and the *Cotton Club* murder. Tune in at seven-thirty this evening for this shocking exposé."

I immediately switched the television off and lay back, staring up and thinking to myself, This is Kafka.

Almost to the day a year before, I had been introduced to a young man named Bill Macdonald. He was handsome, educated, savvy, and desperate to be in the film business. Because he pretended to be in awe of me (an affirmation I so needed), I embraced him. Together we structured a prospectus to raise money to co-finance film production with a major distributor. The concept was original and bore credence.

Aggressively, Bill searched for an investment group. He introduced me to two men, David Knight and David Bryant, the owners of a thriving investment company who were riding high. Beautiful offices, chauffeured cars—you name the accoutrement, they had it. Six months later, a deal was consummated. By far the smallest of any deal of my contemporaries, but to me a new beginning—or so I thought.

Caution took precedence over cost. An army of lawyers from the distinguished law firm Shea Gould, supervised by Alan Schwartz, worked overtime and weekends. They double-checked every dotted *i* and crossed *t*, and checked every detail possible regarding my new partnership. My legal costs alone soared north of $150,000. Finally the papers were signed. It was good for the investors, good for Robert Evans Productions, but . . . the timing was bad. The recessionary 1990s had now begun and business crumbled. The Daves couldn't deliver what they promised.

Robert Evans Productions was on full go, with two major studios competing to be its partner. Then a ghost from hell resurfaced. After a five-year silence, Roy Radin's murder hit the headlines in late October 1988. Now monikered the *Cotton Club* Murder, it made sexy ink for journalists' fodder and prosecutors' careers. Somewhat akin to a fighter who takes one punch too many, the barrage of accusatory blows that followed in the weeks and months to come put me into a tailspin of depression so deep that it was just a hair away from being lethal.

I went cold turkey on every drug I had ever taken, prescription or otherwise. Was it difficult? Almost impossible. But I did it and paid the price for it too. This was when I sold my home to Tony Murray. So deep was my depression that I just wanted to get in a car and go south—one way. Now being but a tenant in my own house, I fell into a far deeper and dangerous abyss.

Thoughts of being an unemployed vagrant haunted my every dream. One night, jolting up from a nightmare in a cold sweat, I took out a bottle containing a hundred Nembutals and dumped a pile of them into my hand. As I raised them to my mouth, I realized that if I took myself out now, I would be judged guilty of the ludicrous innuendos splashing across magazines, newspapers, television, and radio. I couldn't bear to burden my son, Joshua, with this legacy. Throwing the pillows to the floor I buried my head in them, hysterically crying. If it were not for the love of my son, the pills rather than the pillows would have buried me.

To prevent this from happening again, Bill Macdonald climbed into the driver's seat of my green Jaguar and drove me to Scripps Memorial Hospital, a depression clinic where I had decided to check myself in.

Now, forty-eight hours later, having escaped from my self-imprisonment where the examining psychiatrists were considering electric shock therapy, my limo was pulling into the gates of my once-owned

Woodland sanctuary. I had to take control of the never-ending bad dream that my life had become. Never having been psychiatrically oriented, I knew that action—not therapy—was my only shot at survival.

Getting my home, my roots of twenty-five years back, was vital to my survival. There was a big problem: Tony Murray had no intention of selling it back.

Without asking, Jack Nicholson did a Henry Kissinger. He flew to Monte Carlo and begged Tony to sell me back my home. Tony was shocked that Jack would fly halfway around the world to plead on my behalf for what he considered to be just a piece of real estate. Wherever Tony went that summer, he'd tell the story, capping it with "these film people . . . they're all crazy. Imagine Jack Nicholson on his knees to me." The impact of Jack's plea, however, caused Tony to waver.

Meanwhile, a lady friend of mine from years past, Merete Van Kamp, who was now engaged to a Frenchman, Jean-Claude Friederich, visited me many a time, watching me wither away.

"If I get my house back, Merete, it'll give me back the strength I need to get through this hell."

Joshua also saw me withering away before him.

Trying to be positive and not to show my deepest, darkest fears, I kept on saying, "If I get my house back, Joshua, on New Year's Eve you gotta promise me we'll go out together and at the stroke of midnight, we'll kiss each other to bring in the nineties." It was dream talk, but I was desperate to hide my fears and project a positive thought to my son.

By coincidence, Merete's fiancé, Jean-Claude, was a close friend of Tony. As a show of love to Merete's persistent plea on my behalf, Jean-Claude nailed down what Nicholson had started—the return of my home. Call it pity, call it style, Tony did not want to make one dime of profit on a transaction he could have made millions on. What was a token to him was a lifesaver to me. Tony, I owe you a big one.

At the Bistro Gardens that New Year's Eve, Merete, Jean-Claude, and my friends Gary Chazan and Susan Cox joined Joshua and me in ringing in the new decade. When the clock struck twelve, I put my arms around Joshua, hugged him tight, and we kissed smack on the lips. A far-fetched dream come true.

"Happy decade, son."

"Happy decade, Papa."

41

Nervously I opened a small velvet jewel box. I looked inside at a medallion hanging from a gold chain.

"It's the saint of good fortune, your guardian angel," whispered Faye Mancuso. "The jeweler made two of them—one for you, one for Frankie." Frankie was her son, Frank, Jr., who was a close personal pal. His first professional stint was working for me as a gofer on *Urban Cowboy*.

It was Christmas. Around the table sat the entire Mancuso family. I was only the outsider. Our lives had been interwoven for more than two decades, and my fall from grace did not in any way alter our friendship. Quite the contrary—there wasn't a Thanksgiving, a Christmas, an Easter that I was not invited to join their family table. So sincere was their embrace that my last name could have been Mancuso.

Faye was right. The guardian angel medallion brought me heavenly luck. Within the week, the final papers were drawn and Woodland became mine once again.

At the time, I was a producer in name only of *The Two Jakes,* which had already been completed. Unlike *Chinatown,* not only wasn't I a contributor—I was more of a hindrance. Jack had revived *The Two Jakes,* mainly to get it off his conscience, with himself as director and star. Now four years later, the script of *The Two Jakes* was still only 80 percent complete. Bob Towne eighty-sixed Jack, never turning in the last 20 percent of the script, which Jack desperately needed to make *Jakes* work. Today it's paid for—but, yes, still not written.

Four years earlier, I had been co-star and co-producer. Now I was no more than a charity throw-in. It was only Nicholson's insistence that allowed me entrance.

A few days before *Jakes* was to start shooting, the *Los Angeles Herald-Examiner*'s front-page headline read, "ROBERT EVANS NOT RULED OUT AS 'COTTON CLUB' MURDER SUSPECT."

Now they had *The Two Jakes* to shit on as well. Nicholson joked: "Hey, we're making a flick about a murder and the Keed's living it out." His smile on full, "That's notorious for ya."

"Should I take my name off?"

"Sure, and I'll take *mine* off. Fuck 'em all. Let's be arm and arm at the Lakers game together."

Nicholson, a basketball fanatic, has seats right on the floor—front and center, next to the team.

"Hey, Jack—I feel like fuckin' Dillinger on the set."

Crooked smiling me, "You are, Keed. They don't call you 'notorious' for nothin'."

Harold Schneider, my co-producer, was the one who really produced the film as well as protected my ass. By contract I held a single production credit: "A Robert Evans Production." At picture's end, I insisted Harold get credit as presenter as well. If ever anyone deserved it, it was he.

Nicholson wouldn't start his first shot of the flick without my being on the set to share the results.

He also insisted the dailies be shown in my home projection room rather than at the studio. Strange, here's a guy directing and starring, knowing that showing the dailies at my home would cost him a much needed two hours' sleep. But it mattered little. He knew by doing that it gave me a much needed legitimacy. Not quite understanding why they had to be there, each night the entire crew would meet at my home to watch dailies. The Irishman made it clear why; he needed my approving eye (even knowing full well not only couldn't I see straight, but I was on the verge of a breakdown).

The picture opened and closed quickly. This was not Nicholson's fault, except possibly for his naïveté in expecting the last 20 percent of the script to be there for him from his old pal Bob "the Beener" Towne. Alan Finklestein, a producer on the film, specifically remembers that not only did Robert Towne not deliver a completed script, but went to Bora Bora with his wife, claiming he would complete the remaining 20 percent from there. The only line of communication with Towne was to call the main hut between certain hours of the day. The "staff" would then try to locate him because Towne's hut had no direct phone line. That was the last we ever heard from Robert Towne. What a friend.

A new decade, a new year, a house newly back. I was now on the prowl, one hungry cat. Looking for one shot to get my foot back into the door of major studio play.

Knowing that I was iceberg cold, I returned to basics. Learning from success. What originally gained me entrance to an impossible door was owning something that no one else could get. No easy task. But who says success comes easy, especially coming from a coffin?

Concept-orientated was the M.O. of all the studios. "Franchise flicks"—*Superman, Batman, Indiana Jones, Star Wars,* and *Star Trek,* all blockbusters—became the cure-all for box-office cancer. Each studio desperately searched for the fix.

Bill Macdonald showed me a script with a penciled drawing on its cover. For the next nine months, all my efforts were focused. With Alan Schwartz untangling a half century of interwoven rights, I traveled the world on bended knee, knowing this was my one and possibly last shot—and a long shot at that. No studio exec had the time or the passion to untangle its multifaceted web. For me it wasn't mere passion—it was survival.

Faye Mancuso's gold guardian angel shined all the way to heaven. My 100-to-1 shot came in. Its recognition international, a one-line drawing, without even a name. Why? Because it was on the cover of sixty-eight books written over thirty years and was the opening frame on hundreds upon hundreds of television segments. *The Saint*, halo and all, a franchise prize, was now mine. Unlike any hero in the recent past, wit, not brawn, was his M.O.; Cary Grant, not Arnold Schwarzenegger his prototype.

Finally, with all the rights locked up, a visit was paid to my dear friend Frank Mancuso at Paramount. Walking into his office, the outlaw knew he was holding the aces. A few moments of polite conversation, then with sadness Frank questioned my future, asking what I was working on. Me? I laughed.

"This is a strange racket, Frank. As a kid, I got my foot in the door owning something everyone wanted. They had to buy me. Sad, ain't it? I'm in the same position today. Think I own somethin', though, somethin' that everyone wants."

Opening my black satchel, I took out my scriptless script, the haloed saint on its cover.

Mancuso chuckled. "You don't own that."

"Yes I do."

He smile disappeared. "It's impossible! You're talkin' about the most complicated rights situation that goes back fifty years. No one's been able to disentangle them." Then he laughed. "And we've all tried, every studio. Now you're telling me you've unraveled them." Looking at me quizzically. "Bob, come on."

Surely he thought I was stoned.

"True, Frank—I own them."

"Can't be. How?"

"Poverty, Frank. When your back's against the wall, the impossible becomes possible. You're the one who said it to me—I'm a cat, and there's still another life there. Call Schwartz—he'll fill you in."

He did. After fifteen minutes of questioning, Mancuso put the phone down, saying words he thought would never come out of his mouth.

"You're not leaving this office until we make a deal."

At the lowest point in my career, I closed the richest deal of my life.

42

Hey Runt!

Spent over three years writing this. . . . It hurt . . . hurt bad. . . . Reliving your fuckups ain't easy. . . . Then writing 'em and rewriting 'em . . . that's the killer. . . . Did it for you . . . yeah you, you little runt. . . . You deserve it! . . . I wouldn't be here today if it weren't for you. . . . I know it . . . You know it . . . fuck it! . . . I ain't ashamed . . . why keep it a secret?

Knew the pain you were goin' through too . . . showed all over your face. . . . Them pimples you thought of squeezin'? . . . That's how many sleeping pills I thought of takin'.

You pulled one hell of a hat trick, kid . . . that tightrope, you balanced it like a pro . . . your strength stopped my fall.

We've never talked about it, so I'm writin' it . . . set the record straight . . . Talkin' disappears . . . that's why it's on paper. . . . For better or worse, at least you'll know who your ole man really is . . . how much he loves you. . . . It's all that matters.

Pop

Joshua was born on January 16, 1971. Before he was two, he was taken away by divorce decree, to know me only as a "weekend" father for years to come. No kid ever grew up with a more affectionate, caring, involved mother. It was Ali's best role in life. Conversely, my priorities being as fucked up as they were, Joshua was little more than an afterthought for far too many a year. A weekend drop-off rather than the most important parcel of my entire life.

Growing up and surviving the frazzled lives of both his parents was a miracle. Nine out of ten don't make it. One of ten come out stronger; he was that one.

The Hollywood Reporter once printed an interview with Gregory Hines:

Perhaps the most famous story of Hines's stormtrooping tactics is his audition with Robert Evans for The Cotton Club. *"I tap danced on his table to get that part," he says, laughing but nonetheless sincere.*

"He wanted Richard Pryor, and the Richard Gere part was earmarked for Sylvester Stallone. Coppola wasn't involved at that point, and Evans was going to direct, so I went to his house with my hair all slicked back, wearing a '40s jacket, and I said look, I know you don't think I'm right for this part, but if you give it to me I can change. Then I swept everything off his coffee table and jumped on top and did some spins."

Well, dear Gregory, the truth be it, though your fancy steps did count, you really owe your screen breakthrough to my kid.

In July 1982 *An Officer and a Gentleman* had just come out and was a huge hit. Getting Richard Gere signed for the lead in *The Cotton Club* was a coup. At the time Richard Pryor was set for the other lead. In 1982, there wasn't a hotter box-office star than Richard Pryor. A double coup—Gere and Prior.

Paramount was still the financier and distributor of the picture at the time. A Saturday meeting—with Barry Diller, Michael Eisner, Frank Mancuso, and Don Simpson, among others, in attendance—was held at my home. We were there to congratulate ourselves for this great casting coup. More important, we met to work out the complicated billing problems and coordinate what promised to be a blockbuster hit. It was the weekend of one of Joshua's bimonthly visits to his all but absentee father.

The eleven-year-old runt, dripping wet from the pool, interrupted us in the projection room, whispering, "I've gotta talk to you, Daddy."

Angered by his intrusion, I gave him a terse look. "Later, Joshua. Don't you see I'm in an important meeting?"

Twenty minutes passed and again, dripping wet, he stopped the flow of conversation around the table.

"Daddy, I must talk to you *now!* It's important. Please!"

An angered double take, then I asked the knights of the round table to excuse me for a few minutes.

As we walked toward the pool, Joshua's head hardly reached my waist. Looking down at him angrily, I asked, "What's so goddamn important? I'm in there with the entire Paramount brass."

He looked up, "Daddy, do you really think *Cotton Club*'s going to be as big as you say?"

"Is that what you called me out for?"

Without flinching, "Daddy, tell me, please. Do you really think it'll be the big one?"

"What kinda question's that, Joshua?"

Still without a flinch. "Tell me, please."

Trying to hold back my anger, "Ya. Why?"

"Don't use Richard Pryor then. If you do, it'll just be another Richard Pryor movie."

Stopped cold in my tracks? Never before so cold. Putting my hand through his wet hair, realizing the purity of his instincts had more depth than all of us so-called moguls.

Feigning a left, I picked him up and threw him into the pool. Quickly I walked back into the room and repeated the insight of an eleven-year-old to all. Before the meeting was over, we all reached the same conclusion: the canvas is of an era, not a slice of life. If we're looking for *The Godfather* with music, Richard Pryor would hurt it, not help it. Two days later, enter Gregory Hines.

Instinct cannot be bought, taught, or inherited. Less than two years before, Joshua had sat with me during the Thanksgiving holidays while we were working on the final mix, dub, and score of *Popeye*. Dolby Sound, which was state-of-the-art, was the system we were using.

Two weeks before premiere time, we were still feverishly editing it to completion. Paramount surprised us with a new system called Paramount Sound and insisted we use it rather than Dolby. I bowed to the pressure, agreeing to remix the film with Paramount Sound. Joshua, by coincidence, was there when the decision was made.

"You're making a big mistake, Daddy," said the little runt. "Mommy tells me you're having a big opening . . . the whole town's going to be there. I wouldn't take the chance. What if it doesn't work?"

"I'm not dumb, Joshua. It's gonna be checked, rechecked, and rechecked before we show it."

Popeye premiered at the Chinese Theater—the big bash of the year. All the critics and just about the entire industry were invited. *Popeye* didn't hit the screen that night, disaster did. The dialogue inaudible, the music clashing with the effects. What started out a night of glory ended up a night of despair. Many of the audience left before the film was over. The next morning and for the next seventy-two hours, we remixed the entire film back to Dolby.

What can you say about a nine-year-old kid who has more brights than his fifty-year-old father? Instinct. Age is not a factor. You've either got it or you don't. It makes the difference between mediocrity and magic.

For an entire decade, my kid stood watching his father's life fall to shambles. Once I was a king, his mother told him.

As he grew into his teens, he watched his daddy slip from famous to infamous. When he began his eight-year-long education at Crossroads School, his father was royalty. By graduation, though he'll never admit it, he couldn't get a date to the senior prom, three yeses had turned into three nos. His father's an outlaw—maybe a murderer.

It was all but impossible standing next to Ali at Crossroads watching Joshua graduate. That morning, ROBERT EVANS had been in the headlines again. No, I wasn't buying Warner Brothers. Instead: ROBERT EVANS LINKED DIRECTLY TO ROY RADIN MURDER. There I stood, a shell of the man I once was, watching my son graduate.

May I introduce to you now a film legend. The only living producer who has produced two of the hundred films honored and vaulted in perpetuity by the Library of Congress of our country. His filmography reads like a bible. His talent will be remembered long after he is gone. . . .

And on, and on, went William Wolf, a New York film critic introducing that night's guest speaker to his NYU film class.

Three years after that graduation, October 1992, Joshua sits by my side in the overfilled classroom. I was in New York producing *Sliver*. A standing ovation greeted my walk to the podium. It was the proudest moment of my life. My son's first glimpse of his father being hailed, not chastised.

It was Ali's fifty-first birthday. Her party? The family three, feasting at Mr. Chow's. Our connective tissue? Joshua—a spitting image of both, inheriting the best from each.

Hot tea in hand, Joshua stood, toasting his mom.

"I'm the only kid I know who doesn't remember his mom and dad ever living together." Then, looking at the two of us, "Were you really married?"

A double take. The birthday lady took him on: "Look at yourself! What do you think?"

A family laugh, but the runt wasn't finished.

"We've sure gone through it."

Then to his mom, "There's not one kid I know who's closer, more open with his mom than you and me. Happy birthday!"

A fat kiss.

"I love you, Mom!"

Then eyeing his ole man.

"You're somethin' else—no kid has a Pop like you."

Facing two of his family three, he couldn't help but beam. "I'm the luckiest kid I know."

43

The phone kept ringing, awakening me out of a deep sleep. The fuckin' button, god damn it, I forgot to turn it off. I looked at the clock. It wasn't midnight yet. Should I pick it up? I sure in hell didn't win the lottery. It kept ringing. Maybe it's the broad I slipped my number to last night. It's not too late. I'm up now, I hope it's her.

Disguising my voice to protect me from bad news or bad company, I English-accented it, "Evans residence."

Wrong again. It wasn't the broad, but I sure won the fuckin' lottery! Only seventy-two hours earlier Stanley Jaffe had been named chief operating officer of Paramount Communications.

"Sorry for not calling earlier. Suddenly I have so many new friends," Jaffe laughed. "The damn phone doesn't stop. Did I awaken you?"

"Yeah, but you're one hell of a wake-up call. Did you get my note?"

"No, sorry, must be a hundred fifty of them here. Haven't opened one. Haven't had time to zip down my fly, take a piss. Called to tell you one thing. From this day on, the life of Robert Evans is going to be a better one. You're way overdue. You deserve it. Now sleep well, dear," Stanley giggled, "you should."

"Without Robert Evans, the only way we'd be here today, would be if we were dead. That's right, without him Paramount would have been sold off to the graveyard behind us."

Jaffe was telling this to his group of top Paramount executives. A few were a bit surprised.

Jaffe made it clear: "I'm not prone to hyperbole—I was there. I know. I made my bones with him. Unless anyone has any objections, and if you do please speak up, because as of now, Robert Evans is back at Paramount!"

A banner headline across the front page of *Variety*, July 15, 1991:

EVANS BACK TO PARAMOUNT

In a town not conspicuously cordial to comebacks, Robert Evans is making a flamboyant one—and at Paramount, the studio he headed twenty-five years ago. After a decade-long hiatus from active producing, Evans is back behind the Bronson Gate with an arsenal of big-screen titles. . . . "Bob is back," quoted a top Paramount production honcho. "His success has been a remarkable one, and everyone here at Paramount—from Brandon Tartikoff to Stanley Jaffe to Martin Davis—felt he should be back with us. We think this new alliance will reap some very good movies and some real success."

From page, to page, to page, the story continued.

Suddenly they were scurrying for office space—a dictate from the top. A week passed. Jaffe called.

"Bob, if it's okay with you, I'd like you to have your old offices back. Just knowing you're there would give me a smile every time I come to the studio."

From nightmare to dream time, all in a week. It can't be happening. What did I take last night? Being sober, I realized it was not a dream—rather a dream come true.

Do you believe in miracles? I do now! What do you call getting back your dignity?

By Christmas 1991, my newly decorated offices had just been completed and, I swear, I thought I was dreaming. A homecoming. I hadn't had a good Christmas in over a decade—not one. Bring out the champagne, the caviar. I did! It was party time! Sharing my euphoria with everyone—the guards, the Xerox girls, the secretaries, the commissary workers, the chairman of the board, and the junior executives. Warren Beatty, Jack Nicholson, Faye Dunaway, Raquel Welch, and my ex, Ali MacGraw, mingled with hundreds of others throughout the evening. Oddly, Helmet Newton caused the biggest stir. There wasn't a star or executive who didn't want to be introduced to the famed master of the still frame.

A huge Christmas tree filled the entire corner of the main office. A Christmas thought for all to take home, each hand-wrapped. Each package contained a large hand-molded-globe candle, a cigarette lighter with a painted hundred-dollar bill around it and a pill box filled with organic herbs labeled "for health only." Each card said the same, "May the enclosed light up your life with health, love, and a little extra green."

Nicholson grabbed me by the arm. "Let's take a walk." From the lawn outside, we stood, looking into the bay window of my new offices, watching the celebration of the kid's return.

A long silence, then a wide Irish smile. "You know, Keed . . . you were ten thousand to one."

44

Six months behind the gates, and I'm rolling sevens. Three celebrity projects, three top Shakespeares writing them. All on the burner for a go.

One of them was Ira Levin's best-selling novel *Sliver*. Months earlier, Sue Mengers slipped me the galleys on the sly.

"You're the first to read it. Tie it up." Mengers was right—a terrific book and even better movie. There was one problem. Ira Levin didn't want to sell it. Not to me, not to anyone. His agent had strict orders not to entertain any offers.

Industry heat was heavy to acquire the film rights, but every interested studio, director, or producer was stonewalled. I found out why; Roman Polanski was the only filmmaker Levin would trust to bring his new baby, *Sliver,* to the screen. Roman had directed *Rosemary's Baby,* which stood as the only film adaptation that Ira felt had enhanced his written word. Roman's involvement, however, posed a bit of a problem. The entire story takes place in New York City. If Roman were to helm it, he would end up behind bars rather than behind the camera. Unjust as it is, he still remains persona non grata in the good ole U.S.A.

"Send Levin Roman's autobiography," Warren Beatty said. "He writes about you as if you were Thalberg and Selznick combined. Gives you all the credit for *Rosemary's Baby.* Is it true?"

"Of course not."

We both laughed. The laugh turned into a deal. Beatty ain't called the Pro for nothing.

Within a month, I was the proud daddy of Levin's new baby. Within another month, Joe Eszterhas, who penned *Basic Instinct* and was the most sought-after writer in the business, agreed to break precedent and adapt another writer's work. What a coup!

Levin's instinct in wanting Roman to direct was on the money. The Polanski touch could make *Sliver* a genre classic. Not unlike *Rosemary's Baby,* 80 percent of *Sliver* took place indoors. Why not have a top second unit director shoot exteriors, entrances, and exits in New York, and then re-create the interiors in Paris rather than Hollywood? A good try, but no cigar. None of the studio honchos would take the chance, even though I had done it many times before. But it was different then—I was head of the studio, not a "dependent" producer.

Joe Eszterhas's first draft arrived on the Friday of the long Memorial Day weekend. I was off to Palm Springs with the screenplay under my arm. An hour after the sun went down that day, I didn't know whether I was drunk or dreaming, or if my luck really had changed. The best fuckin' screenplay I'd read in a decade (but with the decade I had, I wouldn't have made too big a bet on it).

Before the sun came up the next morning, Stanley Jaffe, Brandon Tartikoff, and John Goldwyn called me. I wasn't losin' it. They felt the same. The best damn script they had read in years. "Could be the big one, let's get it on the screen . . . full speed ahead."

Was I hearing right? In all my years as head of the studio or as a dependent producer, I'd never been given—or gotten—a quicker or more enthusiastic thumbs-up. What a high! What an idiot. Their exhilaration to get *Sliver* into production pronto was for all the wrong reasons—not to make it memorable, but to make a 1993 Memorial Day release. They needed a flick to fill an empty spot in their schedule—suddenly *Sliver* was it. Knowing Levin's instinct on Polanski was on the money, I took a last shot, begging the studio brass to be inventive, do the unexpected and go with Polanski. I might as well have talked to the trees. Philip Noyce was their choice. He had just completed *Patriot Games* for them, which hadn't come out yet—nevertheless, in typical Hollywood fashion, he was momentarily "studio hot." I couldn't criticize their choice: I was a big fan of his talent after seeing a film he had made in Australia, *Dead Calm*. But in my book, there is no one like Roman when it comes to this genre. Since it was my first time at-bat in more than a decade, I couldn't afford the luxury of my usual intransigence. Though I tasted Polanski, I swallowed Noyce, and digested an M.O—compromise . . . compromise . . . compromise—that eventually sped me twice to the emergency room of Cedars Sinai Hospital. Not to pump my stomach, but to check my heart.

The one intransigent stand I did take however was the casting of the female lead, Carly. Sharon Stone was one, two, and three on my dance card. *Basic Instinct* was well on its way to becoming a worldwide blockbuster; her presence on the screen was pure dynamite. Others at the studio preferred Demi Moore, Michelle Pfeiffer, Geena Davis, Kim Basinger—name 'er, they preferred 'er.

"It's Sharon Stone and that's it," I told anyone who tried to question my authority. Again a problem. She didn't want to do it. She felt it was too close to *Basic Instinct*. Now she was yearning to do a comedy. Perversely the studio brass enjoyed my frustration in not being able to hook Stone to the flick. Her manager, Chuck Binder, and her new agent, Guy McElwaine, both pressed her to take the part. She refused. Joe Eszterhas, whose *Basic Instinct* script brought her instant prominence, pressed as well, going so far as doing a complete rewrite just to please her. She disliked the rewrite more than the original. Pleasing a starlet who suddenly becomes a star is one torturous experience. Suddenly they know everything, they've written the book. I've lived through it too many times. The good news ain't worth the bad. But when you want something, you want something.

The more she turned it down, the more I wanted her.

On a Monday, the front office dictate came down. By the close of business Friday, if Sharon Stone doesn't commit, she's out. I immediately called Chuck Binder, lying that Demi Moore was desperate for the role—so much so that her husband, Bruce Willis, would take on the third lead for scale as a favor.

"I'll get back to you tomorrow," Binder said in a flash. "You know I really want Sharon to do it."

"Then move it, Chuck. . . . Moore and Willis ain't a bad parlay for one paycheck."

"I'll go up and twist her arm until she says yes. Okay, Evans? Speak to you in the morning."

The next morning, her answer was no.

Over breakfast my butler brought in the new *Vanity Fair.* Geena Davis was on the cover. With only three days left I took my last shot; calling Binder again. "Chuck, are you bullshitting me or do you really want Sharon to do the picture?"

"I feel like a parrot, Bob, that's how many times I've begged her."

"In five minutes you're gonna have *Vanity Fair* in front of you. Show it to your client. . . . Tell her the girl on the cover is in makeup starting Monday."

"Who's on the cover?"

"You'll see when you get it."

Less than a hour later I was getting into my car, studio bound, when my secretary stopped me.

"Chuck Binder on the horn."

"She's doing it." At first I wasn't sure what he meant. Did he mean, is Geena Davis really doing it? No—he meant his client, Sharon Stone, was. Demi Moore, Michelle Pfeiffer, Julia Roberts wouldn't have bothered her. Ahh, but Geena Davis . . . that touched her cat claws. Call it dumb luck, call it bad luck, call it what you want, but picking Geena Davis's name out of a hat was the only reason she committed. Unbeknown to me it was Geena who turned down *Basic Instinct,* leaving Sharon as the reluctant second choice to fill her shoes. Now staring Sharon in the face was Geena Davis at her most glamorous, on the cover of *Vanity Fair,* no less, bold print heralding her as "Hollywood's new femme fatale." What a come shot for little Miss Muffet stopping Miss Femme Fatale from being in makeup on Monday. Sharon didn't want the part, but she sure in hell didn't want Geena to have it. Did I pay for my transgression? In spades, clubs, diamonds, and hearts.

Many actors were considered for her young male lead, Zeke. A rushed start date was creeping up on us. A thirty-million-dollar flick, with two weeks to cast the male lead. Billy Baldwin was chosen. Miss Stone was underwhelmed by our choice.

Strange vibes were bothering me when meeting after meeting at my house was changed or rescheduled to be held at the studio. Curiosity killed the cat. Well, it almost killed me.

"Is my house off-limits?" I kidded Eszterhas.

"Yeah," he laughed. "The lady made it clear she doesn't want to meet there."

"What lady?"

"Our leading lady."

"She's a lady?"

We both laughed.

"She's told me—told everyone—she'll never walk into your house. A girlfriend of hers, she says, was kept captive there for three and a half years, put in a dog collar and chains, drugged up. Now she weighs three hundred and fifty pounds."

Laughing in Eszterhas's face, "For a top writer, you sure are a second-rate storyteller."

A long Eszterhas look. "Don't believe me, huh?"

"Of course I believe you. Sounds just like me. Not one of my four wives lived with me that long. A dog collar? That's on the nose, it's me again. Never had a dog in my life, don't like 'em. What the hell do you do with a dog collar? Joe, give it to me straight, will ya?"

It was no laughing matter. Eszterhas didn't crack a smile. I did.

"Who's the broad?"

"I don't know."

"How could you? There isn't one. If every broad who said they knew me . . . knew me . . . I'd have to be at least four hundred years old. If one tenth of the people who say they've been to my home had been here, my house would be LAX. The guys at the studio don't believe this shit, do they?"

Eszterhas shrugged. "I'd put a stop to this pronto, Bob. It stinks."

"Put a stop to it? I'll put more than a stop to it."

I didn't. From John Goldwyn to every honcho at Paramount, no one missed out on this one.

"John, she was my choice, but I'm not gonna live with this shit."

"Yes, you are. We're a week away from shooting. If she walks, we won't be in deep shit—you will."

He was right. I took a deep breath, took a deep swallow, and backed away. My day was gonna come.

It didn't—it got worse. Once we started shooting, she let it be known to director Philip Noyce that my presence on the set made her feel uncomfortable. Olivier, Nicholson, Dunaway, Hoffman always wanted Evans near. To Miss Stone, I was an intrusion. Again I swallowed deeply. Not wanting to cramp Miss Stone's style, each day I'd pay a momentary visit to the set and, like a plague, quickly disappear.

When filming was completed I wrote a personal check to my star. A quarter-million-dollar bonus, a gift with one condition: that she prove her concocted lie had an iota of truth. If she could, the quarter million was hers. If she couldn't and was caught with her pants down, she'd have to apologize to me.

Damn it—again the Paramount honchos strongly pressed me not to do it.

"Be professional, Evans. We need her to go out and sell the picture. You'll have your day."

Again I bit my tongue, swallowed deep, and stepped back.

The picture had been shooting on the lot at Paramount for three months. Reminiscent of cheap fiction, it was there Miss Stone put the hit on my then assistant and protégé Bill Macdonald. Macdonald's loyalty to me was such that I was the last to know. The fact that Macdonald had been married in a religious Catholic ceremony six months earlier must have been a turn-on to our star. She wouldn't have to break a sweat seducing this new kid on the block. It was his first outing in Hollywood. His first encounter with a femme fatale. He wasn't the idiot—I was, rehearsing in front of him the way I planned to bring Miss Stone to her knees. Never having the vaguest notion that he had dumped his new bride—a terrific girl he'd gone with for seven years—and was now our star's new squeeze. Everyone else but me knew, and this was a guy I protected . . . reprotected and reprotected. Every exec at the studio wanted him out, each of them telling me that behind my back Macdonald was knifing my reputation to shreds. I didn't believe a word. How could he do it? Here was a guy who was with me during my lowest. Now he's got a shot at reaping the benefits. Learning the film business. His big break, it doesn't add up. Was I wrong! Instead of paying heed to those who knew better, not only didn't I fire him, I pressed to get him a credit on the film. Flatly turned down, I sought Joe Eszterhas's help. Together we took on the front office. Begrudgingly they gifted Macdonald with a co-producer credit. It was the wrong credit. It should have been "off-camera leading man." The irony being that during this entire escapade I was the one paying his salary.

Macdonald's eel-like behavior was a bouquet of gardenias compared to what was to come: he conjured up an outrageous fabrication deserving of nothing less than close psychiatric examination.

Guy McElwaine was confronted at dinner one evening by Bill and Sharon. Sharon feared for her life. Her fiancé, my protégé, convinced her that if she didn't go along with my edit of the film, I'd have her knocked off. It was my M.O. Being my right-hand man for three years, he himself knew of at least three people I put away. It was Bill's way to impress Miss Femme Fatale of his importance to her personal and professional life.

Not for an instant was McElwaine taken in by Macdonald's allegations. Yet he had to be respectful to his client.

"If what you're saying is true," McElwaine told Macdonald, "put your allegations in writing. Then I can present it to the FBI and the powers that be at Paramount."

Naturally, Macdonald never followed through. If he had, he would be serving time by now. He didn't have to. The next day Sharon took it upon herself, cornered Stanley Jaffe at the studio, venting her fright concerning her fiancé's boss. How's that for a sick story? Why didn't I use Geena Davis?

How's this for timing? The next day, Stanley receives a vituperative fourteen-page letter from me concerning my dissatisfaction with the film's edit. Suddenly I'm put on ice—quarantined. From camaraderie I became contagious.

Being sixty-two, not twenty-two, didn't help. I was rushed to the emergency room of Cedars Sinai Hospital with what seemed to be a heart attack. It wasn't—it was a heartache, my blood pressure pressing 220 over 115.

Time passed. Two weeks before the film was to open, Joe Eszterhas and I took a drive to Palm Springs. It was then that the story of my Siberian sentence was unraveled. Eszterhas told me of Macdonald's insidious fabrication. I didn't believe him. How could Bill be so dumb? Perpetuate a mistruth so diabolical. Harbor such disdain. I insisted Joe confront McElwaine with me present. He did. McElwaine not only corroborated what Joe told me but embellished it. As ugly as the story was, at least now I understood why I was put on ice. I deserved it, too. After all, Brutus was on my payroll, not theirs. Angry? Shaking!

"Fellas, I've had it. I'm gonna clean the air but good."

"It's bad timing, Evans."

"Fuck bad timing. I'm tired of hearing the same shit. It's not your name being dragged through the mud."

"Bob, we've put our ass on the line telling you this," McElwaine said. "Joe's been more than stand-up. Don't rock the boat. The lady's doing wall-to-wall interviews around the country. The film opens in two weeks." Again I bit my tongue, zippered my lips.

What started out as a platinum project with a solid gold screenplay and seasoned with the flavor of the year's femme fatale ended up being no more than a silver-plated flick. Its texture still lies on the cutting-room floor. Hunger overpowered passion. A Memorial Day release preempted excellence, leaving *Sliver* shafted rather than crafted.

Poor Philip Noyce. He wasn't given a fair shot. He needed more time. Given the luxury of another week to deliver the international version, he added four minutes of sizzle. What a difference a sizzle makes. Around the world, except in the good ole U.S.A., *Sliver* was a huge box-office smash, bringing heavy change into Paramount's coffers. Imagine if it were good. Damn it! It was all there, not on the silver screen, in the editing room vaults.

Giving the devil her due, however despicable I think Sharon's deportment, I know she's a major box-office star. *Sliver,* without Stone, would have ended up doing a sliver of the business it did. Wherever you are, dear Sharon, that quarter-million-dollar check still awaits you. It's easy money, even for you—just prove your allegations against me are true. If you can't, down on your knees you go—only to apologize, I wouldn't want anything more!

On reflection, I look upon the making of *Sliver* as a continuing exercise in frustration. It never changes. Me? I don't understand it. Fuck being artsy-craftsy, let's talk down and dirty pragmatic. When you've only got one shot—that's it! Either you pull down that beautiful brass ring, or you get them brass knuckles in the balls. No second time around, pal! That's the flick business. Everyone in it knows it.

Why, then, if for no other reason than caution, shouldn't striving for excellence prevail over making a release date? *It doesn't!* Maybe that's why makin' fuckin' flicks is one dangerous business.

45

August 1994.

Half a century? It can't be! Well, it's close. But I feel like a kid. Yeah, but you're not. Okay, okay, I know it.

It was back in 1950 when I first walked through them gates at Paramount, a young "wannabe" actor—razorless, picking up my first check, 125 buckaroos a week, as one of Paramount's many contract pretty faces. I guess my face wasn't that pretty: six months and out the back door I flew. It didn't matter. It was enough time to see a new world open before me. To brush shoulders with Alfred Hitchcock, Bing Crosby, Spencer Tracy. Watch Ronnie Reagan shoot a Paramount cheapie, *Hong Kong.* Screen test for the great director George Stevens, for a co-starring role in *A Place in the Sun.* Damn it! I didn't get it, but I did break bread with Cecil B. De Mille, Alan Ladd, Fred Astaire. When the guards weren't watching, I snuck onto Stage 15. Wow, right before me, Billy Wilder was directing Gloria Swanson and Bill Holden in *Sunset Boulevard.* By the time I got the boot, it was too late—rejection had led to obsession. *Flicks were now my future.* Watch out fifties, here I come, traveling north one way, straight to the top. Got there, too—well, sort of.

As the fifties aged, so did I. *Made it to the big screen!* Beaten up by Errol Flynn, kissed by Ava Gardner, slapped by Joan Crawford, toe-to-toe in close-ups with Jimmy Cagney. Not bad, huh? Not good either. By decade's end, I was sure of one thing: I was a half-assed actor.

The sixties? That's a different story. No back door this time—"run the joint" was the order of the decade. Run it I did—for a decade. Don't understand it. The world of fickle flicks? It's been thirty years now and I'm still here, still standing behind them same gates. Bet your house, it ain't been dull. I've either done it, or gotten it. You name 'em, I've met 'em—well, almost. Either worked with 'em, fought with 'em, hired 'em, fired 'em, laughed with 'em, cried with 'em, figuratively fucked by 'em, literally fucked 'em. It's been one hell of a ride!

Where is everyone? Dead? Most. Wealthy? Some. Destitute? Many. Retired? Suppose so, I ain't seen 'em.

One thing I do know, I ain't dead, I ain't wealthy, I ain't destitute, and I ain't retired. Can't afford any of 'em, gotta keep standin', stay in the picture. Hey, I'm holdin' a platinum platter—*The Saint, The Phantom, Jade, September Affair*—all green lighted, ready to roll. How's that for being in action?

The nineties breezed in plenty of blue sky. Back behind them gates of Paramount. My only kid beaming with pride again, his ole man is back in action. Come October 24, Ali and I are throwing a black-tie, silver anniversary bash. Though divorced twenty-two of the twenty-five years—so what! No couple I know have reached that quarter-of-a-century mark and are better friends, have more laughs with each other than the two of us. That's worth celebrating, isn't it?

Get this, the 1991 Library of Congress selected seventy-five films produced during the twentieth century to be Congressional vaulted, in perpetuity. Hangin' behind my desk at the studio are *two* Congressional certificates. One, for creating *The Godfather,* the other, for producing *Chinatown.* The only guy alive holdin' two aces in their vault is me. If nothin' else, it makes up for the lack of green in my own vault.

Met a sensational lady! Romance? Uh-uh, finance! Best damn partner I've had since making flicks. Christine Peters, her name. But romance did come back into my life. Big time! The 1990s rekindled the only lasting romance I've ever had. A second shot at the brass ring, turning hate into spring fever. It's miracle time. Shhh! Keep it quiet. The love of my life? It's a guy. That's right, a guy—my brother, the only one I have. Don't know if "love's more wonderful the second time around," but it's sure more appreciated.

Still making headlines. Damn it, why can't they be middle of the road? It's either champagne or sedative time. Before one full moon turns into another, I get it in the front. I get it in the back.

Splashed across the Arts & Leisure section of *The New York Times* with a picture more glamorous than any I've taken since playing the bullfighter in *The Sun Also Rises.* Not in suit, shirt, and tie, but jumping out of a pool, dripping wet, gazing into the sun. Macho beefcake time!

Cruise, Nicholson, Costner, Beatty, couldn't expect a more dazzling display, especially from *The New York Times.* But me! Doesn't make sense. Can't deny it, though, it sure was one hell of a boost. Across four columns ran the headline: "THE RISE, FALL AND RISE OF ROBERT EVANS."

This was followed by a two-thousand-word epistle on "the reemergence of a film giant," written by Bernard Weinraub, the *Times* entertainment journalist.

Like the foam on the head of a cold glass of beer, the high was short-lived. Two weeks to the day later, the name Robert Evans again blazed across the top of the page. This time, the *Los Angeles Times,* with an equally large photo. No beefcake this time—law cake. The headline? A bit different!

"THE DEMISE AND RUIN OF PRODUCER ROBERT EVANS."

Being hoisted and dumped within two weeks does not come easy. It's an art form unto itself that few survive. Trust me, I've got a Ph.D. in it.

My life today? More volatile than ever. This last year alone, I've been shot down, bloodied, trampled, accused, threatened, disgraced, betrayed, scandalized, maligned. Tough? Sure, but I ain't complaining. Nothin' comes easy.

Resolve: Fuck 'em, fuck 'em all. . . .